Clinical Approaches
to Violence

Wiley Series in

Clinical Approaches to Criminal Behaviour

Editors

Clive R. Hollin   **Kevin Howells**
University of Leicester   *University of Birmingham*

Clinical Approaches to Violence
Edited by Kevin Howells *and* Clive R. Hollin

Clinical Approaches to Sex Offenders and Their Victims
Edited by Clive R. Hollin *and* Kevin Howells
(forthcoming)

Further titles in preparation

WITHDRAWN

Clinical Approaches to Violence

School of Psychology
University of Birmingham

and

CLIVE R. HOLLIN
Department of Psychology
University of Leicester

JOHN WILEY & SONS
Chichester · New York · Brisbane · Toronto · Singapore

Other Wiley Editorial Offices

John Wiley & Sons, Inc., 605 Third Avenue,
New York, NY 10158-0012, USA

Jacaranda Wiley Ltd, G.P.O. Box 859, Brisbane,
Queensland 4001, Australia

John Wiley & Sons (Canada) Ltd, 22 Worcester Road,
Rexdale, Ontario M9W 1L1, Canada

John Wiley & Sons (SEA) Pte Ltd, 37 Jalan Pemimpin #05-04,
Block B, Union Industrial Building, Singapore 2057

Library of Congress Cataloging-in-Publication Data:
Clinical approaches to violence.
   (Clinical approaches to criminal behaviour ; v. 1)
   Bibliography: p.
   Includes index.
   1. Violence. 2. Clinical psychology. 3. Criminal
psychology. 4. Psychotherapy. I. Howells, Kevin.
II. Hollin, Clive R. III. Series.
RC569.5.V55C56 1989   616.85′82   89-5820

ISBN 0 471 92214 5

British Library Cataloguing in Publication Data:
Clinical approaches to violence.
   1. Violent persons. Psychotherapy
   I. Howells, Kevin II. Hollin, Clive R.
   616.85′82

ISBN 0 471 92214 5

Typeset by Photo·graphics, Honiton, Devon
Printed and bound by Courier International, Tiptree, Essex

KH: To Owen bach

CH: To Felicity Clarkson, who guided my first steps in the world of real offenders

List of Contributors

H. E. BARBAREE, *Department of Psychology, Queen's University, Kingston, Canada.*

RONALD BLACKBURN, *Park Lane Hospital, Liverpool, UK.*

KEVIN D. BROWNE, *Department of Psychology, University of Leicester, UK.*

W. DAVIES, *St Andrew's Hospital, Northampton, UK.*

JONQUIL DRINKWATER, *Park Hospital, Oxford, UK.*

NEIL FRUDE, *Department of Psychology, University College, Cardiff, Wales.*

MALCOLM R. GENTRY, *South Warwickshire District Health Authority, UK.*

GISLI GUDJONSSON, *Institute of Psychiatry, University of London, UK.*

MONIKA HENDERSON, *Ministry for Police and Emergency Services, Victoria, Australia.*

MARTIN HERBERT, *Department of Psychology, University of Leicester, UK.*

CLIVE R. HOLLIN, *Department of Psychology, University of Leicester, UK.*

KEVIN HOWELLS, *School of Psychology, University of Birmingham, UK.*

W. L. MARSHALL, *Department of Psychology, Queens University, Kingston, Canada.*

IAN MCBAIN, *University of Toronto, Canada.*

RAYMOND NOVACO, *Programme in Social Ecology, University of California, Irvine, USA.*

EUGENE B. OSTAPIUK, *Glenthorne Youth Treatment Centre, Birmingham, UK.*

NATHAN POLLOCK, *Clarke Insitute of Psychiatry and University of Toronto, Canada.*

HANS TOCH, *State University of New York, Albany, USA.*

CHRISTOPHER D. WEBSTER, *Clarke Institute of Psychiatry and University of Toronto, Canada.*

WAYNE, L. WELSH, *Programme in Social Ecology, University of California, Irvine, USA.*

Contents

PART 3: Institutional and Professional Contexts

Series Preface

This series around the theme of *Clinical Approaches to Criminal Behaviour* has its origin in a sequence of conferences we organized between 1984 and 1988. Our intention, both then and now, was to make some progress towards re-establishing an approach to changing criminal behaviour which has become unfashionable, unpopular and much maligned in recent years. It should be made absolutely clear that in the present context the term 'clinical' is not intended to imply a medical model, in which criminal behaviour is viewed as pathological, but to define an approach in which the focus is on the individual and on psychological methods of producing change. Having said that, we are not blind to the crucial importance of economic, political and social factors in crime and criminological theory. We agree that change is necessary at all levels to reduce crime, and have no wish to be seen as placing the spotlight of responsibility and blame exclusively on the offender to the exclusion of environmental factors. (As behaviourists, admittedly of differing persuasions within that broad church of theoretical opinion, how could we say otherwise?) However, we would also maintain that it is important not to lose sight of the individual, and it is here that the clinical approach comes into its own. The series is intended to serve two functions: to inform clinicians of developments in the clinical approach to criminal behaviour in its many forms, and to convince others that the clinical approach has a role to play in changing criminal behaviour. There is no reason why social reform and clinical change should be incompatible: others have written on the former approach, we now seek to re-assert the latter.

CLIVE R. HOLLIN
KEVIN HOWELLS

Preface

We undertook the preparation of this book with the hope of rekindling our own (and hopefully others') enthusiasm for the clinical approach to understanding, assessing and changing some forms of violent behaviour. As practising professional psychologists, working in hospital, prison and community settings, we have become aware of the retreat from the clinical approach to 'offending behaviour' in general, under the assaults of 'nothing works' penal philosophies. It has long been our view that the clinical perspective has much to offer in the field of violence prevention, but that the potential contribution of the clinical approach is poorly understood and insufficiently acknowledged among the professions and also in society at large.

For the purposes of this book we use the term 'clinical' to imply not a medical model whereby violent behaviour is seen as pathological but to emphasize the need to focus on the individual, on psychological theories of how people become violent and on psychological methods of producing change.

The different contributions that we have assembled were selected in the light of particular objectives we had for the book. First, we were aware that psychologists, social workers, doctors and other professionals often develop narrow vision in their everyday work. Thus someone may acquire immense knowledge, for example, about physical violence to children (child abuse) but remain ignorant of theories and methods in the fields of spouse abuse, violence in psychiatric hospitals and work on anger-management methods. It is our belief that much is to be gained by learning about clinical methods and research findings in fields that are adjacent to and overlap with our own.

Second, it seemed to us that some degree of theoretical consistency was required for the contributions. We have chosen contributions which we see as broadly consistent with mainstream cognitive and behavioural models in clinical psychology. This is not to say that all contributors share a common theoretical orientation. Indeed, many variations can be observed in individual chapters, with some emphasizing behavioural and others cognitive or social aspects. Nevertheless, we hope that the languages spoken have sufficient in common for mutual understanding to occur.

Third, we have aimed to give the book an international flavour, rather than restricting contributions to one society. Inevitably, this will mean that occasional observations and findings will be idiosyncratic to a particular country rather than generalizable.

Finally, we believe that what is required in this particular field of work is an integration of theory, empirical research and actual clinical practice and realities. For this reason we have selected contributors who, in general, combine a research/theory orientation with involvement in everyday practice. We have asked them to reflect these dual interests in their contributions.

KEVIN HOWELLS
CLIVE R. HOLLIN

Part 1

Concepts and Methods

1

An Introduction to Concepts, Models and Techniques

CLIVE R. HOLLIN
Department of Psychology, University of Leicester, UK

and

KEVIN HOWELLS
School of Psychology, University of Birmingham, UK

This book is about aggression and violence, forms of behaviour which can both endanger and take life as well as produce adverse long-term effects for (surviving) victims. The statistics suggest that serious violent crime is not a common occurrence. Thus, for example, the 1985 Home Office figures for England and Wales reveal 173 convictions for murder, with a further 35 for attempted murder: there were 1254 convictions for wounding or other life-endangering acts. Similarly, Siegel (1986) notes that in 1984 the murder rate in the United States was about 8 per 100 000 of the population. Crime surveys are in accordance with this picture, with few people reporting being the victim of serious physical assault: indeed, 'crimes of violence' account for only 5% of offences in the latest *British Crime Survey* (Hough and Mayhew, 1985). However, with the likely exception of murder, it is also the case that not all acts of violence enter the official statistics or are volunteered in crime survey interviews. There are a number of contexts in which violent acts may remain hidden from public view: if they take place within a relationship; if they are directed towards children; if they take place within an institution; or if the violence has a sexual component.

In inviting contributions to this text we aimed to illuminate the many faces of violence. Specifically, a number of authors were asked to review the research on aggression and violence in their specialist area. This review would then form the basis for a discussion of the role of clinical techniques in the management of violent behaviour. These contributions are contained in Parts

2 and 3. However, to set this research-practitioner stance on a firm basis, Part 1 looks in detail at theories and clinical methods central to a clinical approach to violence.

In this opening chapter we commence with a broad introduction to the psychology of aggression and violence and associated clinical techniques. The following chapters deal in much greater detail with psychopathy, assessment and cognitive and behavioural techniques.

PSYCHOLOGICAL THEORIES OF AGGRESSION AND VIOLENCE

In the literature three terms—'aggression', 'violence' and 'criminal violence'—are in common, sometimes interchangeable, use. Megargee (1982) and Siann (1985) discuss definitional issues and offer the following definitions. Aggression refers to the intention to hurt or gain advantage over other people, without necessarily involving physical injury; violence involves the use of strong physical force against another person, sometimes impelled by aggressive motivation; criminal violence involves directly injurious behaviour which is forbidden by law. While concern here is with psychological theories of violence, there are theories from other disciplines, such as anthropology and biology. A number of texts cover the full range of theories (e.g. Baron, 1977; Siann, 1985; Zillmann, 1979), while Mednick *et al.* (1982) review biological factors, Merikangas (1981) details neurological theories, Riches (1986) discusses the anthropology of violence and Goldstein (1986) covers criminal violence.

Instinct Theories

Freud proposed that human behaviour is driven by two basic instincts: the life instinct (*Eros*) promotes life while the death force (*Thanatos*) seeks to destroy life so as to return the organism to its original, lifeless state. In the conflict between the instincts of life and death, *Eros* seeks to prevent extinction by displacing the destructive energy to the external world. Aggression therefore has a function akin to a safety valve, reducing the energy within the psychic system to acceptable levels. If the aggressive behaviour takes the form of non-destructive and socially acceptable acts then the probability of violence is correspondingly reduced. Such cathartic release might take the form of anger or participating in acceptable aggression such as sport. This 'neutralizing' of the aggressive instinct can go astray so that the aggression becomes 'internalized', potentially culminating in violence, murder or suicide (Kutash, 1978).

Lorenz (1966, 1974) studied aggression from an ethological perspective. From animal studies he proposed that aggression stems directly from an innate 'fighting instinct'. This instinct is seen as having evolved over generations due to its benefits for the survivial of the species—*homo sapiens* included. From this perspective aggressive energy continually builds up within the individual and has, at some point, to be vented. This venting can occur in two ways: a specific environmental aggression-releasing stimulus triggers an aggressive act; or a build-up of unreleased energy culminates in an eruption of violent behaviour.

Storr (1970) sought to fuse psychoanalytic and ethological theories of aggression. He agreed that aggressive behaviour stems from an instinctive impulse, biologically determined, which seeks discharge before reaching critical levels. However, he extends the argument by suggesting that the way in which an individual manifests aggression in later life will result from unconscious motivations derived from childhood emotional experiences. Further, should negative events occur in the period when the individual seeks to deal with the aggressive drive, then the psychopathological aspects of aggression—typified by depression, schizoid behaviour and paranoia—may result from the unresolved drive. Fromm (1977), while primarily working in a psychoanalytic tradition, suggested that it is necessary to go beyond individual factors and consider the role of social, economic and political influences in precipitating aggression and violence.

The criticisms of instinct theories centre on conceptual ambiguities and a lack of empirical verification. There is little hard evidence to demonstrate an instinctual biological drive, nor do there appear to be environmental releasers of aggression in humans. Critics suggest that, in the balance between innate and learned behaviour, instinct theories inadvisably prefer biological to social forces—although Storr, for example, has attempted to meet this point. Bornstein *et al.* (1981, p. 311) summarize the criticisms: 'Lorenz's ethological theory of aggression has taken its place alongside other instinct models, retaining its external strength in literary elegance yet critically weakened by its extremely fragile empirical foundation.'

Drive Theory

As the concept of an innate aggressive instinct fell from favour, so the notion of reactive drives grew to prominence. The 'drive' which motivated a particular behaviour, including violence, was seen as being acquired through experience rather than being innate. As the level of the drive increases so the individual is motivated to find conditions in which behaviours can be acted which reduce the drive. This amalgam of ideas from psychoanalytic and early behavioural psychology was advanced by Dollard *et al.* (1939) as a means of explaining aggression. The theory proposed that if a goal is blocked and expected rewards are not forthcoming, this produces a state of frustration; the frustration instigates aggression, in turn leading to aggressive or violent behaviour. The behaviour may be directed at the source of the frustration or displaced to other targets which have some relationship with the primary source of the frustration. Later work pointed to the distinction between 'hostile aggression' and 'instrumental aggression': with the former the aggression is intended to injure the victim; in the latter it is simply a means to an end, as in, for example, armed robbery (Buss, 1961).

Dollard *et al.*'s (1939) thesis generated a body of research work which led to a number of reformulations of aspects on the initial theory (e.g. Miller, 1941). Berkowitz (1965, 1974) proposed one such modification which has gained prominence. In contrast to the original drive theory, Berkowitz (1965) suggested that frustration acts to produce a state of emotional arousal, or 'anger', which creates a potential for aggression—although the aggression is not inevitable. In order for the potential to be realized, an 'anger-eliciting cue' had to be present: this cue, or stimulus, would be something associated with aggression—another person's behaviour, the presence of a weapon, etc. This argument was taken a stage further with the suggestion that strong environmental stimuli could produce aggression or violence without the prior angry state (Berkowitz, 1974).

One of the strengths of drive theory was that it offered hypotheses which could be tested experimentally: however, as a body of research amassed, it became apparent that the theory lacked explanatory power and attention was diverted elsewhere. As Bornstein *et al.* (1981, p. 316) comment: 'As a result of the deteriorating empirical status of instinct and drive theories of aggression, the social learning perspective . . . has grown rapidly in popularity and support in the past decade.'

Social Learning Theory

Bandura (1973a, b) suggested that there are three crucial aspects to aggression: the *acquisition* of the aggressive behaviour; the process of *instigation* of the aggression; and the conditions which *maintain* the aggression. Social learning theory proposes that the acquisition of behaviour occurs through the process of learning, either through direct experience or by observation. Accordingly, there is empirical evidence to suggest that aggressive behaviour can be acquired through direct reinforcement (e.g. Hayes *et al.*, 1980), and via observation (e.g. Bandura *et al.*, 1963). With regard to instigation, Bandura (1973b) noted that anticipated outcome—in turn, the product of previous learning—was vitally important. The anticipation, signalled by environmental cues previously associated with aggression, not only made aggression more likely it also pointed to the potential victims of the aggression. Alongside anticipated outcome, Bandura also suggested that aversive environmental conditions such as high temperatures, air pollution and crowding can act to raise emotional arousal and facilitate the instigation of aggression (e.g. Anderson, 1987; Rotton and Frey, 1985); while verbal and physical provocation can have a similar effect (e.g. Dengerink *et al.*, 1978). The effects of provocation have been explained both in terms of the anticipated consequences of failing to respond, such as loss of self-esteem, and also in terms of the cognitive appraisal of the provocation. An act perceived as provocative and antagonistic is liable to increase 'angry' arousal and aggression (Novaco, 1976, 1978): although as Novaco (1978) notes, there may be a reciprocal relationship between cognition and anger such that while particular cognitions induce anger, experiencing anger can also lead the individual to think in an aggressive manner. Similar relationships, as shown in Figure 1.1, may function between cognition and behaviour and between anger and behaviour. Finally, from a social learning theory perspective the maintenance of aggression is through the three types of reinforcement; external, vicarious, and self.

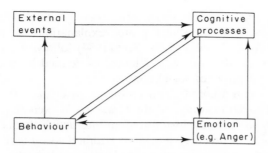

Figure 1.1 Adapted from Novaco (1978)

Siann (1985) makes a number of criticisms of psychological theories of aggression and violence. These include a narrow approach which is a result of laboratory-based research, positivist methodology, and a poor conception of human motivation. Siann suggests that aggression might best be considered as a *social* phenomenon, one best studied 'in the real world of perceived and actual inequalities, environmental stress and political conflict' (p. 165).

Social Accounts

West and Farrington (1977) reported the findings from a longitudinal study of social and other factors in the development of violence. However, as Siann suggests, while helpful from a descriptive viewpoint these findings are not presented in any theoretical framework. Toch (1969) discusses a series of interviews with violent men, attempting to place violence within a social context and so move towards a 'phenomenology of violence'. This work views violence from the offender's perspective, so as to discover the meaning or sense of the act for that person within the social context in which it occurred. Toch describes various uses of violence, such as alleviating tension in awkward social situations or defending reputations. Typically, violence occurs when another person is perceived as a threat and some action is taken to respond to the threat; the other person reacts, the instigator responds again—the *interaction* escalates towards violence. A tradition of social research has followed this style of investigation, with recent work examining the 'rules of disorder' (Marsh and Campbell, 1982; Marsh *et al.*, 1978). This research has shown that some violence, such as between football fans, is rule-bound to the extent that it is agreed that fights should take place between equal numbers and that certain forms of fighting are not allowed.

Other accounts, mainly from sociologists rather than psychologists, have concentrated even further on the social setting. Wolfgang and Ferracuti (1967) argued that subcultures exist, usually involving young men, in which violence is the legitimate norm: the function of the violence is to provide both excitement and a means of achieving status. In seeking to explain these violent subcultures it has been suggested that they are the result of the anger and frustration caused by social and economic inequalities (e.g. Blau and Blau, 1982; Carroll and Jackson, 1983); while others prefer explanations in terms of conflict between cultures (e.g. Miller, 1976). Box (1983) follows a radical criminology approach, suggesting that we see 'violence' as defined by the powerful social classes for their purposes of social control.

As with most social accounts, two problems arise: the difficulty of including the full range of social factors; and the tendency to exclude individual factors. It is difficult to resist the conclusion that an interactive theory is required, one which seeks to place individual behaviour within a social and political context. Psychological research has contributed to both strands in the study of both the situations in which violence occurs and the characteristics of the violent person.

ANALYSIS OF THE VIOLENT SITUATION

The situational approach to understanding violence is firmly established in the psychological literature as one which seeks to analyse the environmental factors associated with violent acts (e.g. Monahan and Klassen, 1982). The focus here is on research which has analysed the contexts in which serious assault, robbery and murder occur.

Serious Assault

Serious assault may be defined as an attack which inflicts severe wounding and physical assault on the victim. Henderson (1986) has reported an exhaustive analysis of violent incidents following interviews with 44 prison inmates serving sentences for wounding, attempted murder, grievous bodily harm and actual bodily harm. The transcripts of the interviews were coded across a range of categories such as victim age and sex, place of incident, time of day, etc. A cluster analysis of the 246 violent incidents described by the interviewees revealed eight distinct types of incident as shown in Table 1.1.

The striking aspect of these findings is the variety of settings, the different types of violence and range of victims involved in the violent act. The majority of offenders reported being involved in more than one of the types of incident, with 'bullying' most common and the 'crime-related with the offender alone' least common. Within this analysis four broad categories are apparent: violence in conjunction with another crime; family violence; 'public violence'; and institutional violence. The first of these is discussed in the following section, the others deserve mention.

Family violence has rapidly become one of the social problems of the 1980s— which is not to say that it has not always existed (see Chapters 6 and 7). Child abuse in particular has attracted a great deal of public and specialist interest (see Chapter 7). Henderson's (1986) analysis shows that family violence, particularly violence towards women, takes place at night without the presence of other people. There is usually a history of violence between offender and victim, with the incident following an argument in which the victim has

Table 1.1 Typology of violent incidents (after Henderson, 1986)

Type of violence	Victim	Most frequent means of assault	Location
Crime-related[a] (individual)	Known[b]	Kicking	Domestic
Crime-related (group)	Unknown	Gun/bottle	Domestic
Prison	Peer	Punching	Prison
Prison	Staff	Strangling	Prison
'Social'	Unknown	Punching	Pub/club
Family	Relative	Gun/knife	Domestic
Gang	Unknown	Knife/kicking	Street
'Bullying'	Young person	Slapping/bottle	Street

[a] Violence during the commission of another crime such as burglary.
[b] Known/unknown to the offender prior to the crime.

retaliated verbally but not physically. Sexual violence, towards either children or women, can take place within relationships or between strangers (Chapter 9).

The dynamics of family violence between husband and wife were described in a study by Dobash and Dobash (1984) of over a hundred battered wives. From both personal interviews and official records Dobash and Dobash constructed a pattern of violence, most often taking place in the family home, which began with a verbal confrontation, often construed by the man as a challenge to his authority. As the pattern unfolds the woman typically attempts to avert the forthcoming violence using strategies such as attempting to withdraw from the situation or trying to reason or debate with the man. As the attack begins, involving slapping, punching, butting or hitting with sticks and other weapons, the woman continues to try to negotiate a way out of the violence. The woman hit back physically in only a very few instances, then out of anger or frustration; the general effect of this was to increase the level of violence. During the majority of assaults there were bystanders present, most often children. They mainly tried to support the woman, either by begging the man to stop or by running for help. After the attack, which resulted in a range of physical injury inflicted on the woman, the men were reported as acting as if nothing had happened, with few expressing remorse or regret. The injured women sought contact with friends, social and medical agencies, or voluntary bodies for both solace and help. Dobash and Dobash suggest that the quality of the response to this search for contact is vital: an outright condemnation of the violence is entirely more supportive than an implicit blaming of the woman by looking for ways in which she might have caused the violence to take place.

'Public violence' is of two types—involving gangs or taking place in pubs or clubs. Henderson describes two types of gang violence. In the first a group attacks a victim at night, usually after drinking hours; the victim is not known to the attackers but is also liable to have been drinking; weapons are used, as well as kicking, which can result in death. The second type of gang violence Henderson describes as 'bullying', in which younger victims are slapped and pushed, resulting in serious injury. Violence associated with pubs tends to be between individuals, with the offender's associates as onlookers rather than fellow attackers. The offender and victim have both been drinking and violence follows an argument instigated by the victim. In the fight both offender and victim sustain injuries.

Violence in institutions is of two types—directed towards fellow inmates or towards authority figures. In Henderson's study the violence was towards other prisoners and police and prison staff, although violence does, of course, occur in other institutions such as prisons and psychiatric hospitals (see Chapters 10, 11 and 12).

Robbery

Robbery is the theft, or attempted theft, of property or money directly from another person; the theft is accompanied by the use of physical force or the threat of physical harm. The robber may be armed, although most armed robbers use their weapons to intimidate rather than to inflict injury (Dinitz *et al.*, 1975)—which is not to say that, given the circumstances, the weapon would not be used. McClintock and Gibson (1961) carried out a study of robbery in London and described five situations in which the offence occurred. The first was a bank or jewellers; the second takes place on the street; the third type was robbery on private premises; and the fourth and fifth types of robbery were either between people who have only a short acquaintance (say, at a party) or between people who have known each other for longer periods. McClintock and Gibson found that stranger-to-stranger robberies are much more common, accounting for over three-quarters of such offences.

Henderson (1986) described two situations in which violence occurred during the course of stealing. In one the violence was directed towards a stranger, often older than the group of offenders, within the victim's home during daylight hours. Weapons are used causing serious injury and the offenders report a lack of emotion in committing the offence. In the second type the offender is alone at night in the victim's house; the violence, typically involving women or elderly people, takes the form of kicking and can be fatal. The offender reports being drunk at the time of the offence, feeling anxious, losing control, and afterwards saying that the victim did not deserve their injuries. These two types of robbery can be seen in terms of the distinction referred to previously between 'instrumental' and 'hostile' aggression (Buss, 1961). In the first instance the violence is simply instrumental in achieving the goal of obtaining money. The second bears the hallmarks of a 'burglary gone wrong': the offender, when discovered, panics and hits out at the householder, control is lost, perhaps due to the effects of drinking, and the simple burglary escalates to a robbery or even murder.

Murder

Murder is the *intentional* taking of the life of another person. The emphasis on intent is crucial: if a life is taken without premeditated intent to kill then the act is termed 'manslaughter'. It is, of course, often a matter for the courts to decide whether an act was premeditated and therefore one of murder, not manslaughter.

Wolfgang (1958) analysed the situations in which 588 murders took place in Philadelphia, USA, between 1948 and 1952. In a substantial number of cases (37%) the killing followed a relatively trivial event such as an argument, threat or insult; in the majority of cases the offender and victim knew each other (87%); the offender and victim were almost always of the same race (94%); most murderers were male (82%), usually less than 35 years of age; most victims were also male (76%); stabbing was the most common means of causing death; the offender, victim or both had usually been drinking (66%); and offenders typically had previous arrest records, usually for violent crime (66%). The murders most frequently occurred in a domestic setting during the summer months, with the hours between 8.00 p.m. Saturday and 2.00 a.m. Sunday the most common times. The incidents which were the most violent in character took place between husband and wife.

Most subsequent surveys broadly agree with Wolfgang's findings, although there are several exceptions. An English study found that the majority (60%) of victims are female (Gibson and Kline, 1961); a study in Chicago found that offender and victim were related in fewer instances (58%), and that firearms were more frequently used (Block, 1977). Goldstein (1986) presents an analysis of the motives for murder from the 1983 American figures, and suggests that about 20% of murders could be related to another crime such as robbery, while 44% were associated with arguments. In total, the general picture is of an incident which commonly takes place between people who are at least acquainted, have argued and have perhaps been drinking.

While the surveys paint an overall picture, a study by Luckenbill (1977) vividly illuminates the fine detail. Luckenbill analysed the interactions between offender and victim in the time immediately before the act of murder. From this analysis he described six stages in 'transactions resulting in murder'. In stage one the opening move comes from the victim in the form of a verbal comment, refusal to comply with a request (mostly in child murder) or some physical act such as flirtation. In some cases an insult was clearly intended, in others the offender interpreted the victim's behaviour as offensive. In stage two the offender seeks confirmation of the insult, by either verbally checking with the victim or with anyone else who might be present; the victim's continuation of the behaviour can also act as confirmation of the insult. In some instances the 'confirmation' is inferred: for example, a child's continued screaming confirms refusal to comply with the instruction to be quiet. At stage three the offender opts not to retreat but to stand his or her ground and retaliate. In most cases the retaliation at this stage is verbal, although in a minority of instances it is physical and the murder results. At stage four the victim replies to the retaliation: as Luckenbill notes, 'The victim's move appeared as an agreement that violence was suitable to the transaction' (p. 183). The victim's move is a continuation of the offensive behaviour, a verbal counterchallenge, or physical attack—a move often supported by onlookers. With stage five, battle commences, usually with a weapon to hand: the act is generally brief. Luckenbill reports that in over half the murders the offender 'dropped the victim in a single shot, stab or rally of blows' (p. 185). In the sixth and final stage the murderer acts in one of three ways: he or she voluntarily waits for the police; is held by others present; or flees the scene.

Luckenbill portrays a crime which is not simply perpetrated by one person: 'Rather, murder is the outcome of a dynamic interchange between an offender, victim, and, in many cases, bystanders' (p. 185). This view of the victim as playing a role, perhaps even a causative one, in determining their fate has been a source of some controversy. Dobash and Dobash (1984), for example, concluded their study of battered wives discussed previously with a note that their research failed to support any interpretation which shifted the blame for the attack from the aggressor to the victim. While not discounting the possibility that Luckenbill's analysis may have some relevance in understanding violence between males, Dobash and Dobash argue that gender and its associated roles and meanings must be considered when male violence is directed at female victims. However, at a general theoretical level, Dobash and Dobash are unhappy with the notion of victim-precipitated violence: 'We would argue that many violent episodes should be understood as often constructed intentionally by the agggressor' (p. 286).

While this interactive model may be efficacious in explaining some murders, particularly domestic ones, there are other types of murder which seem to demand a different level of explanation. The *mass murderer* kills a number of people simultaneously; the *serial killer* is a mass murderer who kills victims over a period of time rather than in one outburst. The victims of the serial killer are often tortured or sexually assaulted before being murdered (Levin and Fox, 1985).

ANALYSIS OF THE VIOLENT OFFENDER

Taxonomies

This approach seeks to classify types of violent offender according to one or more variables. Conklin (1972), for example, suggested that there are four 'specialist' types of robber. The *professional robber* views robbery as a highly effective means of earning a living; the *opportunist robber* steals only small amounts as and when a vulnerable target, such as a young or old person, presents itself; the *addict robber* and the *alcoholic robber* steal to obtain money to purchase more drugs or drink. Similar taxonomies have also been suggested for murder (Morrison, 1973). Megargee (1982) discusses these and other taxonomies in detail. While this general approach is helpful in illustrating that different people commit violent acts for different reasons and under different conditions, it does not say a great deal about the *person* involved. A body of research which has attempted to investigate the psychology of the violent offender is concerned with the link between personality and violence.

PERSONALITY

The model which prompted this line of research was proposed by Megargee (1966): the basis of the model is that violence occurs when the instigation to violence, mediated by anger, exceeds the individual's level of control of aggressive feelings or impulses. The *undercontrolled* person has very low inhibitors, and therefore frequently acts in a violent manner when provocation is perceived. The *overcontrolled* person has extremely strong inhibitors, and violence will only occur if the provocation is intense or has been endured for a very long period of time. Megargee predicted that the overcontrolled personality would be found in those who have committed acts of extreme violence but not among those with histories of frequent minor assaults. Blackburn (1968) compared the personality profiles of a group of 'extreme' violent individuals, convicted of murder, manslaughter or attempted murder, with a group of 'moderate' violent offenders who had committed acts of assault. In keeping with the prediction, the extreme group were significantly more introverted, conforming, overcontrolled and less hostile than the moderate group, although Crawford (1977) failed to replicate this finding. Quinsey *et al.* (1983) and Henderson (1983a) reported that the overcontrolled violent offender showed deficiencies in assertive behaviour. Henderson (1983a) also found that violent offenders who scored low on a psychometric measure of control reported significantly more difficulty in controlling their temper and avoiding fights. While the weight of this research lends support to a distinction based on an overcontrolled–undercontrolled dichotomy, the most significant advances have come from an approach which searches for types or clusters of offenders based on their scores on personality measures.

Blackburn (1971) carried out a cluster analysis of the MMPI scores of 56 male murderers detained in a secure psychiatric hospital. His analysis of MMPI scores showed four clusters of violent offenders: as shown in Table 1.2, two of these clusters were classed as overcontrolled and two as undercontrolled. The *Psychopathic* group is characterized by poor impulse control, high extraversion, outward-directed hostility, low anxiety and few psychiatric symptoms. The *Paranoid–Aggressive* group also displays high impulsivity and

Table 1.2 Typology of violent offenders (after Blackburn, 1971)

Undercontrolled	Overcontrolled
Psychopathic	Controlled–Repressor
Paranoid–Aggressive	Depressed–Inhibited

aggression, but also high levels of psychiatric disorder, particularly psychotic symptoms. These two groups are sometimes referred to as *Primary Psychopaths* and *Secondary Psychopaths*. The overcontrolled classification contains a *Controlled–Repressor* group which exhibits a high degree of impulse control and of defensiveness, and low levels of hostility, anxiety and psychiatric symptoms. The second overcontrolled group is labelled *Depressed–Inhibited*, and is characterized by low levels of impulsivity and extraversion, inward-directed hostility and high levels of depression.

Blackburn (1975) replicated this finding, as did McGurk (1978) with a sample of 'normal' murderers from a prison, rather than hospital, population. Henderson (1982) found essentially the same four types in a sample of violent offenders from the prison population. The evidence therefore supports the fourfold classification of violent offenders. However, before beginning to explain *violent* crime exclusively the prevalence of the four groups in other types of offender must be considered.

In two studies with non-violent prisoners, Holland and Holt (1975) and Widom (1978) found four personality clusters: in both studies three of the clusters corresponded to the original clusters with the exception that the depressed–inhibited group was not found. McGurk and McGurk (1979) similarly found three clusters with non-violent prisoners, and, once again, the groups corresponded to the original ones with no depressed–inhibited group appearing in the analysis. Henderson (1983b) also found four clusters in an MMPI analysis of non-violent offenders, and this time the clusters matched the original analysis; that is, a depressed–inhibited group was found in a non-violent population. Henderson (1983b, p. 676) then compared the non-violent depressed–inhibited group with the same group from the violent population in her earlier study (Henderson, 1982): 'Although the defining characteristics of the two are similar, the violent offender of this [inhibited] group tends to be more disturbed, introverted, anxious and hostile than his non-violent counterpart.' It appears, on balance, that the four personality clusters are to be found in the offender population generally, rather than only in the violent offender population. The depressed–inhibited profile seems the most characteristic of violent offender populations and may therefore give some clues towards explaining at least some violent acts.

The theoretical position is a matter of debate. Bartol (1980) suggests that the low inhibition of the undercontrolled offender corresponds with Eysenck's proposition that anti-social behaviour is the result of a failure to condition impulse control. However, Henderson (1982) found that violent inhibited offenders reported difficulty in making friends and functioning as part of a *social* group. Thus violence can be seen either as resulting from the effects of a stable personality trait; or it can be understood in social terms, with the emphasis on a person–situation interaction (Blackburn, 1983). Blackburn (1986, p. 268) offers a succinct summary of the position to date:

> In the case of the primary and secondary psychopaths, the probability of a violent outcome seems likely to be increased as a result of their typical coercive or hostile approaches to interpersonal problem-solving. For controlled and inhibited

individuals, on the other hand, violence may represent a last resort when attempts to resolve a situation through compliance or avoidance break down. In these terms, this broad classification may provide a first stab at understanding a violent act in the individual case.

While empirical research has supported and refined Megargee's original proposition of undercontrolled and overcontrolled violent individuals, it seems unlikely that this approach will provide an explanation for violent crime in itself. This is not surprising in that theories of aggression and violence which have relied heavily on individual factors—the instinct and drive theories—have been found to be wanting. What is required is a marriage of the situational and individual approaches.

TOWARDS A THEORETICAL PERSPECTIVE

Investigation of violence has focused on three areas: the act itself, the perpetrator and the situation in which the violence occurs. Research has added to our understanding of each of these three areas, with conventional wisdom holding that violence can best be viewed as resulting from an interaction between the 'person' and the 'situation'.

Psychological research has principally been concerned with the 'person' side of the interaction, with a number of studies defining the personality of the violent individual. Situational studies, such as that of Luckenbill (1977), have pointed to the interpersonal transactions and conflicts which often precede violent acts. What is lacking at present is a unifying explanation which accounts for both the person and situation in explaining why a 'violent personality' acts in a violent way given certain situational cues. In some instances this may be clear, as with robbery, where the violence is instrumental in gaining financial reward; however, with murder and serious assault it may be altogether less certain why the crime was committed. While psychological research has attempted to define the violent personality, the *processes* leading to violence are poorly understood. For example, Luckenbill (1977) suggested that the violent offender often 'perceived' insult or provocation. What remains to be answered is how the individual develops such a perceptual set and how this perception leads to violence. In looking for a more complex explanation of aggression and violence, Novaco's (1978) model holds promise in suggesting a complex interplay between physiology, emotion, cognition and behaviour as a response to environmental stimuli. The social, interactive nature of this model is also in keeping with theoretical trends which are moving away from explanations which rest heavily on 'inner' causes of violence—such as instinct and drive—towards a social learning theory. A fusion of social learning theory and the fine detail of Novaco's model appears to offer a way forward for research aimed at understanding violence.

The search for greater understanding of violence is not simply a theoretical quest, it is a matter of considerable professional and public concern. On the one hand, there is the question of the violent individual's future behaviour, which relates to the prediction of dangerousness (Chapter 5), while, on the other, there is the issue of management of the violent person. Imprisonment is one option, although this may do nothing more than shift the violence from one setting to another, achieving little in a rehabilitative sense. While custody may be necessary for the protection of society, this does not negate the potential for clinically oriented intervention in order to attempt to reduce the possibility of future violent acts.

CLINICAL APPROACHES TO VIOLENCE

We will not attempt to discuss here all the various clinical approaches and methods that can and have been used to prevent aggressive and violent behaviour—this is the focus of the chapters to follow. It would be more useful to introduce some general points and concepts which might be useful in assimilating the material in subsequent chapters.

The 'clinical' approach to violence prevention is characterized by primary attention to the psychological characteristics of the individual violent person, both for establishing the aetiology of the violence itself and for producing change. This can be contrasted with social, economic and political levels of analysis and intervention. Clearly, not all forms of violence are appropriately considered in individual clinical terms. One possible criterion for the clinical approach is that the violent behaviour itself constitutes a 'problem' for the perpetrator. Not all violence will be problematic in this way and thus professional 'help' may not be sought. For example, violence may be learned as an effective strategy for manipulating the environment, for obtaining social and material rewards and for preventing aversive behaviour from others. It is not difficult to see how this might be the case, for example, in a prison, where violence may be one of the few operant behaviours open to some individuals for controlling the environment.

Such instrumental uses of violence require a different therapeutic strategy from acts of 'angry' or 'hostile' aggression, where ill-considered violent behaviours are self-defeating for the perpetrator and may even be acknowledged as such. In the former case the therapeutic emphasis would need to be on changing environmental contingencies such that previously preferred behaviours are now ineffective and on establishing alternative, non-violent skills for obtaining rewards.

Many serious forms of violence, including murder, manslaughter, spouse abuse, rape and the physical abuse of children, appear to be acts of angry rather than instrumental aggression (Howells, 1988, 1989), the violent behaviour occurring in the context of provoking environmental events, heightened affect and an intention to hurt the victim as a primary motivator. It is for such angry acts of violence that clinical approaches may be most relevant.

The task of analysis, assessment and intervention in such cases has been considerably facilitated by the preliminary model of angry aggression suggested by Novaco (1976, 1978, 1985 and this volume). Although Novaco has been acknowledged as the instigator of anger-management methods, it seems that his more important contribution has been to identify some of the components of angry aggression and the reciprocal causal relationships existing between them (see, particularly, Novaco, 1978). Theoretical models such as those of Novaco, although preliminary and subject to change, are more richly productive of strategies for assessment and intervention than the detailed techniques and procedures of anger-management programmes themselves.

Novaco distinguishes triggering environmental events (provocations), cognitive processes, physiological/affective arousal and angry behaviours. The implication of this model is that all four components need to be assessed and to become potential areas for intervention. Some progress has been made in specifying triggers for angry aggression in normal populations (Averill, 1982; Mazelan and Howells, 1989), although less is known, directly, about triggering events in violent groups. Threats to self-schemata may be powerful triggers for angry aggression (Blackburn, 1988).

The first part of the clinical assessment task with violent individuals is thus to identify critical triggering events for the person, using formal psychiatric and criminological histories, structured interviews, observations by significant others, direct observation methods and psychometric tests (Howells, 1989). Ascertaining critical triggers for angry violence often suggests direct stimulus control methods for preventing violent incidents (Howells, 1988).

A major feature of Novaco's contribution has been his drawing attention to the crucial role of cognitive processes as a determinant of angry aggressive responses to provocations (Novaco, 1978, 1985 and this volume). Cognitive expectations, appraisals and attributions need to be assessed in violent incidents with a view to detecting biases and information-processing distortions which may predispose the person to violence. Novaco adds to the range of possible assessment methods in his discussion later in this book.

Producing change in cognitive processing is a clear task for clinicians dealing with violent people (Novaco, 1985; Blackburn, 1988; Howells, 1988, 1989). There is a number of studies suggesting that cognitive therapies have some effect, but, unfortunately, too few of them, thus far, are directly concerned with producing change in serious forms of violent behaviour itself (Blackburn, 1988). Cognitive therapy for angry violence will need to face the difficulty that violent people may be less inclined and motivated to stand back from their habitual cognitive styles, in order to change them, than are depressed or anxious people.

The physiological arousal component of Novaco's model suggests the need to assess physiological arousal to provocations and the individual's capacity to control such reactions. Relaxation training has demonstrated some effect on angry responses (Novaco, 1985) and may have a role in relation to violence prevention for some people.

Behavioural reactions to provocations, paradoxically, are not always given the full attention they require in analyses of violence. Although attention is, necessarily, given to violent responses, it is easy to neglect the possibility that the violent act is sometimes the culmination of preceding interactions between the violent person and others in the social environment. This is the 'transactional' aspect of violence suggested by Patterson (1985), Toch (1985) and others. It follows that assessment and treatment need to be directed at what might be called *escalating* behaviours, i.e. aggressive but non-violent behaviours that make a violent outcome more likely. A number of authors have stressed the relevance of social skills training methods for both the analysis and modification of molecular verbal and non-verbal behaviours in violent people (Feindler and Ecton, 1986; Glick and Goldstein, 1987; Howells, 1988, 1989).

In summary, the nature of the assessment and intervention task for the clinician has been clarified by recent analyses of anger and angry aggression. The later chapters in this book add further to our knowledge for particular groups and in particular contexts.

PSYCHIATRIC DISORDER AND VIOLENCE

In this book we shall not be addressing in detail or at length the difficult and controversial issue of the relationship between psychiatric disorder and violence. This topic has been reviewed elsewhere (Howells, 1982; Prins, 1982; Bluglass, 1988), as has the more general issue of the relationships between disorder and criminality (Hollin, 1989). We plan to devote a whole book in this series to this particular topic.

For now it is sufficient to remind the reader of the myriad conceptual, methodological and empirical difficulties in establishing the relationship between these two categories of behaviour (Howells, 1982). It is likely that psychiatric disorder is common in samples of prisoners, including violent ones, but the actual prevalence rate varies considerably, depending on the population studied (Prins, 1980). However, a high rate of mental disorder in offender populations does not establish a causal link between the disorder and criminal or violent acts. The correlation sometimes observed between violent crime and disorder may be a function of the mentally ill being less skilled at avoiding detection (Teplin, 1984), or the potency of prison and similar environments in producing mental disorder in inmates (Gunn, 1977). Studies attempting to follow up psychiatric populations to determine whether the mentally ill have higher subsequent rates of violent or other crime are equally equivocal, because of a range of confounds existing in this kind of research (Rabkin, 1979; Howells, 1982).

Attempts have been made to relate *particular* disorders and conditions to the causation of violent behaviour. Recent reviews by Bluglass (1988) and Prins (1988) cover psychopathic disorders (see Blackburn, this volume), epilepsy, EEG abnormality, alcohol intoxication, schizophrenia, mental handicap, depression and other abnormalities. Schizophrenia and depression are, perhaps, the most plausible contenders as disorders making a significant, albeit small, contribution to the aetiology of violence.

The general public probably associates schizophrenia with violence (Spry, 1984) and there is some evidence that schizophrenics are slightly more likely to commit violent offences than other disordered groups or the general population (Sosowsky, 1978; Taylor and Gunn, 1984). A relationship may exist between paranoid ideation and violence, the victims of a schizophrenic's violent attacks often being the same people who figure in their delusions (Häfner and

Böker, 1982, Planansky and Johnston, 1977). Delusional crimes of this type are probably particularly likely to catch the public imagination. Craft (1984) notes the case of Ian Ball, in which delusional thought processes were manifest in a plot to kidnap a member of the royal family. Prins (1983, 1986) discusses the crimes of Peter Sutcliffe, the 'Yorkshire Ripper', there being some controversy as to the role of his paranoid schizophrenia in the murders he committed. It should be stressed, however, that the publicity generated by such cases is in inverse proportion to their frequency. Only a tiny proportion of deluded and paranoid people commit such crimes. Mental illness is thus neither a necessary nor a sufficient cause of violence.

While schizophrenia may be directly related to violence, links other than delusions may be important. Taylor (1982, p. 280) suggests that

> It is not unusual to find that the violent act of a schizophrenic cannot be directly explained by the current psychopathology. This does not, however, negate the relevance of the illness . . . social and illness variables must be considered together.

The point Taylor makes is an important one: as well as searching for a causal relationship between schizophrenia and violence, attention should also be paid to the similarities in social, environmental and organic antecedents common to both violence and schizophrenia. More recent findings by the same researcher reinforce this point. From a survey of 121 psychotic offenders, Taylor (1985, p. 497) concluded that '20% of the actively psychotic were directly driven to offend by their psychotic symptoms, and a further 26% probably so'. When social factors such as homelessness were considered along with the nature of the crime, so that 'the direct and indirect consequence of psychosis are considered together, then over 80% of the offences of the psychotic were probably attributable to their illness' (p. 497).

Similar complexities exist in the relationship between depression and violence. Depression and violence may be correlated for a number of reasons, without there being a causal relationship. Suicidal symptomatology is common in domestic homicides, and it is likely that some serious acts of violence of this sort reflect a desire to kill self and family for 'depressive' reasons (West, 1965).

In summary, we must conclude that some psychiatric disorders, particularly schizophrenia and depression, are probably over-represented among those who engage in serious violence. The exact nature of the relationship between the disorder and violent acts, however, remains problematic. The published research on this relationship would seem to have a number of implications for the practitioner. First, the great majority of violent acts the practitioner will encounter are unlikely to be explicable in terms of mental disorder, unless he or she works in a setting with patients where a violence–disorder link is selectively referred. Thus, in general, violence will require explanation and intervention in terms of 'normal' psychological principles. Second, when a client is encountered in whom violence and disorder co-exist the relationship between the disorder and the violence may not be a linear causal one. Thus when a violent schizophrenic, for example, is encountered, there should be caution about assuming that the disorder is implicated in the causation of the violence. Equally, improvement in the psychiatric state of such a patient does not imply that the probability of violence is thereby reduced.

Third, when disorder and violence *are* found to be causally related (this could be demonstrated, for example, by looking at the covariation over time between the disorder and the occurrence of violence) this should not be the end of the story in terms of psychological analysis. The task then becomes to identify the specific psychological dysfunctions in the disordered patients that increase the probability of violence. Thus, having discovered, for example, that psychotic episodes precede and probably cause violence in a particular person, we then need to determine what features of the psychosis are significant. Is it, for example, delusional beliefs with a particular content? Indeed, investigation of such cases may give important clues as to the nature of *general* instigators of violence. The importance of delusions, for example, may alert us to the possibility that for all people, not just the mentally disordered, cognitive beliefs about other people and their behaviours are an important determinant of violence. In this sense a psychiatric diagnosis should be the beginning rather than the end of the search for an explanation.

References

Anderson, C. A. (1987). Temperature and aggression: Effects on quarterly, yearly, and city rates of violent and nonviolent crime. *Journal of Personality and Social Psychology*, **52**, 1161–173.

Averill, J. R. (1982). *Anger and Aggression: An Essay on Emotion*. New York: Springer-Verlag.

Bandura, A. (1973a). *Aggression: A Social Learning Analysis*. Englewood Cliffs, NJ: Prentice-Hall.

Bandura, A. (1973b). Social learning theory of aggression. In J. F. Kautson (ed.), *The Control of Aggression: Implications from Basic Research*. Chicago, IL: Aldine.

Bandura, A., Ross, D., and Ross, S. A. (1963). Imitation of film-mediated aggressive models. *Journal of Abnormal and Social Psychology*, **66**, 3–11.

Baron, R. A. (1977). *Human Aggression*. New York: Plenum Press.

Bartol, C. R. (1980). *Criminal Behavior: A Psychosocial Approach*. Englewood Cliffs, NJ: Prentice-Hall.

Berkowitz, L. (1965). The concept of aggressive drive: Some additional considerations. In L. Berkowitz (ed.), *Advances in Experimental Social Psychology*, Vol. 2. New York: Academic Press.

Berkowitz, L. (1974). Some determinants of impulsive aggression: Role of mediated associations with reinforcement for aggression. *Psychological Review*, **81**, 165–76.

Blackburn, R. (1968). Personality in relation to extreme aggression in psychiatric offenders. *British Journal of Psychiatry*, **114**, 821–8.

Blackburn, R. (1971). Personality types among abnormal homocides. *British Journal of Criminology*, **11**, 14–31.

Blackburn, R. (1975). An empirical classification of psychopathic personality. *British Journal of Psychiatry*, **127**, 456–60.

Blackburn, R. (1983). Psychopathy, delinquency and crime. In A. Gale and J. A. Edwards (eds), *Physiological Correlates of Human Behaviour, Vol. 3: Individual Differences and Psychopathology*. London: Academic Press.

Blackburn, R. (1986). Patterns of personality deviation among violent offenders. *British Journal of Criminology*, **26**, 254–69.

Blackburn, R. (1988). Cognitive–behavioural approaches to understanding and treating aggression. In K. Howells and C. Hollin (eds), *Clinical Approaches to Aggression and Violence: Issues in Criminological and Legal Psychology*. Leicester: British Psychological Society.

Blau, J., and Blau, P. (1982). The cost of inequality: Metropolitan structure and violent crime. *American Sociological Review*, **47**, 114–29.

Block, R. (1977). *Violent Crime*. Lexington, MA: Lexington Books.

Bluglass, R. (1988). Psychiatric approaches to aggression and violence. In K. Howells and C. Hollin (eds), *Clinical Approaches to Aggression and Violence: Issues in Criminological Legal Psychology* Leicester: British Psychological Society.

Bornstein, P. H., Hamilton, S. B., and McFall, M. E. (1981). Modification of adult aggression: A critical review of theory, research, and practice. In M. Hersen, R. M. Eisler, and P. M. Miller (eds.), *Progress in Behavior Modification*, Vol. 12. London: Academic Press.

Box, S. (1983). *Power, Crime and Mystification*. London: Tavistock.

Buss, A. H. (1961). *The Psychology of Aggression*. New York: Wiley.

Carroll, L., and Jackson, P. I. (1983). Inequality, opportunity and crime rates in central cities. *Criminology*, **21**, 178–93.

Conklin, J. (1972). *Robbery and the Criminal Justice System*. New York: Lippincott.

Craft, M. (1984). Low intelligence, mental handicap and criminality. In M. Craft and A. Craft (eds), *Mentally Abnormal Offenders*. London: Baillière Tindall.

Crawford, D. A. (1977). The HDHQ results of long-term prisoners: Relationships with criminal and institutional behaviour. *British Journal of Social and Clinical Psychology*, **16**, 391–4.

Dengerink, H. A., Schnedler, R. W., and Covey, M. V. (1978). The role of avoidance in aggressive responses to attack and no attack. *Journal of Personality and Social Psychology*, **36**, 1044–53.

Dinitz, S., Dynes, R., and Clarke, A. (1975). *Deviance*. Oxford: Oxford University Press.

Dobash, R. E., and Dobash, R. P. (1984). The nature and antecedents of violent events. *British Journal of Criminology*, **24**, 269–88.

Dollard, J., Doob, L. W., Miller, N. E., Mowrer, O. H., and Sears, R. R. (1939). *Frustration and Aggression*. New Haven, CT: Yale University Press.

Feindler, E. L., and Ecton, R. B. (1986). *Adolescent Anger Control: Cognitive–Behavioral Techniques*. New York: Pergamon Press.

Fromm, E. (1977). *The Anatomy of Human Destructiveness*. Harmondsworth, Middlesex: Penguin.

Gibson, E., and Kline, S. (1961). *Murder*. London: HMSO.

Glick, B., and Goldstein, A. P. (1987). Aggression replacement training. *Journal of Counseling and Development*, **65**, 356–67.

Goldstein, J. H. (1986). *Aggression and Crimes of Violence* (2nd edn.). Oxford: Oxford University Press.

Gunn, J. (1977). Criminal behaviour and mental disorder. *British Journal of Psychiatry*, **130**, 317–29.

Häfner, H., and Böker, W. (1982). *Crimes of Violence by Mentally Abnormal Offenders: A Psychiatric and Epidemiological Study in the Federal German Republic*. (Trans. H. Marshall), Cambridge: Cambridge University Press (original work published in 1973).

Hayes, S. C., Rincover, A., and Volosin, D. (1980). Variables influencing the acquisition and maintenance of aggressive behaviour: Modeling versus sensory reinforcement. *Journal of Abnormal Psychology*, **89**, 254–62.

Henderson, M. (1982). An empirical classification of convicted violent offenders. *British Journal of Criminology*, **22**, 1–20.

Henderson, M. (1983a). Self-reported assertion and aggression among violent offenders with high or low levels of overcontrolled hostility. *Personality and Individual Differences*, **4**, 113–5.

Henderson, M. (1983b). An empirical classification of non-violent offenders using the MMPI. *Personality and Individual Differences*, **4**, 671–7.

Henderson, M. (1986). An empirical typology of violent incidents reported by prison inmates with convictions for violence. *Aggressive Behavior*, **12**, 21–32.

Holland, T. R., and Holt, N. (1975). Personality patterns among short-term prisoners undergoing presentence evaluations. *Psychological Reports*, **37**, 827–36.

Hollin, C. R. (1989). *Psychology and Crime: An Introduction to Criminological Psychology*. London: Routledge.

Hough, M., and Mayhew, P. (1985). *Taking Account of Crime: Key Findings from the second British Crime Survey*. London: HMSO.

Howells, K. (1982). Mental disorder and violent behaviour. In P. Feldman (ed.), *Developments in the Study of Criminal Behaviour, Vol. 2: Violence*. Chichester: Wiley.

Howells, K. (1988). The management of angry aggression. In W. Dryden and P. Trowers (eds), *Developments in Cognitive Psychotherapy*. London: Sage.

Howells, K. (1989). Anger—management methods in relation to the prevention of violent behaviour. In J. Archer and K. Browne (eds). *Human Aggression: Naturalistic Approaches*. London: Routledge.

Kutash, S. B. (1978). Psychoanalytic theories of aggression. In I. L. Kutash, S. B. Kutash, and L. B. Schlesinger (eds.), *Violence: Perspectives on Murder and Aggression*. San Francisco: Jossey-Bass.

Levin, J., and Fox, A. F. (1985). *Mass Murder*. New York: Plenum Press.

Lorenz, K. (1966). *On Aggression*. New York: Harcourt Brace World.

Lorenz, K. (1974). *Civilized Man's Eight Deadly Sins*. New York: Harcourt Brace Jovanovich.

Luckenbill, D. F. (1977). Criminal homicide as a situated transaction. *Social Problems*, **25**, 176–86.

Marsh, P., and Cambell, A. (Eds.). (1982). *Aggression and Violence*. Oxford: Blackwell.

Marsh, P., Rosser, E., and Harré, R. (1978). *The Rules of Disorder*. London: Routledge & Kegan Paul.

Mazelan, P. and Howells, K. (1989). *Temper and Temperateness: the Experience of Anger in Everyday Life*. London: Sidgwick and Jackson. In press.

McClintock, F. H., and Gibson, E. (1961). *Robbery in London*. London: Macmillan.

McGurk, B. J. (1978). Personality types among normal homicides. *British Journal of Criminology*, **18**, 146–61.

McGurk, B. J., and McGurk, R. E. (1979). Personality types among prisoners and prison officers—an investigation of Megargee's theory of control. *British Journal of Criminology*, **19**, 31–49.

Mednick, S. A., Pollock, V., Volavka, J., and Gabrielli, W. F. (1982). Biology and violence. In M. E. Wolfgang and N. A. Weiner (eds.), *Criminal Violence*. Beverly Hills, CA: Sage Publications.

Megargee, E. I. (1966). Undercontrolled and overcontrolled personality types in extreme antisocial aggression. *Psychological Monographs*, **80**, (3, Whole No. 611).

Megargee, E. I. (1982). Psychological determinants and correlates of criminal violence. In M. E. Wolfgang and N. A. Weiner (eds.), *Criminal Violence*. Beverly Hills, CA: Sage Publications.

Merikangas, J. R. (1981). The neurology of violence. In J. R. Merikangas (ed.), *Brain–Behavior Relationships*. Lexington, MA: Lexington Books.

Miller, N. E. (1941). The frustration–aggression hypothesis. *Psychological Review*, **48**, 337–42.

Miller, W. (1976). Youth gangs in the urban crisis era. In J. F. Short (ed.), *Delinquency, Crime and Society*. Chicago: University of Chicago Press.

Monahan, J., and Klassen, D. (1982). Situational approaches to understanding and predicting individual violent behavior. In M. E. Wolfgang and N. A. Weiner (eds.), *Criminal Violence*. Beverly Hills, CA: Sage Publications.

Morrison, W. A. (1973). Criminal homicide and the death penalty in Canada: Time for reassessment and new directions: Toward a typology of homicide. *Canadian Journal of Criminology and Corrections*, **15**, 267–96.

Novaco, R. W. (1976). The functions and regulation of the arousal of anger. *American Journal of Psychiatry*, **133**, 1124–8.

Novaco, R. W. (1978). Anger and coping with stress. In J. P. Foreyt and D. P. Rathjen (eds.), *Cognitive Behavior Therapy*. New York: Plenum Press.

Novaco, R. W. (1985). Anger and its therapeutic regulations. In M. A. Chesner and R. H Rosenman (eds), *Anger and Hostility in Cardiovascular and Behavioral Disorders*. New York: Hemisphere Publishing.

Patterson, G. R. (1985). A microsocial analysis of anger and irritable behavior. In M. A. Chesney and R. H. Rosenman (eds). *Anger and Hostility in Cardiovascular and Behavioral Disorders*. Washington: Hemisphere Publishing Co.

Planansky, K., and Johnston, R. (1977). Homicidal aggression in schizophrenic man. *Acta Psychiatrica Scandinavia*, **55**, 65–73.

Prins, H. (1980). *Offenders, Deviants or Patients? An Introduction to the Study of Socio-Forensic Problems*. London: Tavistock.

Prins, H. (1982). *Criminal Behaviour: An Introduction to Criminology and the Penal System* (2nd ed.). London: Tavistock.

Prins, H. (1983). Diminished responsibility and the Sutcliffe case: Legal, psychiatric and social aspects. *Medicine, Science and the Law*, **23**, 17–24.

Prins, H. (1986). *Dangerous Behaviour, the Law and Mental Disorder*. London: Tavistock.

Prins, H. (1988). Mental illness and criminal behaviour. Paper presented to conference on '*Clinical Approaches to the Mentally Disordered Offender*'. Leicester, September.

Quinsey, V. L., Maguire, A., and Varney, G. W. (1983). Assertion and overcontrolled hostility among mentally disordered murderers. *Journal of Consulting and Clinical Psychology*, **51**, 550–6.

Riches, D. (Ed.). (1986). *The Anthropology of Violence*. Oxford: Blackwell.

Rabkin, J. G. (1979). Criminal behaviour of discharged mental patients: A critical appraisal of the research. *Psychological Bulletin*, **86**, 1–27.

Rotton, J., and Frey, J. (1985). Air pollution, weather, and violent crimes: Concomitant time-series analysis of archival data. *Journal of Personality and Social Psychology*, **49**, 1207–20.

Siann, G. (1985). *Accounting for Aggression: Perspectives on Aggression and Violence*. London: Allen & Unwin.

Siegel, L. J. (1986). *Criminology* (2nd edn.). St. Paul, MN: West Publishing Co.

Sosowsky, L. (1978). Crime and violence amongst mental patients reconsidered in view of the new legal relationship between the State and the mentally ill. *American Journal of Psychiatry*, **135**, 33–42.

Spry, W. B. (1984). Schizophrenia and crime. In M. Craft and A. Craft (eds), *Mentally Abnormal Offenders*. London: Baillière Tindall.

Storr, A. (1970). *Human Aggression*. Harmondsworth, Middlesex: Penguin.

Taylor, P. J. (1982). Schizophrenia and violence. In J. Gunn and D. P. Farrington (eds), *Abnormal Offenders, Delinquency, and the Criminal Justice System*. Chichester: Wiley.

Taylor, P. J. (1985). Motives for offending among violent and psychotic men. *British Journal of Psychiatry*, **147**, 491–98.

Taylor, P.J., and Gunn, J. (1984). Violence and psychosis II—effect of psychiatric diagnosis on conviction and sentencing of offenders. *British Medical Journal*, **289**, 9–12.

Teplin, L. A. (1984). Criminalizing mental disorder: The comparative arrest rate of the mentally ill. *American Psychologist*, **39**, 794–803.

Toch, H. (1979). Perspectives on the offender. In H. Toch (ed.), *Psychology of crime and criminal justice*. London: Holt, Rinehart & Winston.

Toch, H. (1985). The catalytic situation in the violence equation. *Journal of Applied Social Psychology*, **15**, 105–13.

West, D. J. (1965). *Murder Followed by Suicide*. London: Heinemann.

West, D. J., and Farrington, D. P. (1977). *The Delinquent Way of Life*. London: Heinemann.

Widom, C. S. (1978). An empirical classification of female offenders. *Criminal Justice and Behavior*, **5**, 35–52.

Wolfgang, M. E. (1958). *Patterns in Criminal Homicide*. Philadelphia: University of Pennsylvania Press.

Wolfgang, M. E., and Ferracuti, F. (1967). *The Subculture of Violence: Towards an Integrated Theory in Criminology*. London: Tavistock.

Zillman, D. (1979). *Hostility and Aggression*. Hillsdale, NJ: Lawrence Erlbaum Associates.

2

Behavioural Approaches to Violent Crime

Monika Henderson

Ministry for Police and Emergency Services, Victoria, Australia

Behavioural approaches to the management of violent behaviour rely on the basic assumption that the behaviour has been learnt and, like any other learnt response, can be 'unlearnt' and replaced by an alternative, non-violent behaviour. Traditional behaviourist theories emphasized a straightforward stimulus–response model as the determinant of behaviour, with the behaviour both initially established and subsequently maintained by reinforcement. In these terms, violence would be considered a straightforward response to specific triggering stimuli, which continues because the behaviour results in some sort of reward. For example, the victim exhibits unpleasant behaviour (e.g. argument or threatened aggression) which elicits a violent response by the aggressor. The violence stops the victim's unpleasant behaviour, which is rewarding to the aggressor, so the likelihood of a further violent response under future similar circumstances is strengthened.

Such a simplistic model has obvious limitations in explaining complex human behaviours. In its simplest form, it cannot explain why the same individual may respond violently in one situation but not in another seemingly similar one, nor why considerably different degrees of violence can be triggered by similar circumstances across different individuals. In particular, the simple stimulus–response model takes no account of the importance of cognitive processes on the expression and the inhibition of behaviour.

The application of behavioural theory to the explanation of human behaviour is increasingly incorporating aspects of cognitive theory. The links between situational variables and the subsequent response are mediated by various cognitive processes. The individual's perception and appraisal of the situation, the person's interpretation of his or her own emotional state, the perceived goal of the act, personal motivations and other cognitive factors have a significant impact on the particular behavioural outcome. Even reinforcement

Clinical Approaches to Violence. Edited by K. Howells and C. R. Hollin
© 1989 John Wiley & Sons.

processes, whether in the form of tangible rewards, social rewards or self-reward, are subject to cognitive and emotive processes that determine how they will govern the behaviour.

These theoretical developments have been paralleled in therapeutic and other intervention strategies. Current intervention methods are placing increasingly greater emphasis on the importance of cognitive processes in the determination of human behaviour, and tailoring intervention strategies accordingly.

The position taken in this chapter is that the expression and inhibition of violent behaviour is a function of previous learning history and current social and situational determinants, mediated by internalized norms, attitudes and cognitions. Consequently, the appropriate approach to the control and management of violent behaviour is by replacing the learnt violent response with an alternative non-violent one, and that this can best be achieved through affecting both the underlying behavioural skills and cognitive processes.

BEHAVIOURAL APPROACHES

A variety of behavioural approaches has been applied to the management of violence. These include both direct control methods through the manipulation of reinforcement contingencies and indirect control of violence by the teaching of non-violent alternatives, and most intervention strategies will use both direct and indirect methods.

Direct control methods include traditional behaviour-modification techniques such as punishment, extinction, time out and overcorrection. These are reviewed in detail in Fehrenbach and Thelen (1981), and focus on aggression as the main target behaviour or as part of a general improvement in interpersonal behaviour within larger behavioural programmes and token economies. Contingency management techniques have also been usefully applied to aggression, as have self-control techniques (Goldstein et al., 1979). Although there has been little systematic research in this specific area, most available studies in extinction of general behaviour show direct methods to be less effective when used in isolation than when combined with teaching of an alternative response.

Various indirect control methods have been used in teaching non-violent alternatives. The most common is social skills training, which is discussed in more detail below. Other methods include conflict-management techniques, such as negotiation and contracting methods, and problem-solving approaches (Goldstein et al., 1979).

Social skills training is by far the most commonly used method in this area. It has achieved considerable popularity over the past decade in the treatment and management of human behaviour across a range of target populations. The technique has been embraced by clinical and correctional workers, and applied to psychiatric and offender populations in most countries. Its application to the control of violent behaviour has been less extensive to date, but an increasing number of studies is now being reported.

The term 'social skills training' covers a range of techniques and programmes, but is characterized by the use of five common component processes: information giving, modelling, behavioural rehearsal, corrective feedback and social reinforcement. Central to the social skills training process is the identification of the target behaviour (in this case, violence), within a situation-specific context (i.e. under what circumstances and specific situations it occurs for that individual), followed by the teaching of alternative responses to the situation (e.g. modelling a non-violent assertive response to that situation) and the practice of such alternative behaviours, with the aim of generalizing the new learnt behaviour to those real-life situations that previously elicited the less desirable (i.e. violent) behaviour.

Social skills training methods have met with considerable success in improving general social skills in various target groups, particularly psychiatric patients. Its application to violent behaviour is less extensive, and the few reported studies are reviewed below and described in more detail in the case illustration outlined later in this chapter.

SOCIAL SKILLS TRAINING APPROACHES TO AGGRESSION MANAGEMENT: A LITERATURE REVIEW

One of the earliest reports of applying social skills training techniques to the control of aggression is an uncontrolled single case reported by Kaufman and Wagner (1972). They described a systematic treatment programme (BARB) and its use with an aggressive adolescent. No data were given on treatment gains. Wallace et al. (1973) used assertive training and contingency contracting with a 22-year-old handicapped aggressive male. This was also an uncontrolled treatment study, and few data are available. However, Wallace et al. reported that only a single incident of indirect aggression occurred during 9-month follow-up for their client, when he had shown a pretreatment history of frequent and regular outbursts.

Rimm et al. (1974) reported one of the earliest applications of social skills training methods to aggression among non-clinical populations, with seven male volunteers who responded to a newspaper advertisement asking for men with temper-control deficits. Six other volunteers acted as controls. Trainees showed significantly greater improvement than controls on ratings of global assertiveness to role-played anger-provoking situations and on self-rated anxiety and anger after training in assertion. There were no significant differences in self-rated confidence or on a self-reported measure of assertion. No follow-up or generalization data were reported. Rimm (1977) also described an earlier study with collaborators using adult psychiatric patients institutionalized for anti-social aggression. The training group showed significantly greater improvement on social skills measures than placebo controls, and Rimm stated that informal follow-up observation by staff and relatives suggests that training reduced hostility and aggression among these patients.

Several other single-case or small-sample studies with aggressive psychiatric patients report similar findings. Foy et al. (1975) treated a male psychiatric patient hospitalized for explosive outbursts of rage using modelling followed by modelling plus instruction. They found that modelling improved assertive behaviour and reduced aggressive and other inappropriate behaviours, while the addition of instruction augmented these effects. The learnt skills were maintained at six months and appeared to generalize to the natural environment. Frederiksen *et al.* (1976) also obtained improvement in five molecular ratings and a molar rating of skill by social skills training methods with two verbally abusive adult psychiatric patients. Improvement generalized to new role-play situations and new role-play partners, as well as to the ward situation. Matson and Stephens (1978) reported similar improvement in four aggressive female chronic schizophrenics which was maintained at 3-month follow-up, and which also generalized to the ward setting.

Galassi and Galassi (1978) presented a study with female college students reporting low assertiveness and high aggression and hostility. Training resulted in significantly greater improvement on self-reported assertive behaviour and on some role-play ratings when compared to controls but there were no significant group differences on verbal hostility. Lehman and Olson (1975) treated female college students reporting problems with hostility towards men, using assertion training and rational-emotive therapy procedures. They obtained significant improvement in self-reported hostility and anger and on behavioural measures compared to discussion and no treatment control groups. Rahaim *et al.* (1980) used social skills training with a male client seeking help in controlling physical and verbally aggressive outbursts during his work as a police officer. They assessed treatment gains by both behavioural and cognitive measures and found improvement in self-reported assertion and anger and in assertive and aggressive verbal responses to role-played situations. Generalization to novel role-plays was reported as 'only moderate', although no figures were given. Improvement on some measures was obtained at 8-month follow-up. The authors concluded that behavioural intervention alters cognitions, so that a specific cognitive therapy programme is unnecessary.

Fehrenbach and Thelen (1981) selected 40 male students from a sample of over 1000 on the basis of self-rated anger control difficulty and rated aggression in a pretest role-play. Half received assertion training either with or without modelling, and the rest were allocated to either an attention placebo or assessment-only control group. Both training groups showed significantly greater total assertiveness scores in role-played responses to anger-inducing situations than controls. Both training groups and attention placebo controls were significantly less aggressive than the assessment-only group, but did not differ among each other. Improvement on the assertion but not aggression measures generalized to novel role-plays for the modelling training group only. Fehrenbach and Thelen's results show only limited support for the role of training in reducing aggression. However, as noted by the authors themselves, their treatment involved brief analogue therapy of only two 30-minute sessions, and is therefore not a realistic test of social skills training, which generally involves at least 10–15 hours of training.

Recent studies with clinical populations have also used these techniques with aggressive groups. Elder *et al.* (1979) used a multiple-baseline design to assess training with four adolescents. Three target behaviours (interruptions, response to negative communication and requests for behaviour change) showed improvement which generalized to novel role-played scenes and to the ward setting. Although there was no systematic follow-up evaluation of treatment effects, three trainees who had been discharged as patients were adequately maintaining themselves in the community nine months after training. Kolko *et al.* (1981) also found improvement in three aggressive adolescent psychiatric patients after social skills training in a well-designed and evaluated treatment study. The patients showed generalization to novel role-plays, therapy and ward-adjustment ratings, and observational ratings of a simulated *in vivo* situation.

One study specifically selected physically assaultive individuals for social skills training. Rice and Quinsey (1980) reported the results of an earlier study with physically assaultive patients in a maximum-security hospital. They achieved positive results with patients who were not frequently assaultive and less 'deteriorated' than most of their high-incidence assaulters, but found no significant change on any measure for highly assaultive patients.

The early studies share many of the methodological problems common to social skills studies in general. Assessment method and selection of target measures are not always methodologically rigorous, training methods are poorly described, evaluation uses clinical or 'informal' rather than statistical criteria and control groups (or adequate single-case design methods) are often lacking. However, most report improvement in aggressive behaviour, with some generalization to non-training settings and maintenance over time. Later studies show stricter methodologies and improved evaluation techniques. These results are not as consistently positive as earlier ones, and some studies report negative findings on certain measures while others fail to achieve acceptable generalization or maintenance effects. However, it is encouraging that Kolko *et al.*, who report the most methodologically rigorous study of those reviewed above, found generalized skill acquisition after training.

As a group, these studies emphasize the control of verbal aggression, and where the trainees have been described in detail, referral has tended to be for verbal outbursts or temper loss. Although there are some treatment programmes specifically aimed at anger control and assertion in non-patient populations with physically violent backgrounds, such as incarcerated delinquents (e.g. Neill, 1982), these tend not to be experimentally validated or reported.

Other studies have used social skills training with aggressive children (e.g. Bornstein *et al.*, in press; Gittleman, 1965) or with criminal populations such as sex offenders or arsonists whose offence may be defined as 'aggressive' but who do not necessarily show direct interpersonal physical violence (e.g. Crawford, 1979; Crawford and Allen, 1977; Burgess *et al.*, 1980; Rice and Chaplin, 1979; Becker *et al.*, 1978; Whitman and Quinsey, 1981). Social skills training has also been used with mixed-offence incarcerated or probationer adults or delinquents, where trainees may be a predominantly violent or aggressive, but this is not the focus of treatment nor a criterion for selection (e.g. Gilmour *et al.*, 1981; Rice, 1983; Twentyman *et al.*, 1978; Bornstein *et al.*, 1979; Priestly, 1978; Spence, 1983; Lowe and Stewart, 1983; Golden *et al.*, 1980; Werner *et al.*, 1975; and the 15 studies with delinquents reviewed in Henderson and Hollin, 1983).

To summarize, social skills training studies with self-referred adult aggressives and clinical populations show positive treatment gains, with some generalization and maintenance effects. However, they are limited to verbal aggression, and the lack of published controlled studies using social skills training methods specifically with physically violent non-patient adult samples is obvious. Discussion of the issues relating to implementation is therefore based on direct experience with such intervention strategies.

ISSUES RELATED TO IMPLEMENTATION

Applying social skills training methods to the management of violent crime involves a number of major implementation issues, related to both practical and ethical concerns, in particular to adequacy of assessment and the consequences of dealing with what is predominantly an incarcerated target group. These are discussed in detail below.

Assessment

As with any behavioural method, social skills training with violent offenders requires accurate and appropriate assessment to take place, both of the level and nature of social skills deficit. Assessment methods have traditionally relied on self-report measures and behavioural ratings of role-played situations. Other less frequently employed techniques include *in vivo* observation, physiological measures and assessment of actual effectiveness. Limitations of these methods have been well discussed in a number of reviews (e.g. Henderson and Hollin, 1986) and centre around the unreliability of self-report, the artificiality of role-play situations and the poor correlation with real-life behaviour.

A particular issue for any assessment of violent behaviour is its low frequency of occurrence. Any assessment of the efficacy of treatment or intervention on violent behaviour must therefore rely on indirect measures, such as self-reported likelihood of behaving violently or measurement of anger or hostility.

A second issue is the situational specificity of violent behaviour. Research on violent crime or aggressive behaviour clearly indicates that these are often highly situation-specific for an individual person. Methods for enhancing assessment include:

(1) Use of a multi-method approach, combining role-play assessment, self-rating and rating by significant others, such as staff or peers, in the non-training situation;
(2) Use of situation-specific measures that adequately sample the range of both skills and behavioural situations in which violence may occur;
(3) Use of macro rather than micro-assessment of performance where appropriate; for example, a macro-rating of 'competence' or 'anxiety' may

be more valid, albeit less reliable, than a micro-rating of 'level of eye contact' or 'fidgeting';

(4) Development and use of situations of personal relevance to the trainee and, where appropriate, taken from his or her personal experience; these are more likely to elicit and assess skills and responses relevant to violent behaviour for that individual;

(5) Where role-plays are used, techniques that enhance the naturalness of the role-play, such as instructing role-play partners to respond as they would in a normal interaction, providing contextual and situational information to both trainee and role-play partners, etc.

Training Procedures

Most social skills training methods use four basic techniques: focused instruction, modelling the skilled behaviour, behavioural rehearsal of the skills behaviour often using role-play, and corrective feedback with social reinforcement often using videotaped playback of the role-play. Studies contrasting the relative efficacy of these techniques show the strongest effects with combined use of the methods (Thelen *et al.*, 1979; Edelson and Seidman, 1975; Hung and Rosenthal, 1981).

Group training has benefits over individual training, as it is more resource effective on staff time, allows use of peer-group trainees as role-play partners or models and enhances social validation by providing peer-group reinforcement and discussion of subculture norms and conventions. However, selection of a compatible group with enough similarity in terms of level and type of social skills deficit to make a cohesive and effective group learning situation is more difficult with this target group. Assessment of individual skill levels, as well as judicious matching of trainees within the group by the trainer, is critical.

Training procedures may be enhanced by:

(1) Limiting group size to about six trainees to allow a diversity of role-play partners within a manageable group size;

(2) Course content targeted towards the skill requirements of the group based on detailed assessment of skill deficits and designed around situations of personal relevance to group trainees, rather than totally prestructured;

(3) Focused instruction ensuring a limited number of learning points relevant to each targeted skill to be learnt per session and practised to overlearning stage;

(4) Emphasis on general principles rather than micro-behaviours in isolation; for example, frequency of eye contact and smiling related to the importance of rewardingness in intimate interactions;

(5) Diversity of role-play partners within each role-play situation to enhance generalization;

(6) Use of 'personalized' role-plays selected and developed by the trainee based on personal experience;

(7) Immediate feedback on each role-played performance, first from the role-play partner, emphasizing his or her feelings during the interaction in response to the trainee, then generally from other trainees and trainer;

(8) Review of the trainee's own feelings and thoughts of key points in the role-play interaction, to examine and modify cognitive appraisals of the situation for consistency with skilled behaviour;

(9) Emphasis on the interactive nature of social behaviour and on the role of personal control and reciprocal interaction of any personal exchange. The fact that the individual's own behaviour has a direct consequence on the feelings and behaviour of other interactants, which in turn affects how the trainee feels and behaves, is often a new lesson learnt by many trainees;

(10) Motivating trainees to view the learning of social skills as both personally relevant and rewarding by emphasizing that skilled behaviour allows own goals and needs to be met in a manner that is most effective and beneficial to the self and others in the long term;

(11) Training in 'back-up skills', such as emphasizing that skilled behaviour may not always result in desired goals for any number of reasons unrelated to the trainee's performance, and encouraging trainees to examine other possible causes for apparent failure instead of attributing negative outcome to own behaviour.

Generalization

One of the major criticisms of social skills training methods has been the failure of skills learnt in structured training situations to generalize to the real-life situation. Techniques to maximize transfer of these learnt skills to real-life situations centre around maximizing the 'naturalness' and variability of training, and on extending the training situation as far as possible into the natural setting through the use of 'homework' or practice assignments. In this way, the learnt skills are applied to an unstructured situation selected by the trainee outside the non-training environment. By reviewing these practice situations in subsequent training sessions, mistakes can be analysed and skills enhanced even further.

This is particularly critical for interventions with violent behaviour, where the 'real-life' situation is often compounded by factors not present in the training one. For example, physiological arousal, a high level of anger or other negative affects, effects of alcohol, and social situational variables such as the presence of significant others as audience may all operate to enhance the likelihood of an aggressive response in the real-life situation, because strategies to deal with these factors, or their combination, have not been specifically learnt in the training setting. Again, success is contingent upon first, the extent to which training has been effective in producing situations that are natural, and therefore involve a high level of participation by the trainee, to the extent of creating physiological and emotional states experienced in the real-life situation. By learning the control of these states in the training setting, skills are developed that can then be applied in the real-life setting. Second, success is also enhanced if training is extended to the natural setting, by practice assignments, homework or *in vivo* training sessions.

Generalization effects may be enhanced by:

(1) Use of relevant homework and practice assignments outside the group which are reviewed in detail at the subsequent session;
(2) Encouraging trainees to practise newly learnt skills as often as possible outside training and homework sessions;
(3) Teaching self-reinforcement skills to be employed when successfully performing homework of practice assignment.

The Institutional Environment

In addition to the practical difficulties associated with introducing an intervention programme of this type into an institutional environment there are also ethical and moral considerations. As with any institution-based programme, issues about consent and voluntary participation must be addressed.

CASE ILLUSTRATION

A social skills training programme was developed and implemented for male prisoners at a British maximum-security prison in 1982 and groups were run over a two-year period. Although originally designed to provide a programme exclusively for violent offenders, the programme was extended to other non-violent prisoners with significant social skills deficits. The results for those 12 prisoners who had convictions for direct interpersonal violence (i.e. homicide, wounding and grievous or aggravated bodily harm) and completed the programme are reviewed below.

The programme was developed around three major skill areas relevant to violent behaviour:

(1) *Assertion*: i.e. the ability to express negative feelings or to respond to undesired behaviour in others in a manner that achieves the desired goal (not submissive) without infringing the rights of others (not aggressive). Violence may occur as a means of achieving the desired goals that cannot be obtained by non-violent (assertive) methods.
(2) *Self-control*: i.e. the ability to control anger, arousal and inhibit loss of temper or irritability when provoked. This is particularly relevant in anger-induced aggression. Violence may occur because of inability to identify or control feelings of anger or arousal before they are expressed behaviourally.
(3) *Social anxiety*: individuals may react aggressively to events which are perceived as threatening or give rise to anxiety. Violence may be used to

neutralize the source of anxiety or to reduce arousal.

A multi-method approach was used to assess these areas of social skill deficit and general social competence. Measures used were:

(1) Rated assertion, aggression, anxiety and general skills on a videotaped role-play assessment, and a rating of predicted outcome of the role-play interaction by the role-play partner;
(2) Prison staff ratings of assertive behaviour, aggression, irritability, self-control, anxiety, confidence and general social skills over the preceding two-week period;
(3) Self-rating by the prisoner of items similar to (2) above;
(4) Self-report questionnaires, including the Rathus assertion inventory (Rathus, 1973), the Social Anxiety and Distress Scale (Watson and Friend, 1969) and a 60-item inventory of self-reported difficulty with social situations (Henderson, 1984), incorporating subscales of assertion, aggression and social anxiety.

Training sessions involved groups of six to eight trainees and two co-trainers, using modelling by trainers and other trainees, focused instruction, videotaped behavioural rehearsal and feedback and group discussion. Processes outlined earlier to enhance training and generalization effects were employed. The assessment measures outlined above were completed on each trainee at the end of the training programme and at 4-month followup.

Training resulted in significant improvement in rated assertion, improved social skills and a likelihood of acceding to the request by the role-play partner. Staff ratings showed a significant improvement in rated self-confidence and social skills, although mean scores on most measures show improvement over time for all ratings. The most marked effect is in self-ratings and self-report measures, where all results showed significant improvement. These changes were maintained or showed continued improvement at follow-up.

In summary, the strongest effect appears for global measures of social skills. Results are also strong for social anxiety. There is some improvement in assertiveness, but little change in aggression control across the 12 prisoners as a whole. However, individual prisoners show significant change in areas of specific skill deficit.

For example, John is a 23-year-old prisoner serving a 5-year sentence for wounding and has a history of other violent convictions, including grievous bodily harm and various counts of assault. He also relates a number of fights for which he has not been convicted, including one in which be believes he fatally stabbed his victim. John also has a prison-management history of major and minor disciplinary infractions involving physical violence, threat of assault and verbal abuse, and regularly faces disciplinary hearings.

His descriptions of the pre-prison violent incidents reveal a similar pattern. Most occur in pubs, clubs or other social situations, in front of other people, and all follow arguments, often over minor issues such as a spilt drink or minor provocation or alleged slight. All follow arguments, in which he describes himself as feeling helpless and tongue-tied. He says:

> I have no difficulty standing up for myself. I usually belt them if I'm pushed too far. If someone disagrees with me I'd punch him.

The prison incidents also tend to involve public situations where John perceives he is being provoked or 'put down' in front of other people and becomes violent in response. In interview, he describes his violent episodes as unpredictable and uncontrollable when they actually occur, but relates precipitating incidents in full detail, together with his feelings of being frustrated, helpless, 'cornered' and humiliated. His explanation for each violent response is that he feels he has to stand up for himself in order to deal with the situation, and that he reaches a point where he is unable to control, or even predict, the occurrence of physical violence.

A detailed assessment of John's level of social competence across the various measures shows a consistent pattern of low assertion, poor aggression control and high social anxiety, particularly in public situations with an audience of same-age peers. He also shows low self-confidence and poor general social skills.

Role-play scenes given particular attention for John were developed around the theme of responding assertively in public situations where he received minor provocation from a same-age male peer. Techniques also included discussion of John's interpretation of the behaviour of the antagonist and of implication of subsequent responses; identification of John's physiological and emotional state during the interaction; practice of anger-control techniques; relaxation methods, etc.

John showed substantial improvement in self and staff-rated aggression control, as well as enhanced assertion skills. Comments by staff and other prisoners also showed marked attitudinal change and improved skills in a variety of unrelated situations. These changes were maintained throughout the follow-up period until his reclassification to a minimum-security prison, prior to release. Staff attribute his earlier than expected transfer to this marked attitudinal and behavioural change. Informal follow-up over another 12 months shows that John completed his prison term without further disciplinary incident.

In summary, social skills training with this group of violent offenders resulted in significant improvements in social competence and in specific skills such as assertion. As a group, there is no systematic reported change in aggression control, which may in part be due to the nature of the assessment measure or to an overlap between the concepts of assertion and aggression by both staff raters and prisoners themselves. However, to the extent that improved social competence and assertion are pro-social alternatives to violent behaviour, social skills training appears an effective intervention method for violent offenders. Additionally, the programme has strong support from staff and trainees themselves as to its usefulness and success.

CONCLUSIONS

Behavioural methods, particularly social skills training, provide practitioners with a useful and effective intervention strategy for the management of violence, particularly when combined with techniques that also address the cognitive processes underlying the expression of violent behaviour.

References

Becker, J., Abel, G., Blanchard, E., Murphy, W., and Coleman, E. (1978). Evaluating social skills of sexual aggressives. *Criminal Justice and Behavior*, **5**, 357–67.

Bornstein, M., Bellack, A., and Hersen, M. (in press). Social skills training for highly aggressive children in an inpatient psychiatric setting. *Behavior Modification*.

Bornstein, P., Winegardner, J., Rychtarik, R., Paul, W., Naifeh, S., Sweeney, J., and Justman, A. (1979). Interpersonal skills training: evaluation of a programme with adult male offenders. *Criminal Justice and Behavior*, **6**, 119–32.

Burgess, R., Jewitt, R., Sandham, J., and Hudson, B. (1980). Working with sex offenders: a social skills training group. *British Journal of Social Work*, **10**, 133–42.

Crawford, D. (1979). Modification of deviant sexual behaviour: the need for a comprehensive approach. *British Journal of Medical Psychology*, **52**, 151–6.

Crawford, D., and Allen, J. (1977). A social skills training programme with sex offenders. Paper presented at the International Conference on Love and Attraction, Swansea.

Edelson, R., and Seidman, E. (1975). Use of videotaped feedback in altering interpersonal perceptions of married couples: a therapy analogue. *Journal of Consulting and Clinical Psychology*, **43**, 244–50.

Edler, J., Eldelstein, B., and Narick, M. (1979). Adolescent psychiatric patients: modifying aggressive behaviour with social skills training. *Behavior Modification*, **3**, 161–78.

Fawcett, B., Ingham, E., McKeever, M., and Williams, S. (1979). Social skills group for young prisoners. *Social Work Today*, **10**, 16–18.

Fehrenbach, P., and Thelen, M. (1981). Assertive-skills training for inappropriately aggressive college males: effects on assertive and aggressive behaviours. *Journal of Behavior Therapy and Experimental Psychiatry*, **12**, 213–17.

Fehrenbach, P., and Thelen, M. (1982). Behavioural approaches to the treatment of aggressive disorders. *Behaviour Modification*, **6**, 465–97.

Foy, D., Eisler, R., and Pinkston, S. (1975). Modelled assertion in a case of explosive rages. *Journal of Behavior Therapy and Experimental Psychiatry*, **6**, 135–7.

Frederiksen, L., Jenkins, J., Foy, D., and Eisler, R. (1976). Social skills training to modify abusive verbal outbursts in adults. *Journal of Applied Behaviour Analysis*, **9**, 117–25.

Freedman, B., Rosenthal, L., Donahoe, C., Schlundt, R., and McFall, R. (1978). A social behavioural analysis of skill deficits in delinquent and nondelinquent adolescent boys. *Journal of Consulting and Clinical Psychology*, **46**, 1448–62.

Galassi, J., and Galassi, M. (1978). Assertion: a critical review. *Psychotherapy: Theory, Research and Practice*, **15**, 16–29.

Gilmour, D., McCormick, I., and De Ruiter, (1981). Group assertion training for adult male offenders: internal validity. *Behavior Therapy*, **12**, 274–9.

Gittleman, M. (1965). Behavioural rehearsal as a technique in child treatment. *Journal of Child Psychology and Psychiatry*, **6**, 251–5.

Golden, K., Twentyman, C., Jensen, M., Karan, J. and Kloss, J. (1980). Coping with authority: SST for the complex offender. *Criminal Justice and Behavior*, **7**, 147–59.

Goldstein, A., Carr, E., Davidson, W., and Wehr, P. (1979). *In Response to Aggression: Methods of Control and Prosocial Alternatives*, New York: Pergamon Press.

Henderson, M. (1984). Personality and social skills in violent offenders. DPhil thesis, Oxford University.

Henderson, M., and Hollin, C. (1983). A critical review of social skills training with young offenders. *Criminal Justice and Behavior*, **10**, 316–41.

Henderson, M., and Hollin, C. (1986). Social skills and delinquency. In C. R. Hollin and P. Trower (eds), *Handbook of Social Skills Training, Vol. 1: Applications Across the Life Span*. Oxford: Pergamon Press.

Hung, J., and Rosenthal, T. (1981). Therapeutic videotaped playback. In J. Fryrear and B. Hashman (eds), *Videotherapy in Mental Health*, Illinois: Charles C. Thomas.

Kaufman, L., and Wagner, B. (1972). BARB: a systematic treatment technology for temper control disorders. *Behavior Therapy*, **3**, 84–90.

Kolko, D., Dorsett, P., and Milan, M. (1981). A total assessment approach to the evaluation of SST: the effectiveness of an anger control program for adolescent psychiatric patients. *Behavioral Assessment*, **3**, 383–402.

Lehman, A., and Olson, P. (1975). Cognitive behavioural approaches to the reduction of anger and aggression. *Dissertation Abstracts International*, **35**, 5118B–19B.

Lowe, P., and Stewart, C. (1983). Women in prison. In S. Spence and G. Shephard (eds), *Developments in Social Skills Training*, London: Academic Press.

Matson, J., and Stephens, R. (1978). Increasing appropriate explosive chronic psychiatric patients with a social skills training package. *Behavior Modification*, **2**, 61–76.

Neill, A. (1982). Personal Communication.

Priestley, P. (1978). Release courses: a new venture for prison officers. *Prison Service Journal.*, April.

Rahaim, S., Lefebvre, C., and Jenkins, J. (1980). The effects of SST on behavioural and cognitive components of anger management. *Journal of Behavior Therapy and Experimental Psychiatry*, **11**, 3–8.

Rathus, S. (1973). A 30-item schedule for assessing assertive behaviour. *Behavior Therapy*, **4**, 398–406.

Rice, M. (1983). Improving the social skills of males in a maximum security psychiatric setting. *Canadian Journal of Behavioral Science*, **46**, 360–1.

Rice, M., and Chaplin, T. (1979). Social skills training for hospitalised male arsonists. *Journal of Behavioral Therapy and Experimental Psychiatry*, **10**, 105–8.

Rice, M., and Quinsey, V. (1980). Assessment and training of social competence in dangerous psychiatric patients. *International Journal of Law and Psychiatry*, **3**, 371–90.

Rimm, D. (1977). Treatment of antisocial aggression. In G. Harris (ed.), *The Group Treatment of Human Problems*, New York: Grune & Stratton.

Rimm, D., Hill, G., Brown, N., and Stuart, J. (1974). Group assertive training in the treatment of expression of inappropriate anger. *Psychological Reports*, **34**, 791–8.

Spence, S. (1981). Differences in social skills performance between institutionalised juvenile male offenders and a comparable group of boys without offence records. *British Journal of Clinical Psychology*, **20**, 163–71.

Spence, S. (1983). Adolescent offenders in an institutional setting. In S. Spence and G. Shephard (eds), *Developments in Social Skills Training*, London: Academic Press.

Thelen, M., Fry, R., Fehrenbach, P., and Frautschi, N. (1979). Therapeutic videotape and film modelling: a review. *Psychological Bulletin*, **86**, 701–20.

Twentyman, C., Jensen, M., and Kloss, J. (1978). SST for the complex offender: employment-seeking skills. *Journal of Clinical Psychology*, **34**, 320–6.

Wallace, C., Teigen, J., Liberman, R., and Baker, V. (1973). Destructive behaviour treated by contingency contracts and assertive training: a case study. *Journal of Behavior Therapy and Experimental Psychiatry*, **4**, 273–4.

Watson, D., and Friend, R. (1969). Measurement of social-evaluative anxiety. *Journal of Consulting and Clinical Psychology*, **33**, 448–57.

Werner, J., Minkin, L., Minkin, B., Fixsen, D., Phillips, E., and Wolf, M. (1975). 'Intervention package': an analysis to prepare juvenile delinquents for encounters with police officers. *Criminal Justice and Behavior*, **2**, 55–83.

Whitman, W., and Quinsey, V. (1981). Heterosexual skills training for institutionalised rapists and child molesters. *Canadian Journal of Behavioral Science*, **13**, 105–14.

3

Anger Disturbances: Cognitive Mediation and Clinical Prescriptions

RAYMOND W. NOVACO and WAYNE N. WELSH
Program in Social Ecology, University of California, Irvine, USA

Paradoxically, anger is both satisfying and frightening. Its mobilizing and self-justifying qualities have distinctly adaptive functions, but as an activator of harm-doing behavior it has a conspicuously problematic character. In contemporary Western society, where life too often entails converging pressures and constraints, the ability to regulate and manage anger has important implications for well-being. However, this mysterious companion of everyday life and recurring ingredient of industrialized society is frequently entangled in acts of individual and collective violence. Although certain anger-driven acts of violence may be valued rather than disparaged, depending upon social–political perspective, those in the helping professions are confronted with the pathological features of uncontrolled anger. The links between anger, aggression, and psychological disturbances present clinicians with salient problems.

Normal emotion is recognizably different from provocation-proneness. The anger–aggression connnection demarcates this with relative clarity, and it has become increasingly recognized that anger has adverse effects on physical health (e.g. Chesney and Rosenman, 1985). While anger is neither necessary nor sufficient for aggression to occur, it is nonetheless a central activator of both individual and collective violence and is significantly involved in a wide range of mental health disturbances, including disorders of personality, childhood and adolescence, organic syndromes, paranoia, depression, explosivity, dissociative states and post-traumatic stress. The delineation of anger as a clinical and social problem is given in Novaco (1986). The inability to regulate anger constitutes a risk factor for both harm-doing to others and for multiple impairments affecting health, performance, and relationships.

Clinical Approaches to Violence. Edited by K. Howells and C. R. Hollin
© 1989 John Wiley & Sons.

Problems of anger and aggression present some unique difficulties for counselors and therapists. The alarming features of the problem constellation, the impatient nature of the client's personality and the instrumentality of anger and aggression constitute special challenges (Novaco, 1985). Recent treatment studies (Benson *et al.*, 1986; Hazaleus and Deffenbacher, 1987; Stermac, 1987) have shown the continued success of cognitive–behavioral interventions with an increasing variety of populations, and emerging programs such as that of Feindler and Ecton (1986) for adolescents represent significant extensions of anger-control treatment.

Cognitive mediation is clearly a central avenue for anger regulation. First systematized into a therapeutic method (combined with arousal reduction and behavioral coping) by Novaco (1975), the principles of the cognitive regulation of anger originate in ancient Eastern philosophy and in Roman Stoicism. This chapter will explore some new ways of looking at cognitive mediation beyond the attentional focus, expectation and appraisal mechanisms previously developed. Information-processing approaches have much to offer with regard to how we understand interpersonal transactions involving anger and aggression, particularly as such exchanges are viewed in a contextual perspective. Ideas about cognitive deficits will be presented with regard to their clinical implications for assessment and treatment.

Conceptions of anger as a dysfunctional emotional state are rooted in historical notions about anger as a passion. Themes of insanity and destructiveness associated with anger arousal spring from this passion perspective which separates anger from rationality. Although ancient passion theorists did recognize that mental states (opinions and beliefs) influenced the production of anger, the cognitive operations were usually understood as interpretive templates imposed over an event. Similarly, contemporary thought about cognitive mediation of anger is too often restricted to an event-interpretation tandem process. This misses the automaticity of cognitive appraisal as embedded in the perception of events and neglects how ingrained cognitive structures influence what receives attention, how it is processed, and what responses are enacted. Before proceeding to ideas about cognitive mediation and their clinical implications, we will first present the portrayal of anger as passion and its association with insanity and destructiveness.

ANGER, PATHOLOGY AND PASSION

As an affective disturbance, anger is significantly involved in many psychiatric disorders; but unlike anxiety and depression, which have a number of diagnostic categories, anger has no formal classification.* While anxiety and depression are clinical conditions, anger (like fear and sadness) is an emotion. Although there is some divergence in thinking about how emotions are defined (cf. Plutchik, 1980), there is considerable consensus that emotions have subjective

---

* Explosive disorder, 'an impulse control dysfunction, intrinsically involves anger and aggression, but this is an extreme and very rare condition (cf. Novaco, 1986).

phenomenological properties, involve physiological arousal (autonomic and somatic), are transitory states rather than enduring conditions and have expressive qualities. Anxiety and depression constitute a varied combination or patterning of fundamental emotions (Izard, 1972), whereas anger has a more unified constellation of component features.

Because anger is a normal emotion and part of the human fabric, it has no automatic status as a problem. It has been an attribute of many heroic and creative personalities, but it also has taken abnormal forms in the lives of disturbed individuals. For some people, it is an effective force, used as it naturally occurs in problem situations. In such cases, anger is rarely out of control. In its problematic manifestations the experience and expression of anger are more volatile, erupting frequently and impulsively, unchecked by consideration of the consequences.

Unusual cases make convenient illustrations, and a fascinating portrait of pathological anger can be found in the intriguing book of Thomas and Morgan-Witts (1983) here reconstructed:

Each morning as he arises, a young man in Yesiltepe, Turkey, spreads his prayer rug, prostrates himself, touching his forehead to the ground, and quietly speaks the name of the God he worships. He does this several times. Then he ritualistically and fervently recites his long list of hatreds.

There on his treasured prayer mat, Mehmet Ali Agca each day repeats this tortured litany of persons and collectivities who evoke his deepest rage. He needs a long time to finish the list. The years of his young life fueled an incredible resentment and animosity. The list includes landlords, Russian tsars, NATO, and Sheik Yamani whom he felt should have crippled the West with Arab oil. America especially is the subject of Agca's anger for its hamburgers, Levi's, and television programs. He devotes five minutes just to get through the America segment of his list.

He hates those who use and deal in heroin, made from the poppy of the surrounding villages. He hates the drug bosses, especially those on the other side of the world who pay the poppy farmers $15 per pound but sell the refined product in New York for $200 000 a pound. But Agca puts all profiteers and employers on his list—his father's employer had refused to pay his last week of salary after he was killed in an accident. Yet his memory of his father is hardly beatific, remembering mostly his calloused, violent hands that bashed his mother. He had smiled at his father's funeral.

His family's poverty brought misery and depression. With his mother's encouragement, they thought that he could rid himself of the despondency by hating. This produced his list, which grew as the years passed. And he became attracted to the Gray Wolves, a group of Turkish anarchists.

Agca's mental state was precarious. He was an insomniac as a teenager. Obsessive–compulsive behavior, depression, and social isolation marked his personality, his list of hatreds being only one of many rituals and ruminations. And at the end of the list were the most virulent and consuming ones. These were his religious hatreds, which he had reduced to one unmistakeable representation. The image was that of an old man, dressed in white robes with a skullcap, who lives in a huge palace in Rome. He believed that this old man is the leader of the enemies of Islam. In his exercise book, Agca kept faded newspaper photos and stories of the old man's travels to places where he spread his hateful message that eroded the foundations of Islam. With this passionate list of hatreds, this young man resolved to kill that man in Rome or whoever succeeded him.

Mehmet Ali Agca indeed attempted to assassinate Pope John Paul II, who later went to his jail cell to grant him forgiveness. Agca, of course, was the one thought to be crazy.

Such highly publicized cases of violent behavior often portray the attacker as insane, although political assassinations in Italy are much less likely to be viewed as being carried out by a psychotic person than when they occur in the United States. In the United States, those who attempt to assassinate government leaders are automatically assumed to be mentally deranged. In fact, except in the case of Oscar Collazo and Griselio Torresola, members of the Puerto Rican Nationalist Party who attempted to assassinate President Harry S. Truman in 1950, there has been considerable psychiatric evidence to support the US belief that presidential assassins are mentally disturbed (Taylor and Weisz, 1970). After the assassination of John Kennedy, there were attempts to kill Gerald Ford and Ronald Reagan by individuals found to be insane. However, John Hinckley, who made the attempt on Reagan, was not angry at his target:

> John Hinckley was a 25-year-old man from Evergreen, Colorado, born of religious parents in Oklahoma. He was described by those who knew him as cordial and friendly, although he was a loner. His father was a wealthy oilman, but the son dropped out of college, becoming a drifter looking for odd jobs. When he was 22, he joined a neo-Nazi group, but disengaged from it because it was insufficiently militant.
>
> He became obsessed with a movie actress, Jodi Foster, to whom he wrote many letters. At this time he was 25 years old. To prove his love for this actress whom he idolized, he attempted to assassinate the President of the United States. When he fired many shots at Ronald Reagan at close range, Hinckley was mostly concerned about whether the television cameras got all the action. Extensive psychiatric analysis found no anger by Hinckley toward Reagan; in fact, he had a mild admiration for him.

The Hinckley case is a dramatic example of aggression or violence without anger toward the victim. Anger is neither necessary nor sufficient for aggression. Organized crime executions motivated by 'business' concerns rather than anger, as well as people like Hinckley seeking notoriety through violence, exemplify the non-necessity of anger. More commonly, there are cases of murder–suicide by a family member driven by hopelessness and despair, without anger at the murdered one. However, less commonly recognized crimes of violence also fit this absence of anger configuration. Quite different from the clinical variety of violent behaviors are the typically neglected cases of corporate violence (Monahan and Novaco, 1980), where deliberate decisions having harm-doing consequences are made by corporate executives. When such decisions about products or their manufacturing present unreasonable risks to employees, consumers or otherwise affected citizens, and those decisions are made with knowledge of the likelihood of harm-doing, then such behavior ought to be considered violent. Such decisions are made without anger and without intention to harm particular individuals, but they are violent just the same. One is just as dead from exposure to toxic wastes or from a faulty piece of equipment that results in a crash as one is from a bullet or a knife.

These examples of aggression without anger stand apart from common conceptions of human destructiveness; and anger is often misconceived as a cauldron of tumultuous forces that cannot be moderated and which is largely irrational. Anger, especially when intense, has semantic ties to concepts of insanity. Becoming enraged suggests being rabid, which connotes a diseased state of mind. The involvement of cognition in anger arousal and prolongation is easily misunderstood from this standpoint.

The eruption of anger in a syndrome of temporary insanity or lasting psychosis is common enough in many cultures. In cases of 'wild man' and 'amok' behavior (cf. Averill, 1982) this is highly systematized. Angry outbursts are easily recognized as a protest against the constraints of life or perhaps unusual injustices, but insanity is often in the picture. In the American movie, *Network*, the character Howard Beale is a veteran anchorman of the Universal Broadcasting Company who becomes a mad prophet for national television audiences in the movie when he implores everyone to go to their windows, stick their heads out and yell, 'I'm as mad as hell, and I'm not going to take it anymore'.

Howard Beale touched a nerve not only in the fictional television audiences of the movie but in the real audiences of the movie theater. His crazed chanting enjoins us to revolt against the adversities of everyday living with its bureaucratic snarls and impersonal thwartings: 'Things have got to change. But first you've got to get mad.' This role of anger in converting feelings of helplessness to taking charge of one's destiny is unmistakeably part of social protest movements from the French Revolution to the more or less contemporary punk subculture. Whether it be the 'conquerors of the Bastille' or merely the Sex Pistols, anger is a vehicle for self-assertion and revolt. This is anger's 'potentiating' function (Novaco, 1976), meaning that it potentiates a sense of control or mastery, which may very well be illusory. In the case of Howard Beale, the suggestion of insanity exists at more than one level, because in the movie he is eventually assassinated on the air. More tragically, a dramatic performance of televised suicide was duplicated in reality in 1987 by Pennsylvania State Treasurer, R. Budd Dwyer, who indeed put a 0.357 magnum pistol into his mouth and pulled the trigger. Some news stations actually showed this event in its horrendous entirety. Dwyer, of course, was the one thought to be crazy. No one doubted the sanity of the 'news' directors.

The association of anger with insanity has never been more fully drawn than by Shakespeare in *King Lear*, whose irascible temperament and inability to control his easily activated rage were main features of his character. At the opening of the play, King Lear proposes the division of his kingdom among his three daughters, apportioned according to a test of love that he presents to them. When his youngest daughter, Cordelia, fails to proclaim the greatness of her love for her father ('I cannot heave my heart into my mouth'), the King becomes enraged, disowning and disinheriting the one that he loves best.

Although it is Cordelia who speaks with sincerity, Lear's wrath destroys the relationship that he needs most. Later, his eldest daughter, Goneril, has a confrontation with him that provokes incredible anger. Suspecting that her father was planning to reclaim his throne, she dismisses his retinue, which she thinks has conspirators against her. In their quarrel over this, Lear unleashes a venomous curse: 'Into her womb convey sterility! Dry up in her organs of increase.' Such an explosion of anger toward his pregnant daughter shows the complete absence of control, and Lear himself senses that he has gone mad. His outbursts of rage poison his family relationships and lead to their collective ruin.

When an agitated person does something violent, the question of mental illness inevitably arises. Yet thinking of anger as a product or precursor of mental imbalance is to overgeneralize from extreme cases and derives from long-standing views of anger as a passion that seizes control of the personality. This view of anger denies its adaptive functions and misses social context influences. However, ideas about the role of cognition in the activation and maintenance of anger can be traced to early passion theorists.

Prior to the eighteenth century, what we now call emotions were commonly called *passions*, by which the personality was 'gripped', 'seized' or 'torn' (Averill, 1974). Anger is perhaps the prototype of emotions understood as passions. Anger arousal seems to flood the personality, overriding reason and leading to impulsive actions. Movements, words and thoughts become antagonistic and turbulent. Becoming angry seems to signify that one is out of control, being driven by uncivilized forces that ultimately must be checked. This view of anger as a passion that takes control of the personality is rooted in many ancient philosophical beliefs, including those of Roman Stoic philosophers, such as Lucius Seneca and Marcus Aurelius.

Philosophical thought about the passions originated with Plato, followed by Aristotle; it continued with the Stoics and then the philosophers of the Middle Ages, the Renaissance and the Enlightenment. Descartes, Spinoza, Hobbes and Hume wrote extensively about the passions, carrying forward ideas about passions like anger expounded by St Thomas Aquinas in medieval times and by Seneca and Plato before him (Averill, 1982). Hutcheson's (1742) *An Essay on the Nature and Conduct of the Passions and Affections* was probably the last major book to use the terms in its title (McReynolds, 1969). Hutcheson was a moral philosopher, born in Ireland and educated in Scotland, where he later became a professor at the University of Glasgow. He characterized anger as 'a Propensity to occasion Evil to another, arising upon apprehension of an Injury done by him' (p. 75). Passion theorists all recognize the role of cognition in the arousal of anger, yet consistently treat it as an irrational state.

The separation of the passions from rationality was served by the distinction between the mortal and the immortal soul drawn by Plato in *Timaeus* (a very difficult dialogue). The immortal soul, which Plato associated with reason, was located in the head. The mortal soul, found in the trunk of the body, was irrational and contained the passions. The neck was an isthmus and boundary. The passions were thus located in visceral regions, superior and inferior. Anger, a spirited passion, was located in the superior region, with the heart as the central organ. This allegedly provided some control from the head and cooling from the lungs. The inferior region contained the appetitive cravings for hunger, sex and avarice. This linking of emotion to bodily regions and physiological change has been traced by Averill (1974) historically and called 'psychophysiological symbolism', which, he asserts, hinders our understanding of emotions, preventing us from seeing their social construction.

Following Plato's division of the mortal from the immortal soul, anger was dissociated from the intellectual faculties. Examining problems of will or volition in *Ethica Nicomachea*, Aristotle stated, 'For choice is not common to irrational creatures as well, but appetite and anger are . . . Still less anger, for acts due to anger are thought to be less than any other objects of choice' (Ross, 1963, Section iiii, 10–19). Aristotle also wrote in his *Physiognomica* that 'when we are mastered by a fit of temper we become more obstinate and totally intractable; we grow headstrong and violent and do whatever our temper impels us to do' (Ross, 1963, Section 809, 35). The ancients thought that anger seizes control of the personality, and because of its separation from the intellect, it is clearly viewed as a problem. Marcus Aurelius stated that 'he who is excited by anger seems to turn away from reason' (Long, 1925, p. 146).

For the Stoic philosophers, the passions upset the balance of the soul and were disturbances that could become diseases if the person chronically indulged in them. While Plato and Aristotle taught that emotions should be regulated, the Stoics believed that they should be entirely subordinated to reason. Passions, like anger, were mental disturbances that must be prevented, avoided and suppressed if ever experienced.

Because the ancient philosophers had no word for emotion and understood passion as something quite strong, there can be some dispute about whether the Stoics thought all feelings should be suppressed (Sandbach, 1975). However, on the topic of anger specifically, there is no mistake about the views of the Stoics—anger has no value and is to be completely avoided. Nowhere is this more clear than in the treatise *De Ira*, by the Roman, Lucius Seneca, who was the first anger scholar. Seneca began this little-known but important work in a way that unmistakeably conveys his sentiment:

> We are here to encounter the most outrageous, brutal, dangerous, and intractable of all passions; the most loathsome and unmannerly; nay, the most ridiculous too; and the subduing of this monster will do a great deal toward the establishment of human peace (Seneca, 41/1917, p. 215).

For Seneca, anger is never warranted or useful, even in the case of terrible insults or if harm had been done to one's family. Asked whether an honorable man could be allowed to be angry about the murder of his father or the raping of his wife, daughter or sister before his very face, Seneca would say no. Anger is never warranted. However, he was no saintly advocate of turning the other cheek, as he makes it clear that seeking retribution is quite proper. Retaliation can be done without being confused by emotion, '. . . not in any transport of passion, but in honor and conscience. Neither is there any need for anger where reason does the same thing' (p. 226). To be angry at offenders was, for Seneca, to be weak and wicked. Anger was a disturbance always to be avoided, but being temperate did not preclude being vigorous.

ANGER, PASSION AND AGGRESSION

Viewing anger as a passion separates it from the intellect and sees only its disturbing qualities. The passion idea also overemphasizes the association with aggression. The intensity, turbulence and non-reasoned connotations of passion states suggest this connection. Although there are conspicuous fusions of anger and aggression in various cases of criminal violence and in warfare, the connection is overdrawn and diverts attention from the health consequences of chronic anger reactions.

Becoming angry does not automatically produce aggression, nor does it always help one to fight. Claudius said that 'Rage supplies all arms. When an angry man thirsts for blood, anything will serve him as a spear'; but Seneca disputed the view that anger can be useful in warfare:

> Some people are of the opinion that anger inflames and animates the soldier; that it is a spur to bold and arduous undertakings . . . but where there is any ardour of mind necessary, we may rouse ourselves, and be more or less brisk and vigorous as there is occasion: but all without anger still (p. 227).

Calling attention to the discipline of Roman armies who defeated brave, hardy and more numerous Germanic opponents, Seneca argued that a man need not be angry to be valiant, whether he be a commander or common soldier.

> [A] good swordsman watches his opportunity, and keeps himself upon his guard, whereas passion lays a man open: nay it is one of the prime lessons in fencing school to learn not to be angry . . . No man is courageous in his anger that was not so without it (p. 228).

Here, of course, Seneca is not alone, as such thoughts about competence and valor are very much a part of the Eastern philosophies of Taoism and Buddhism that underlie Oriental martial arts training.

The views of Seneca regarding anger as a desire for revenge and as a vice that makes us destroy one another carried through to the seventeenth century in the works of Descartes, who believed that anger was almost always accompanied by the desire to aggress. In his treatise, *The Passions of the Soul*, Descartes wrote:

> 'Anger is also a species of hatred or aversion which we have towards those who have done some evil or have tried to injure not any chance person but more particularly ourselves. Thus it has the same content as indignation . . . But it is incomparably more violent than these three other passions, because the desire to repel harmful things and to revenge oneself, is the most pertinent of all desires' (Haldane and Ross, 1931, p. 420).

The long history of philosophical thought on the nature of passions dissociates anger from reason and strongly ties it to aggression.

This association between anger and aggression, fixed in our thinking for at least two millennia, engenders the belief that anger is negative or harmful because it is expected to result in harm-doing. Newspaper stories about persons consumed by fits of rage who perform violent acts can be found almost daily, especially if one looks at tabloids that search for sensational stories. In the United States there have been numerous incidents of mass murder by individuals who became uncontrollably angry over work situations. Among the worst in 1988 occurred in Los Angeles, when an angry retaliation against a former boss by a disgruntled airline worker was expanded by the perpetrator to also kill the passengers and crew of a jetliner. Thinking of anger and its expression in terms of the enactments of abnormal personalities is to see only the bizarre manifestations. King Lear and psychotic criminals do not represent the expression of anger with the purpose of solving relationship problems, overcoming obstacles in the social structure, or responding to moral injustice. The constructive expression of anger is a very different matter than destructive and impulsive explosions of wrath or revenge.

FALLACIES OF THE PASSION VIEW

There are several difficulties with viewing anger as a passion that takes control of the personality, constitutes a mental disturbance and leads to aggressive acts. One problem is that it defines anger exclusively in negative terms, overlooking its positive functions. Indeed, anger-arousal has disruptive, instigational and other maladaptive effects, but it also has energizing, expressive and discriminative functions (cf. Novaco, 1976). The view of anger promulgated by the Stoics, though, is overly negative. Seneca's characterizations of anger as never warranted, as dissolving of social bonds and as having no purpose is an extreme position that is alien to our present-day social norms.

Another difficulty with viewing anger as a passion is the overemphasis on aggressive behavior or violence when considering the harmful effects of anger. Although harm-doing behavior toward others is clearly a serious risk when anger becomes intense, the more common problems associated with chronic anger involve impairments to one's own psychological well-being and physical health. Personal relationships and work performance also suffer from recurrent and prolonged anger episodes, which may involve emotional reactions that are not so intense or passion-like. Thinking of anger as a passion implies a high degree of arousal, but intensity is only one problem dimension—frequency, duration and mode of expression are others. Anger that occurs too frequently or which lasts too long is indicative of maladjustment.

Aggressive expression of anger is certainly a problem, but there are problematic non-aggressive expressions of anger as well, such as fleeing from or avoiding conflict situations that require resolution. Running away or freezing and being stubborn may not be aggressive expressions, yet they are problem reactions that fail to take constructive steps toward conflict resolution. Seeing anger as a passion that seizes the personality overlooks these disturbances to personal well-being. When gauging the harmful effects of anger, looking only at aggression misses much that is under the surface.

The idea of anger as passion also divorces it from reason. Just as Plato separated emotions from the head, locating them in the viscera, the role of mental processes in the production of anger is easily misunderstood. Anger is certainly something experienced both above and below the neck. The loss of control associated with strong anger reactions engenders worries about mental stability. Indeed, when an agitated person does something violent, the question of mental illness inevitably arises. Like King Lear, who reacts entirely out of proportion to the situation, an enraged person seems to suffer from a deranged mind.

The influence of cognitive processes on the occurrence of anger was not at all missed by the Stoics. Marcus Aurelius, Seneca and the Greek, Epictetus, had many insightful things to say about how thought influences emotion, and their wisdom was noted in the development of an expectation and appraisal model of cognitive mediation for anger (Novaco, 1979). However, their understanding of cognitive influences is limited to general processes of interpretation, judgement, meaning and opinion. Contemporary theory is also often fixed on mental operations that are brought to bear on some occurring event or one that has transpired. This limitation misses the automatic character of cognitive mediation in perception, as well as the programming function of cognitive scripts. Provocation episodes can usefully be understood with regard to information-processing errors and perceptual/behavioral scripts for anger and aggression. We will map some existing research with respect to these points and then present ideas regarding their clinical implications.

COGNITION AND ANGER

Far too often, cognitive mediation of anger is understood as an intermediary process interposed between the exposure to some stimulus and the resulting physiological and behavioral reactions. As previously argued (Novaco, 1986), cognitive 'mediation' should be understood as an automatic and intrinsic part of the perceptual process, as well as explicit thinking or otherwise conscious operations that might be involved in an event–thought–reaction sequence. In the field of human aggression, critics of cognitive mediation views (e.g. Berkowitz, 1983) fail to treat cognitive appraisal as anything other than an operation tandem to the observing. Furthermore, the selection of what receives attention and ultimately functions as a provocation is very much influenced by cognitive dispositions such as expectations, schemas and scripts.

Information-processing concepts have been applied to the explanation of a wide variety of important social behaviors, including clinician judgements (Chapman and Chapman, 1982), risk perception (Slovic et al., 1982), stereotypes (Nisbett and Ross, 1980), jury decision-making (Thompson and Schumann, 1987), depression (Beck et al., 1979), and a variety of clinical disorders (Ingram, 1986). Very little research in the area of human aggression has involved this cognitive science orientation. Here we will not present a formal information-processing analysis of the provocation of anger, which is a task beyond the scope of this chapter. However, we will outline some ideas from this orientation that can enrich understanding of the cognitive determinants of anger.

Despite the now-prominent interest in cognition among behaviorally oriented clinicians, there is an absence of guiding conceptual perspectives (Ingram and Kendall, 1986). The information-processing approach does provide an umbrella over a variety of cognitive therapies which share paradigmatic assumptions regarding the conceptualization of cognition. Ingram and Kendall propose a useful cognitive taxonomy that includes four main categories of cognitive activity: structures, propositions, operations and products. Cognitive structures are functional mechanisms that store information; cognitive propositions are the content of the structures; cognitive operations are procedures by which information is processed (attention, encoding, recall); and cognitive products are thoughts that result from the interaction of information, structures, propositions and operations.

Cognitive products have been the major focus of clinical research, with little attention to the other components of the Ingram and Kendall taxonomy. The cognitive biases which we discuss below fall into the categories of cognitive operations (attentional cueing and perceptual matching) and cognitive propositions (fundamental attribution error, false consensus and anchoring effects).

Attentional cueing and perceptual matching derive from general notions of pattern recognition, which concerns how we recognize each stimulus event as matching or exemplifying some earlier experience. Pattern recognition is thought to consist of three stages of processing: encoding, comparison and decision. Comparison and decision processes can be influenced by stimulus context and prior knowledge by at least three strategies:

(1) Selectively activating certain categories in memory through priming from the environment or through internal processes (e.g. expectations) or states (e.g. moods);
(2) Limiting comparisons to selected domains of categories in classifying the stimulus; and
(3) Biasing the decision process such that a particular category is selected to represent the stimulus, despite a lack of confirming sensory evidence.

The first type of strategy includes what we call 'attentional cueing'; the third includes 'perceptual matching'.

A basic assumption of the information-processing approach is that few stimuli are approached in a novel manner by adults (Nisbett and Ross, 1980). Instead, they are processed through pre-existing systems of beliefs, knowledge and propositions. These structures, called schemas, influence the type of stimuli given attention, whether and how such stimuli are encoded and stored in memory, and how such transformed stimuli are recalled to interpret new information. In general, such structures help people to process information rapidly. The price for such mental economy, however, is potential bias in judgements and/or adverse behavioral outcomes induced by the activation and application of simplistic or normatively inappropriate information-processing strategies (Nisbett and Ross, 1980).

Cognitive processing that is predisposed toward anger and aggression can be viewed in terms of five information-processing biases:

(1)   Attentional cueing;
(2)   Perceptual matching;
(3)   Attribution error;
(4)   False consensus; and
(5)   Anchoring effects.

Attentional Cueing

William James once said that in order to get angry about something you must first pay attention to it. Indeed, preoccupation and rumination are cognitive processes by which chronically angered persons self-generate provocation, prolonging anger reactions beyond normal dissipation periods (Novaco, 1986). Regarding the first-hand, immediate experience of provocation, situational cues have differential salience across perceivers. What receives attention is very much a matter of dispositional variables, including anger itself. This proposition, of course, has its psychological origins in the 'New Look' perception research in the 1940s and 1950s, when investigators such as Jerome Bruner and his colleagues began to challenge the veridical perspective of classical perceptionists. Personality factors, needs and defenses began to be studied for their influences on perception. Instead of the 'cool' context of laboratory displays (as William James would put it), research shifted to 'hot' contexts (as Richard Lazarus put it) regarding stimuli that had personal meaning to the subject. Thus, Bruner and Goodman (1947) found that poor children consistently overestimated the size of coins significantly more than did rich ones, although they were very good at estimating the size of cardboard discs. Another study found that hungry subjects were more likely to see food in ambiguous pictures, and this tendency increased with the fasting period. Similarly, as traditional clinicians would know, Murray's need-press theory generated the Thematic Apperception Test (Murray, 1943).

Human needs and emotions increase the response saliency of particular perceptual categories and make us 'vigilant' for particular stimuli. Just as hunger can make us vigilant for food-related stimuli, the arousal of anger may direct attention to aggressive cues. Scherer et al. (1975) suggest that an angered person may be sensitized to cues for aggression that would thereby justify an attack. They speculated that incidents like the Kent State massacre (when Ohio National Guardsmen opened fire on university students on 4 May 1970) can be understood in terms of oversensitization. Laboratory research has clearly shown that arousal (anger or general arousal) facilitates aggression in the presence of aggressive cues (Rule and Nesdale, 1976). Regarding the anger and aggression responses of groups, Allport (1958) discussed cognitive processes of selective attention and sensitization in his classic work on prejudice.

Perceptual Matching

Previous experience with provocation hypothetically will facilitate the perception of antagonistic elements in a situation. The more someone has been exposed to aggressive stimuli, the more readily he or she will perceive aggression (Scherer *et al.*, 1975). This proposition is a representativeness heuristic (Nisbett and Ross, 1980), concerned with the recognition and categorization of stimuli.

Two studies by Toch and his colleagues provide support for this idea with regard to aggressive scenes. Toch and Schulte (1961) used a binocular rivalry technique, reminiscent of Bagby's (1957) cross-cultural study of whether Mexicans or Americans more readily perceived a bullfight or a baseball game. They showed two different images simultaneously presented to each eye of the subject for a fraction of a second. One scene showed a man pointing a gun at another; the other scene showed a man plowing a field. Advanced police administration students were more likely to report the violent image than a control group of psychology students. Rookie police students were no more likely to see the violent images than the psychology students. This technique was also used by Shelley and Toch (1968) with institutionalized offenders. Nine violent scenes and nine corresponding neutral ones were presented in pairs. They found that men with more violent institutional records and more violent case histories were more likely to perceive violent scenes than non-violent prisoners. These authors report that case histories of the violent offenders revealed early signs of a relative inability to control themselves and a tendency to actively express hostility and violence. It seems plausible, therefore, that violent offenders' early exposure to violent events resulted in many violent schemas being encoded and stored, rendering them highly available for recall as problem situations arose.

Attribution Error

The fundamental attribution error refers to the tendency for people to overattribute the behavior of actors to dispositional rather than situational causes. In other words, people tend to believe that others behave the way they do because of their character or personality. Perceived situational influences on behavior are minimized (Nisbett and Ross, 1980). Might such a bias be conducive to anger-arousal or aggression?

Dyck and Rule (1978) hypothesized that the recipient of an attack should retaliate more when the causal basis for the attack is attributed to the personal characteristics of the attacker (an internal cause) than when cause is attributed to features of the situation (an external one). Indirect confirmation for this hypothesis comes from well-replicated studies showing that information about an attacker's intent (e.g. benign versus malicious) serves to increase or decrease retaliation (Dyck and Rule, 1978; Zillman, 1979).

To test their hypothesis more directly, Dyck and Rule (1978) manipulated consensus by instructing subjects that aversive noise delivered by partners in a learning task was either typical of most people (high consensus) or atypical (low consensus). Subjects were subsequently given an opportunity to retaliate against their partner by delivering shock. In the low-consensus condition, subjects made significantly more personal attributions to their partner for the aversive stimulation. They responded with greater retaliation than did subjects in the high-consensus condition.

Aggressive individuals may routinely make dispositional attributions. Driscoll (1982) had high- and low-aggressive subjects view a videotape depicting an incident between an instigator and a victim. He found that persons high in aggression (measured by self-reported aggressive experience) perceived greater injury, more negative reactions and more domineering on the part of the stimulus person than did low-aggressives.

False Consensus

'False consensus' refers to the tendency to assume that a larger proportion of others behave as oneself does than is actually the case, and the imagined consensus also extends to opinions. A corollary bias involves the tendency for an individual to assume that events have undue relevance for the self. This perceptual error is related to the deficiencies in role-taking commonly found among angry and aggressive populations.

Short and Simeonsson (1986) note that research with adolescents has consistently demonstrated that delinquent children are more immature in several aspects of cognitive development, including perspective-taking. Perspective-taking enables the individual to perceive and interpret others' reactions to his or her behavior accurately. Such ability has important implications for information-processing:

> In order to perceive these reactions correctly, the individual must be able to see past his own perspective; that is, he must be able to recognize that other persons see things differently from him and to accurately assess that viewpoint instead of attributing his own viewpoint to others (p. 170).

As predicted, highly aggressive delinquents were less able to perceive others' viewpoints than were low-aggressive delinquents, as measured by Chandler's Index of Social Egocentrism (Short and Simeonsson, 1986, p. 162). Such egocentric mechanisms of information processing may shape the cumulative selection, encoding, storage and recall of information over time, and thus influence the content and availability of certain types of schemas in adult life.

Self-preoccupied schematic structures were described by Yochelson and Samenow (1976), whose analysis of the criminal personality was based upon numerous interviews with adults and adolescents. Not only did criminals tend to display an inability to see the perspective of their victims, but they also made egocentric attributions of their own values to all other persons. Criminals in the sample often believed that their crime was typical of everyone else's desires, but their personal misfortune or lack of power led to a higher likelihood of being apprehended and convicted. They asserted that they just had the 'guts' to get what they wanted.

Anchoring Effects

A third type of mechanism, called 'anchoring', refers to the tendency of one's initial judgement to become resistant to change, even when subsequent information dictates that revision (or complete abandonment) is appropriate. For example, first impressions in social interactions carry disproportionate weight in evaluating another person (Nisbett and Ross, 1980).

Research has shown that subjects fail to adequately revise their attributions of personal causality to a provoker when additional (mitigating) information is given. Mitigating information suggests the influence of situational rather than personal causes for aggressive behavior. Kremer and Stephens (1983) found that a victim retaliates less when a provoking event is seen as unintentional, justified or occurring under other mitigating circumstances. Using Kelley's (1967) discounting principle, they suggest that the perceived role of a given cause (the provoker) in producing an effect (an attack) will be discounted if other plausible causes (situational factors) are also present.

The conditions under which such additional information is provided may influence its effects considerably. Kremer and Stephen's subjects who heard prior mitigating information retaliated less than those who (1) heard it following a provocation or (2) not at all, and made significantly more external (situational) attributions than either of the two groups. However, a fourth group of subjects received (a) prior mitigating information, (b) an initial provocation and (c) a second provocation. In this fourth group, the effect of early mitigating information was completely eliminated. Thus, the mitigational influence may be only conditional, awaiting further information about personal characteristics. Unfortunately, in this experiment attributions were measured only once, leaving change unassessed.

Whether anger is aroused or reduced by mitigation depends on the perceiver's information-processing goals, current emotional state and strength and timing of information concerning harm. Johnson and Rule (1986) found that high-mitigation information (i.e. strong situational excuses for the confederate's rude behavior) delivered prior to provocation, rather than afterward, resulted in less physiological arousal (measued by blood pressure) and less retaliation.

Those in prior mitigation conditions also recalled more details of the co-worker's speech, suggesting that the increased arousal in the post-mitigation group led to a perceptual narrowing by subjects. Elevated arousal may have blocked revision of their original, person-centered attributions for provocation. The effect of anger arousal may thus be a crucial determinant of schema or script activation, acting to limit the search or retrieval of suitable interpretive strategies.

Cognitive Scripts

Mental economy is also produced by scripting. A cognitive script is a mental programming of an event sequence involving the self as an actor or observer. Scripts are usually relevant to particular situational contexts and contain notions of causality and temporal order. For example, a 'restaurant script' may consist of entering, being seated, ordering, talking, eating etc. Scripts, like schemas, generally make new events quickly predictable and comprehensible, but can also lead to distortions. With regard to aggression, very little research has examined aggressive schemas or scripts. Rule and Dobbs (1986) provide some initial evidence for such cognitive structures using marital disputes as the research example. Finding high consistency in the judgements and rank-ordering of script elements, they suggest that aggressive scripts tend to have a prototypic representation and are conceived of as series of events unfolding over time.

In situations where there are salient cues for aggressive behavior, cognitive scripts of aggression embedded in the experience of the individual can potentiate an aggressive behavior chain. The psychological idea of a script pertains to how social information is cognitively represented and organized (Abelson, 1976; Bower et al., 1979; Higgins et al., 1981), and has alternatively been called a 'social episode' by Forgas (1979, 1986), referring to cognitive representations of stereotypical interaction sequences. Forgas (1986) has begun to study implicit representations of aggression situations for understanding everyday reactions. The script idea, however, was implied in Toch's (1969) analysis of violent men, for example, when he wrote that violence was habit forming, viewed violent incidents as composed of stages and asserted that offenders saw themselves as participants in violent games: 'Most importantly, they start seeing elements of past violent encounters as they approach fresh situations and begin to respond routinely' (p. 186).

The concept of an aggressive script, then, is that of a mental programming of antagonistic behavior in a particular context whereby situational cues activate various subroutines for an actor's responses. Automobile driving is an emerging context for anger and aggression, from freeway shootings to rampaging drivers and suicide car crashes (Novaco, 1988). Roadway situations are impregnated with cues linked to aggressive scripts, such as the way the automobile is symbolized, traffic-related provocation and countless media portrayals of aggression in driving scenarios—for example, the prototypic chase scenes of *Bullitt* and *The French Connection*. Exposure to scripts which suggest or even legitimize violence have reduced inhibitions as well as programmed the mind with mental images. Combined with other disinhibitory influences, cognitive scripts for antagonistic behavior may be particularly potent in driving situations, making aggression difficult to deter.

CLINICAL ASSESSMENT IMPLICATIONS

Clinical intervention typically focuses much more on what a person thinks than how a person thinks. From both an assessment and treatment standpoint, much is to be gained from understanding cognitive operations and propositions regarding anger and aggression. The clinical prediction of violent behavior has proved to be a perplexing challenge (Monahan, 1981), but a conspicuous shortcoming of existing approaches to assessing the risk of harm-doing is that anger-proneness and regulatory capacity have been ignored. Present methods of anger-assessment rely exclusively on self-report inventories or scales, and clinical validation of existing instruments is generally absent. Importantly, no existing methodology for assessing anger is derived from a theoretical model that delineates component systems (cognitive, physiological and behavioral), and few theoretical approaches to anger emphasize contextual determinants. Our attempt here has been to further understanding of cognitive systems, and we now sketch some ideas concerning how the just-discussed cognitive factors might be assessed and treated.

A useful technique for assessing cognitive operations and propositions is the Meichenbaum and Butler (1980) videotape reconstruction procedure. Subjects or clients are videotaped while performing some task, such as a provocative, structured role-play (Novaco, 1975), and later asked to view the videotape and attempt to 'reconstruct' their thoughts and feelings as accurately as possible. The shorter the time between the videotaped assessment and the verbal reconstruction, the better. Similar assessments also could be carried out with standardized written or videotaped scenarios to which the subject is asked to react. The role-play procedure is favored where resources allow, however, because of potentially higher subject involvement and less artificiality. Such procedures indeed activate the arousal of anger and have been shown to be both valid and reliable (Novaco, 1975).

The fundamental attribution error can be assessed by such a technique. Role-plays should be constructed so as to provide for a range of personological versus situational attributions. Group norms can be established for anger-prone versus 'normal' groups to determine if angry clients do indeed tend to ascribe more blame to the person than the situation. How this varies across types of provocation or with regard to characteristics of the provocation also might be gauged. An instrument such as the Novaco Provocation Inventory (Novaco, 1975, and in press) which measures anger intensity across a range of 80 situations can be useful in identifying the contexts in which anger is easily triggered.

Similarly, following laboratory research, clients can be given hypothetical mitigating information about their own reported provocation experiences. This could be varied in terms of how much it 'discounts' the role of the provocateur, calling for more situational attributions for the provoker's annoyance or insult. Anchoring effects can thus be assessed. Does an anger-prone client fail to adequately revise attributions of blame toward the provoker in the light of the discounting information? Does this deficit occur across a wide range of situations or only for particularly provocative situations? Do they reappraise with low mitigational information (slight situational consideration) or high mitigational information (considerable situational causality)? It is expected that clients with anger problems would fail to adequately shift toward situational explanations, especially under low-mitigation information. The factors influencing this deficit then become the focus for interventions of cognitive restructuring and arousal reduction. It is most important that the client's level of arousal be assessed (e.g. blood pressure and heart rate), since arousal probably mediates attributions of causality (Johnson and Rule, 1986).

Assessment of the false consensus bias can be done with some innovation. Chandler's Index of Social Egocentrism (Chandler, 1973) has been used mainly with juvenile populations, but has been successfully applied to adult offender populations as well (Ross and Fabriano, 1983). A similar test, less well developed, is Selman's (1980) Test of Social Perspective-Taking. Selman's test is based on moral dilemmas which require the subject to present strategies for reducing conflict, while Chandler's requires the subject to differentiate between his or her own knowledge and that of a hypothetical 'bystander' presented in several scenarios. However, both tests have been criticized for time-consuming, subjective scoring and lengthy administration procedures (Ross and Fabiano, 1983).

A potentially useful assessment again might be obtained through role-play scenarios (alternatively, written scenarios or standardized videotapes) simply by asking the subject to estimate how his or her responses compared to that of other people. In his opinion, did he behave more/less aggressively than others would behave? In his opinion, did he assign more blame to the person than others would have done? In his opinion, did he shift his attributions when faced with mitigating information more/less than others would have? We hypothesize that anger-prone clients will generally display an impairment (and perhaps even reluctance) in comparing their perceptions and behaviors to those of others. They will tend to attribute their own perceptions and behaviors to others as well, seeing such responses as 'normal'. Obviously, a wide range of perceptions and behaviors could be called upon for comparison with 'what others would think or do'.

Attentional cueing and perceptual matching easily lend themselves to the suggested procedures (videotape reconstruction, standardized videotapes or written scenarios). One could examine whether anger-prone versus normal clients perceive more aggressive cues or report greater arousal or display greater aggression when faced with situations varying in aggressive and ambiguous cues (e.g. presence of weapons, ambiguous challenges or implied threats, prior goal-blocking, etc.). Are angered or anger-prone subjects more likely to 'see' threat and provocation in ambiguous circumstances (i.e. are they more vigilant for violent cues than 'normals')? Even traditional assessment procedures such as the Thematic Apperception Test (TAT) (Murray, 1943) also may be useful in this regard.

The binocular rivalry technique (e.g. Shelley and Toch, 1968) has great potential for assessing perceptual matching, simultaneously presenting (for fractions of a second) corresponding pairs of violent versus non-violent slides. The clinician with institutional resources could assess whether anger-prone clients were more likely to perceive scenes with violent versus non-violent content, as well as assessing contextual determinants of the perceptual bias.

Psychometric assessments of perceptual matching also could require subjects to generate different alternatives to conflict situations, plan a set of actions to achieve a goal and anticipate short- and long-term consequences of different alternatives. A variety of psychometric tests are used for these purposes, including (1) Means–Ends Problem-Solving Procedure; (2) Optional Thinking

Test; (3) Awareness of Consequences Test; and (4) Causal Thinking Test (Spivack *et al.*, 1976). These types of deficits in interpersonal problem solving have been found in offenders versus non-offenders, and such deficits have been linked to aggression and impulsivity (Ross and Fabiano, 1983). We would hypothesize that anger-prone clients would generate more aggressive alternatives, but fewer acceptable ones; they also would display greater deficits in planning actions to achieve goals and anticipating consequences than 'normals'.

SUMMARY

Cognitive influences on the production and prolongation of anger have been recognized since the writings of ancient philosophers, who understood anger as a passion that seizes control of the personality. Because anger, once activated, was viewed as divorced from reason and because of its colloquial association with insanity, the understanding of cognitive factors mediating anger-arousal was, for the most part, restricted to undifferentiated notions of appraisal or interpretation. Contemporary psychology ought not to be similarly limited in its theory and intervention regarding anger, which continues to receive less attention than disorders of anxiety and depression, despite its enormous societal significance. Potentially dangerous psychiatric patients, incarcerated offenders, juveniles and adults on probation and perpetrators of family violence are frequently the subjects of public concern, but little progress has been made in understanding the anger-proneness aspects of their psychological disposition and problem behavior.

In this chapter we have suggested a path of inquiry regarding cognitive determinants of anger that adds to the expectation and appraisal mediators developed previously (Novaco, 1979, 1985). The information-processing approach is a rich source of ideas about how angry clients think, which is needed to complement our understanding of what they think. There are a number of cognitive–behavioral intervention strategies for modifying dysfunctional cognitions, but the identification of the targets of these therapeutic efforts ought to be improved. It is our hope that we have been at least partially successful in suggesting the utility of the information-processing paradigm for understanding anger and aggression disorders.

References

Abelson, R. P. (1976). Script processing in attitude formation and decision making. In J. Carroll and J. Payne (eds), *Cognitive and Social Behavior*, Hillsdale, NJ: Lawrence Erlbaum Associates.

Allport, G. W. (1958). *The Nature of Prejudice*, Garden City, NY: Anchor Books.

Averill, J. (1974). An analysis of psychosocial symbolism and its influence on theories of emotion. *Journal of the Theory of Social Behavior*, **4**, 147–90.

Averill, J. (1982). *Anger and Aggression: An Essay on Emotion*, New York: Springer-Verlag.

Bagby, J. W. (1957). A cross-cultural study of perceptual predominance in binocular rivalry. *Journal of Abnormal and Social Psychology*, **54**, 331–44.

Beck, A. T., Rush, A. J., Shaw, B. F. and Emery, G. (1979). *Cognitive Theory of Depression*, New York: Plenum.

Benson, B. A., Rice, C. J., and Miranti, S. V. (1986). Effects of anger management training with mentally retarded adults in group treatment. *Journal of Consulting and Clinical Psychology*, **54**, 728–9.

Berkowitz, L. (1983). The experience of anger as a parallel process in the display of impulsive, 'angry' aggression. In R. G. Green and E. I. Donnerstein (eds), *Aggression: Theoretical and Empirical Reviews*, Volume 1, New York: Academic Press.

Bower, G. H., Black, J. B., and Turner, T. J. (1979). *Cognitive Psychology*, **11**, 177–220.

Bruner, J. S., and Goodman, C. C. (1947). Value and need as organizing factors in perception. *Journal of Abnormal Psychology*, **42**, 33–44.

Chandler, M. J. (1973). Egocentrism and antisocial behavior: the assessment and training of social perspective taking skills. *Developmental Psychology*, **9**, 326–32.

Chapman, L. J., and Chapman, J. (1982). Test results are what you think they are. In D. Kahneman, P. Slovic and A. Tatersky (eds), *Judgment under Certainty: Heuristics and Biases*, New York: Cambridge University Press.

Chesney, M. A., and Rosenman, R. H. (1985). (eds.) *Anger and Hostility in Cardiovascular and Behavioral Disorders*, Washington: Hemisphere.

Driscoll, J. M. (1982). Perception of an aggressive interaction as a function of the perceiver's aggression. *Perceptual and Motor Skills*, **54**, 1123–34.

Dyck, R. J., and Rule, B. G. (1978). Effect on retaliation of causal attributions concerning attack. *Journal of Personality and Social Psychology*, **36**, 521–9.

Forgas, J. P. (1979). Multidimensional scaling: A discovery method in social psychology. In G. P. Ginsburg (ed.), *Emerging Strategies in Social Psychology*, London: Academic Press.

Forgas, J. P. (1986). Cognitive representations of aggression. In A. Campbell and J. Gibbs (eds), *Violent transactions: The Limits of Personality*, Oxford: Blackwell.

Haldane, E. S., and Ross, G. (1931). *The Philosophical Works of Descartes*, Volume 1, Cambridge: Cambridge University Press.

Hazaleus, S. L., and Deffenbacher, J. L. (1986). Relaxation and cognitive treatments of anger. *Journal of Consulting and Clinical Psychology*, **54**, 222–6.

Higgins, E. T., Herman, C. P., and Zanna, M. P. (1981). *Social Cognition: The Ontario Symposium*, Volume I, Hillsdale, NJ: Lawrence Erlbaum Associates.

Hutcheson, F. (1742). *An Essay on the Nature and Conduct of the Passions and Affections*, London: Ward *et al*.

Ingram, R. E. (1986). *Information Processing Approaches to Clinical Psychology*, New York: Academic Press.

Ingram, R. E., and Kendall, P. C. (1986). Cognitive clinical psychology: Implications of an information processing perspective. In R. E. Ingram (ed.), *Information Processing Approaches to Clinical Psychology*, New York: Academic Press.

Izard, C. E. (1972). *Patterns of Emotions: A New Analysis of Anxiety and Depression*. New York: Academic Press.

Johnson, T. E., and Rule, B. G. (1986). Mitigating circumstance information, censure, and aggression. *Journal of Personality and Social Psychology*, **50**, 537–42.

Kelley, H. H. (1967). Attribution theory in social psychology. In D. Levine (ed.), *Nebraska Symposium on Motivation*, Volume 15, Lincoln: University of Nebraska Press, pp. 192–238.

Kremer, J. F., and Stephens, L. (1983). Attributions and arousal as mediators of mitigation's effect on retaliation. *Journal of Personality and Social Psychology*, **45**, 335–43.

McReynolds, P. (1969). Introduction to Hutcheson's essay (*op. cit.*). Gainesville, FLA: Scholars Facsimiles and Reprints.

Meichenbaum, D., and Butler, L. (1980). Cognitive ethology: assessing the streams of cognition and emotion. In K. R. Blankenstein, P. Pliner and J. Polivy (eds), *Advances in the Study of Communication*, Volume 6, New York: Plenum.

Monahan, J., and Novaco, R. W. (1980). Corporate violence: a psychological analysis. In P. D. Lipsitt and B. D. Sales (eds.), *New Directions in Psychological Research*. New York: Van Nostrand.

Monahan, J. (1981). *The Clinical Prediction of Violent Behavior*, Rockville, MD: NIMH.

Murray, H. A. (1943). *Manual of Thematic Apperception Test*, Cambridge, MA: Harvard University Press.

Nisbett, R., and Ross, L. (1980). *Human Inference: Strategies and Shortcomings of Social Judgment*, Englewood Cliffs, NJ: Prentice-Hall.

Novaco, R. W. (1975). *Anger Control: The Development and Evaluation of an Experimental Treatment*, Lexington, MA: D. C. Heath.

Novaco, R. W. (1976). The function and regulation of the arousal of anger. *American Journal of Psychiatry,* **133**, 1124–8.

Novaco, R. W. (1979). The cognitive regulation of anger and stress. In P. C. Kendall and S. D. Hollon (eds), *Cognitive–behavioral Interventions*, New York: Academic Press.

Novaco, R. W. (1985). Anger and its therapeutic regulation. In M. A. Chesney and R. Rosenman (eds), *Anger and Hostility in Cardiovascular and Behavioral Disorders*, New York: Hemisphere.

Novaco, R. W. (1986). Anger as a clinical and social problem. In R. Blanchard and C. Blanchard (eds), *Advances in the Study of Aggression*, Volume 2, New York: Academic Press.

Novaco, R. W. (1988). Automobile driving and aggressive behavior: effects of multiple disinhibiting influences. In W. Wachs (ed.), *The Car and the City*. Submitted manuscript.

Plutchik, R. (1980). *Emotion: A Psychoevolutionary Synthesis*. New York: Harper and Row.

Ross, W. D. (1963). *The Works of Aristotle*, Volume IX, Oxford: Oxford University Press.

Ross, R. R., and Fabiano, E. A. (1983). *The Cognitive Model of Crime and Delinquency Prevention and Rehabilitation: I. Assessment procedures*, Ottawa: Ontario Ministry of Correctional Services.

Rule, B. G., and Dobbs, A. R. (1986). *Scripts for Aggression*. Paper presented at the Forty-seventh Annual Conference of the Canadian Psychological Association, Toronto, Canada, June.

Rule, B. G., and Nesdale, A. R. (1976). Emotional arousal and aggressive behavior. *Psychological Bulletin*, **83**, 851–63.

Sandbach, F. H. (1975). *The Stoics,* London: Chatto and Windus.

Scherer, K. R., Abeles, R. P., and Fischer, C. S. (1975). *Human Aggression and Conflict: Interdisciplinary Perspectives*, Englewood Cliffs, NJ: Prentice-Hall.

Selman, R. L. (1980). *The Growth of Interpersonal Understanding, Development and Clinical Analysis,* New York: Academic Press.

Seneca, L. (41/1917). *Seneca's Morals*, New York: Harper.

Shelley, E. L. V., and Toch, H. H. (1968). The perception of violence as an indicator of adjustment in institutionalized offenders. In H. Toch and H. C. Smith (eds), *Social Perception: The Development of Interpersonal Impressions. An Enduring Problem in Psychology*, Princeton, NJ: D. Van Nostrand.

Short, R. J., and Simeonsson, R. J. (1986). Social cognition and aggression in delinquent adolescent males. *Adolescence, 21*, 159–76.

Slovic, P., Fischoff, B., and Lichtenstein, S. (1982). Facts versus fears: understanding perceived risk. In D. Kahneman, P. Slovic and A. Tversky (eds), *Judgment under Uncertainty: Heuristics and Biases*, New York: Cambridge University Press, pp. 463–89.

Spivack, G., Platt, J. J., and Shure, M. B. (1976). *The Problem-solving Approach to Adjustment: A Guide to Research and Intervention*, San Francisco, CA: Jossey-Bass.

Stermac, L. E. (1987). Anger control treatment for forensic patients. *Journal of Interpersonal Violence*, **1**, 446–57.

Taylor, R. L., and Weisz, A. E. (1970). American presidential assassination. In D. Daniels, M. Gilula and F. Ochberg (eds.), *Violence and the Struggle for Existence*. Boston: Little, Brown and Co.

Thomas, G., and Morgan-Witts, M. (1983). *Pontiff*. New York: Signet.

Thompson, W. C., and Schumann, E. L. (1987). Interpretation of statistical evidence in criminal trials: the prosecutor's fallacy and the defense attorney's fallacy. *Law and Human Behavior*, **11**, 167–87.

Toch, H. (1969). *Violent Men*, Chicago, IL: Aldine.

Toch, H. H., and Schulte, R. (1961). Readiness to perceive violence as a result of police training. *British Journal of Psychology*, **52**, 389–93.

Yochelson, S., and Samenow, S. E. (1976). *The Criminal Personality*, New York: Aronson.

Zillman, D. (1979). *Hostility and Aggression*, Hillsdale, NJ: Lawrence Erlbaum Associates.

4

Psychopathy and Personality Disorder in Relation to Violence

RONALD BLACKBURN
Park Lane Hospital, Liverpool, UK

INTRODUCTION

Clinicians concerned with individual acts of personal violence or interpersonal conflict typically construe aggression as behaviour which has harmful or injurious consequences. Everyday use of the term focuses on vigorous action perceived as malevolently intended and contrary to social norms, and hence tends to exclude passive acts of harm-doing and injurious behaviour which is socially legitimated, such as disciplinary punishment or self-defence. The identification of an act as aggressive is, therefore, highly dependent on the attributions and values of the observer, and aggression cannot be defined on the basis of observed behaviour alone (Bandura, 1983).

There are advantages in subsuming aggression under the broader rubric of *coercion*, i.e. the use of threats or punishments to influence social interaction (Tedeschi *et al.*, 1977). This emphasizes the interpersonal context and functions of harmful behaviour, and in particular, the social processes of power and control. It also directs attention to the motives for harmful action. Aggression is therefore construed here as coercive action, of which violence, or the use of physical force, is an extreme form. It is distinguished from the emotional state of *anger*, which is relatively independent of aggression. While most instances of extreme aggression are probably motivated by anger, aggression is not a necessary consequence of anger, nor is all aggression accompanied by a state of anger. These terms are further distinguished from *hostility*, which is used to denote negative evaluations of others as expressed in attitudinal statements of resentment or mistrust.

Given that punitive and damaging behaviour is relatively commonplace, there would appear to be nothing inherently pathological about human violence,

Clinical Approaches to Violence. Edited by K. Howells and C. R. Hollin
© 1989 John Wiley & Sons.

and intervention in instances of coercive action which society deems illegitimate is clearly a selective process. The traditional justification for clinical intervention with violent people is that their violence is a function of more general psychological abnormality. While this may sometimes take the form of psychosis or organic brain pathology, violence and other deviant behaviour is commonly held to be a consequence of relatively enduring deficiencies or dysfunctions described as personality disorders, and more particularly *psychopathic personality*.

These terms have always been contentious. Critics have noted their lack of agreed meaning, and have seen them as an attempt to medicalize deviance. Some have argued that the primary causes of violence reside in social conditions rather than in individual problems, and during the past two decades psychologists have debated the utility of concepts of personality which imply cross-situational consistency in behaviour. Social learning theorists, in particular, have maintained that aggression is more a function of specific person–situation interactions than of generalized tendencies. In this chapter it will be argued that generalized attributes of the person contribute significantly to violence, and that although not sufficient to account for a violent act, concepts of personality deviation or disorder are both defensible and necessary in the explanation of aggressive behaviour.

AGGRESSION AS A DISPOSITION

Personality, Traits and Dispositions

It is important to distinguish the *occurrence* of a violent act from the *tendency* to repeat such acts. As is described later, an act of violence does not necessarily imply an 'aggressive personality'. However, to attribute a trait of aggressiveness to someone implies that they are inclined to exhibit aggressive behaviour with some consistency across time and setting. Since the concept of *trait* has been at the centre of the 'person–situation' debate, its status needs to be examined.

The concept of personality is often reified, and treated as some mystical entity or force which 'exists' beyond social behaviour, emotions, cognition or whatever. This, however, is true only insofar as the organized whole differs from the sum of its components. In psychological theories, personality refers to behavioural regularities which distinguish and differentiate individuals, i.e. traits, and to the processes and structures which a theory postulates as responsible for those regularities. Traits are also central to current clinical concepts of personality disorder. In the *Diagnostic and Statistical Manual* (DSM-III: American Psychiatric Association, 1980), they are defined as 'enduring patterns of perceiving, relating to, and thinking about the environment and oneself'. They constitute personality disorder when they are 'inflexible and maladaptive' and cause impaired social functioning or subjective distress.

Mischel (1968) concluded that the empirical data did not justify conceptualizing personality in terms of 'underlying states and traits' or 'broad response dispositions'. Although he has subsequently modified this position, and much of the controversy has subsided in the wake of interactionism, many clinicians continue to be suspicious of trait concepts. However, the issues surrounding their utility are as much conceptual as empirical (Alston, 1975; Levy, 1983).

First, there is nothing particularly problematic about traits as *dispositions*, since dispositional terms are indispensable to lawlike statements. Trait terms such as 'shy' or 'aggressive' have the same status as 'depressed', 'anorexic' or 'pedophile'. All describe tendencies or *capacities* which reside in the person, but which are manifest only under relevant conditions. The question of breadth is perhaps more central to the objection to traits, and Mischel (1973) proposes cognitive alternatives to traits, such as outcome expectancies, which are 'specific' to particular situations. However, he adds that these are 'relatively specific'. How specific or general is not explicit, but, as Alston (1975) notes, if the only objection to traits is their breadth, it is a simple matter to narrow them. This is precisely the interactionist solution. Thus, rather than describing people as 'aggressive' it may be more useful to distinguish the kind of response shown in particular situations, such as 'verbally aggressive in school'. This is nonetheless still trait description.

A further issue is the predictive utility of trait measures. Traits are weak predictors of behaviour in specific situations, and responses supposedly indicative of the same trait commonly intercorrelate at a low level. However, it is the function of traits to summarize behaviour *in the average*, and it is unreasonable to expect them to predict single occurrences. When measures of generalized traits, including aggressiveness, are related to relevant behaviours averaged over settings, validity coefficients well above the 0.30 level are obtained (Hogan *et al.*, 1977; Olweus, 1980). Furthermore, traits cannot be inferred from single responses, any more than IQ can be inferred from the response to a single item of an intelligence test. As Epstein has shown (Epstein and O'Brien, 1985), when specific responses are aggregated over time and occasions, substantial stability can be demonstrated for a wide range of social and emotional traits. It is, then, aggregated and not specific behaviours which are predicted by trait description, and there is sufficient stability in behaviour to make useful probability statements about a person's proclivities on the basis of trait measures which do not specify situations. Indeed, outside the laboratory, situations are not usually predictable in advance.

Since traits describe average and probable rather than invariant behaviour, they cannot provide a fundamental account of behaviour. The notion of 'underlying' traits is misleading, since few personality theorists view traits as explanatory constructs. Alston (1975) suggests that personality variables fall into two groups, i.e. trait concepts, which describe frequency dispositions, and 'purposive–cognitive' concepts, such as goals, beliefs or expectancy. Only the latter constructs have an explanatory function. It will be noted that the cognitive variables of social learning theorists fall into this category. However, defenders of trait description also appeal to cognitive–motivational variables to *explain* behaviour (Epstein and O'Brien, 1985; Olweus, 1979).

The utility of traits, then, lies in describing the prominent features of a person's behavioural repertoire. They provide a useful first step in accounting for behaviour, but are not in themselves explanatory. However, if there is consistency of behaviour across situations in the average it must be accounted for in terms of what individuals carry with them, and this would suggest processes of greater generality than social learning theorists have been prepared to concede.

The Stability of Aggression

Cogent evidence for the utility of trait concepts comes from longitudinal studies of the stability of aggression. Olweus (1979) reviewed evidence on the stability of aggression as measured by observer ratings, peer nominations and direct observation, and identified twelve investigations in which assessments had been made on at least two occasions, which ranged from 6 months to 21 years apart. The average raw correlation between the two assessments was 0.63, which after correction for attenuation rose to 0.79. Some of these studies involved re-assessment by different means and in different contexts after extended periods of development and life experiences. Olweus therefore concluded that there is substantial stability in aggression which cannot be attributed to situational constancy.

Several subsequent studies are consistent with Olweus's findings. For example, Feshbach and Price (1984) found that among schoolchildren, two-year retest correlations for ratings of aggression were 0.55 for teachers and 0.68 for parents. Cross-situational consistency was also indicated by correlations between ratings made at home and those made at school ranging from 0.39 to 0.59. Long-term stability has been shown in a community sample by Huesmann *et al.* (1984). Peer nominations of aggression made at age 8 showed a correlation of 0.46 with self- and spouse-reported aggression 22 years later. People can, then, be meaningfully differentiated in terms of aggressive tendencies which are relatively enduring personal attributes.

Habitual criminal violence appears to be a function of such a disposition. For example, Farrington (1978) found that 70% of delinquents who had records of violent crime by the age of 21 had been rated as among the most aggressive of their peers at age 12, in comparison with 23% of non-delinquents. Robins (1978) has also found that fighting in childhood consistently predicts violent behaviour in adults. Moreover, more persistent violence is associated with greater social deviance. Wolfgang (1975) identified a core of chronic offenders who made up less than a fifth of known delinquents, but who were responsible for almost three-quarters of all homicides, rapes, robberies and aggravated assaults. Farrington also found that violent offenders were more likely to be multiple-recidivists, while in a younger group, Loeber and Dishion (1984) observed that boys who were most consistently aggressive were more likely to be delinquent. In Robins's research, fighting in childhood was part of a syndrome which included delinquency, truancy, under-age drinking, sexual precocity and school dropout. All types of deviant behaviour in childhood predicted adult anti-social behaviour. Thus, across several studies, about three-quarters of adults displaying more serious anti-social behaviour had displayed the syndrome of childhood anti-social behaviour. These findings have been influential in recent conceptions of anti-social or psychopathic personality disorder.

Origins of Consistency in Aggression

Persisting aggression is commonly assumed to originate in family modelling and reinforcement. Violent adults frequently report a history of witnessing violence and experiencing physical abuse in childhood, and Huesmann *et al.* (1984) found that aggression was perpetuated in families across three generations. Inadequate supervision of the child's behaviour and parental failure to punish deviant behaviour or reward pro-social behaviour is also a common finding in studies of aggressive children. However, Patterson (1979) observed that coercive responding by children in the home is *negatively* reinforced, i.e. it terminates aversive behaviours from other family members, although aggression in school may be positively reinforced.

Aggression may also be influenced by genetic factors, and a recent twin study by Rushton *et al.* (1986) found evidence for substantial heritability for self-reported aggressiveness. This is not inconsistent with learning analyses, but suggests that the child may be an active contributor to the learning of aggression. Genetic factors most probably exert their influence through relatively non-specific characteristics such as general activity or hormonal level. For example, an overactive child is likely to create more opportunities for aversive exchanges with caretakers or siblings, thereby increasing the likelihood of reciprocal aversive control.

Social learning theory proposes that behavioural stability is cognitively mediated. Mischel (1973) and Bandura (1983) view reinforcing contingencies as antecedent sources of information about appropriate behavioural outcomes, which create expectations of similar outcomes on future occasions. Expectancies are thus crucial mediators, providing rules about stimulus- and response-outcomes which guide behaviour. Once established as relatively general rules, expectancies may override the objective contingencies in a situation, and become self-fulfilling prophecies (Carson, 1979).

Failure to discriminate between present and past events is, however, commonly regarded as dysfunctional, and this is implied by the clinical concept of personality disorders as traits which are 'inflexible and maladaptive'. Greater consistency of aggression may therefore be more characteristic of maladjusted individuals. For example, Raush (1965) found that while hyperaggressive and normal boys were similar in following an unfriendly antecedent with an unfriendly response, the aggressive boys were more likely to follow a friendly antecedent with an unfriendly response. They were thus less able to differentiate between events, responding to friendly events as if they had a hostile meaning. Similarly, when asked to describe their responses to thwarting or provoking situations, mentally disordered offenders showed greater consistency and less discrimination between situations than did students (Blackburn, 1984). Recent work by Mischel (1984) also suggests that consistency in aggression is a function of maladjustment or skill deficits. Among problem boys, cross-situational consistency of rated aggression was significant though modest ($r = 0.37$) when the boys' skills matched those required by the situations, but was much higher $r = 0.73$) when the competence requirements of the situations exceeded those possessed by the boys. While not accounting for the origin of these behaviours, Mischel interprets these findings as indicating that lack of 'construction competencies' with which to cope with a situation is stressful and leads to indiscriminate responding. Also relevant is the finding that in role-played responses to conflict situations, offenders were more aggressive than non-offenders but lacked non-aggressive assertive skills (Kirchner *et al.*, 1979).

A critical construct in current analyses of expectancy and personality is that of the *schema*. Schemata are generic cognitive structures through which knowledge is organized and stored, and which permit rapid identification of meaningful events, but at the cost of distortions in everyday interaction (Singer and Kolligian, 1987). Emotional schemata are relatively specific, but relevant to individual differences is the concept of the *script* (Abelson, 1981). Scripts are cognitive schemata by which sequences of events are anticipated, and represent the linking together of related experiences to form dominant themes guiding cognitive processing and social interaction. Scripts are formed at different levels of generality, from the concrete to the abstract. Metascripts are abstract representations subsuming more concrete categories, and their formation provides a basis for normal personality variation. An aggressive disposition could thus represent a bias to select hostile cues and to 'run off' coercive sequences to influence a transgressor. For example, Dodge and Newman (1981) found that aggressive boys showed an attributional bias to interpret social cues from others as displays of hostility, which was associated with more rapid speed of judgement and selective inattention to non-hostile cues. However, emotional scripts are amplified with extended experience, and may become overgeneralized metascripts. Aversive childhood experiences of abuse or rejection, for example, may be perpetuated into adult life as maladaptive reactions to diverse situations appraised as equivalent. This is seen to be a result of analogical thinking rather than simple stimulus generalization.

PERSONALITY AND AGGRESSION

Even among those characterized by an aggressive disposition, acts of physical aggression are relatively infrequent, and an observed disposition cannot itself explain the occurrence of a violent act. A trait of aggression implies a readiness to react with a range of functionally equivalent responses to a particular class of situations, but whether aggression occurs in those situations depends on more proximal factors such as the antagonist's behaviour and status, the anticipation of rewards and punishments, the arousal of competing tendencies or the availability of alternative coping skills or competencies. Other personal attributes, as well as current situational factors, must therefore enter into explanations of violence.

Personality Variables in the Inhibition of Aggression

Psychodynamic and early learning theorists viewed aggression as a natural response to frustration, and saw individual differences as residing in the acquisition of emotional inhibitions restraining harmful behaviour, such as anxiety, guilt, empathic concern and concomitant tolerance for frustration. Lack of such reactions has been central to the conception of psychopathic personality. McCord and McCord (1964), for example, described the psychopath as 'an asocial, aggressive, highly impulsive person, who feels little or no guilt, and is unable to form lasting bonds of affection with other human beings'. Correlational studies support these assumptions insofar as aggression is closely associated with a personality dimension which includes impulsivity and extrapunitive hostility (Blackburn, 1972, 1986; Quay, 1979).

The importance of inhibitory tendencies has been demonstrated by Olweus (1973). He found that, among adolescent boys low on a test of inhibitions against aggression, the relation between a test of aggression and peer ratings of aggressiveness was +0.62. Among those high in inhibition, a significant *negative* correlation of 0.55 was found. This is an example of a moderator effect, and when inhibitory tendencies were not taken into account there was no significant relation between test and rating measures of aggression. Blackburn (1987) found that among hospitalized violent offenders who reported low social anxiety the correlation between self-reported and observer-rated aggression was 0.75. Among more withdrawn and anxious patients the correlation was a non-significant 0.26, although overall, the aggression scale was in this case significantly related to observer ratings ($r = 0.54$). Those who experience frequent anger and hostility may therefore be less likely to express these feelings directly in overt aggression when social anxiety and avoidance is high.

Generalized inhibitions against aggression are central to the concept of the *overcontrolled* assaultive offender (Megargee, 1966). Megargee proposed that *undercontrolled* offenders have weak inhibitions, and are likely to respond aggressively to provocation with some regularity. They are also likely to be identified as psychopathic personalities. Overcontrolled offenders, in contrast, have strong inhibitions and will aggress only when instigation (anger-arousal) is sufficiently intense to overcome inhibitions. They are therefore expected to attack others rarely, but with extreme intensity if they do so. They should hence be found more commonly among those who have been extremely assaultive. In support of this hypothesis, Megargee found that boys with a record of extreme assault were rated as more controlled and unaggressive, and showed greater control and conventionality on personality tests than moderately assaultive and non-violent delinquents. Further support was obtained in a study of mentally disordered offenders (Blackburn, 1968). Extreme assaultives were significantly more controlled, inhibited and defensive on psychological tests than moderate assaultives, and were significantly less likely to have a prior criminal record or to be diagnosed as psychopathic personality. In a subsequent study of 56 murderers almost half showed such characteristics (Blackburn, 1971).

Megargee developed a scale of overcontrolled hostility (OH), and Lane and Kling (1979) found that OH differentiated male forensic patients with a history of infrequent but intense violence. On the basis of test correlates of the scale, they considered that high scores on OH reflected rigidity, excessive control, repression of conflicts and a reluctance to admit to psychiatric symptoms. Walters *et al*. (1982) also found that psychiatric outpatients scoring high on OH were more likely to be described by their therapists as prone to chronic but rigidly suppressed anger and hostility. Murderers scoring highly on OH have also been found to be characterized by lack of assertiveness in role-plays and by less anger expression in response to provocation (Quinsey *et al*., 1983).

While the overcontrol hypothesis sheds some light on why typically *unaggressive* individuals are found among violent offenders, its theoretical basis is open to question. It is proposed that the intensity of aggression in the overcontrolled aggressor represents an accumulation or summation of anger-arousal to repeated provocation, but such an energy model is not in accord with current knowledge of aggression. Nevertheless, this aspect of the model can be salvaged, since anger can be self-produced and maintained by the cognitive rehearsal of grievances (Zillmann, 1979). Such rehearsal may bias a person to perceive and respond more readily to subsequent provocation. The model does not, however, clarify whether it is the arousal of anger, its expression or the lack of aggressive habits which is problematic for overcontrolled individuals.

There is evidence for two overcontrolled patterns (Blackburn, 1971, 1986), one characterized by relatively strong anger experiences, social anxiety and control over overt aggression, the other denying angry or hostile tendencies, while being sociable, non-anxious and conforming. Both groups appear to have acquired non-aggressive, avoidant ways of coping with conflict situations, but the defensive denial of the latter group implies cognitive avoidance. Clinical observations suggest that such offenders are strongly dependent on approval, and that their offences commonly involve threatened loss of status. Those in the more anxious subgroup are least likely to have a history of repeated violence, although their offences often involve sexual coercion (Blackburn, 1984). They are also more clearly characterized by low self-esteem. As Tedeschi *et al*. (1977) note, low self-esteem may make a person vulnerable to threat, but people with low self-esteem may also adopt coercive means of social influence because they lack non-coercive skills with which to achieve power and status.

Personality Variables in the Facilitation of Aggression

Recent theories have paid more attention to factors which facilitate aggression, such as the arousal of anger, and to the cognitive processes which mediate facilitation or inhibition. It is, for example, clearly established that frustration instigates aggression only if it is judged to be unwarranted. Similarly, the inhibitory effects of threatened punishment depend on its perceived justification (Zillmann, 1979). Cognitive appraisals and inferences therefore play a significant role in determining aggressive behaviour.

Although experimental research on aggression has tended to ignore individual differences, many of the variables identified in social learning and social cognitive analyses are likely to be influenced by stable personal attributes. In social learning theory, aggression is seen as one of several possible coping responses to situations which are aversive, or which have strong incentive value. Classes of aversive event include physical assault, threat or insult and frustrative non-reward, while incentives may be social reinforcers, such as status or approval, or material rewards. What constitutes threat or positive goals will clearly vary between people. Self-concept and esteem, for example, were implicated in Toch's (1969) observations of violent encounters between police and delinquents, which suggested that threats to masculine self-image and self-image promotion or defending were significantly associated with violence.

Zillmann (1979) focuses attention on the importance of cognitive guidance in conflict situations, and emphasizes the role of causal attributions in the arousal of anger. As he notes, retaliation and punishment are *moral* concepts, dependent on prior standards of what constitutes transgression and what represents equitable compensatory reaction. Similarly, Ferguson and Rule (1983) propose that the arousal of anger is related not simply to the degree of perceived aversive treatment by others but also to judgements of whether the aversion is intentional, malevolent, foreseeable and unjustified. Such inferences derive from what the individual construes *ought* to be the case, and therefore reflect what is important in terms of personal values, rights and self-esteem. Individual differences in ease of anger arousal may therefore relate to moral value systems and to expectancies and judgemental processes which bias appraisals of interpersonal events. For example, anger-prone people are likely to be unrealistically perfectionist (Zwemer and Deffenbacher, 1984).

PSYCHOPATHY, PERSONALITY DISORDER AND VIOLENCE

Psychopathic Personality and the Classification of Personality Disorder

As it originated in German psychiatry, psychopathic personality meant literally a *psychologically damaged* person, but in the course of a complex history it has been narrowed to denote a specific category of *socially damaging* individuals. Particularly significant in this respect has been Cleckley's conceptualization of psychopathic personality, which has influenced the research of North American psychologists, notably Hare (Cleckley, 1976; Hare, 1986). Cleckley viewed psychopathic personality as 'a distinct clinical entity' characterized by deficiencies in emotional reactivity and concern for others, and he proposed 16 criteria by which psychopaths could be identified. These include traits such as superficial charm, unreliability, lack of remorse, egocentricity and interpersonal unrespon-siveness. Cleckley's concept, however, has been criticized as a misleading stereotype (Vaillant, 1975), and unresolved are issues of its relation to the classification of personality disorders, the homogeneity of the category and whether a dimensional concept of psychopathy is more appropriate than that of a category.

The term 'psychopath' no longer appears in formal psychiatric classifications, but it is represented by *anti-social personality disorder* in DSM-III, which is one of eleven categories of personality disorder. These are grouped on the basis of similarities into the following clusters:

(1) Disorders characterized by 'odd' or eccentric behaviours (paranoid, schizoid and schizotypal);
(2) Those in which individuals display dramatic, emotional, or erratic behaviours (histrionic, narcissistic, anti-social and borderline);
(3) Those comprising individuals with anxious or fearful tendencies (avoidant, dependent, compulsive and passive–aggressive).

The DSM-III classification drew on the theoretical scheme proposed by Millon (1981), which combines four patterns of self–other orientation (dependent, independent, ambivalent, detached) with approach or avoidance tendencies (active versus passive) to yield eight coping patterns. Millon regards paranoid, schizotypal and borderline disorders as severe manifestations of his eight basic patterns rather than as distinct categories, and disagrees with the DSM definition of anti-social personality disorder. In Millon's scheme, this is identified as an *aggressive* coping pattern, corresponding to the active maintenance of independence, with a narcissistic personality representing the passive form. Millon proposes that the dominant traits of the aggressive personality are hostile affectivity, social rebelliousness, vindictiveness and disregard for danger.

The DSM concept of anti-social personality, however, was influenced by the research of Robins (1978), and the category is defined by detailed criteria of delinquent and socially undesirable behaviour involving violation of the rights of others. Reference to personality traits is limited to irritability and aggressiveness, impulsivity and recklessness. These criteria are inconsistent with the aim of defining personality disorders in terms of traits. Anti-normative or deviant acts may or may not be a consequence of personality characteristics, but they are not in themselves traits, and they belong in a different universe of discourse (Blackburn, 1988). Personality disorder and socially deviant behavior are not, in other words, mutually exclusive classes, and a person may display either, neither or both. Socially deviant behaviour is, therefore, neither a necessary nor sufficient criterion for defining a disorder of personality, and there is no logical reason for expecting those who are homogeneous in terms of a history of social deviance to be homogeneous in personality traits.

Blackburn (1988) argues that, as a result of the confounding of socially deviant behaviour with personality traits, current concepts of psychopathic or anti-social personality do not denote a single category of individuals who are deviant in personality. In England, the Mental Health Act category of *psychopathic disorder* is identified essentially by anti-social behaviour, and the definition contains no reference to personality ('a disorder or disability of mind

. . . which results in abnormally aggressive or seriously irresponsible conduct on the part of the person concerned'). Patients assigned to this category are not, in fact, homogeneous in personality (Blackburn, 1975). In the United States the term 'psychopathic' has also been equated with antisocial, and has been used interchangeably with *sociopathic*, a term denoting any form of socially deviant behaviour. Hare suggests that Cleckley's criteria and those for the DSM anti-social personality disorder identify broadly the same group of people. However, Cleckley's criteria also appear among those for other DSM personality disorders, in particular histrionic, narcissistic and borderline. Also, many of those in the anti-social personality disorder category have been found to meet the criteria for these other disorders. Psychopathic or anti-social personality does not, then, appear to be the distinct entity which Cleckley claimed, and covers several more specific categories. The notion of a unique category of people who are socially deviant and prone to aggression is therefore misleading (Wulach, 1983).

Personality Types and Violence

Most of the recent formulations of psychopathy include aggressiveness as a central defining trait. Although this is not explicit in Cleckley's concept, Hare and McPherson (1984) found that within a prison sample the majority of those meeting Cleckley's criteria had a history of serious violent crimes, and were also more likely to behave aggressively in prison. Nevertheless, while repetitive aggressive behaviour would indicate a trait of aggression, it has been stressed that the occurrence of a single act of violence is not itself an indicator of such a disposition. Indeed, the concept of the overcontrolled aggressor suggests that a violent act may sometimes be associated with a disposition *not* to aggress. It is therefore unlikely that those who have committed violent crimes will be homogeneous in personality.

Blackburn (1971) carried out a cluster analysis of MMPI data obtained from 56 murderers in a forensic psychiatric security hospital, and found four distinct personality patterns. These have subsequently been shown to be the main patterns among violent offenders within the category of psychopathic disorder (Blackburn, 1975) and among violent mentally disordered offenders more generally (Blackburn, 1986). These same types have been identified among 'normal' murderers (McGurk, 1978) and violent male criminals (Henderson, 1982). From their predominant personality characteristics, these four types have been described as *primary psychopaths* (impulsive, aggressive, hostile, extraverted), *secondary psychopaths* (impulsive, aggressive, hostile, socially anxious and withdrawn), *controlled* or *conforming* (defensive, sociable, unaggressive) and *inhibited* (unaggressive, withdrawn, introverted). The former two groups are similar in showing relatively strong impulsive and aggressive tendencies, but the differences between them indicate that more than one type of abnormal personality is associated with anti-social behaviour. The latter two groups represent two forms of overcontrol, as was noted earlier. Consistent with the overcontrol hypothesis, 52% of primary psychopaths but only 8% of the inhibited group were found to have a history of repeated violence (Blackburn, 1984). The two psychopathic groups also describe themselves as significantly more likely to react to interpersonal threat with angry aggression (Blackburn and Lee-Evans, 1985).

These four groups represent combinations of extremes on two dimensions labelled *psychopathy* (PY) and *social withdrawal* (SW) (Blackburn, 1986). As was described earlier, SW moderates the relationship between aggressive tendencies (PY) and observed aggressive behaviour, probably because SW is related to inhibitory tendencies and lack of assertiveness. Heilbrun (1982) has found that IQ also moderates the relationship between psychopathy and violence. Prisoners scoring highly on a measure of psychopathy, but low in IQ, were more likely to have a history of violent crime than psychopaths with a higher IQ, and also scored lower on measures of empathy and impulse control. Heilbrun suggests that more effective information processing in the higher IQ group permits greater cognitive control, but may be associated with sadistic rather than impulsive violence. When further distinctions were made on the basis of SW, Heilbrun and Heilbrun (1985) found that the combination of psychopathy, low IQ and high SW was associated with the highest level of violent behaviour within the prison.

Although these studies suggest systematic relationships between personality variables and violent behaviour, it must be reiterated that such variables are not in themselves sufficient to account for violence. Hostile attitudes or low self-esteem may bias people to perceive malevolent intent more readily, while an aggressive disposition and limited cognitive and social skills make attempts to resolve conflict by coercive means more likely. However, these characteristics are not confined to violent offenders. It is probable that the majority of aggressive personalities do not exhibit flagrant anti-social behaviour, even though they may be prone to conflict with those around them (Millon, 1981).

Dimensional Classification of Personality Disorder

Research on psychopathy and overcontrol has developed independently of the psychiatric classification of personality disorders. Some correspondence between the empirically derived types described above and clinical categories of personality disorder nevertheless seems likely. Thus, primary psychopaths seem to show characteristics of anti-social, narcissistic and histrionic categories, while secondary psychopaths appear more likely to meet criteria for anti-social, borderline and paranoid disorders. The controlled group shows traits which define dependent and compulsive personalities, while the inhibited one may include avoidant, schizoid and passive–aggressive personalities.

However, a dimensional classification may more appropriately represent the relationship between classes of personality disorder. It was suggested earlier that Cleckley's concept of psychopathy does not identify a single category. It may, however, identify a *dimension* of personality which is common to more than one class of disorder. Several factor analytic studies have, in fact, found a general factor of psychopathy which is defined by traits which are prominent among Cleckley's criteria, such as ecocentricity, irresponsibility and lack of interpersonal warmth (e.g. Tyrer and Alexander, 1979; Hare, 1980).

Blackburn and Maybury (1985) demonstrated that this factor corresponds to a dimension of hostility, which, together with an independent dimension of dominance–submission, forms the basic element of the *interpersonal circle* (Wiggins, 1982). In this two-dimensional system, segments of the circle around the hostility and dominance axes define different interpersonal styles which have clear parallels in the categories of personality disorder (Widiger and Frances, 1985a). However, as these segments are continuous and do not have precise boundaries, the notion of discrete categories of disorder becomes simply a convenient fiction. Such a system more realistically portrays the continuity between normal and abnormal personality, and between different forms of personality deviation.

How DSM categories might relate to this scheme is shown in Figure 4.1. The continuous circle of interpersonal traits is marked by summary labels of hostile, withdrawn, etc. The inner circle represents the normal range and the outer one the more extreme variations corresponding to inflexible styles reflecting different combinations of hostility and dominance. Primary and secondary psychopaths would be those occupying adjacent positions around the hostile dominant quadrant. Millon's 'aggressive' pattern is preferred to the label of 'anti-social', since in this scheme, anti-social personality is a misleading concept. While styles in the hostile–dominant quadrant may be associated with an increased likelihood of interpersonal conflict, there is no necessary association between anti-social behaviour and any particular style.

This approach has implications for explanation and intervention. The interpersonal model proposes that social exchanges generally follow a comp-

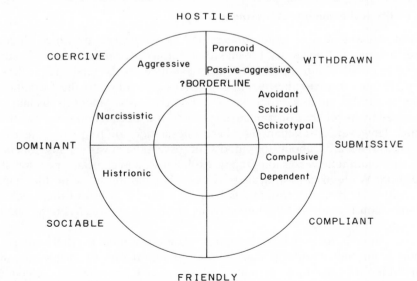

Figure 4.1 Hypothesized relations of DSM-III personality disorders to the interpersonal circle

lementary pattern, i.e. social behaviours 'pull' either opposite (dominant-submissive) or congruent (friendly–friendly or hostile–hostile) behaviours from other people (Kiesler, 1983). Carson (1979) suggests that there is a causal link between beliefs or expectancies about how others are likely to react, the enactment of behaviours consistent with these expectations and confirmatory reactions from others. A hostile–dominant person, for example, expects hostility from others as a result of aversive experiences, and behaves in a way which elicits confirmation of these expectancies in the reactions of others. Inflexible interpersonal styles thus come to be maintained as self-fulfilling prophecies which impede the learning of more appropriate skilled behaviour. Invalidation of these dysfunctional beliefs is therefore a central goal of therapy.

THE ASSESSMENT OF PERSONALITY DISORDER IN VIOLENT POPULATIONS

The viewpoint developed above implies that, without information about the typical characteristics which the violent person brings to an encounter, the analysis is incomplete, and that personality assessment should therefore be part of the psychological investigation of violent people. Currently, this is by no means common practice as a result of the decline of psychologists' interest and hence training in assessment methods. Competent assessment is, however, an integral part of therapy, and assessment skills have an increasingly high priority in forensic services, where the most significant function of the psychologist is often to advise others on appropriate intervention for a violent offender.

The Utility of Personality Assessment

Clinical assessment is generally understood as the *process* by which clinicians gather information necessary for making informed decisions about a client. It therefore entails both interactive and cognitive skills, and, regardless of discipline, this involves the testing of hypotheses leading to the formation of a model of the client's problems. Psychological assessment is usually distinguished by its reliance on objective *methods* of data collection and hypothesis testing. However, assessment has been the subject of frequent controversy centred on debates about the merits of psychodiagnosis versus functional analysis, nomothetic versus idiographic explanation and clinical versus statistical prediction. While discussion of these issues is beyond the scope of this chapter, the utility of personality testing has been of central concern in these debates, and some consideration of the implications of current approaches to personality is appropriate.

First, while a focus on traits shares with traditional psychodiagnosis an emphasis on molar aspects and internal determinants of behaviour, it is compatible with the more specific and structured approach of behavioural analysis. Owens and Bagshaw (1985), for example, indicate how traits enter into a functional analysis of aggression. From the standpoint of social cognitive theory, however, personality measures are not simply discrete variables to be added to situational antecedents and consequences in such an analysis. Their significance lies in providing signposts to the way in which the person classifies situations, and anticipates consequences. For example, Carson's interpersonal model would suggest that a violent act which is a feature of a more general coercive style is supported by expectations of aversive outcomes in a range of social interactions, and a belief in the efficacy of coercion as a means of control.

Trait assessment is part of the nomothetic tradition. Given that a person may be characterized in terms of aggressiveness, social avoidance, low self-esteem or whatever, we attempt to predict future behaviour on the basis of what is known about such attributes in general. Prediction is integral to clinical decision making, and successful prediction, whether of future violence or response to treatment, is commonly taken as the benchmark for the utility of assessment methods. However, there are inherent limitations on our ability to predict future behaviour from nomothetic laws. From a cognitive perspective, we may differentiate people at one level of abstraction in terms of sharing particular classes of expectations or rules. However, at the concrete level, rules are individual and idiosyncratic. As has been emphasized, traits are merely a first stab at explanation, and explanation of an individual's behaviour must therefore entail assessment of the person's own rules. Although nomothetic and idiographic approaches are complementary, clinical assessment must ultimately be idiographic.

Mischel (1964) suggested that the primary function of assessment is to render the individual's behaviour *intelligible*. Postpositivist philosophy of science also proposes that prediction has been over-emphasized at the expense of explanation, and that attempts to predict specific events on the basis of observed regularities are misplaced (Manicas and Secord, 1983). Human dispositions or capacities can be recognized and explained in terms of their component structures and organization. However, the natural environment is an open system subject to many indeterminacies, and capacities are not necessarily activated in the open world. An adequate assessment can therefore reveal what a person has the *capacity* to do, but not what he or she *will* do.

It is suggested, then, that the primary purpose of gathering information about personality is to facilitate *explanation* of an individual's behaviour. In these terms, the major function of an assessment of the violent person is to answer the questions of what enabled him or her to act in this way on that occasion, whether this implies the possibility of future recurrence, and what attributes, whether broad or specific, need to change to reduce this possibility. These questions need to be repeated throughout therapy.

Methods of Assessing Personality Disorder

Foulds (1971) made important distinctions between traits, deviant traits, states and symptoms. These are not mutually exclusive categories, and individuals who exhibit personality disorder may also commonly exhibit disturbed emotional states or the symptoms of other psychiatric disorder. Since our concern is with 'inflexible and maladaptive traits', this section focuses on methods of trait assessment.

There is no precise definition of what constitutes an 'inflexible' or 'maladaptive' trait. However, Foulds's concept of deviant traits focuses on stable attributes which are more likely to be associated with social dysfunction and personal distress, i.e. those which are maladaptive, examples being egocentricity, impulsivity and extrapunitive hostility. Although it is unlikely that the current psychiatric classifications of personality disorder represent optimal ways of describing patterns of deviant traits, DSM-III attempts to specify a comprehensive range of such traits.

Clinicians infer traits most commonly through interviews and case-history reports. A trait may be attributed on the basis of a person's own statements of behavioural regularity, on corroborating non-verbal behaviours or on the reports of others. There are two major problems in such an assessment. One is conceptual, and derives from the fact that a trait is a summary abstraction of a broad class of behaviours and does not have any precise definition or explicit rules of application. The observer's own norms may dictate the criteria for applying such a term. The second problem is the more practical one of determining whether a particular behaviour pattern is a stable or regular feature of a person's repertoire. People vary in the accuracy with which they can identify regularities in their own behaviour, and in psychiatric populations, behavioural consistencies may be masked by abnormal mood states. Similarly, a clinician's judgements of what is typical for an individual are derived from a limited sample of observations, and may be biased by an isolated but recent or striking example of trait-relevant behaviour.

These inherent difficulties of trait ascription account for the typical unreliability of interview-based judgements of personality disorder. Some improvement can be achieved with structured interviews, in which traits are rated on interval scales, and which have the advantage of comprehensive coverage of a range of deviant behaviours (Tyrer and Alexander, 1979; Stangl et al., 1985). A recent development draws on cognitive research which has shown that the class concepts of natural language generally, and traits in particular (Buss and Craik, 1983), are not typically applied on the basis of necessary and sufficient criteria but rather through the identification of central or *prototypical* features shared by most but not all exemplars of a category. Widiger and Frances (1985a) suggest that the traits of personality disorder may be redefined in terms of prototypical behavioural indicators, and Livesley (1986) has shown that this may lead to improved reliability in clinical assessment.

Psychologists more typically rely on the use of structured tests, most frequently *self-report inventories* but also *observer rating scales*. These survey behaviour samples of varying comprehensiveness, and are designed to meet minimal psychometric standards of reliability and validity. Self-reports are potentially most informative because the individual is in the best position to identify what is typical and long-standing, and attitudinal traits relating to the self or others may not be readily apparent to an observer. Each method carries its own limitations. Self-reports rely on the person's concept of his or her own behaviour. Concealment or distortion is possible, although in clinical samples deliberate falsification is probably less of a problem than the effects on self-appraisal of limited self-knowledge or temporary mood. Observer ratings have parallel problems in the judgemental biases resulting from the observer's own norms, and in the limited opportunities for observation. Ideally, then, multi-method assessment is desirable, although not always feasible.

A considerable number of scales has been developed for the assessment of personality deviation, many for use with anti-social populations (see Brodsky and Smitherman, 1983). Only a few of the more commonly used measures will be mentioned here. The only test which purports to measure the DSM-III categories of personality disorder is the Millon Clinical Multiaxial Inventory (Millon, 1983). This is generally regarded as the most serious competitor to the MMPI, and has the advantage of a scoring system which takes account of population base rates. The MMPI continues to be used widely in the assessment of personality deviation, due in particular to its rich sampling of psychological problems and extensive accumulated research data. However, its standard scales are psychometrically deficient, and confound deviant traits with symptoms. Moreover, there is considerable redundancy in the item pool, since more than half of the items and most of the scales relate to the general dimension of anxiety or neuroticism, which has recently been described as one of 'negative affectivity' and a correlate of self-esteem (Watson and Clark, 1984). Some of its scales, notably *Pd* (Psychopathic Deviate), *Ma* (Hypomania) and *Si* (Social Introversion) are relevant to personality deviation, and some additional scales pertinent to hostility and aggression have been developed (Blackburn, 1972). The fourfold typology of personality deviation in violent offenders described earlier was derived from MMPI patterns (Blackburn, 1975), but has subsequently been shown to be reproduced by two relatively brief dimensional scales (Blackburn, 1987).

Foulds and Bedford (1978) developed the Personality Deviance Scale to assess the traits of extrapunitive and intropunitive hostility, and dominance, and several self-report scales have been used to measure psychopathy. Apart from MMPI scales, these include *So* (Socialization: Gough, 1965) and factor-analytic scales derived by Quay (1979). Self-report measures of aggression and hostility are provided by the Buss–Durkee Hostility Inventory (Buss and Durkee, 1957), which assesses traits of assault, indirect hostility, irritability, negativism, resentment, suspicion and verbal hostility. Similar in some respects is the Interpersonal Behaviour Scale (Mauger and Adkinson, 1980), which distinguishes aggression from assertiveness, and provides subscales of these general dimensions. The Anger Inventory (Novaco, 1975) seems to be partly overlapping with these latter measures, but employs descriptions of particular situations rather than response variables. The S–R Inventory of Hostility assesses both, and has been used to measure anger (Blackburn and Lee-Evans, 1985).

Observer-rating scales have been less commonly developed. The Psychopathy Checklist (Hare, 1980) employs a combination of structured interview and case history data to measure variables relevant to the concept of the psychopath. Quay (1984) has developed the Adult Internal Management System, which categorizes offenders into five groups by means of life history data and observer ratings, one group being described as aggressive–psychopathic. Blackburn and Maybury (1985) describe a rating scale to measure the dimension of psychopathy or aggression and an orthogonal dimension of social withdrawal. Items of these scales demonstrate the circular relationship of the interpersonal circle, suggesting that deviant interpersonal styles can be identified in relatively simple rating measures. A sophisticated rating system for assessing interpersonal behaviour is the Structured Analysis of Social Behaviour described by Benjamin (1981).

The measurement of cognitive aspects of personality has recently begun to emerge in the cognitive–behavioural literature (Landau and Goldfried, 1981), but has had little impact on the assessment of personality disorder or violence. However, Howells (1978) has demonstrated the use of the *repertory grid* with a poisoner, and the writer has employed a method of *semantic differential* analysis originating with Kear-Colwell and McAllister (1970) to identify the personal meaning of violent acts to offenders. This entails cluster analysis of the person's ratings of significant events, people and emotional states to determine what interpersonal or emotional themes might be associated with violence.

THE TREATMENT OF PERSONALITY DISORDERS

To the extent that violence is a function of personal attributes beyond the focal problem of aggressive behaviour, these must be a target of treatment. Specific approaches to the management of aggression and anger are dealt with elsewhere in this volume, but there has been little systematic outcome research on the treatment of personality disorder (Widiger and Frances, 1985b). This reflects the lack of clinical interest in personality disorders, other than psychopathic personality, prior to the advent of DSM-III, and behaviourally oriented clinicians in particular have been antipathetic to the relevance of personality variables to treatment. However, it has become clear that half or more of those in clinical or anti-social populations meet the criteria for at least one DSM category of personality disorder. It is therefore likely that therapists commonly deal with personality disorders but choose to call them something else. What are commonly identified as social skill deficits, for example, include social avoidance and anxiety, lack of assertiveness and inappropriate anger expression, which appear among the criteria for personality disorders. Such response dispositions are among those likely to be of concern in the treatment of violent individuals.

Personality disorders are not diseases, and their treatment is more analogous to remedial education than to medical treatment. Personal change rather than 'cure' is therefore the appropriate goal, although the provision of specific self-control and coping skills may often be the most attainable target. Most methods of psychological treatment are of potential relevance to personality disorders. Psychodynamic therapists have emphasized this class of disorders, and there have recently been attempts to incorporate clinical concepts of personality disorder into a behavioural framework. Marshall and Barbaree (1984), for example, conceptualize personality disorders as unskilful social behavioural repertoires which fail to engender rewarding or non-aversive outcomes from others. The interpersonal model also suggests a focus on the strengthening of adaptive skills, but it gives particular weight to changing the dysfunctional expectations about self and others which support particular inflexible styles. This is congruent with the aims and methods of cognitive–behavioural therapies, but adds attention to motivation and communication processes (Safran, 1984).

Treatment Outcome Research

Case reports of personality disorder have appeared periodically in the psychoanalytic literature, but outcome studies are confined largely to the effects of various treatment regimes on psychopathic personality in anti-social populations. While problems of aggression are prominent in such populations, the concept of psychopath has typically been used without clear definition, and it has been noted that even the more specific concepts developed recently do not refer to a homogeneous category of personality disorder. Reviewers almost invariably end up reviewing the treatment of delinquents or criminals in general. This literature has only marginal implications for the question of personality change. Psychodynamic programmes, for example, have tended to identify only vague goals such as 'responsibility', 'maturity' or 'self-awareness', while behavioural programmes have often been concerned with targets such as institutional compliance, grooming habits or skills whose relevance to anti-social behaviour is undocumented.

Apart from failures to differentiate personality disorders, this literature is marred by methodological problems. Levine and Bornstein (1972) examined almost three hundred reports on the treatment of psychopaths, but were able to identify only ten outcome studies which met minimal methodological requirements (homogeneous samples of anti-social personality, untreated controls, follow-up and specific outcome criteria). Nevertheless, of these ten, eight described significant effects on anti-social behaviour. Suedfeld and Landon (1978) reviewed the extensive literature on individual and group therapy, milieu therapy, somatic treatment and behaviour modification reported up to 1975. They felt that consistently inadequate criteria of psychopathy precluded anything more than the following tentative conclusions: therapy should be conducted with firm rules and non-gullible supportiveness, drugs may enable the psychopath to achieve rapport with the therapist, a therapeutic community may be helpful and time is a good healer.

The handful of studies reported subsequently does not permit more substantive generalizations. Psychotherapists have described uncontrolled outcome studies which justify cautious optimism in the treatability of psychopaths. Vaillant (1975) described four case studies in which inpatient containment, firm behavioural control, confrontation rather than dynamic interpretation and peer-group support apparently achieved successful personality change. Carney (1977) also reported that at least 'symptom-orientated solutions' were achieved among aggressive offenders exhibiting personality deviation who attended outpatient group therapy. On the other hand, a controlled study of drug abusers found that anti-social personalities showed little psychological change with psychotherapy unless they were also depressed (Woody *et al.*, 1985). Effects of the therapeutic community on anti-social behaviour also continue to be equivocal. McCord (1983) reports significantly reduced recidivism among young delinquents exposed to such a programme, but Gunn *et al.* (1978) found no such effects for adult offenders released from a therapeutic prison. Data obtained by Copas and Whiteley (1976) suggest that this kind of regime is beneficial only for those who already possess an adequate repertoire of interpersonal skills.

A few behavioural programmes for undifferentiated personality disorders have been described which achieved successful reductions in social dysfunction. Although the token economy is now generally regarded as ineffectual in promoting durable behaviour change, a programme combining a token economy, individualized contingency management and social skills training was found by Moyes *et al.* (1985) to reduce aggressive and disruptive behaviour and self-mutilation in personality-disordered youths. However, an ambitious token economy programme in which offenders were also assigned to differential treatment on the basis of Quay's classification system failed to produce any significant reduction in recidivism (Cavior and Schmidt, 1978).

The utility of anger-management training for aggressive individuals with interpersonal problems has received some recent attention (see Chapter 3), but applications of cognitive–behavioural methods with this group remain otherwise relatively unexplored. Templeman and Wollersheim (1979) described a cognitive–behavioural programme which employed fixed-role therapy, problem-solving training and the use of self-instructions to teach psychopaths to obtain goals of sensation and self-gratification in socially acceptable ways, but reported no outcome data. Frederiksen and Rainwater (1981) conceptualized explosive personality disorder in terms of negative interpersonal expectations and deficient assertion. They treated voluntary patients with a short but intensive programme of social skills training, cognitive restructuring and self-control, and found reductions in explosive outbursts for those followed up, although some continued to have social problems.

There are still insufficient empirical data to justify any single approach to the treatment of aggressive individuals who are deviant in personality. Examples can be found of successful outcomes for most forms of psychological treatment, but the evidence suggests that none is consistently successful. As with the treatment of other psychological problems, it remains likely that characteristics of treatment setting, therapist and client may be as important to outcome as specific technique.

A Case History

The treatment of aggressive individuals is a complex and demanding task, and some of the issues are illustrated by the following description of the treatment of a violent sex offender detained in a maximum-security hospital.

Peter was a single man aged 30 at the time of his admission following a violent attempted rape. He had ten previous convictions for assault, wounding and burglary. Most of his offences were directed to females, and included several serious assaults on prostitutes, involving beating, abuse, bondage and forced intercourse. He had longstanding difficulties in relating to females, and of a few short-lived affairs, the longest lasted for two weeks. Experience of normal sexual intercourse was limited, and had often been accompanied by erectile failure. Since the age of 18, he had experienced sadistic fantasies of subjecting women to terror and sexual degradation. These were not invariably accompanied by sexual arousal, and he found masturbation disgusting and unenjoyable.

Peter was an only child, with a family history of a stormy and often violent relationship between his parents. His father was extremely vindictive, belittling him and punishing him for his interest in sex. As it subsequently emerged, angry confrontations with his peers readily elicited recall of his father's violence. Also, during assaults on prostitutes, he imagined that he *was* his father. This 'identification with the aggressor' is susceptible to both learning and psychodynamic explanations. At school, he was isolated and a target of bullying, and never established close friendships with peers. He resorted to heavy drinking to cope with social anxiety, and this typically increased aggression and preceded several of his offences.

When first seen by the writer, his sadistic fantasies had declined, but he was frequently involved in angry confrontations with other patients, which were followed by periods of avoidance and withdrawal to his room. During initial interviews he expressed fears that his assaults on females could escalate to murder, but also felt that he had problems of tension, anger-control and fears that his verbal aggression would lead to mutual violence. Assessment procedures included tests of personality deviation, attitudes to self and others, self-ratings of heterosexual anxiety and efficacy, sexual knowledge, ward behaviour ratings and penile plethysmography. He showed characteristics of anti-social, schizoid, avoidant and passive–aggressive personality disorders, and was describable as a secondary psychopath. More specifically, he showed pervasive fears and avoidance of close relationships with males and females, and a limited capacity for non-aggressive, assertive self-expression. However, he also showed extreme intolerance and hostility, and a coercive style of relating to peers, which included frequent denigrating remarks, verbal threats and occasionally physical assaults. Although he did not describe low self-esteem, he made exaggerated claims of adequacy in some areas of his life and blamed others for most of his difficulties, and self-statements elicited during therapy revealed fears that others would judge him inadequate. Sexual difficulties were apparent in heterosexual anxiety and low efficacy expectations, sexual ignorance, prudishness and guilt, and marked arousal to sexual violence.

Treatment goals related to his hostile expectations and attributions, anger-arousal and tension, social and sexual anxieties, and interpersonal skill deficits. Treatment proceeded for two and a half years, and consisted of individual sessions of cognitive therapy focusing on anger management and expectations of self and others, sex education, and an orgasmic conditioning procedure aimed at increasing positive feelings about normal sex, and he eventually joined a cognitively oriented social skills training group.

Assessment was repeated at approximately yearly intervals. After one year, results indicated reduced tension, anger, hostility and avoidance, improved knowledge and positive feelings about sex, but continuing problems of coercive interaction and heterosexual anxiety. These were subsequently found to be reduced following social skills training, and significant reductions in reactions to sexual violence were also found. Peter progressed through a rehabilitation programme of phased outings from the hospital, and four years after commencing treatment was discharged to a hostel, with a condition of continued psychological support and supervision by a probation officer.

During the first four months he was relaxed in everyday social interactions, had no desire for heavy drinking, felt confident in his ability to manage stress and avoid further violence, and made active efforts to find work. He resorted to prostitutes on a few occasions, but had no problems of sexual performance and felt no sadistic urges. He eventually established a relationship with a woman, Cath, in which he was able to engage in intimate interactions for the first time in his life, but she terminated the relationship after some two months when he told her of his past offences. He appeared to cope with this with support, but subsequently began to complain about feeling threatened by hostel residents. A month later, he was found to be drinking heavily, and shortly after, he was arrested after abortively attacking a prostitute with a knife.

Following his re-admission, assessment revealed that previous problems had returned to their earlier level. He attributed this to the stresses imposed by the hostel. However, it emerged that the termination of his relationship with Cath had made him feel inadequate, and that he had also felt resentment to her for rejecting him. Eventually, after getting drunk, he reverted to previous sadistic activities with prostitutes, imagining that he was punishing Cath for humiliating him.

This case illustrates the multi-faceted problems likely to be shown by violent offenders and the need to attend to multiple targets of change. It also shows the lengthy nature of treatment and the problems of sustaining change. Significant changes were demonstrated during treatment, and there was clinical agreement that progress was sufficient to justify a return to the community, where treatment gains should be consolidated. However, while Peter's interpersonal skills and his self-efficacy had apparently improved, these changes were, in retrospect, tenuous. Given the significance of damage to his self-esteem resulting from his rejection by Cath, and its relationship to the return of his fears of intimacy and his desires for sadistic punishment, it would appear that changes in significant emotional schemata, and in his more central, 'core' beliefs about self and others, had not occurred (Safran, 1984). Attaining this 'personal revolution' remains the crucial issue for the psychological treatment of personality disorder.

References

Abelson, R. P. (1981). Psychological status of the script concept. *American Psychologist*, **36**, 715–29.

Alston, W. P. (1975). Traits, consistency, and conceptual alternatives for personality theory. *Journal of the Theory of Social Behaviour*, **5**, 17–48.

American Psychiatric Association (1980). *Diagnostic and Statistical Manual of Mental Disorders*, 3rd edition, Washington, DC.

Bandura, A. (1983). Psychological mechanisms of aggression. In R. G. Geen and E. I. Donnerstein (eds), *Aggression: Theoretical and Experimental Reviews*, Volume One, New York: Academic Press, pp. 3–40.

Benjamin, L. S. (1981). A psychosocial competence classification system. In J. D. Wine and M. D. Smye (eds), *Social Competence*, New York: Guilford Press, pp. 189–231.

Blackburn, R. (1968). Personality in relation to extreme aggression in psychiatric offenders. *British Journal of Psychiatry*, **114**, 821–8.

Blackburn, R. (1971). Personality types among abnormal homicides. *British Journal of Criminology*, **11**, 14–31.

Blackburn, R. (1972). Dimensions of hostility and aggression in abnormal offenders. *Journal of Consulting and Clinical Psychology*, **38**, 20–6.

Blackburn, R. (1975). An empirical classification of psychopathic personality. *British Journal of Psychiatry*, **127**, 456–60.

Blackburn, R. (1984). The person and dangerousness. In D. J. Muller, D. E. Blackman and A. J. Chapman (eds), *Psychology and Law*, Chichester: Wiley, pp. 102–11.

Blackburn, R. (1986). Patterns of personality deviation among violent offenders: replication and extension of an empirical taxonomy. *British Journal of Criminology*, **26**, 254–69.

Blackburn, R. (1987). Two scales for the assessment of personality disorder in antisocial populations. *Personality and Individual Differences*, **8**, 81–93.

Blackburn, R. (1988). On moral judgements and personality disorders: the myth of the psychopathic personality revisited. *British Journal of Psychiatry*, **153**, 505–12.

Blackburn, R., and Lee-Evans, J. M. (1985). Reactions of primary and secondary psychopaths to anger evoking situations. *British Journal of Clinical Psychology*, **24**, 93–100.

Blackburn, R., and Maybury, C. (1985). Identifying the psychopath: the relation of Cleckley's criteria to the interpersonal domain. *Personality and Individual Differences*, **6**, 375–86.

Brodsky, S. L., and Smitherman, H. O. (1983). *Handbook of Scales for Research in Crime and Delinquency*, New York: Plenum.

Buss, A. H., and Durkee, A. (1957). An inventory for assessing different kinds of hostility. *Journal of Consulting Psychology*, **21**, 343–9.

Buss, D. M., and Craik, K. H. (1983). The act frequency approach to personality. *Psychological Review*, **90**, 105–26.

Carney, F. L. (1977). Outpatient treatment of the aggressive offender. *American Journal of Psychotherapy*, **31**, 265–74.

Carson, R. C. (1979). Personality and exchange in developing relationships. In R. L. Burgess and T. L. Huston (eds), *Social Exchange in Developing Relationships*, New York: Academic Press, pp. 247–69.

Cavior, H. E., and Schmidt, A. A. (1978). Test of the effectiveness of a differential treatment strategy at the Robert F. Kennedy Centre. *Criminal Justice and Behaviour,* **5**, 131–9.

Cleckley, H. (1976). *The Mask of Sanity*, 6th edition, St. Louis, MO: Mosby.

Copas, J. B., and Whiteley, J. S. (1976). Predicting success in the treatment of psychopaths. *British Journal of Psychiatry*, **129**, 388–92.

Dodge, K. A., and Newman, J. P. (1981). Biased decision-making processes in aggressive boys. *Journal of Abnormal Psychology*, **90**, 375–9.

Epstein, S., and O'Brien, E. J. (1985). The person–situation debate in historical and current perspective. *Psychological Bulletin*, **98**, 513–37.

Farrington, D. P. (1978). The family backgrounds of aggressive youths. In M. Berger and D. Schaffer (eds), *Aggression and Antisocial Disorder in Children*, London: Pergamon Press, pp. 98–122.

Ferguson, T. J., and Rule, B. G. (1983). An attributional perspective on anger and aggression. In R. G. Geen and E. I. Donnerstein (eds), *Aggression: Theoretical and Empirical Reviews*, Volume 1, New York: Academic Press, pp. 41–74.

Feshbach, S., and Price, J. (1984). The development of cognitive competencies and the control of aggression. *Aggressive Behaviour*, **10**, 185–200.

Foulds, G. A. (1971). Personality deviance and personal symptomatology. *Psychological Medicine*, **1**, 222–33.

Foulds, G. A., and Bedford, A. (1978). *Personality Deviance Scale*, Windsor: National Foundation for Educational Research.

Frederiksen, L. W., and Rainwater, N. (1981). Explosive behaviour: a skill development approach to treatment. In R. B. Stuart (ed.), *Violent Behaviour: Social Learning Approaches to Prediction, Management and Treatment*, New York: Brunner/Mazel, pp. 211–34.

Gough, H. G. (1965). *Manual for the California Psychological Inventory*, Palo Alto, CA: Consulting Psychologists Press.

Gunn, J., Robertson, G., Dell, S., and Way, C. (1978). *Psychiatric Aspects of Imprisonment*, London: Academic Press.

Hare, R. D. (1980). A research scale for the assessment of psychopathy in criminal populations. *Personality and Individual Differences*, **1**, 111–19.

Hare, R. D. (1986). Twenty years of experience with the Cleckley psychopath. In W. H. Reid, D. Dorr, J. Walker and J. W. Bonner (eds), *Unmasking the Psychopath: Antisocial Personality and Related Syndromes*, New York: W. W. Norton, pp. 3–27.

Hare, R. D., and McPherson, L. M. (1984). Violent and aggressive behaviour by criminal psychopaths. *International Journal of Law and Psychiatry*, **7**, 35–50.

Heilbrun, A. B. (1982). Cognitive models of criminal violence based on intelligence and psychopathy levels. *Journal of Consulting and Clinical Psychology*, **50**, 546–57.

Heilbrun, A. B., and Heilbrun, M. R. (1985). Psychopathy and dangerousness: comparison, integration, and extension of two psychopathic typologies. *British Journal of Clinical Psychology*, **24**, 181–95.

Henderson, M. (1982). An empirical classification of convicted violent offenders. *British Journal of Criminology*, **22**, 1–20.

Hogan, R., DeSoto, C. B., and Solano, C. (1977). Traits, tests, and personality research. *American Psychologist*, **32**, 255–64.

Howells, K. (1978). The meaning of poisoning to a person diagnosed as a psychopath. *Medicine, Science and the Law*, **18**, 179–84.

Huesmann, L. R., Eron, L. D., Lefkowitz, M. M., and Walder, L. O. (1984). Stability of aggression over time and generations. *Developmental Psychology*, **20**, 1120–34.

Kear-Colwell, J. J., and McAllister, J. (1970). A new method for the analysis of individual meaning systems. *British Journal of Medical Psychology*, **43**, 49–56.

Kiesler, D. J. (1983). The 1982 Interpersonal Circle: a taxonomy for complementarity in human transactions. *Psychological Review*, **90**, 185–214.

Kirchner, E., Kennedy, R., and Draguns, J. (1979). Assertion and aggression in adult offenders. *Behaviour Therapy*, **10**, 452–71.

Landau, R. L., and Goldfried, M. R. (1981). The assessment of cognitive schemata: a unifying framework for cognitive, behavioural, and traditional assessment. In P. C. Kendall and S. D. Hollon (eds), *Assessment Strategies for Cognitive–Behavioural Interventions*, New York: Academic Press, pp. 363–99.

Lane, P. J., and Kling, J. (1979). Construct validity of the overcontrolled hostility scale of the MMPI. *Journal of Consulting and Clinical Psychology*, **47**, 781–2.

Levine, W. R., and Bornstein, P. E. (1972). Is the sociopath treatable? The contribution of psychiatry to a legal dilemma. *Washington University Law Quarterly*, 693–717.

Levy, L. H. (1983). Trait approaches. In M. Hersen, A. E. Kazdin and A. S. Bellak (eds), *The Clinical Psychology Handbook*, New York: Pergamon Press, pp. 123–42.

Livesley, W. J. (1986). Trait and behavioural prototypes of personality disorder. *American Journal of Psychiatry*, **143**, 728–32.

Loeber, R., and Dishion, T. J. (1984). Boys who fight at home and school: family conditions influencing cross-setting consistency. *Journal of Consulting and Clinical Psychology*, **52**, 759–68.

McCord, W. M. (1983). *The Psychopath and Milieu Therapy*, New York: Academic Press.

McCord, W. M., and McCord, J. (1964). *The Psychopath: an Essay on the Criminal Mind*, New York: Van Nostrand.

McGurk, B. (1978). Personality types among normal homicides. *British Journal of Criminology*, **18**, 146–61.

Manicas, P. T., and Secord, P. F. (1983). Implications for psychology of the new philosophy of science. *American Psychologist*, **38**, 399–413.

Marshall, W. L., and Barbaree, H. E. (1984). Disorders of personality, impulse, and adjustment. In S. M. Turner and M. Hersen (eds), *Adult Psychopathology and Diagnosis*, New York: Wiley, pp. 406–49.

Mauger, P. A., and Adkinson, D. R. (1980). *Interpersonal Behaviour Survey*, Los Angeles, CA: Western Psychological Services.

Megargee, E. I. (1966). Undercontrolled and overcontrolled personality types in extreme antisocial aggression. *Psychological Monographs*, **80**, whole No. 611.

Millon, T. (1981). *Disorders of Personality: DSM-III, Axis II*, New York: Wiley.

Millon, T. (1983). *Millon Clinical Multiaxial Inventory*, 3rd edition, Minneapolis, MINN: Interpretive Scoring Systems.

Mischel, T. (1964). Personal constructs, rules, and the logic of clinical activity. *Psychological Review*, **71**, 180–92.

Mischel, W. (1968). *Personality and Assessment*, New York: Wiley.

Mischel, W. (1973). Toward a cognitive social learning reconceptualisation of personality. *Psychological Review*, **80**, 252–83.

Mischel, W. (1984). Challenges and convergences in the search for consistency. *American Psychologist*, **39**, 351–64.

Moyes, T., Tennent, T. G., and Bedford, A. P. (1985). Long-term follow-up study of a ward-based behaviour modification programme for adolescents with acting-out and conduct problems. *British Journal of Psychiatry*, **147**, 300–5.

Novaco, R. W. (1975). *Anger Control: The Development and Evaluation of an Experimental Treatment*, Lexington, MA: Lexington Books.

Olweus, D. (1973). Personality and aggression. In J. K. Cole and D. D. Jensen (eds), *Nebraska Symposium on Motivation*, Lincoln: University of Nebraska Press.

Olweus, D. (1979). Stability of aggressive reaction patterns in males: a review. *Psychological Bulletin*, **86**, 852–75.

Olweus, D. (1980). The consistency issue in personality psychology revisited: with special reference to aggression. *British Journal of Social and Clinical Psychology*, **19**, 377–90.

Owens, R. G., and Bagshaw, M. (1985). First steps in a functional analysis of aggression. In E. Karas (ed.), *Current Issues in Clinical Psychology*, Volume Two, New York: Plenum, pp. 285–307.

Patterson, G. R. (1979). A performance theory for coercive family interaction. In R. Cairns (ed.), *Social Interaction: Methods, Analysis, and Illustration*, Hillsdale, NJ: Lawrence Erlbaum Associates, pp. 119–62.

Quay, H. C. (1979). Classification. In H. C. Quay and J. S. Werry (eds), *Psychopathological Disorders of Childhood*, 2nd edition, New York: Wiley, pp. 1–42.

Quay, H. C. (1984). *Managing Adult Inmates*, American Correctional Association.

Quinsey, V. L., Maguire, A., and Varney, G. W. (1983). Assertion and overcontrolled hostility among mentally disordered murderers. *Journal of Consulting and Clinical Psychology*, **51**, 550–56.

Raush, H. L. (1965). Interaction sequences. *Journal of Personality and Social Psychology*, **2**, 487–99.

Robins, L. (1978). Sturdy predictors of adult antisocial behaviour: replications from longitudinal studies. *Psychological Medicine*, **8**, 611–22.

Rushton, J. P., Fulker, D. W., Neale, M. C., Nias, D. K. B., and Eysenck, H. J. (1986). Altruism and aggression: the heritability of individual differences. *Journal of Personality and Social Psychology*, **50**, 1192–8.

Safran, J. D. (1984). Assessing the cognitive–interpersonal cycle. *Cognitive Therapy and Research*, **8**, 338–48.

Singer, J. L., and Kolligian, J. (1987). Personality: Developments in the study of private experience. *Annual Review of Psychology*, **58**, 533–74.

Stangl, D., Pfohl, B., Zimmerman, M., Bowers, W., and Corenthal, C. (1985). A structured interview for the DSM-III personality disorders. *Archives of General Psychiatry*, **42**, 591–6.

Suedfeld, P., and Landon, P. B. (1978). Approaches to treatment. In R. D. Hare and D. Schalling (eds), *Psychopathic Behaviour: Approaches to Research*, New York: Wiley, pp. 347–76.

Tedeschi, J. T., Gaes, G. G., and Rivera, A. N. (1977). Aggression and the use of coercive power. *Journal of Social Issues*, **33**, 101–25.

Templeman, T. L., and Wollersheim, J. P. (1979). A cognitive–behavioural approach to the treatment of psychopathy. *Psychotherapy: Theory, Research and Practice*, **16**, 132–9.

Toch, H. (1969). *Violent Men*, Harmondsworth: Penguin Books.

Tyrer, P., and Alexander, J. (1979). Classification of personality disorder. *British Journal of Psychiatry*, **135**, 163–7.

Vaillant, G. E. (1975). Sociopathy as a human process: a viewpoint. *Archives of General Psychiatry*, **32**, 178–83.

Walters, G. D., Greene, R. L., and Solomon, G. S. (1982). Empirical correlates of the overcontrolled hostility scale and the MMPI 4–3 highpoint pair. *Journal of Consulting and Clinical Psychology*, **50**, 213–18.

Watson, D., and Clark, L. A. (1984). Negative affectivity: the disposition to experience aversive emotional states. *Psychological Bulletin*, **96**, 465–90.

Widiger, T. A., and Frances, A. (1985a). The DSM-III personality disorders: perspectives from psychology. *Archives of General Psychiatry*, **42**, 615–23.

Widiger, T. A., and Frances, A. (1985b). Axis II personality disorders: diagnostic and treatment issues. *Hospital and Community Psychiatry*, **36**, 619–27.

Wiggins, J. S. (1982). Circumplex models of interpersonal behaviour in clinical psychology. In P. C. Kendall and J. N. Butcher (eds), *Handbook of Research Methods in Clinical Psychology*, New York: Wiley, pp. 183–221.

Wolfgang, M. (1975). Contemporary perspectives on violence. In D. Chappell and J. Monahan (eds), *Violence and Criminal Justice*, Lexington, MA: D. C. Heath, pp. 2–19.

Woody, G. E., McLellan, A. T., Luborsky, L., and O'Brien, C. P. (1985). Sociopathy and psychotherapy outcome. *Archives of General Psychiatry, 42*, 1081–6.

Wulach, J. (1983). Diagnosing the DSM-III antisocial personality disorder. *Professional Psychology: Research and Practice, 14*, 330–40.

Zillmann, D. (1979). *Hostility and Aggression*, Hillsdale, NJ: Lawrence Erlbaum Associates.

Zwemer, W. A., and Deffenbacher, J. L. (1984). Irrational beliefs, anger, and anxiety. *Journal of Counselling Psychology, 31*, 391–3.

5

Clinical Decision Making and the Assessment of Dangerousness

NATHAN POLLOCK
Clarke Institute of Psychiatry, Canada

IAN MCBAIN
University of Toronto, Canada

and

CHRISTOPHER D. WEBSTER
Clarke Institute of Psychiatry and University of Toronto, Canada

Clinicians undertaking assessments for legal purposes face several problems associated with the fact that the professions of science and law approach theoretical and practical issues from widely different points of view (Webster, 1984a). As Grisso (1987, p. 127) notes:

> Assessments to assist in making legal decisions must employ somewhat different designs and data collection methods than are found in traditional clinical assessments. This is because legal questions usually are not synonymous with clinical questions.

To avoid becoming entangled in a web of conceptual confusion, clinicians in the justice system must have an understanding of the legal process and a clear idea of their function in judicial proceedings. Unwary clinicians can easily be drawn into territory beyond the limits of their competence and into roles more appropriate to judges, juries, parole officers or police detectives. Further, clinicians must be alert to divergent and shifting role demands and be prepared to respond appropriately. Depending on the circumstances and legal strategies of a particular case, a clinician might be called upon to provide an explanation

Clinical Approaches to Violence. Edited by K. Howells and C. R. Hollin
© 1989 John Wiley & Sons.

of behaviour, a prediction of behaviour, an opinion about disposition or perhaps all three.

'Dangerousness' is a prime example of a concept which challenges the clinician's ability to negotiate the maze of conflicting demands and role expectations encountered in the judicial process. Offering a clinical opinion in court about dangerousness is often a balancing act between scientific integrity and social responsibility. To make matters more difficult, the scientific literature typically fails to reflect the complexity of the legal realities, and so offers little useful guidance to the confused and beleaguered clinician. Historically, the role of the clinician assessing dangerousness has been shaped more by the pragmatic demands of the justice system than by careful consideration by mental health professionals of the scope of their competence and expertise. As a result, the clinical assessment of dangerousness has come to be regarded as having a single purpose—accurate prediction. As Halleck (1987, p. 87) aptly remarks, the clinician:

> can play the important role of telling decisionmakers more about the social situations and the biological and psychological incapacities of the individuals who are the subject of their decisions. Alas, that rarely happens, . . . [r]ather we get put into the role . . . of the Wizard, a role with many perils.

One effect of this single-minded emphasis on predictive accuracy has been a polarization of opinion about the role of clinicians in judicial deliberations about dangerousness. There are those (e.g. Stone, 1985) who argue that because the scientific support for the accuracy of clinical prediction is scant, clinicians should decline to participate in such deliberations. Others (e.g. Dietz, 1985) believe that clinicians can make substantial contributions to legal predictions of dangerousness and see this as a social responsibility. Kozol (1982, p. 244), in this vein, has written that when it comes to assessing dangerous potential 'the profession of psychiatry has a responsibility to assist in the administration of justice sincerely and without reservation or equivocation'. Among those who do argue for the participation of clinicians in predictive decision making there is considerable disagreement about which approach is the more appropriate. Some reject the clinical method in favour of the statistically based actuarial approach, arguing that it is the more accurate and only scientifically justified procedure (e.g. Gottfredson, 1987). Others continue to value the idiographic clinical approach, believing it to be the more thorough and adaptable method (Holt, 1978; Halleck, 1987).

Accuracy in prediction is clearly a worthwhile aim but it is not the only consideration for forensic clinicians. Recently, a new perspective on the prediction of dangerousness has begun to emerge which emphasizes accountability over accuracy (e.g. Marra et al., 1987). From this point of view, the central issue is not the prediction itself but the clinical decision-making process; and the test of clinical prediction is not its overall accuracy or 'hit rate' but rather how defensible the prediction is in terms of the social realities and the current state of scientific knowledge. Monahan (1981) was one of the first to focus attention on clinical decision making in predicting dangerous behaviour. In his central text on the topic, he argues that, despite his earlier misgivings, he now believes there are times when it is appropriate for some clinicians to offer projections about future violent conduct. The clinician's responsibility is to decide when prediction is warranted, which predictive approach is indicated and how much confidence to place in the conclusions. Monahan's synthesis of the literature on the prediction of dangerousness and his recommendations for clinical decision making have provided new impetus to the predictive enterprise.

This chapter is an effort to disentangle some of the confusion surrounding the clinical assessment of dangerousness for judicial decision making. In the course of this analysis we draw attention to the idea that there is more to assessment than prediction, and that to act responsibly the clinician must first clarify the clinical task. Our point is that some appreciable portion of the difficulty associated with the task of assessing dangerousness is due to the fact that, so far, relatively little attention has been paid to the compatibility of different clinical functions. For example, the clinical explanation of dangerous behaviour may not always assist (and in fact may hinder) the prediction of violence. Further, we put forward the idea that existing research, depending as it does on statistically manipulable measures, fails to recognize the complexities of the clinical task, and so can scarcely be expected to cast light on actual clinical capability. Instead, what is needed is a clinical–research paradigm which emphasizes the theoretical underpinnings of the clincal decision-making process. The chapter concludes with a discussion of new approaches to the assessment of dangerousness and practical guidelines for clinical decision making about dangerous behaviour.

IDENTIFYING THE CLINICAL TASK: EXPLANATION OR PREDICTION

When the issue is dangerousness, the responsibilities of the clinician must extend beyond the examination of the patient to a careful scrutiny of the clinical task. To conduct a responsible and relevant assessment the clinician must be aware of his or her role in the judicial process and the intended purpose of the evaluation. The reason for the referral (Shah, 1978), the possible application of the assessment findings (Monahan, 1981) and the clinician's theoretical bias (Pfohl, 1978) may be crucial considerations in the assessment of dangerousness.

Although today prediction is arguably the most pressing demand upon forensic practitioners assessing dangerousness, in fact it is a relatively recent development in clinical practice. Foucault (1978) traces the evolution of the concept of dangerousness and its prediction in his analysis of the history of psychiatry and the law. At the beginning of the nineteenth century the law began to attempt 'to adapt the modalities of punishment to the nature of the criminal' (p. 9). Whereas previously it was sufficient for the courts to punish according to the severity of the crime, it became necessary to understand what lay behind the criminal act in order appropriately to mete out punishment. The emphasis shifted from a focus on what had occurred to why it had occurred, and the central legal issue became the distinction between criminal acts which were 'psychologically determined' and those which were 'gratuitous and undetermined' (p. 11). Only in cases of psychologically determined crime could the perpetrator be considered legally responsible and punishable. Otherwise the individual might be absolved of blame and receive treatment instead of punishment. In this social climate the courts began to turn to doctors as 'specialists in motivation' who could offer explanations for apparently senseless (and usually violent) criminal acts (p. 10).

As the penal system proved unable to live up to the ideal of reforming the criminal, the emphasis again shifted, this time from the issue of the legal responsibility of the individual to the protection of society. With this development, clinical assessment, in addition to explaining the criminal act, was expected to evaluate the risk the individual might present to the safety of the community (Greenland, 1985). By the beginning of the twentieth century the concept of the 'dangerous being' had become an established concept in the criminal law (Petrunik, 1983). Increasingly, mental health professionals were being called upon to assist the courts in identifying potentially dangerous individuals.

Despite this historical progression, the role of clinical assessment as an explanation of behaviour has not been supplanted by the demand for prediction, and the courts still look to mental health professionals for answers to the question 'why?'. The role of explanation in the clinical assessment of dangerousness is perhaps best exemplified by questions of moral accountability and criminal responsibility. Prins (1986) has recently noted that 'in cases where serious personal harm has been caused to others, often in bizarre and unusual circumstances, questions of explanation and exculpation arise' (p. 9). Prins cites three specific instances in which personal accountability is an issue: (1) insanity as a defense, (2) fitness to stand trial and (3) diminished responsibility. To establish the degree of accountability in such cases, the courts look to clinicians for an explanation of the defendant's behaviour. The court's decision is largely determined by the extent to which this behaviour is deemed to have been voluntary as opposed to being due to factors beyond his or her control (e.g. mental illness, lapses of consciousness, seizure activity, etc.), and the clinician's explanatory account may be instrumental in determining the court's perception of the offence and decisions about disposition.

This distinction between the explanatory and predictive functions of the assessment of dangerousness has a direct bearing on clinical practice. Whether, in requesting an assessment of dangerousness, the court is looking for an explanation or a prediction of the defendant's behaviour to a large extent defines the clinical task. The court's purpose also has important implications for the making of decisions about the appropriate clinical assessment approach and the correct application of the assessment findings. Consider this example:

> An 83-year-old man with no prior criminal convictions or psychiatric illness was referred for psychiatric assessment after being charged with murdering his wife. His wife had suffered from a degenerative brain disease for several years and he

had cared for her alone. More recently, she had become almost completely disoriented and had to be supervised continuously lest she wander away from the house in a confused state. The accused was himself in bad health. Three days prior to the incident he had returned home from the hospital, where he had been placed on insulin after a diagnosis of diabetes.

His recollection of the incident was sketchy. He recalled eating breakfast and feeling a bit lightheaded and dizzy. He remembered his wife becoming agitated and accusing him of being an imposter. Despite his efforts to calm her, she became increasingly upset and attempted to run away. Exasperated and unable to stop her, he reached for a board on the kitchen counter and hit her over the head.

The clinical assessment did not uncover evidence of psychiatric illness or a propensity for violent or other anti-social behaviour. Instead the report submitted to the court emphasized two points. First, the accused had been under extraordinary stress considering his age, poor health and the unusually demanding task of caring for his ailing wife. Second, the fact that the accused had recently been placed on insulin was noted as a possible contributing factor. The opinion was that poorly stabilized blood-sugar may have affected the accused's psychological functioning at the time of the incident, since hypoglycemia has been known to precipitate transient confusional states, memory impairment and aggressive outbursts.

In a case such as this the court is primarily concerned with deciding an appropriate disposition, and so is less interested in a prediction of dangerousness than in an explanation of the occurrence. A clinician applying an actuarial approach in the assessment of this individual might have correctly concluded that, given the individual's age and the absence of a history of violence, the likelihood of recurrence would be slight. However, here such a conclusion would clearly be beside the point.

Too often, forensic clinicians either ignore or confuse the dual tasks of prediction and explanation in the assessment of dangerousness (Scriven, 1964). Neither task is straightforward nor are the two necessarily complementary. How clinicians should go about predicting dangerousness or whether they should even try remain disputed issues. The explanatory task is equally complex, since the kind of explanation which the criminal justice system demands, and the kind of explanation traditional science provides, are rarely equivalent. Scientists use the word 'explanation' in a restricted technical sense. A phenomenon is explained to the extent it can be predicted. This kind of scientific explanation, however, may have little to say about the meaning of human action, and the kind of account which gives meaning to past behaviour may not lend itself to accurate behavioural prediction.

MATCHING THE METHOD TO THE TASK

Sarbin (1986) makes an important distinction between clinical prediction and clinical inference. He argues that these two processes rely on different modes of thought or organizing principles, the conceptual and the narrative. The conceptual mode is concerned with 'establishing equations, causality hypotheses, and other features of the world view of mechanistic science' (p. 363). The narrative mode involves the 'process of organizing or integrating happenings

and actions into a comprehensible story' (p. 366). This process is called
'emplotment'. Along similar lines, Hitt (1969) has argued for two distinct but
equally valid models of man (the behaviouristic and the phenomenological),
each useful for different scientific purposes.

The narrative approach to understanding human behaviour, as described by
Sarbin, is not construed as arbitrary or subjective. As with the conceptual
approach, it is subject to test according to rigorous validity criteria. Whereas
the truth test of conceptual thought is the degree of correspondence between
prediction and outcome, the test of the narrative explanation is coherence,
that is, how well the story hangs together. For Sarbin the question is not which
is the better approach but rather 'under what conditions and for what purposes
should we choose the test of correspondence or the test of coherence?' (p. 368),
and it is the clinician's responsibility to decide which approach is most
appropriate. Sarbin argues that the conceptual mode in the form of statistical
prediction is appropriate 'in circumstances where the personal and societal
costs of the inevitable false positives and false negatives are morally defensible'
(p. 368), and that the narrative mode is often essential to the psychotherapeutic
process.

Sarbin's distinction between the conceptual and narrative modes has important
implications for clinical practice in the assessment of dangerousness. The
conceptual mode, since it provides the basis for the traditional scientific
enterprise, is well suited to the task of prediction. The narrative mode, because
it has its roots in intentions and goal-directed actions (Bruner, 1984), is ideally
suited to providing the kinds of explanation which can satisfy the need for
understanding motives in the ascription of culpability. Sarbin warns, however,
that if the clinical objectives are unclear or the clinician selects an approach
inappropriate to the clinical task, there can be a serious misapplication of
clinical methods.

Yet this is precisely what often seems to occur when clinicians predict
dangerousness for the courts. While historically the role of the forensic clinician
assessing dangerousness has grown to include prediction as well as explanation,
a corresponding development in clinical practice and research has largely failed
to materialize. Many clinicians have continued to apply to the predictive task
what are essentially narrative methods, best suited to explanation and moral
evaluation. Assessments based on psychodynamic hypotheses, medical diagnosis
or psychometric evaluations may have explanatory value and may assist in
decisions about legal responsibility but usually have little to offer when
prediction is the goal.

Monahan (1981) also warns that the application of inappropriate clinical
methods to the predictive task can result in gross overestimation of the potential
for dangerous conduct. He cites the four most common sources of clinical
error;

(1) The lack of specificity in defining a criterion of violent or dangerous
    behaviour;
(2) The overwhelming tendency for clinicians to ignore statistical base rates

even though such information is clearly the most important with regard to making predictions;

(3) The reliance upon illusory correlations;
(4) The failure to incorporate environmental information.

Webster *et al.* (1985) have dealt with these and other factors at some length (pp. 25–34).

Einhorn (1986) argues that much of clinical judgement involves backward reasoning or hindsight. The hazard here is that once a person's life history is reconstructed so as to 'explain' a mental illness or aberrant behaviour it is difficult to imagine events having turned out any other way. Once the clinician has developed a narrative explanation of dangerous behaviour there is a risk of that explanation colouring clinical judgement about future dangerousness. The conclusion that past violence is explainable can lead to serious under- or overestimation of future dangerousness, depending on the circumstances of the behaviour and the clinician's theoretical perspective.

Fischoff (1975) and his colleagues have demonstrated that knowledge of an outcome results in a gross overestimation of prior probability. Furthermore, available evidence is processed in such a way as to overemphasize that which seems related to the outcome while ignoring the rest. In this way, what was a low base-rate event (hence of low probability) can come to be construed as having been inevitable (highly probable). The overprediction of dangerous behaviour may, in part, be the result of this kind of cognitive bias. A clinician who is called upon to explain the occurrence of a particular dangerous act will review the perpetrator's history with the expressed purpose of finding the 'evidence' to support a causal account of the act. Once such an account is constructed, the crime seems to have been predetermined. This 'creeping determinism', as Fischoff calls it, will subsequently hamper any attempt of the clinician to make an accurate evaluation either of the crime's prior probability or of its likelihood of recurrence.

The pitfall of hindsight bias stresses the need for a rigorous and impartial approach to both the tasks of explanation and prediction. These two aspects of clinical assessment need to be refined in tandem, particularly if clinicians are to be expected to perform optimally at both. A subjective, unvalidated approach to the tasks of explanation and prediction can only lead to arbitrary and unjust decisions about culpability and the likelihood of future dangerous behaviour. To proceed towards more effective and responsible clinical decision making, clinicians must adopt scientifically substantiated models of dangerousness.

THE CLINICAL METHOD: PRACTICE IN SEARCH OF THEORY

One of the principal functions of modern criminal law, Foucault (1978) argues, is 'to reduce as much as possible . . . the risk of criminality represented by the individual in question' (p. 16). The law's responsibility to defend society from future wrongdoing demands that predictions be made about the individual's potential for dangerous behaviour towards others. It is to the issue of prediction that we now turn our attention.

In the courts the prediction of dangerous behaviour has become an everyday reality. It is a routine and unremarkable event, instrumental to the administration of justice and largely taken for granted. Consider, for example, this excerpt from a newspaper article about indeterminate prison sentences for individuals declared to be Dangerous Offenders in Canada:

> OTTAWA—A section of the Criminal Code that lets judges send dangerous offenders to prison indefinitely does not violate the Charter of Rights and Freedoms, the Supreme Court of Canada says.
> The court ruled 5–2 yesterday that the dangerous offender law is not cruel and unusual punishment because it applies only to individuals identified as likely to continue a pattern of dangerous and violent behaviour.
> 'Such a sentence serves both a punitive and preventive role and its purpose, the protection of society, underlies the criminal law in general and sentencing in particular,' Mr Justice Gerard La Forest wrote.
> The law enables the court to adjust to the 'common-sense reality that the present condition of the offender is such that . . . future violent acts can quite confidently be expected of that person' (*Toronto Star*, 16 October 1987).

The clinical perspective, in contrast to this matter-of-fact legal point of view, regards the prediction of dangerousness as a difficult and complex problem, perhaps without solution (Scriven, 1964). Three decades of vigorous research have failed to provide the scientific knowledge needed to predict violent behaviour. Outcome studies of clinical prediction have consistently demonstrated below chance levels of accuracy. These disappointing results and the low base rate of violence in the general population suggest that, most often, a global prediction of non-dangerousness will produce the most accurate overall results (Menzies *et al.*, 1985a).

Assuming non-dangerousness in every case may be defensible from a strictly statistical standpoint, but it is obviously not of much help to the courts charged with settling moral and practical problems. For the safety of the community there must be an attempt to identify potentially dangerous people, and for the protection of individual rights this must be done fairly and responsibly. The law and science approach the issue of dangerousness from two quite different perspectives. One sees the prediction of dangerousness as a moral imperative and a *sine qua non* of the administration of justice. The other regards it as a difficult technical and theoretical problem which, as yet, has no satisfactory solution. Mental health professionals in the courts find themselves having to contend with the two often incompatible roles of 'expert' and 'scientist'. As experts, they are called upon to contribute their knowledge to the solution of serious social problems (such as how best to protect society from potentially dangerous people) but, if properly informed, as scientists they realize how limited their expertise really is.

Much has been written about the limitations and inaccuracies of clinical predictions of behaviour (Meehl, 1954), including the prediction of dangerousness (Steadman and Cocozza, 1974; Quinsey and Maguire, 1986). On this basis, hardliners have strongly urged clinicians to give up the predictive enterprise entirely (Dickens, 1985; Stone, 1985). One of the key elements of the controversy surrounding behavioural prediction is the clinical–actuarial debate which began in the 1940s. The original controversy, involving Paul Meehl (1954), Robert Holt (1958) and Theodore Sarbin (1943) as key figures, was a contest of competing views of the science of human behaviour. A thoughtful analysis of this debate as it applies to the prediction of dangerousness is presented by Monahan (1981). He concludes that in fact the distinction between the clinical and actuarial approaches is an artificial one, and that 'they are merely *ends of continua* regarding the collection of data and methods for transforming data into predictions' (p. 64).

The literature on dangerousness often seems sidetracked by artificial and poorly defined distinctions which are irrelevant to the practical concerns of clinicians. Haynes (1985) has termed this the 'isolation of research from clinical practice' (p. 83). Different researchers hold different notions of what constitutes clinical prediction. In some cases, studies of clinical prediction designed to identify discrete predictors of violent behaviour (e.g. Lothstein and Jones, 1978; Selby, 1984) can more correctly be described as actuarial analyses of clinical data. Such studies, as Holt (1978) points out, do not accurately represent the complexity of the clinical method. Other studies attempt to evaluate outcomes of clinical prediction by following up in the community individuals who, at one time, had been judged by clinicians to be dangerous (Kozol *et al.*, 1972; Steadman, 1972; Steadman and Cocozza, 1974). Typically, these studies skirt the issue of defining the clinical method by regarding it as whatever is done by clinicians in the field.

The clinical method, when it is defined at all in the scientific literature, is most often dismissed as intuitive and subjective (Elstein, 1976). Our position, however, is that the clinical method is not as vague and imprecise as it is sometimes characterized, and that the 'intuition' of the competent clinician is not a mysterious talent. It is a theoretically based decision-making process which proceeds by posing and testing clinical hypothesis derived, at least implicitly, from a theoretical model of human personality and behaviour. What is needed is a clear theoretical rationale for decisions about dangerous behaviour which will allow clinicians to recognize and appropriately assess causal relationships between relevant factors in the individual's personality and environment and the violent act. Yet, as Hall (1984, p. 79) remarks in his critical review of the research in this area, 'except for a few notable exceptions . . . where violence is examined in controlled experimental contexts, most of the human studies are correlational in nature . . . thus not allowing for causal interpretations'.

Before advances can be made in the clinical prediction of dangerous behaviour, more attention must be paid to the theoretical basis of clinical assessment. As the research now stands, we know that, in general, clinical prediction (at least as it has been studied so far) is not particularly accurate. However, we have little idea which theoretical models, if any, show promise; nor can we say what can be done to improve the theoretical underpinnings of the clinical assessment of dangerousness. Decisions about which data to include, how various factors interact and which variables deserve emphasis depend on theoretical constructs underlying the clinical decision-making procedure. Quinsey and Maguire (1986, p. 169), noting the poor showing of studies of clinical prediction, remark that:

> Future research must employ a radically different strategy if progress is to be made in the prediction of dangerousness . . . . Research efforts in the future must be guided by theories that specify which sorts of variables should be related to certain sorts of outcomes in specific postrelease conditions.

As Meehl (1986, p. 373) notes, 'In order to use theoretical concepts fruitfully in making predictions for concrete cases, one requires a well-corroborated theory, which has high verisimilitude and includes almost all the relevant variables . . . '. In the following sections we will consider how the clinician can use existing scientific knowledge to make defensible, theoretically based, clinical decisions about the clinical methods to be employed, the reporting of the clinical findings and the degree of confidence in the clinical conclusions.

CLINICAL DECISION MAKING: ACCOUNTABILITY VERSUS ACCURACY

It is time that clinicians and researchers abandoned the search for empirically derived 'predictors' of violence and focused instead on the development of theoretically based decision-making procedures for arriving at defensible clinical decisions about dangerousness. Monahan (1981, p. 50) makes it clear that there are presently no valid psychometric measures for the prediction of dangerous behaviour. Given the complexity of the task, this is perhaps not difficult to understand. One of the principal difficulties is that an instrument, scale, test or other device requires a very large number of items, not all of which will be applicable in a given case. Moreover, the various items would have to be weighted differently according to the patient or prisoner under consideration (Bem and Allen, 1974; Bem and Funder, 1978).

The preoccupation in the clinical–research literature with the discovery and development of predictors of violence in large part reflects clinicians' efforts to satisfy the expectations of the justice system. Marra et al. (1987) point out that forensic clinicians are often caught between the limitations of their ability to predict violent behaviour and the growing demand from the courts to assist in the identification of dangerous individuals. Given these circumstances, they argue, clinical decisions about dangerousness should emphasize accountability rather than accuracy. They advocate adopting a clinical strategy for the assessment of dangerousness based on a conceptually valid clinical decision-making model. Conceptual validity is defined in terms of the intercorrelation of each area of assessment with the theoretical construct of dangerousness: 'In the purest sense, factorial stability is the standard in conceptual validity as opposed to external predictive ability' (p. 293). They conclude that 'clinicians can function within professional and ethical parameters in dealing with issues of dangerousness if their conclusions are founded in an approach and strategy that allows for a critical evaluation of the internal consistency of the data base through conceptual validation' (p. 299).

The scientific literature has generally tended to neglect theoretical issues in favour of empirically based studies of predictive accuracy. Consequently, there has been little progress towards establishing the theoretical constructs necessary for the development of defensible clinical strategies for prediction. There are a few exceptions to the atheoretical, empirical approach characteristic of the research on the clinical prediction of dangerousness. Menzies *et al.* (1985b), for example, have attempted to apply Megargee's (1976) conceptual framework, described in more detail below, to the development of a systematic clinical procedure for evaluating dangerousness. They report on a scale called the Dangerous Behaviour Rating Scheme (DBRS), based on Megargee's article and also influenced by the opinion of several experienced forensic clinicians. This scheme comprised 22 items, each to be rated on a seven-point continuum (from 'extremely low' to 'extremely high'). Examples of items were: passive–aggressive, hostility, anger, rage, emotionality, guilt, capacity for empathy, capacity for change, self-perceptions as dangerous, control over actions, tolerance, environmental stress, environmental support, likelihood of dangerous behaviour increasing under the influence of alcohol and drugs, and perceived degree to which the patient was manipulative during the interview. A definition manual was developed for use by clinicians and raters. This scheme was then applied by members of the assessing team and by two uninvolved raters to some 200 consecutive forensic patients given brief psychiatric pre-trial assessments.

The DBRS data from the raters, but not the clinicians, have so far been analyzed (Menzies *et al.*, 1985b). These do at least show that coders can be trained to attain acceptable levels of inter-rater reliability. On all but one item they achieved correlations above +0.50. Menzies *et al.* found it necessary to drop some items for varied reasons, leaving 15 predictor items intact. Correlation coefficients between these items and a composite outcome score based on violent conduct over a two-year period were modest, ranging from +0.06 to +0.32. The authors conducted factor analyses on the scale, isolating four dimensions (potential for violence, interpersonal responsibility, dangerousness to self and controlled aggression). The aggregate of all four factors yielded the most accurate prediction of dangerous behaviour (+0.34). This accounts for but 12% of the variance. It would appear that the exercise was more useful from a theoretical than a directly practical point of view. The authors felt constrained to warn readers that the DBRS was intended for research rather than clinical use. They say:

> The prediction of dangerous behaviour can be justified only under the most rigorous qualifications. Incorporation of psychometric instruments must await further testing and higher standards (p. 66).

What are clinicians to do without definitive theoretical guidelines and effective technology for making defensible decisions about dangerousness? Must they simply demur until more conclusive research has been undertaken, or does an adequate theoretical foundation now exist for making defensible clinical judgements? Mulvey and Lidz (1984) point out that theoretical frameworks are already at hand for explaining violent and dangerous behaviour. These include the classical frustration–aggression model (e.g. Dollard *et al.*, 1939), the social learning model (e.g. Bandura, 1973) and sociological models (e.g. Wolfgang and Ferracutti, 1967). They argue that while each of these theories has its limitations, 'information does exist to construct a logical model for clinical decision making regarding dangerousness, even if the absolute predictive value of this information is still unproven (pp. 395–6).

This attitude reflects a new perspective on the 'dangerousness' issue which emphasizes the validity of the clinical process as the primary consideration in the assessment of dangerousness. Those who advocate this approach acknowledge that predicting dangerousness is inevitably imperfect, and that all clinicians can do is make the most responsible decisions possible under less than ideal circumstances. This view of the clinical assessment procedure as a theoretically based decision-making procedure is examined more closely in the following section.

MODELS FOR CLINICAL DECISIONS ABOUT DANGEROUSNESS

Megargee, whose well-known 1976 paper has already been mentioned, was one of the first to describe a theoretically based approach to predicting dangerousness. He acknowledges the limitations inherent in clinical predictions of dangerousness, but argues that mental health professionals have a social obligation to contribute their expertise to the predictive enterprise, in spite of inevitable errors. Although he recognizes that the most accurate approach is to predict non-dangerousness, in all cases he advocates 'a decision model that minimizes the possible adverse consequences for all concerned, the predictee, the potential victim, and society' (p. 17).

Megargee presents a conceptual framework for examining the prediction of dangerousness which consists of 'three broad classes of personality variables: motivation, internal inhibition, and habit strength' (p. 6), and emphasizes the importance of situational factors. The evaluation of motivation includes the distinction between angry aggression and instrumental aggression and the assessment of the individual's hostility level. Examples of internal inhibitions are pro-social values, empathy and self-regulatory mechanisms which suppress or repress the aggressive response. Habit strength is defined as 'the extent to which aggressive responses have been reinforced in the past' (p. 9). Finally, situational factors include the availability of a weapon, the presence of a potential victim and the level of environmental stress. To assess dangerousness the clinician must evaluate the individual's motivation and the aggressive habit strength, based on developmental and historical considerations, and weigh these against personality and situational factors which may inhibit or disinhibit violent behaviour.

In addition to a conceptual framework to guide clinical decision making,

Megargee offers suggestions for making higher-order decisions about the appropriateness of prediction in specific cases and methodological considerations. These include considering the consequences of an incorrect prediction decision, limiting prediction to high base-rate populations, recognizing when prediction is not possible and confining prediction to cases in which situational factors are well understood. He concludes that 'in addition to modifying and improving the prediction process to minimize the number of errors, it is time for mental health professionals to accept the responsibility to consider in each case the ethical and social implications of their predictions' (pp. 19–20).

Monahan's (1981) work is representative of this new attitude towards the problem of the assessment and prediction of dangerousness. He argues that legal pragmatics dictate that predictions of dangerousness are necessary and that mental health professionals are the most qualified for the task. Monahan urges clinicians predicting dangerousness to adopt statistical techniques in combination with their clinical skills. He outlines the clinical indicators and actuarial variables which have been found to have some utility in the prediction of violence, and discusses decision rules for evaluating the applicability of these data in individual cases. Furthermore, he suggests a number of explicit decision rules to guide the clinician in determining the task demands, deciding issues of professional competence and ethics, gathering and synthesizing relevant data and evaluating the reliability of the assessment conclusions.

Others have taken similar approaches to reconsidering the extensive literature on the assessment of dangerousness and have constructed theoretical models of assessment which can address the task of prediction from a scientifically defensible standpoint. Mulvey and Lidz (1984), for example, write that 'clinicians do have a substantial literature of empirical research and clinical observation to guide their decision making' (p. 379). They note that there are two aspects of dangerous behaviour mentioned repeatedly in the scientific literature:

> First, it is a relative, context bound behavior with multiple definitions. Second, it is attributable to a complex interaction of individual predispositional and situational factors (p. 379).

In their synthesis of the literature on dangerousness, Mulvey and Lidz (1984) outline predispositional factors and situational factors which have been linked to violent behaviour. These include physiological substrate, present personality characteristics, general demographics and socialization experiences. They point out that, although relatively little is known about situational influences, factors such as the family environment and the availability of victims, weapons and alcohol may be important considerations. Mulvey and Lidz also contrast these empirically defensible predictive factors with factors which clinicians have been found to consider in making predictions about dangerous behaviour.

Mulvey and Lidz conclude that 'observations of clinical decision making show only a few variables as having any real discriminatory power for explaining these determinations as they occur' (p. 396). Their point is that, in general, clinicians need to reconsider the appropriateness of their clinical methods in light of the available empirical evidence. As with Megargee and Monahan, these authors encourage clinicians to step back from the predictive process itself and to consider the legal, social and ethical contexts in which decisions about dangerousness are made:

> Being aware that this process may be influenced by a variety of contextual and practical factors is a necessary first step in improving performance of this difficult clinical task. Even a perfect combined model using all of the reviewed factors would not predict dangerousness very accurately. The best that can be hoped for is an informed judgment (p. 396).

Marra *et al.* (1987), as mentioned above, describe a clinical strategy for predicting dangerousness which emphasizes clinical accountability rather than predictive accuracy. This approach is based on categories of variables demonstrated in the literature to be conceptually linked with a potential for dangerous behaviour. These categories, which are intended to provide a focus for assessing risk elements, include:

(1) History of dangerous behaviour;
(2) Institutional record;
(3) Stressors and means to violence;
(4) Victim and environmental issues;
(5) Mental disorder;
(6) Psychological testing;
(7) Actuarial scales;
(8) Moderator variables.

Factors in each category are evaluated and a category risk rating is assigned. Marra *et al.* argue that this approach 'facilitates depth, breadth and flexibility in assessment' while 'providing a structure from which internal consistency is assessed' (p. 294).

Greenland (1985), from his experience as an observer of clinical decision-making tactics, has proposed a typological approach to categorize violent individuals into different conceptual groupings. These are:

(1) Anti-social, habitually aggressive, undercontrolled, substance abusers;
(2) Psychotic individuals who experience a build-up of tension before acts of violence;
(3) Clinically depressed people who kill for 'altruistic' reasons;
(4) Those whose violence can be attributed to disinhibitory factors such as brain damage, cyclic alcoholism or major mental illness.

Greenland emphasizes the need for a more thorough understanding of the dynamics of violence before prediction can be attempted. He further describes the clinical assessment as a self-reflective process set in a broader social context. He warns clinicians to be aware of the limits of their professional competence and to take care not to stray into aspects of the judicial process which lie beyond their areas of expertise.

Perhaps the most systematic effort to construct a decision model of clinical prediction from available empirical findings has been presented by Hall (1984, 1987). In his discussion of the literature he writes that 'a rudimentary phenomenological network appears to have emerged in terms of predictor/ subject characteristics and dangerousness prediction accuracy' (p. 80). Hall proposes a dangerousness typology based on the perpetrator's relationship to the victim and the direction and degree of violence. In addition, he cites three principal clusters of factors to be evaluated in predicting dangerousness:

(1) Baseline and developmental characteristics which may determine a violent habit pattern;
(2) Reinforcing social and psychological factors which lower the threshold for dangerousness to occur;
(3) Transient situational stimuli, including interpersonal stress and substance intoxication which set violent behaviour in motion.

Hall (1987) rates these factors according to the degree of support they receive in the literature as correlates of dangerous behaviour, and he spells out the rules to be applied in estimating the probability of future violence.

Hall (1987, p. 113) proposes a 'dangerousness prediction decision tree', which outlines the clinical decision-making process inclusive of decisions about the appropriateness of the referral question and the degree of confidence in the prediction. He also specifies a dozen common errors committed by clinicians in deciding about dangerousness. These include failure adequately to consider the mental health–law interface, lack of an adequate forensic database, failure to account for data distortion, predicting in the absence of past violence, being influenced by illusory correlations between evaluation responses and supposed dangerousness, predicting from diagnosis and ignoring relevant base rates.

The approaches reviewed here share a common view of the assessment of dangerousness as a theoretically based decision-making procedure. While predictive accuracy may remain an important objective, the primary consideration of these approaches is the clinician's ability to make scientifically defensible decisions about dangerous behaviour. In the following section the application of a decision-based approach to assessing dangerousness is considered.

MAKING DECISIONS ABOUT DANGEROUSNESS: APPLYING THE MODEL

Vander Mey and Neff (1986) describe a process of 'building inductively from specific observations to general statements', which they term 'grounded theory' (p. 74). In this section we take such an approach to defining a scientifically defensible model for clinical decision making about dangerousness. This model is derived from our understanding of the existing literature on the assessment of dangerousness and, in particular, our perceptions of the common features of the theoretically based approaches discussed above. Our intention is to demonstrate that existing scientific knowledge can provide a clinical decision-making model to help clinicians make responsible decisions about dangerousness.

Generally speaking, clinical decisions about dangerousness fall into three broad categories:

(1) Whether the assessment should be undertaken;
(2) How the assessment should be conducted; and
(3) How the assessment findings should be represented.

These categories are by no means independent of each other. Whether the assessment is undertaken may depend on how it is to be conducted. For example, a clinician may decline an assessment because the appropriate clinical approach is outside his or her area of expertise. Further, the selection of the clinical method may depend on how the results are to be reported. Actuarial methods may have little to avail the clinician offering an opinion on treatment considerations. Nonetheless, this categorization of clinical decisions can serve as a useful heuristic device for purposes of the present discussion.

Whether to Do the Assessment

To decide whether the assessment of dangerousness should in fact be undertaken the clinician must first be satisfied that the purpose of the assessment is clear. For example, is the referral source asking for an explanation of the behaviour in question or is a prediction of future conduct expected? Is an evaluation of treatment potential and treatment needs relevant to the referral issues? Is the referral question in fact a disguised request for a determination of guilt or innocence?

It is not appropriate for the clinician simply to do a broad spectrum assessment in the absence of an explicit referral question. Because the prediction of dangerousness is an inexact science it should be attempted only when clearly justified by legal considerations. Of course, this is not to say that a clinician concerned about imminent dangerousness in a particular individual should not take some responsible action. However, when the question of dangerousness is more a hypothetical, legal issue, as it usually is in such cases, it is not the clinician's role, nor is it within the realm of his or her expertise, to raise the matter in court. If the purpose of the referral is to explain behaviour or to offer an opinion about treatment, the clinician should stick to these issues. If the referral question is not explicit, the clinician's first task is to seek clarification. Also if, despite all efforts, the referral question cannot be clarified the assessment should be declined.

Once the purpose of the assessment has been determined, the clinician must decide if he or she is competent to proceed. An expert in the actuarial prediction of dangerous behaviour, for instance, might have little to offer in the way of treatment recommendations; and a skilled psychotherapist might not have the qualifications to give an informed opinion about future violence.

Along with others mentioned above (Hall, 1987; Kozol, 1982; Monahan, 1981), we believe that, at least in some cases, mental health professionals do have something of value to offer the courts in matters of dangerousness. It is the clinician's responsibility, however, to answer some fundamental questions about professional competence and conduct. Is the clinician familiar with the theoretical, methodological, clinical and research literature on the assessment of dangerous behaviour? Is he or she acquainted with the legal framework in which the assessment will be conducted? Have issues of personal or professional ethics been satisfied? Should consultations from other specialists be sought? Should the assessment be passed on to a better-informed colleague?

Before proceeding with the assessment the clinician should also decide if the referral question is justified. If, for example, the referral issue is really a request for a confirmation of guilt, the assessment should be refused. In cases where a defendant denies criminal charges of a violent nature and the factual evidence is inconclusive, referrals are often made in the hope of discovering whether the individual would have been capable of committing the act. Clinicians must be careful not to be cast in the role of 'lie detector'.

Finally, if predicting dangerousness is the referral issue and there is no known history of violence, the referral must be considered inappropriate. Marra *et al.* remark that 'unless a consistent pattern develops in the evaluation, the clinician ethically must not render an opinion until further evaluation resolves inconsistencies' (p. 298). Since clinical prediction relies on determining patterns of violence, in the absence of a history of dangerous behaviour the clinician lacks sufficient information to proceed. Violence simply cannot be accurately predicted in the absence of a history of violent behaviour (Monahan, 1981; Kozol, 1982; Hall, 1987).

How to Conduct the Assessment

The purpose of the assessment to some extent determines the methods to be employed. As argued above, the narrative approach is more appropriate when the task is explaining dangerous behaviour, whereas a more conventional empirically based approach is suitable for predictive decision making. However, decisions about which data to include, which factors bear closer examination and how the various factors interact depend largely on the theoretical principles underlying the clinical method.

What do we mean by 'the clinical method'? First, we do not regard this method as subjective or intuitive; nor do we believe that it can be accurately described as non-actuarial. In fact, with Monahan (1981) we see statistically grounded considerations as an important aspect of the overall clinical process. What distinguishes the clinical method is the scientifically and theoretically based approach to discovering patterns of behaviour in the individual. The skilful clinician assessing dangerous behaviour formulates and tests a series of clinical hypotheses to define patterns of violence in the individual's history. Once defined, these patterns can be applied to the explanation and prediction of violence in that individual. Measures or clinical indicators of known validity may be used to prove or disprove the clinical hypotheses, but no one measure or group of measures will be definitive or even relevant in every case. Each person will show a different pattern of violence, and every assessment will pursue a different set of hypotheses. Despite these individual differences, to be scientifically defensible the patterns described by the clinician and the hypotheses developed must be consistent with a general theory of dangerous behaviour.

As Marra *et al.* (1987) describe the process, the clinician 'applies known correlates of violence, producing direction to hypothesizing, and generating specific ideas about variables relevant to that individual: (1) questions emerge; (2) thoughts about past patterns and contingent variables project possible futures; and (3) dangerousness-linked hypotheses develop' (p. 293). Simply administering a large battery of tests or conducting a wide-ranging interview in search of possible signs of dangerousness cannot be justified scientifically. In conventional research it is well understood that by increasing the number hypotheses under consideration the experimenter increases the probability of spurious significant findings. Similarly, if the clinician indiscriminately applies every available clinical measure the chances of finding an 'indicator' of dangerousness become very high. Unless the assessment process is guided by clinical hypotheses the clinician runs the risk of seriously misjudging the causes and likelihood of dangerous behaviour.

How can the clinician formulate suitable hypotheses? Although developing appropriate hypotheses depends, to some extent, on clinical acumen and experience, there are a few well-established principles to guide decision making about clinical hypotheses.

First, violent behaviour depends on an interplay of predisposing and countervailing influences in the individual's life. In assessing dangerousness the clinician should consider both facilitating and inhibiting factors. What historical, environmental, physiological or psychological factors might potentiate violence, and which factors might counteract (or fail to counteract) violent impulses in the individual? Is there a history of repeated exposure to violence in childhood? What can be determined about the person's affective state and fantasy life around the time of the behaviour in question? How accurate are the individual's social perceptions and self-perceptions? Does the person show a pro-social or anti-social orientation? How well can the individual form sensible plans and effectively regulate his or her actions? Can past violence be attributed to inadequate or unreliable social coping abilities?

A second basic principle is that dangerous behaviour is the result of an interaction of factors in the individual (i.e. developmental, historical and personality factors) and transient or enduring situational factors. The clinician should carefully evaluate the influence of situational factors on the individual's behaviour. What are the sources of vocational, social and familial stress in the person's current environment? Is there a pattern of violence associated with periods of stress? Is there a pattern to the kinds of victims selected? Are weapons easily accessible? What are the attitudes towards violence in the person's subculture? What social supports are available to the individual?.

Situational influence on behavioural expression is widely recognized as a central issue in predicting future conduct (e.g. Bronfennbrenner, 1977; Mischel and Peake, 1982). Hall (1987) rates situational factors such as the termination of a central love relationship or a sudden worsening of financial situation as related to violence with a high degree of confidence. He regards such environmental stresses superimposed on a history of violence as one of the best predictors of dangerousness. Monahan (1981) also stresses the importance of considering situational factors. He argues that short-term 'emergency' predictions are likely to be more accurate, because 'there is a small situational and temporal "gap" between the behavior used as a predictor and the outcome that is being predicted' (p. 59). Mulvey and Lidz (1984) note, however, that despite the acknowledged importance of situational factors 'the amount of literature on the situational components of [violent behaviour] is limited' (p. 390). Werner et al. (1983), in their study of decision-making strategy in the clinical prediction of imminent dangerousness, discuss some of the problems involved in this kind of research.

A third principle is that dangerous behaviour, in some cases, results from a kind of behavioural entropy. Violence often reflects a state of psychological disorganization resulting from a deficiency or disruption in the self-regulatory capacity of the individual. Under such circumstances, behaviour loses its structure and becomes erratic, poorly controlled and therefore possibly destructive. This may happen, for example, when an individual becomes intoxicated or is subjected to extreme and unusual stress (Megargee, 1976). Hall (1984) refers to such disinhibiting events as 'triggering stimuli'. It is important to note whether acts of violence in the past have been associated with periods of disinhibition and disorganization. Brain damage, severe depression, psychotic decompensation and substance abuse should be investigated as possible disinhibitory factors.

These simple principles can guide the clinician's initial decisions in formulating preliminary hypotheses. Sometimes this may happen through a process of elimination. Suppose, for example, that no evidence exists in a particular case for an association between violent behaviour and situational or disinhibitory factors. The clinician might therefore assume that the behaviour is attributable to predisposing personality or social learning factors. Perhaps the individual has a hostile, anti-social orientation or, if a sexual assault was involved, perhaps the individual has sadistic tendencies. These avenues can then be pursued through clinical interviews, psychological assessment or phallometric testing (Freund, 1976). Depending on the findings, the initial hypotheses may be confirmed or other hypotheses may be formulated and tested.

Often the evidence is quite direct. For example, sometimes there is an obvious pattern of violence associated with behavioural disorganization. In such cases, when prediction is the issue, a defensible argument can be made for a continuing potential for violent behaviour provided that the risk of future disorganization is high. If, for instance, a particular individual behaves violently only when intoxicated or only during psychotic episodes, and if the likelihood of continuing alcohol abuse or psychotic decompensation can be evaluated, then something useful can be concluded about the probability of future violence. As an example, consider the following case history:

A 25-year-old college student was admitted to the forensic unit of a psychiatric hospital after tying his maternal grandmother to her bed and beating her severely. The grandmother was hospitalized with head and back injuries and listed in serious condition. The patient was living in the family home at the time of the assault. In interview he insisted that his grandmother had been conspiring with other family members to manipulate him into marrying a young woman he had once known in high school. He said she had persisted in her efforts in spite of his protests, and finally he felt compelled to attack her.

A review of criminal and medical records showed no history of criminal convictions. However, on two previous cocasions the patient had assaulted his mother and his father. He had been hospitalized following these incidents and both times had been diagnosed paranoid schizophrenic and placed on the appropriate medication. Apparently, he had responded well to treatment during these previous admissions, and after several weeks was able to understand that he had been mistaken about his family's intentions. He was encouraged to continue with his medication regimen and at discharge was helped to find independent accommodation. Unfortunately, on both occasions following discharge, he did not comply with treatment. Nor did he secure his own accommodation but instead remained in the family home.

In this case there is a clear connection between psychotic decompensation and violent behaviour. The clinician assessing this young man might hypothesize that his violent behaviour is, in large part, attributable to the disorganizing effects of a psychotic episode, possibly influenced by familial stress. The repetitive nature of violent behaviour directed at family members and associated with paranoid delusions suggests a well-defined pattern. Investigations to confirm the clinical hypothesis might include psychometric testing to establish evidence of psychotic process, a second psychiatric opinion regarding the diagnosis and a thorough social work consultation to evaluate family dynamics. If the hypothesis were confirmed, the clinician in this situation could state with considerable confidence that, should a psychotic episode recur while the patient was still living with his family, the risk of violence would be high. The history of poor medication compliance and his continued dependence on his family would further increase the probability of future assaults.

This example is particularly instructive, since it highlights the importance of a theoretically based model of assessment and illustrates the weakness of a strict actuarial approach in certain circumstances. The clinical conclusions in this case, linking psychosis with violence, are only defensible if based on a clear theoretical rationale. From an atheoretical, statistical perspective these data have nothing to offer the prediction of dangerousness, since mental illness in general has not been found to be a reliable predictor of dangerous behaviour (Mulvey and Lidz, 1984; Monahan, 1981).

Most often, dangerous behaviour reflects a complex interaction of psychologcial, situational and disinhibitory factors, as illustrated by the following case:

A 41-year-old man convicted of indecent assault was referred by the court to evaluate his potential for dangerous behaviour and for management recommendations. According to documents supplied by the court, he had broken into a house while intoxicated and sexually assaulted an eleven-year-old girl. At the time of the incident he had been unemployed and on welfare for eight months. He had a lengthy history of similar violent sexual offences committed under the influence of alcohol.

In interview he maintained that he had been wrongfully accused. He explained that he had mistakenly entered the wrong home after an evening of drinking and had left without incident after realizing his error. He complained bitterly about having been mistreated by the legal system and expressed some paranoid ideas about a judicial conspiracy. He denied any psychological problems.

The clinical impression was that this man's violent behaviour was attributable to a combination of factors, including predisposing personality and behavioural features (an anti-social orientation and an established pattern of violent sexual behaviour), situational stress (eight months' unemployment) and disinhibitory factors (poor impulse control, alcohol intoxication). Psychological testing was administered to evaluate cognitive functioning, anti-social tendencies and substance dependence. Intellectual assessment indicated average intelligence. However, Rorschach performance showed cognitive disorganization, suggesting a potential for serious failures of judgement and impulsive behaviour. The Minnesota Multiphasic Personality Inventory indicated an anti-social orientation, unreliable controls and a potential for alcohol dependence.

The clinical report submitted to the court cited a need for treatment, including counselling for alcohol dependence, vocational guidance and life skills training. However, based on this man's denial of his psychological difficulties, treatment potential was evaluated as poor. The probability of future violence was considered to be high due to a clear pattern of violent sexual offences while intoxicated and the likelihood of continuing alcohol abuse.

He was sentenced to several years in prison and eventually released on parole. Shortly after his release he was again arrested on a charge of sexual assault. He was convicted and received an indeterminate prison term as a Dangerous Offender.

In this case an estimate of the probability of future violence based on statistical considerations might have reached similar conclusions. This man showed several characteristics commonly seen in repeat offenders, including prior convictions for violent offences, a history of deviant sexual behaviour, unemployment and alcohol abuse. In actuarial terms his reference group had a high base rate of violence. This raises an important question. When should actuarial methods be applied in the clinical assessment of dangerousness?

A decision-making model can help the clinician determine when actuarial techniques are likely to be of value. As mentioned above, the process of formulating and testing clinical hypotheses aims to uncover factors in the individual's environment or psychological make-up which are causally related to dangerous behaviour. Depending on the factors under consideration and the available technology, establishing causality may be a relatively simple matter or it may be virtually impossible. As Meehl (1954, p. 373) remarks, usually clinical prediction depends on:

> an accurate technology of measurement, including access to the initial and boundary conditions of the system to be predicted and negligible influence of . . . 'contingency factors'. None of these conditions is met in our routine clinical forecasting situation.

When the objective is prediction, and when realistic and sensible causal hypotheses cannot be established, the actuarial approach is likely to prove superior.

As a rule, clinical hypothesis testing will be more appropriate than a purely actuarial method when disinhibitory or situational factors are clearly implicated. When disinhibitory factors are of primary importance, the ability to predict dangerous behaviour does not depend on an understanding of the intricacies of a well-regulated behavioural system. Instead, it depends on the clinician's ability to forecast a gross disruption of the individual's self-regulatory capacity. It is generally far more difficult to anticipate precisely how a system will function than to predict that the system will break down entirely.

When situational factors are prominent as part of a pattern of dangerous behaviour, predictions based on clincial hypotheses can also be made with a fair degree of certainty. In part, this is because situational factors can often be evaluated and monitored with some precision. Whereas the clinician rarely, if ever, can be certain of the individual's psychological state at the time of a violent act, information about situational factors is frequently available through family members, eye-witness accounts and police reports.

When dangerous behaviour shows no clear pattern of association with situational or disinhibitory factors and instead is assumed to reflect underlying psychological variables, it is likely to be no more predictable using theoretically based methods than any other complex behaviour. Under circumstances where personality factors appear to govern violence (or at least where disinhibitory and situational factors are not apparent) the clinician is better off relying on actuarial approaches. Hypotheses about personality dynamics and psychological constructs are likely to be more important in the explanation of past behaviour than in prediction. The personality dynamics and behavioural principles of violence are not well enough understood to establish the kinds of causal connections necessary to make reliable theoretically based predictions. We simply do not yet have the required theoretical and technological sophistication. As Kozol (1982, p. 254)) remarks:

> Dangerous potential is not detectable through routine psychiatric examination. Nor is it detectable by any single test or combination of stereotyped tests.

Consider the following case, in which a psychologist correctly and successfully defends in court the actuarial approach to prediction:

> The defendant was a 35-year-old woman, a schoolteacher by training. She had suffered from paranoid schizophrenia, off and on, for many years. The police were telephoned during an altercation between her and her father. In the course of a scuffle, she pushed a police officer backward down the stairs. He hit his head on the wall, necessitating some stitches. Subsequently, she was arrested and charged with assaulting a police officer. In due course she was remanded from detention to a psychiatric facility for assessment. Because she did not meet the criteria for civil commitment under provincial law, and for other reasons, the examining psychiatrist suggested to the court that there might be grounds for a finding of 'Not Guilty by Reason of Insanity'. In Canada persons so found can be detained indefinitely in a secure hospital. The psychiatrist's intent was to bring

treatment to bear. Yet the woman's lawyer felt that such a course would infringe her basic rights; that his client did not want or even need treatment. Although not directly relevant to the question of legal sanity, the issue of dangerousness had been raised in the psychiatrist's report and was of particular interest to the court.

Crown: Could you please tell the court, Doctor, whether or not you have examined the patient?
Psychologist: I have not.
Crown: Since you have not assessed her can you indicate to the court what possible use your testimony might be, if any?
Psychologist: I am interested in statistical prediction, on actuarial considerations and in the processes involved in clinical assessment and prediction.
Crown: Do these bear on the present case?
Psychologist: I would think so, yes.
Crown: Tell me, Doctor, do you know any families with three and a half children?
Psychologist: No. I take it that you wish to imply that statistical averaging can never apply to an individual case such as the one before the court.
Crown: Yes, I question the relevance of your testimony. Indeed I would ask His Honour to disqualify you as a witness.
Judge: No, I am not willing to do that. We have heard his credentials and I am satisfied that his testimony could assist the court.
Crown: We have from the examining psychiatrist, Dr Jones, an opinion that Ms Smith is dangerous. He has examined her and come to this conclusion most carefully. Do you wish to discredit him?
Psychologist: No. I know Dr Jones and have the utmost respect for his expertise. I am here to talk about the research on predicting dangerousness and the implications for clinical and actuarial prediction.
Crown: Which is more important, clinical or statistical prediction?
Psychologist: Generally speaking, they are equally important considerations.
Crown: Really, you must come down on one side or the other. Surely the clinical side, that dealing with the individual, is more vital?
Psychologist: I would not agree. In fact in some cases I'd say that actuarial considerations are more important than clinical. In other cases it may be the other way round.
Crown: I simply cannot accept this!
Judge: I have found this discussion most interesting and useful. I accept the idea of the importance of statistical considerations and I'm going to remand the prisoner for further assessment. What I expect is a discussion of the statistical factors pertinent to this case.

Note that a theoretically based prediction in this case, drawing a causal link between a diagnosis of paranoid schizophrenia and violent behaviour, would be scientifically unjustifed. Unlike the case cited previously, there is nothing to suggest a pattern of violence in the defendant associated with psychological disturbance. Despite the defendant's history of paranoid schizophrenia, in this instance there is no established causal connection between mental illness and the assault on the police officer.

To the extent that the clinician is unable to develop theoretically or empirically defensible causal hypotheses about an individual's violent behaviour, statistical approaches will likely prove superior. The clinician should not hesitate to rely on statistical approaches under such circumstances. In cases such as the one described above, those who choose to make clinical predictions of dangerousness based on conclusions about psychological functioning and personality dynamics should do so with caution.

Reporting the Assessment Findings

Once the assessment has been conducted and the relevant data have been collected and analyzed the clinician must decide how to synthesize and represent the findings. For example, in reporting the clinical opinion the clinician must be careful not to misrepresent the degree of confidence in the clinical conclusions. For a number of reasons, the clinician's opinion may be less than conclusive. An important item of information might have been missing or the individual under assessment might have concealed some facts and exaggerated others. Also, when the issue is prediction it may be that for technical reasons (e.g. no available base-rate data, no discernible pattern of violence) neither the actuarial approach nor a theoretically oriented one is able to provide useful estimates of the likelihood of violence.

When an opinion is expressed about violence potential it is the clinician's responsibility to state the opinion in probabilistic and conditional terms, taking into account mitigating situational factors (Webster, 1984b). If violence is predicted, the clinician should indicate how likely it is, where and when it might occur and who the likely victims are. Once the prediction is stated, the clinician should also indicate the degree of confidence to be placed on the opinion. Hall's (1987) discussion of 'distortion analysis' offers useful guidelines for arriving at an estimate of the confidence level of the clinical findings.

Clinicians must also be careful not to confuse explanatory and predictive hypotheses. Because of hindsight bias, an explanatory account of dangerous behaviour applied to the predictive task can result in the construction of an impression of dangerousness where no danger exists (Pfohl, 1978). Finally, clinicians must take care not to present a clinical opinion as though it were factual evidence. Often evidence which is otherwise inadmissible in court may find its way into legal proceedings under the guise of expert opinion.

CONCLUSION

In this chapter we have attempted to illustrate how a relatively simple model of clinical decision making can promote accountability for decisions about violent behaviour. Our intention, of course, has not been to present the definitive model of clinical assessment. We simply wish to point out that by adopting a clinical decision-making model the clinician can make informed decisions about whether to conduct an assessment of dangerousness, which methods to employ, how to weigh responsibly the various elements contributing to an individual's violent acts and how to regard and report the clinical findings. Although accurate measurement and prediction of violence potential is not always possible, by adopting a theoretically based decision-making approach the forensic clinician can make defensible decisions about dangerousness while maintaining a balance between scientific and social responsibility.

References

Bandura, A. (1973). Social learning theory of aggression. In J. Knutson (ed.), *The Control of Aggression*, Chicago, IL: Aldine.

Bem, D., and Allen, A. (1974). On predicting some of the people some of the time: the search for cross-situational consistencies in behavior. *Psychological Review*, **81**, 506–20.

Bem, D., and Funder, D. (1978). Predicting more of the people more of the time: assessing the personality of situations. *Psychological Review*, **85**, 485–501.

Bronfennbrenner, U. (1977). *The Ecology of Human Development*, Cambridge, MA: Harvard University Press.

Bruner, J. (1984). *Narrative and Paradigmatic Modes of Thought*. Invited Address, Division I, American Psychological Association Conference, Toronto, August 1984.

Dickens, B. M. (1985). Prediction professionalism and public policy. In C. D. Webster, M. H. Ben-Aron and S. J. Hucker (eds), *Dangerousness: Probability and Prediction, Psychiatry and Public Policy*, New York: Cambridge University Press.

Dietz, P. E. (1985). Hypothetical criteria for the prediction of individual criminality. In C. D. Webster, M. B. Ben-Aron and S. J. Hucker (eds), *Dangerousness: Probability and Prediction, Psychiatry and Public Policy*, New York: Cambridge University Press.

Dollard, J., Doob, L., Miller, M., Mowrer, O., and Sears, R. (1939). *Frustration and Aggression*, New Haven, CT: Yale University Press.

Einhorn, H. J. (1986). Accepting error to make less error. *Journal of Personality Assessment*, **50**(3), 387–95.

Elstein, A. (1976). Clinical judgment: psychological research and medical practice. *Science*, **194**, 696–700.

Feinsten, A. R. (1967). *Clinical Judgement*, Baltimore, MD: Williams and Wilkins.

Fischoff, B. (1975). Hindsight = foresight: the effect of outcome knowledge on judgement under uncertainty. *Journal of Experimental Psychology: Human Perception and Performance*, **1**, 288–99.

Foucault, M. (1978). About the concept of the 'dangerous individual' in 19th century legal psychiatry. *International Journal of Law and Psychiatry*, **1**, 1–19.

Freund, K. (1976). Diagnosis and treatment of forensically significant anomalous erotic preferences. *Canadian Journal of Criminology and Corrections*, **18**(3), 181–9.

Gottfredson, S. D. (1987). Statistical and actuarial considerations. In F. N. Dutile and C. D. Foust (eds), *The Prediction of Criminal Violence*, Springfield, IL: Charles C. Thomas.

Greenland, C. (1985). Dangerousness, mental disorder and politics. In C. D. Webster, M. B. Ben-Aron and S. J. Hucker (eds), *Dangerousness: Probability and Prediction, Psychiatry and Public Policy*, New York: Cambridge University Press.

Grisso, T. (1987). Psychological assessments for legal decisions. In D. N. Weisstub (ed.), *Law and Mental Health: International Perspectives, Volume 3*, New York: Pergamon Press.

Hall, H. V. (1984). Predicting dangerousness for the courts. *American Journal of Forensic Psychology*, **4**, 5–25.

Hall, H. V. (1987). *Violence Prediction. Guidelines for the Forensic Practitioner*, Springfield, IL: Charles C. Thomas.

Halleck, S. (1987). Clinical applicability for prediction. In F. N. Dutile and C. D. Foust (eds), *The Prediction of Criminal Violence*, Springfield, IL: Charles C. Thomas.

Haynes, R. B. (1985). The predictive value of the clinical assessment for the diagnosis, prognosis, and treatment response of patients. In C. D. Webster, M. B. Ben-Aron and S. J. Hucker (eds), *Dangerousness: Probability and Prediction, Psychiatry and Public Policy*, New York: Cambridge University Press.

Hitt, W. D. (1969). Two models of man. *American Psychologist*, **24**, 651–8.

Holt, R. R. (1958). Clinical and statistical prediction: a reformulation and some new data. *Journal of Abnormal and Social Psychology*, **56**, 1–12.

Holt, R. R.. (1978). *Methods in Clinical Psychology: Prediction and Research*, Volume 2, New York: Plenum.

Holt, R. R. (1986). Clinical and statistical prediction: A retrospective and would-be integrative perspective. *Journal of Personality Assessment*, **50**(3), 376–86.

Kozol, H. L. (1982). Dangerousness in society and law. *The University of Toledo Law Review*, **13**, 241–67.

Kozol, H., Boucher, R., and Garofalo, R. (1972). The diagnosis and treatment of dangerousness. *Crime and Delinquency*, **18**, 371–92.

Lothstein, L. M., and Jones, P. (1978). Discriminating violent individuals by means of various psychological tests. *Journal of Personality Assessment*, **42**, 237–4.

Marra, A. M., Konzelman, G. E., and Giles, P. G. (1987). A clinical strategy to the assessment of dangerousness. *International Journal of Offender Therapy and Comparative Criminology*, **31**, 291–9.

Meehl, P. E. (1954). *Clinical Versus Statistical Prediction*, Minneapolis: University of Minnesota Press.

Meehl, P. E. (1986). Causes and effects of my disturbing little book. *Journal of Personality Assessment*, **50**, 370–5.

Megargee, E. I. (1976). The prediction of dangerous behavior. *Criminal Justice and Behavior*, **3**, 3–22.

Menzies, R. J., Webster, C. D., and Sepejak, D. S. (1985a). Hitting the forensic sound barrier: predictions of dangerousness in a pretrial clinic. In C. D. Webster, M. H. Ben-Aron and S. J. Hucker (eds), *Dangerousness: Probability and Prediction, Psychiatry and Public Policy*, New York: Cambridge University Press.

Menzies, R. J., Webster, C. D., and Sepejak, D. S. (1985b). The dimensions of dangerousness: evaluating the accuracy of psychometric predictions of violence among forensic patients. *Law and Human Behaviour*, **9**, 35–56.

Mischel, W., and Peake, P. K. (1982). Beyond *déja vu* in the search for cross-situational consistency. *Psychological Review*, **89**, 730–55.

Monahan, J. (1981). *Predicting Violent Behavior: An Assessment of Clinical Techniques*, Beverly Hills, CA: Sage.

Mulvey, E. P., and Lidz, C. W. (1984). Clinical considerations in the prediction of dangerousness in mental patients. *Clinical Psychology Review*, **4**, 379–401.

Petrunik, M. (1983). The politics of dangerousness. *International Journal of Law and Psychiatry*, **5**, 225–46.

Pfohl, S. J. (1978). *Predicting Dangerousness: The Social Construction of Psychiatric Reality*, Lexington, MA: D. C. Heath.

Prins, H. (1986). *Dangerous Behaviour, the Law, and Mental Disorder*. London: Tavistock.

Quinsey, V., and Maguire, A. (1986). Maximum security psychiatric patients: actuarial and clinical prediction of dangerousness. *Journal of Interpersonal Violence*, **1**, 143–71.

Sarbin, T. R. (1943). A contribution to the study of actuarial and individual methods of prediction. *American Journal of Sociology*, **48**, 593–602.

Sarbin, T. R. (1986). Prediction and clinical inference: forty years later. *Journal of Personality Assessment*, **50**(3), 362–9.

Scriven, M. (1964). Views of human nature. In T. W. Mann (ed.), *Behaviorism and Phenomenology: Contrasting Bases for Modern Psychology*, Chicago, IL: University of Chicago Press.

Selby, M. J. (1984). Assessment of violence potential using measures of anger, hostility, and social desirability. *Journal of Personality Assessment*, **48**, 531–44.

Shah, S. A. (1978). Dangerousness: a paradigm for exploring some issues in law and psychology. *American Psychologist*, **33**, 224–38.

Steadman, H. J. (1973). Some evidence on the inadequacy of the concept and determination of dangerousness in law and psychiatry. *Journal of Psychiatry and Law*, **1**, 409–26.

Steadman, H. J., and Cocozza, J. J. (1974). *Careers of the Criminally Insane: Excessive Social Control of Deviance*, Lexington, MA: D. C. Heath.

Stone, A. A. (1985). The new legal standard of dangerousness: fair in the theory, unfair in practice. In C. D. Webster, M. B. Ben-Aron and S. J. Hucker (eds), *Dangerousness: Probability and Prediction, Psychiatry and Public Policy*, New York: Cambridge University Press.

Vander May, B. J., and Neff, R. L. (1986). *Incest as Child Abuse*, New York: Praeger.

Webster, C. D. (1984a). On gaining acceptance: why the courts accept only reluctantly findings from experimental and social psychology. *International Journal of Law and Psychiatry*, **7**, 407–14.

Webster, C. D. (1984b). How much of the clinical predictability of dangerousness is due to language and communications difficulties? Some sample questions and some inspired but heady answers. *International Journal of Offender Therapy and Comparative Criminology*, **28**, 159–67.

Webster, C. D., Dickens, B. M., and Addario, S. (1985). *Constructing Dangerousness: Scientific, Legal and Policy Implications*, Toronto: University of Toronto Centre of Criminology.

Webster, C. D., and Menzies, R. J. (1987). The clinical prediction of dangerousness. In D. N. Weisstaub (ed.), *Law and Mental Health: International Perspectives*, New York: Pergamon Press.

Werner, P. D., Rose, T. L., and Yesavage, J. A. (1983). Reliability, accuracy and decision-making strategy in clinical predictions of imminent dangerousness. *Journal of Consulting and Clinical Psychology*, **51**, 815–25.

Wolfgang, M. E., and Ferracutti, F. (1967). *The Subculture of Violence*, London: Tavistock.

A shorterned version of this paper was presented at the *XIVth International Congress on Law and Mental Health*, Montreal, 1988.

C. D. Webster and R. J. Menzies acknowledge with thanks support under Social Science and Humanities Research Council Grant No. 410–85–1429.

Part 2

Family and Sexual Violence

6

Family Violence: Spouse and Elder Abuse

KEVIN D. BROWNE
Family Violence Research Group, Department of Psychology, University of Leicester, UK

INTRODUCTION

Until the last decade, the subject of family violence was poorly documented. Research into aggression and violence was dominated by laboratory rather than naturalistic approaches (Archer and Browne, 1989b) and thus did not centre on the social context of the family. 'Abusive' violence was commonly thought to be rare and only to occur in problem families, whereas other aggressive acts between members of the family were considered to be 'normal' and socially acceptable.

The widespread nature of extreme forms of aggression within the family was determined in the 1970s and has been substantiated ever since (e.g. Straus *et al.*, 1980; Van Hasselt *et al.*, 1987). This has dispelled the myth that the family home is a peaceful, non-violent environment. In fact, 'people are more likely to be killed, physically assaulted, hit, beaten up, slapped or spanked in their own homes by other family members than anywhere else, or by anyone else in our society' (Gelles and Cornell, 1985, p. 12).

Violence has recently been described as 'the exercise of physical force so as to cause injury or forceably interfere with personal freedom' (Archer and Browne, 1989a). When applied to the family situation, this definition embraces three aspects of violence by adults; child abuse, spouse abuse and elder abuse, and two aspects of violence by children; sibling abuse and parent abuse.

Research has examined each type of abuse separately, one possible reason being that each one evolved as a recognized social problem at a different time. Each type of abuse can, however, be characterized in the same way, and dichotomized into 'active' and 'passive' forms: active abuse involves violent acts (as defined above) in a physical, emotional or sexual context; passive abuse refers to neglect, which can only be considered violent in the metaphorical

Clinical Approaches to Violence. Edited by K. Howells and C. R. Hollin
© 1989 John Wiley & Sons.

sense as it does not involve physical force. Nevertheless, it can cause both physical and emotional injury.

This chapter is primarily concerned with the incidence, causes, prevention and treatment of two aspects of violence exhibited by adults in the family. It concentrates on first, violence between couples (spouse abuse), and second, on the abuse and neglect of elderly relatives dependent on the family.

While these types of family violence are discussed in isolation from other forms such as child abuse (see Chapter 7) or sibling and parent abuse (see Chapter 8), it is important to realize that all forms of violence in the family are interrelated and have an impact on the family as a whole. This is reflected in a number of recent publications that take a holistic approach to the causation and maintenance of family violence (Browne, 1989; Gelles, 1987a), and to intervention and treatment when *working with violent families* (Bolton and Bolton, 1987). There are close links, for example, between wife abuse and child physical abuse (e.g. Gayford, 1975; Merrick and Michelsen, 1985; Milner and Gold, 1986; Browne and Saqi, 1988) and child sexual abuse (e.g. Dietz and Craft, 1980; Truesdell *et al.*, 1986). However, the implications of these contingencies for the recognition and prevention of family violence have yet to be determined. Indeed, Finkelhor and Hotaling (1988) have outlined in their book, *Stopping Family Violence*, a number of urgent research questions. This urgency becomes painfully obvious when the pervasive nature of spouse and elder abuse is contemplated.

THE NATURE AND DEFINITION OF SPOUSE ABUSE

The term 'spouse abuse' refers to physical and/or psychological violence by a man or a woman towards his or her intimate partner. This involves both married and unmarried couples, whether they are living together or apart from each other. Physical violence in this context has been defined by Gelles and Cornell (1985, p. 20) as 'an act carried out with the intention, or perceived intention of causing physical pain or injury to another person'. They claim that slaps, pushes, shoves and spankings are frequently considered to be an acceptable part of family life, and therefore are examples of 'normal violence', whereas punches, kicks, bites, chokings, beatings, attempted stabbings and shootings are examples of 'abusive violence', as these acts have a high probability of injury.

Psychological violence is less apparent and more difficult to dichotomize into what is generally considered to be acceptable and unacceptable. Edleson (1984) defined psychological violence as 'Verbal or non-verbal threats of violence against another person or against that person's belongings'. This may be of an emotional or environmental nature; for instance, threatening suicide, destroying pets, punching walls and throwing objects (Purdy and Nickle, 1981). It is important to consider psychological violence as 'abusive', because it carries with it the continual threat of actual physical violence and so creates an atmosphere of tension and uncertainty in the home which produces degradation and humiliation in the victimized partner. Early definitions of spouse abuse (e.g. Gayford, 1975; Martin, 1976; Gelles and Straus, 1979) focused purely on acts of physical damage directed towards the partner. However, it is now widely recognized that spouse abuse also includes material deprivation, emotional and sexual abuse, marital rape and pornography (London, 1978).

Thus spouse abuse may be said to have occurred when there is evidence of any physical or psychological injury, sexual assault or forced relations that has been inflicted upon the victims by their intimate partner. It should be pointed out that the asexual language of this definition is deliberate. Studies of randomly selected families have shown that women report themselves to be at least as violent as men in terms of hitting or throwing things at their partners (Steinmetz, 1977a; Bland and Orn, 1986).

Physical aggression, abusive violence and sexual assault have become accepted as male rather than female attributes in intimate relationships. However, there is some evidence to show that this is not always the case. Brand and Kidd (1986) compared physical and sexual violence in heterosexual and female homosexual partners. They found that in 'committed relationships', forced sex (9%, 7%) and physical abuse (27%, 25%) had a similar percentage of occurrence for both groups. From a US National Incidence Survey of 2143 families, Straus (1978) reported that 4.6% of the wives surveyed had engaged in abusive violence towards their husbands. The number of wives who threw things was twice as large as that of husbands. Kicking, hitting and threatening with a knife or gun was also higher in frequency for wives, while pushing, shoving, slapping, beating up and using a knife or gun was higher for husbands.

Thus violence is not always unidirectional (men to women). Indeed, Gelles (1987a) and Straus et al. (1980) suggest that 'marital violence' is often bidirectional, with similar rates of aggressive behaviour for husbands and wives.

THE EXTENT OF SPOUSE ABUSE

Marital Violence

Research on the prevalence and incidence of spouse abuse has been hindered by a general lack of awareness about the problem, a general acceptance and normalization of family violence and a denial that a problem exists (Star, 1980). Nevertheless, a number of sources have been used to measure the amount of spouse abuse reported, such as police records, medical case notes, divorce applications, family interviews and surveys of violent crime, but there is still widespread ignorance about the extent of spouse abuse and the form it takes (Binney et al., 1981).

In the UK there are no regularly updated statistics on wife abuse but the problem is thought to be extensive. McClintock (1978) reported that 15% of all indictable crimes against the person in England were commited within the family. For spouse and parent abuse combined, he found the victims to be 74% women and 26% men. From court and police records in Scotland, Dobash and Dobash (1979, 1987) reported that the second largest category of interpersonal violence was assault on wives (25.1%), the most common form of violence being between unrelated males (37.2%). Of the 1051 cases of violence within the home recorded by the police, 'wife-beating' represented 76.8%, 'child-beating' 10.5% and 'husband-beating' 1.2% of cases. While 97.4% of the offending family members were male, 94.4% of the victims were female.

Borkowski *et al.* (1983) estimated the extent of wife assault from the study of divorcing couples conducted by Levinger (1966). The study reported that 32% of middle-class and 40% of working-class couples mention physical abuse as a major complaint in divorce proceedings. On the assumption that one third of all marriages end in divorce (Haskey, 1982), it becomes possible to roughly predict that between 11% and 13% of marriages will experience some form of physical violence. This, of course, is probably an underestimate, as the sample was restricted to divorce cases. The findings from another restricted sample were reported by Fergusson *et al.* (1986), who carried out a study in New Zealand which followed a group of parents over seven years. During that time 8.5% of the women had been assaulted. A rather more disturbing area of study is that of abuse of pregnant women. In a study of 290 pregnant women, Helton (1986) found that 15.2% reported battering before their current pregnancies and 8.3% reported battering during their current pregnancy.

A large survey in the United States (Straus, 1978; Straus *et al.*, 1980) has shown that 'marital violence' occurs once a year or more in 16% of families. Overall, 28% of marriages reported experience of marital violence at some time. Within these violent homes approximately a quarter of the couples had just a male offender, a quarter had just a female offender and in half the couples both partners were reported to be violent.

In terms of 'abusive' violence, the same study revealed that 3.8% of the wives and 4.6% of the husbands were battered by their partners during the previous twelve-month period. When these data were first reported as evidence of a 'battered-husband syndrome' (Steinmetz, 1977b) they received much criticism, as the survey did not detect whether the wives' violence was in retaliation or self-defence, and therefore the data may have been misinterpreted (Pleck *et al.*, 1978).

Indeed, for a number of women who have killed their husbands, the US courts have declared the act legally justified as self-defence (Ewing, 1987). The incidence of domestic murders has been reported to be between 20% and 40% of all homicides in the United States (Curtis, 1974). From his review of US criminal records, Curtis states that 'In 1974, 844 husbands were killed by their wives where 1009 wives were slain by their husbands'.

Marital and Courtship Rape

There have also been studies that indicate the extent of marital rape or forced sex as an expression of spouse abuse. For example, a UK survey of 1236 women living in London (Hall, 1985) revealed that 9% had at some time been forced by their spouse to have sex. Russell (1982), in her work on this subject, interviewed 930 women in San Francisco, 644 of whom were married. For respondents who were married, 4% had experienced forced sex but no other physical violence, 14% had been raped and battered and 12% had been battered but not raped. Finkelhor and Yllo (1982, 1985) put the question, 'Has your spouse ever used physical force or threat to try to have sex with you?' to a randomized sample of women. The response was that '10% said yes'.

Studies of female college students in the United States reveal even higher figures for 'date rape'. There is general agreement that between 14% and 15% of female students report having 'forced sex' during a date (Wilson and Durrenberger, 1982; Levine and Kanin, 1987). The issues of sexual violence to women are discussed by W. Marshall and H. Barbaree in Chapter 9 of this volume.

Courtship Violence

The occurrence of physical violence also is not restricted to married or co-habiting couples. In the UK, Dobash et al. (1978, 1985) found that 20% of battered women claim that the first violent assault occurred prior to marriage or cohabitation. Previous research in the United States has shown that between 21% and 52% of unmarried student couples report at least one episode of physical violence in their dating history as either the victim or the aggressor (see Table 6.1).

With respect to current relationships, most of the violence is reciprocal (21% on average), with no significant difference between the sexes (Arias and O'Leary, 1984; De Maris, 1987). However, gender differences are evident for the remainder (see Table 6.1), with males reporting victimization more than

Table 6.1 Dating and courtship violence in US undergraduate students. (Number in sample ranges from 270 to 484)

	Year	Sex	Violence in current relationships		Violence in dating history
			Aggressor (%)	Victim (%)	(%)
Makepeace	1981		–	–	21
Cate et al.	1982		–	–	22
Bernard and Bernard	1983		–	–	30
Arias and O'Leary[a]	1984	Male	–	30	–
		Female	–	35	–
Rose and Marshall	1985		–	–	52
Deal and Wampler	1986	Male	25	36	47
		Female	27	26	
Arias et al.	1987	Male	30	49	50
		Female	32	26	
De Maris	1987	Male	24	29	–
		Female	31	26	–

[a]Couples one month prior to marriage.

females, while violence reported by the offender are similar for both sexes (Deal and Wampler, 1986; Arias *et al.*, 1987).

It is interesting that some of the studies support Steinmetz's (1977b) 'battered-husband syndrome'. There may be two possible reasons for this:

(1) Aggression by men is seen as more natural and is either forgotten or downplayed, and thus possibly under-reported;
(2) Aggression by women, on the other hand, being 'unnatural', would be remembered more. Since women are stereotypically seen as less aggressive than men, it may take less aggression on the part of a woman for her to be labelled violent. This may then lead to an over-reporting of woman's aggressive acts (Deal and Wampler, 1986).

In conclusion, there is now considerable evidence for the interactive nature of spouse abuse. It must be pointed out, however, that 'When men hit women and women hit men, the real victims are almost certainly going to be the women' (Gelles, 1981, p. 128). The data available on dating violence tell us nothing of the outcome of that violence. As in the case of marital violence, the damage caused by violent men is likely to be greater than that caused by violent women, because males are usually stronger and larger than their female partners. In addition, men usually have more social resources at their command, so the physical or social consequences of courtship and marital violence are limited when the male is the victim. Therefore, spouse abuse is primarily a problem of victimized women (Wardell *et al.*, 1983; Pagelow, 1979, 1982, 1984; Johnson, 1985; Dobash and Dobash, 1979, 1987).

Women in the UK Who Seek Refuge and Shelter

In their book *Leaving Violent Men*, Binney *et al.* (1981) reported a survey of 150 refuges in England and Wales. From this they estimate that 11 400 women and 20 850 children used the accommodation in a one-year period (September 1977 to September 1978). A survey of 656 women who were in the 150 refuges at the time of their study showed that the majority of women had left home to escape physcial violence to themselves (90%) and sometimes to their children (27%). Other forms of ill-treatment were also mentioned, such as psychological abuse and not being given enough money to live on. Many of the women had experienced several kinds of ill-treatment. Of the women they interviewed, 68% claimed that 'mental cruelty' was just one of the reasons they left; usually this happened in conjunction with physical violence, although 10% said that they had suffered mental cruelty on its own. In some cases the women had been kept virtual prisoners, and in others they had been verbally tormented and threatened until they were confused about their own sanity. Dobash and Dobash's (1979) in-depth interview with 106 'battered' women shows that violence during a typical physical assault falls into the following categories: punching the face and/or the body, 44%; kicking, kneeing or butting, 27%; pushing into a non-injurious object, 15%; hitting with an object, 5%; and attempted smothering or strangling, 2%. In 89% of cases the violence started after marriage, or after the woman began living with the man. In some cases it was only when the violence also began to be directed at the children that the woman felt justified in leaving home.

Pahl (1985) carried out detailed interviews with 42 refuge occupants in South-east England. Her study revealed the following:

(1) In 38 (90%) of the couples there was a *child under five* in the household when the violence was taking place;
(2) For 15 (36%) of these families the woman was *pregnant* when violence began. In most of the cases this was the first child for the prospective parents.

The majority (81%) of the women interviewed were aged between 20 and 34 years old with an average of two to three children. The violence these women suffered had often occurred for a considerable length of time, the average being 7 years (ranging from a few months to 30–40 years). Over half the sample (59%) had been abused for three years or more.

To emphasize the desperation of women who *finally* seek refuge, Ashby and Pizzey (1974) described a number of case histories. For example:

> Sonia, who has three children, came to Women's Aid from Wales where her husband owned a shop. He is seriously mentally ill and undergoing psychiatric treatment, and the hospital insisted that Sonia remained with him because he was so sick. He beat her brutally and also beat the second child. He made the children sit and watch the beating and Sonia was not allowed to stand up after being beaten until she had crawled across the floor and licked his feet (p. 23).

However, it would be wrong to assume from this one case that such awful experiences happen only to women who are supporting their husband through mental illness. There are many other reasons why violence may occur in the family.

CAUSES OF VIOLENCE TO SPOUSE

Lystad (1975) identified three levels of explanation for violence in the home: those which explain the causes within the cultural values of society; those involving social and structural factors; and those involving psychological variables.

Cultural Explanations

The most broad viewpoint (Gil, 1978; Straus, 1980; Levine, 1986; Goldstein, 1986) holds that cultural values, the availability of weapons and the exposure to unpunished models of aggression affect personal attitudes towards violent behaviour. These, in turn, influence an individual's acceptance of aggression as a form of emotional expression and as a method of control over others.

Finn (1986) states that traditional sex-role attitudes are the most powerful predictor of attitudes supporting marital violence, while the person's race and sex play a relatively unimportant part. According to research on high-school dating violence, between 12% and 35% of adolescent couples are aggressive. One quarter of the victims and three tenths of the offenders interpret the violence as a sign of love (Henton *et al.*, 1983). The study of courtship violence suggests that the patterns of spouse abuse emerge long before a person gets married. Research clearly demonstrates similarities between courtship and marital violence, and suggests that for many women, both young and old, physical abuse alone is not sufficient grounds to terminate a relationship (Roscoe and Benaske, 1985; O'Keefe *et al.*, 1986).

Dobash and Dobash (1979) recognize the contribution of patriarchy to family violence, and propose that the source of violence lies in the social and economic processes that directly and indirectly support a patriarchal social order and family structure which leads to the domination of women by men. Hanmer (1977, 1978) has expanded this idea into a theory incorporating the whole political system (which represents men), and in her view the policies of the welfare state induce dependency in women. For further discussion on radical, feminist and marxist analyses of the subordination of children and women in the family see Marsden (1978).

Social and Structural Explanations

Less dramatic sociological perspectives emphasize the important of socio-economic and structural factors within the family which can promote violence, such as low wages, unemployment, poor housing, overcrowding and social isolation (O'Brien, 1971). These alienating conditions are seen by Gelles's (1987b) 'Economic' model as causing frustration and stress for the individual, which may lead to violence. Gelles claims that violence is an adaptation or response to structural or situational stress, which is not confined to families in lower socio-economic groups.

Other sociological attempts to explain violence emphasize that conflict is produced by the unequal distribution of resources and asymmetric social relationships within the family (Goode, 1974; Ball-Rokeach, 1980). Goode proposes a 'resource theory', and argues that the family, like other social institutions, relies to some degree on force or threat to maintain order. He postulates that the more alternatives (or 'resources') an individual can command, or perceive to command, the less he or she will use force (itself a 'resource') in an overt manner. O'Brien (1971) shows a similar line of thought in his 'status inconsistency' hypothesis. He focuses on the economic problems of the husband and the possible disparity in the educational achievements of husband and wife that may result in his lower status in the family. Violence is seen as an option to remedy a low-status position and increase self-esteem. Giles-Sims (1983) and Straus (1980) support this idea in the context of a general systems approach, and refer to deviant authority structures in the family. They claim that the level of violence is likely to be greatest when the wife is dominant in decision making. Goldstein and Rosenbaum (1985) provide evidence for an association between wife abuse and low self-esteem in abusive husbands, and state that the abusive husbands were more likely to perceive their wives' behaviour as threatening to their self-concepts.

Gelles (1983) has analysed the causes of family violence in terms of cost and benefit. His 'exchange theory' considers that the private nature of the home environment reduces the cost of overt aggression in terms of official reprimand. This, in turn, leads to a higher probability of aggression in the home, where there are fewer social constraints on behaviour. Thus privacy makes family violence less detectable and easier to commit. Indeed, it has recently been estimated by Dutton (1987) that the probability of 'wife assault' being detected by the criminal justice system in Canada is about 6.5%. If detected, the probability of arrest is 21.2%. Overall, the offender has a 0.38% chance of being punished by the courts.

Generally, the sociological perspective has moved away from simple explanations of family violence, such as poverty, to one involving the transactions that occur between the abuser and the abused within the structure of the family.

Psychological Explanations

Psychological approaches can also be divided into those which focus on the individual and those which are interactive in nature.

Individually focused explanations have concentrated on the personality characteristics of abusive spouses (e.g. Rosenbaum and O'Leary, 1981). The research suggests that men who engage in spouse abuse are very insecure, with many anxieties over inferiority, inadequacy and abandonment (Weitzman and Dreen, 1982). However, they show no personality differences from non-abusive men, other than being less assertive. Nevertheless, spouse abuse has been significantly linked to psychiatric disorder (Faulk, 1974; Bland and Orn, 1986; Jacob, 1987), although Coleman (1980) found that less than 25% of the abusive men she interviewed reported a psychiatric history.

An area of research that has attracted the largest amount of interest relates spouse abuse to the use of alcohol and drugs (Edleson *et al.*, 1985). In the UK, Gayford's (1975) sample of battered women described their husband's drunkenness as a contributing factor to violence on a regular (52%) or occasional (22%) basis. In the United States, surveys of battered women typically show that 60% of their partners have an alcohol problem and 21% also had a drug problem (Carlson, 1977; Roberts, 1987). A substantial number of other studies confirm the association of alcohol and drug abuse with violence towards spouse (e.g. Ball, 1977;. Bayles, 1978; Gerson, 1978; Walker, 1979; Fagen *et al.*, 1983; Pahl, 1985; Van Hasselt *et al.*, 1985; Gelles, 1987b). Some authors propose that it is the major cause (e.g. Weissberg, 1983), but Moore (1979) gives a convincing explanation for its frequent representation. She suggests that alcohol consumption relieves the man of the responsibility for his behaviour, and gives the wife justification for remaining in the relationship in the hope that he will control his drinking which will end his aggressiveness. A similar point has been made by Dobash and Dobash (1987). The role of circulating testosterone and its hormonal effects on male aggression has also been suggested as a biological factor contributing to violence (Persky *et al.*, 1971; Mazur, 1983).

In contrast to biological determinism, social learning explanations of spouse abuse emphasize the abusive individual's exposure to family violence as a child (Giles-Simms, 1985). This is based on the assumption that people learn violent behaviour from observing aggressive role models (Bandura, 1973). In support of this argument, Roy (1982) has stated that four out of five abusive men (*n* = 4000) were reported by their partners as either observing their fathers abusing their mothers and/or being a victim of child abuse themselves. This was in comparison to only a third of the abused women. Findings from many other studies have supported this observation (e.g. Gayford, 1975; Carroll, 1977; Rosenbaum and O'Leary, 1981; Kalmuss, 1984; Lewis, 1987; Straus *et al.*, 1980).

There is evidence that violence between parents affects the children in a family. The behaviour and psychiatric problems discovered in children of violent marriages include truancy, aggressive behaviour at home and school, and anxiety disorders (Levine, 1975; Hughes and Barad, 1983; Jaffe *et al.*, 1986; Davis and Carlson, 1987). It is suggested that such children learn aversive behaviour as a general style for controlling their social and physical environments, and this style continues into adulthood (Gully and Dengerink, 1983; Browne and Saqi, 1987). Lewis (1987) claims that some women also learn to accept violent behaviour towards themselves as a result of childhood experiences.

Interactional approaches

Due to past experiences, some abusing couples tend to establish aggressive relationships because they are familiar, and therefore comfortable, with violence as an expression of intimate concern and attachment. Indeed, Hanks and Rosenbaum (1978) have commented on the striking similarity between the abused woman's current marital relationship and that of her parents.

Many battered women and abusive men lack the social competence and personal skills or resources to develp healthy relationships. This may be a result of inadequate parents and poor socialization (Walker and Browne, 1985).

Another factor involved in the formation of violent relationships is the way in which males and females are differently socialized during childhood.. Walker and Browne (1985) state that women typically learn that they are supposed to be weak and unable to cope with violence. They do not develop techniques for avoiding or stopping abuse, and rather than responding assertively they submit to violence, believing that they have no alternative to being abused. However, men are typically socialized to believe that they should be active, aggressive and dominant over women. It is therefore clear that the risk of abuse increases if the couple consists of a dominant male and a possessive female. In relation to this, Gayford (1976) distinguished ten types of 'battered wives', offering names and descriptions which imply that the cause of violent behaviour lies also with the victim.

Walker (1979) previously described a cycle of violence which exists periodically in an abusive relationships. The cycle is made up of three phases: a tension-building phase; a period of acute violence; and a state of reconciliation. Once this sequence is entered into it can be very difficult to escape from.

Frude (1989), in Chapter 7 of this volume, takes a similar perspective and puts forward the notion of a causal chain leading to an incidence of child abuse which can equally be applied to spouse and elder abuse: first, the presence of a stressful situation; second, the assessment of the situation as threatening (which may be unrealistic); third, anger and emotional distress as a response to the situation, and fourth, a lack of inhibitions with regard to violent expression. This finally results in the individual being more easily provoked to show aggression. With respect to anger arousal, Novaco's (1978) work (see also Chapter 3 of this volume) emphasizes the role of cognitive processes such as appraisal and expectations in the assessment of external events as threatening.

The above theoretical approaches suggest that the causes of family violence cannot be explained at a purely individual, societal or cultural level. They indicate that a multi-variate model is more appropriate.

An Integrated Approach to the Causation of Family Violence

The study of social interactions and relationships can be seen as occupying a central and potentially integrating place in the study of family violence (Figure 6.1). Gelles (1987a, b) and Browne (1989) present complex models of the causes of family violence that combine psychological, cultural, social and structural explanations. They assume that violence in the family is influenced

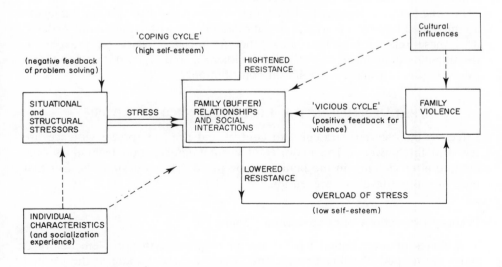

Figure 6.1 The causation of family violence (adapted from Browne, 1989)

by (1) situational stressors, such as distorted family relationships, low self-esteem, unwanted or problem children and other dependants, and (2) structural stressors, such as poor housing, overcrowding, unemployment, social isolation, and financial and health problems. However, Browne (1989) expands on Gelles's (1973) original formulation to demonstrate that the chances of these situational and structural stressors resulting in family violence are mediated by and depend on the interactive relationships within the family (see Figure 6.1). A secure relationship between family members will 'buffer' any effects of stress and facilitate coping strategies on behalf of the family. By contrast, insecure or anxious relationships will not 'buffer' the family under stress, and 'episodic overload', such as an argument, may result in a physical or emotional attack.

This will have a negative effect on the existing interpersonal relationships and reduce any 'buffering' effects still further, making it easier for stressors to overload the system once again. Hence, a positive feedback ('vicious cycle') is set up which eventually leads to 'systematic overload', where constant stress results in repeated physical assaults. This situation becomes progressively worse without intervention and could be termed 'the spiral of violence'.

According to Rutter (1985), aggression is a social behaviour within everyone's repertoire, and he suggests that it is under control when the individual has high esteem, good relationships and stress is appropriately managed. However, the quality of relationships and responses to stress in the family will depend on the participant's personality and character traits and their pathology, such as low self-esteem, poor temperament control and psychological disorders. This may be a result of the early social experiences. As indicated earlier, culture and community values may also affect attitudes and styles of interaction in intimate relationships which, in turn, will be influenced by the social position of the individuals in terms of their age, sex, education, socio-economic status, ethnic group and social class background.

In conclusion, it is suggested that stress factors and background influences are mediated through the interpersonal relationships within the family. Indeed, it is these relationships that should be the focus of work on prevention, treatment and management of family violence, and it is at this level that psychologists can make a significant contribution.

PREVENTION STRATEGIES FOR SPOUSE ABUSE

Effective intervention strategies to control and prevent spouse violence are few and far between. The majority of current intervention techniques only operate after violence in the family has occurred. This is despite the fact that there are three levels of prevention.

Primary Preventions of Fundamental Change

Techniques of intervention which attempt to prevent the problem before it starts are termed 'Primary Preventions'. Usually these operate at the societal level through public-awareness campaigns and advocacy groups, and then are realized by social, legal and educational processes of change. Gelles and Cornell (1985) suggest the following actions for the primary prevention of spouse abuse:

(1) Eliminate the norms that legitimize and glorify violence in the society and the family, such as the use of violence as a form of media entertainment.
(2) Reduce violence-provoking stress created by society, such as poverty and inequality.
(3) Incorporate families into a network of kin and community and reduce social isolation.
(4) Change the sexist character of society and educational development.
(5) Break the cycle of violence in the family by teaching alternatives to violence as a way of controlling children.

The above proposals call for fundamental changes in family life and society as a whole. If they are not unrealistic, they are at least long-term solutions.

Secondary Preventions of Prediction and Identification

In the short term, intervention techniques aimed at the early identification of potential or actual spouse violence are more realistic. This is considered to be secondary prevention, and includes professionals involved in counselling, telephone helplines, home visits and clinic, health centre or hospital care. Such professionals can be instructed to routinely screen all families who come into contact with the service they are providing.

Predictive characteristics

It is difficult to predict the chances of family violence in the family, as some spouses resort to violence inconsistently while others may do so only under extreme stress. However, studies on the causes of family violence have identified factors that are usually present when spouse abuse occurs. Thus the checklist in Table 6.2 may be useful in establishing those men and women at high risk for abusive violence.

Men and women are often reluctant to admit relationship problems and may feel ashamed of their violent interactions. Predictive characteristics are helpful, therefore, in identifying the possibility of violence for both the family and the therapist. Where there is undue concern about the possibility of spouse violence, the problem should be referred to a more appropriate professional who may fully assess the couple's relationship and adverse factors affecting the family, such as stress and conflict at work (Barling and Rosenbaum, 1986).

Assessment procedures

Barling *et al.* (1987) claim that the most frequently used measurement of marital and courtship violence is the Conflict Tactics Scales (CTS—Straus,

Table 6.2   Predictive characteristics of spouse violence

(1)   History of violence, threatening behaviour and the use of weapons.
(2)   Exposure to violence as a child.
(3)   Feelings of low self-esteem and helplessness.
(4)   Feelings of social withdrawal, isolation and lack of social support.
(5)   Feelings of jealousy and accusations of infidelity.
(6)   Presence of non-accidental injuries such as scratch marks or a black eye.
(7)   Presence of a provocative victim that escalates arguments and shows reciprocal
      aggression.
(8)   Presence of an overdependent victim, possibly due to poor health, sexual
      problems or difficulties during pregnancy and childbirth.
(9)   History of alcohol or drug abuse.
(10) History of psychological disorders such as anxiety and depression.
(11) Behavioural problems in children, especially anti-social behaviour.
(12) Socio-economic problems such as unemployment and financial difficulties.
(13) Stress at work and job dissatisfaction.
(14) Recent adverse life-event such as separation from spouse or death of a
      parent or child.

1979). This is a self-administered 18-item scale assessing the behaviours that an individual might exhibit during an argument with his or her partner (e.g. reasoning, verbal aggression or physical force). The last eight items make up a violence index, ranging from throwing an object to using a knife or gun. Studies using the CTS have found it to be valid with regard to whether a relationship is violent or not, but usually both men and women report more violence for their partner than themselves. Husbands tend to see their marriage as mutually violent, whereas wives call it 'husband violent' (Browning and Dutton, 1986). A criticism of the CTS is that it does not consider the consequences or context of violence and so tends to equate male and female aggressive acts. The Index of Spouse Abuse (ISA) accounts for some of these shortcomings, as it is a 30-item scale designed to measure the severity of abuse inflicted on a woman by her partner (Hudson and McIntosh, 1981.)

Indicators of individual differences in impulsive aggression have also been developed, such as the Irritability and Emotional Susceptibility Scales (Caprara et al., 1985). However, Edmunds and Kendrick (1980) conclude from their study of the measurement of aggression that indices of social interaction are required. Indeed, the ratio of positive to negative comments is an important indicator of affection in relationships (Patterson, 1976; Browne, 1986). These data can be derived from the Marital Interaction Coding System (MICS), which is an observational measure of spouse interaction developed by Weiss et al. (1973). The MICS technique consists of three assessment stages: (1) videotaping a couple's interaction during a discussion of relationship conflict, (2) coding the observed interaction according to 30 behavioural items, and (3) scoring the interaction. Scoring is based on the relative frequencies of behaviour which are classified into positive and negative verbal and non-verbal categories.

A Positivity Index is obtained for the couple that represents the ratio of positive to negative behaviours. The MICS procedures have been shown to successfully discriminate distressed couples from happily married ones, and have also been used to evaluate the effects of behavioural marital therapy (Weiss and Summers, 1983).

A more economical observational measure of spouse interaction entitled the Communication Skills Test (CST) has been developed by Floyd and Markmann (1984). In contrast to the relatively minute behavioural units coded with the MICS, the observer judges the degree to which an entire statement represents either disruptive or facilitative communication and rates the statement on a five-point scale, i.e. (1) very negative, (2) negative, (3) neutral, (4) positive and (5) very positive. Relative frequency scores are then obtained by dividing the number of statements in each category by the total number of statements. However, the validity of this test is in question, as comparative scores derived from the MICS and the CST do not significantly correlate (see Floyd et al., 1987).

Other measures of spouse relationships can be obtained from marital and family questionnaires. These should not be seen as alternatives to observational techniques for marriage and family assessment, but should be used in conjunction with behavioural methods. This is because both indirect and self-reports of events may not correspond to actual ones. Nevertheless, how a respondent thinks or feels may be crucial. Thus when time and finances permit, assessment should contain data collected using both approaches, as a multi-method technique allows interview/questionnaire data to be validated against directly observed behaviour and vice versa (Browne, 1986).

A major review of marital and family questionnaires, together with some observation techniques for marriage and family assessment, has been compiled by Filsinger (1983). To give just one example, the Positive Feelings Question-naire is designed to assess positive affect and love for one's partner. The PFQ has been shown to be reliable and sensitive to treatment changes, and its validity has also been demonstrated in terms of high correlations with other measures of relationship satisfaction (O'Leary et al., 1983).

Measures of stress in the family can also be obtained by questionnaires and checklists. McCubbin and Patterson (1983) have developed the Family Inventory of Life Events and Changes (FILE). This is a 71-item self-report instrument designed to record the hardships, stresses and strains a family has experienced within the past year. These are grouped into nine subscales:

(1) Intrafamily strains such as parental problems;
(2) Marital strains such as sexual difficulties or separation;
(3) Pregnancy and childbearing strains;
(4) Finance and business strains;
(5) Work/family transitions and strains such as periods of unemployment;
(6) Illness and family-care strains;
(7) Family losses or breakdowns;
(8) Family transitions such as family members moving in and out;

(9) Family legal strains such as court appearances.

The total number of family demands is referred to as the 'family pile-up' score, which may be useful, as both the reliability and validity of this instrument has been demonstrated to be high.

More general measures of stress, such as the Family Stress Checklist (Orkow, 1985) and the Parenting Stress Index (Abidin, 1983) have previously been associated with studies on child abuse (e.g. Browne and Saqi, 1987). Nevertheless, they can usefully be applied to spouse and elder abuse. For example, the PSI is a screening instrument that provides scores related to the parent's sense of attachment, competence, social isolation, relationship with spouse, and mental and physical health. In addition to an assessment of life-stress events, it also provides scores on the child's demands, mood, activity, adaptability and acceptability, as perceived by the parent. In future it will be of interest to see whether research can establish an association between styles of spouse interaction and high or low ratings of stress.

TREATMENT AND CONTROL OF SPOUSE ABUSE

At the tertiary level of prevention, techniques are employed when violence between the spouses has actually been determined. Without secondary prevention this will be only after many repeated episodes of family violence have occurred and have become enmeshed in the family system. Tertiary prevention programmes are by far the most common form of intervention for controlling spouse abuse, and may be classified into three categories:

(1) Refuges and shelters;
(2) Police intervention and legal controls;
(3) Psychological treatments.

Most of these interventions are aimed at battered women, although it is well recognized that both spouses contribute to the cycle of family violence (Bolton and Bolton, 1987; Gelles, 1987a, b; Straus *et al.*, 1980). Of course, this may be a result of men being reluctant to identify themselves and seek treatment for violent relationships.

Characteristics of Battered Women Who Seek Help

Finn (1985) showed that battered women are typically under serious stress from a number of sources, i.e. money, work, children, relatives, physical illness, jealousy, sexual relationship, deciding who is boss, settling arguments, alcohol and drug use. The study demonstrated that, as stress increased, there was a corresponding decrease in the use of positive coping mechanisms such as acquiring social support. This is despite the fact that intervention by friends, relatives and neighbours, or the threat of such intervention, tends to make spouse abuse less common and less severe (Levinson, 1985; Jaffe *et al*, 1986).

Finn (1985) reported that battered women were more likely to use passive coping mechanisms of minimal reactivity, or show avoidant strategies such as drugs and social withdrawal.

These solutions to the problem result in less control over the situation. Less control results in increased stress, and so a cycle develops, with a gradually decreasing use of coping techniques. Thus it is not surprising that Weitzman and Dreen (1982) describe battered women as typically having limited coping mechanisms, high dependence on partners, anxiety, depression and low self-esteem. Women who are continually battered often develop a state of learned helplessness, where they perceive themselves to have no control over their lives or environment (Walker, 1979).

It has been found that many women experiencing learned helplessness have tried on several occasions to seek outside intervention (Hendricks-Matthews, 1982). However, agencies such as the police and social and medical services are very often unwilling to help. Family life is still often seen as being sacred, and agencies are reluctant to intrude into private family matters. Police place domestic disturbances at the bottom of their list of priorities, and are reluctant to prosecute husbands who assault their wives. Social services try to keep the couple together, often when continued violence is certain. Failed attempts at seeking help only serve to reinforce the abused woman's feelings of helplessness. Very often abused women have a low locus of control, and they attribute any success to be due to external factors such as good luck. Failure is seen as the woman's own fault; lack of success is attributed to internal factors.

Fincham and Bradley (1988) emphasize the importance of causal attribution in distressed marriages. This is where the woman places the blame for the violence inflicted on her. If she sees the man as the cause of the violence then this may have positive effects on her coping strategies. However, in a state of learned helplessness the woman will often attribute the blame to herself, thus compounding her feelings of impotence. In fact, as abused wives are often persuaded by their husbands that they are incompetent, hysterical or frigid and, as a result of their distorted self-image, they may genuinely come to believe that they provoked the attack.

Learned helplessness is the reason often cited why women remain in an abusive relationship. Walker and Browne (1985) describe how women who are repeatedly abused gradually perceive themselves to have fewer and fewer options. They feel that they can exert no control over their situation and that nothing they do will change anything. Efforts to find ways of escaping the violence cease, and instead they learn to endure and adapt to the abuse. Gelles (1987a) claims that women are more likely to remain in an abusive relationship if they experienced violence as a child. In addition, Truninger (1971) suggests that women are entrapped in marriage through a lack of resources and economic constraints (see Table 6.3)

Thus there are two types of women who need different kinds of help: those who have left violent relationships and those who are unable to leave. The first group requires assistance in the form of shelters, starting a new life, finding employment, etc. For the second group, counselling is required to help them to overcome feelings of helplessness and inadequacy.

Table 6.3   Reasons for remaining in a violent
relationship (Truninger, 1971)

---

(1) Negative self-concept;
(2) Learned helplessness;
(3) Husband will reform;
(4) Economic hardship of leaving too great;
(5) Children need father;
(6) Cannot cope alone;
(7) Divorces are stigmatized;
(8) Difficulties in getting a job and meeting
     new friends.

Refuges and Shelters

In 1971 the first refuge for battered women opened its doors (Pizzey, 1974).
Ten years later there were about 175 in the UK, most of which were affiliated
to the National Women's Aid Federation (NWAF). At any one time there
were approximately 1000 women and 1700 children living in these shelters
(Dobash and Dobash, 1987). The Select Committee on Violence in Marriage
(1975) recommended that there should be one refuge place available per 10 000
of the population, and concluded that refuges were meeting an important need
but were inadequately coping with the demand for places (i.e. there is one
refuge place per 60 000). The main objective of the refuges is to provide
shelter from further abuse for women and their children (Martin, 1976),
although they also offer protection, accommodation, support and advice (Pahl,
1978). Conditions in the shelters are not really suitable for long-term stay due
to overcrowding and the general communal nature of the houses, but they do
provide a 'breathing space' which is necessary for the woman to come to terms
with separation and sort out financial, legal and housing matters. The average
length of stay in British refuges is five and a half months, but many stay for
over a year (Binney et al., 1981). The effectiveness of the shelters is difficult
to assess, but Binney et al. (1981) found that 75% of the women felt that the
refuge had helped them.

A minority of refuges (for example, Chiswick Family Rescue (formerly
Chiswick Women's Aid)) operate a counselling service on an individual basis
to get the woman to understand the relationship she was in, and the roots of
the relationship. Also they try to make her feel positive about herself, but not
by raising her consciousness of herself as part of an oppressed sector of society.
By contrast, the majority of refuges run by the NWAF feel that a woman
should be encouraged to discuss battering and other personal experiences in
relation to the general position of women in society. Thus rather than
'counselling' being given, group discussions are encouraged. Indeed, the
'therapeutic' relationship is viewed by the NWAF in a negative light, in line
with their feminist principles.

Table 6.4 Steps to therapy: reality therapy received by battered women in shelter (Whipple, 1985)

---

(1) Client is made to feel accepted and cared for:
    — She is allowed to relate details of experiences;
    — Assurance is given that she is not different;
    — Help is offered.
(2) Ask 'What did you do to end abuse in the past?'
    — A change in her own behaviour is emphasized.
(3) Each description is evaluated.
(4) Client's goals for change are identified.
(5) A realistic and immediate plan is formulated.
(6) Client's commitment is evaluated.
(7) Independence and self-help is emphasized.
(8) Repeated therapeutic contact is recommended.

To support the case for individual counselling and therapy, Whipple (1985) wrote a report on the use of reality therapy with battered women in a refuge. She identified eight steps to the therapy (see Table 6.4).

It has been claimed that the provision of shelters for battered women breaks the cycle of violence (Berk *et al.*, 1986). Indeed, Pizzey (1974) stated that '. . . in providing refuge today we may remove the need for refuge in the future'. However, this view is overoptimistic, as many of the women (20%) returned home to their abusive husbands and further violence. Binney *et al.* (1981) found that they returned because of accommodation problems or to give their partner another chance. A minority returned for the sake of the children and some were forced back. A further aspect of returning home was related to the attitudes and personality of the woman. In their follow-up study (eighteen months later) of 84 women who had returned home, Binney *et al.* found that 34% had suffered life-threatening attacks or had been hospitalized for serious injuries (e.g. broken bones). Assaults included being kicked, pushed into fires or through glass, thrown against walls or down stairs, being punched or having had their hair pulled out.

Police Intervention and Legal Control

Under the UK Domestic Violence Act 1976 there are two main types of injunction, Non-molestation Orders and Exclusion Orders. Non-molestation Orders say that the husband must not use violence against the woman or the children. This incorporates assault, pestering or otherwise interfering (mental cruelty is therefore also included). Exclusion Orders mean that the husband must leave the matrimonial home and stay away from it. The court is also empowered to attach subsidiary orders to the main one (for example, an interim Custody Order, or the Penalty of Arrest).

The police do have the power to arrest the husband for 'actual bodily harm' or for 'behaviour likely to cause a breach of the peace', but the attitudes of the police in general are not very helpful in this respect, although the Criminal Evidence Act 1986 now allows the police to compel women assaulted by their husbands to give evidence against them (Horley, 1986). Nevertheless, if the husband is put in prison, usually it is not for the violence but for contempt of court.

The effects of arrests were shown in a study by Berk and Newton (1985) to substantially decrease the incidence of wife battering and apparently deter the abuser from rebattering. Arrest emphasizes to the abuser that domestic violence is both illegal and unacceptable. If violence has not yet reached the stage of chronic abuse then intervention may be possible in the form of marriage counselling (e.g. Beech, 1985). This can help both partners to appreciate the nature of the problem and to see how they can change their lifestyle in order to remove the cause of violence. Nevertheless, it is essential for those battered women who are unable to leave or wish to remain with their abusive husbands to receive expert psychological help for themselves and their partners.

Psychological Treatments

Goldstein (1983) has identified three main strategies for psychological intervention:

(1) Treating the battered woman;
(2) Treating the abusive man;
(3) Conjoint treatment.

Treating the battered woman

This has included both individual and group psychotherapy. The aim of this therapy is to help the woman to achieve a realistic goal and build or restore her self-esteem and sense of competency. If the goal is to leave her husband then it is hoped that by following certain steps (see Table 6.4), and having repeated contact to maintain support, the woman will gain independence (Whipple, 1985).

Psychotherapy may also help the woman to recognize her feelings of anger at being abused, and finally help her to plan her changes in the future, whether she stays or leaves her male partner. During the course of therapy it is sometimes necessary to challenge the commonly held myths that violence is a 'normal' part of intimate relationships, and to re-address the woman's causal attributions that it is all her own fault (Goldstein, 1983). If the woman attributes the blame for the violence to her husband, then the likelihood of intervention being successful is far greater than if she thinks of herself as the cause of violence. Similarly, women with an internal locus of control have a better prognosis than those with an external one.

Hendricks and Matthews (1982) suggest that when a battered woman is being counselled it is important to assess how receptive to intervention she is, as her helplessness can vary from being limited to the abusive relationship to being present in all aspects of her life.

Marital rape victims can resemble battered women and non-marital rape victims. They are characterized by feelings of humiliation, anger, depression, self-blame, poor self-esteem, negative reactions towards men and lack of interest in or enjoyment of sex. Although many victims are in need of counselling for rape, they do not seek help, or they seek help for a different marital problem. Many of the reasons for this are similar to those for battered wives—for example, learned helplessness, fear of retribution, stigmatization and fear of being blamed. They may see the marital rape as a part of battering and not as a problem in its own right (Hanneke and Shields, 1985).

Treatment programmes for men

These have concentrated on cessation of violence and the restructuring of attitudes towards the use of violence in the family (e.g. Hall and Ryan, 1984). It is generally agreed that a husband's unwillingness to admit to or work on the problem of his aggression is a major stumbling block in preventing further abuse.

Recently there has been emphasis on increasing the treatment programmes available for abusive men (e.g. Saunders, 1984, 1986). An example of a group programme aimed at teaching abusive men to observe themselves and change their violent behaviour has been described by Edleson and his colleagues (1984, 1985b), who used the following techniques in combination:

(1) *Self-observation.* For many men the events leading up to a violent incident are unclear. They cannot connect prior events with the violent act. While aggression may have satisfying effects for the man in the short term, he may fail to see the long-term effects on the relationship. Self-observation helps abusive men to clarify behavioural chains of events and identify precursors of violence in the future.

(2) *Cognitive restructuring.* This is a process in which individuals are helped to analyse thought patterns and then change the assumptions and attitudes on which they are based. An abusive man often has a rigid set of beliefs relating to how his partner should behave. This justifies confrontation over his wife's behaviour and allows him to put blame on her for causing him to lose his temper.

(3) *Interpersonal skills training.* As we have already seen, abusive men and abused women are often deficient in coping skills, and so have difficulty in defusing stressful situations before they lead to violence. This type of

training is therefore very beneficial to both men and women. It may begin by identifying a specific situation in which a person has experienced difficulties. It is then analysed to find the 'critical moment', that is, the point during the interaction when a different behaviour might have produced a more positive outcome. With the help of others the appropriate type of behaviour is decided upon, and the situation acted out as a role-play so that the person can practise.

(4) *Relaxation training*.   A major link in the chain of events leading to a violent outburst is increased tension. If this tension can be recognized and dissipated, another link in the chain has been broken.

(5) *Small-group format*.   Although many men who batter express regret about what they may have done, they continue to blame their partners for the abuse (Bernard and Bernard, 1984) and sometimes receive mixed messages from male peers condoning their actions (e.g. 'Sometimes you've got to keep them in line'). The small-group format provides counterconditioning for such men, as they are surrounded by others who want to change their aggressive behaviour. However, there is a need for systematic evaluation of the effectiveness of most of these approaches applied to abusive husbands (Gondolf, 1987).

Conjoint treatment

Given the reciprocal nature of spouse violence, it is thought that abused and abuser integrated group programmes help both men and women to perceive the similarity of their concerns and hence enable them to solve their problems together. This approach to marital violence regards both men and women as victims of stress and deficient coping abilities. Therefore, stress management techniques (see Meichenbaum, 1985; Boss, 1988) could be suggested for the treatment of couples. Indeed, anger-control training for battering couples has shown an 85% success rate, with no further violence up to six months later (Deschner and McNeil, 1986). The clinical implications of research on the control of aggression has been reviewed by Goldstein (1983), and these implications have been applied to the study of spouse abuse (Steinfield, 1986).

Conclusion

Help for the battered woman has concentrated on removing the immediate threat of violence by providing shelters, safe homes and refuges, followed by help in leaving the violent relationship. However, many women choose to remain in the relationship and see violence as being only one of a number of stressors. Because of this, programmes which focus on a single strategy (e.g. communication training or anger control) will have poor success. The overall level of stress in the family must be reduced by increasing the repertoire of coping skills available to both men and women.

The major problem of intervention is that most instances of violence·go unreported and undetected. This may be due to a fear of retribution by the husband, of stigma or of being blamed and an absence of the belief that the situation can change. It is often only when a sensitive helping professional asks the right question that the victim will admit to the problem. Sensitive methods for interviewing violent families are discussed by Gelles (1987a) and Bolton and Bolton (1987).

There has been much criticism of both the quality and quantity of services provided for prevention and treatment of abusive men and battered wives. Traditional sources of help have been accused of aggravating problems by failing to provide assistance, deflecting blame onto the woman seeking help and increasing her sense of isolation. The following history illustrates these views:

> First, she went to a doctor, who gave her tranquillizers to calm her and stop her hysteria. Next, she went to a priest, who explained the importance of patience and tolerance: her husband was simply insecure and frustrated, he needed her support and forgiveness. Once she called the police, who responded by asking her husband to take a walk around the block to calm down. Finally, she went to a community mental health agency, where she was told that it was really her husband who needed help and unless she could get him to come in for counselling there was really nothing the agency could do for her (Davis, 1984).

It is essential that professionals take a more responsible and informed attitude to spouse violence.

THE NATURE AND DEFINITION OF ELDER ABUSE

Although Western society is gradually becoming aware of elder abuse, the problem remains the least-researched area of family violence (Eastman, 1989). This is reflected in the amount of literature that is available on the subject, which, in comparison to spouse abuse, is extremely limited (see Johnson and O'Brien, 1985). Nevertheless, a number of recent review publications have emerged (Eastman, 1984; Pillemer and Wolf, 1986; Quinn and Tomita, 1986; Steinmetz, 1988).

Since 1975, when Baker first coined the phrase 'granny bashing', no clear agreement on a definition of elder abuse has been reached (Valentine and Cash, 1986). In the UK 'Granny battering has been described as the systematic and continuous abuse of an elderly person by the carer, often, although not always, a relative on whom the elderly person is dependent for care . . .' (Cloke, 1983, p. 2).

The US Congress Select Committee on Aging (1981) gave a much broader definition as 'The wilful infliction of physical pain, injury or debilitating mental anguish, unreasonable confinement, or wilful deprivation by a caretaker of services which are necessary to maintain mental and physical health'. Of course, this description is not confined to domestic settings, and might include the policies of the government itself.

With respect to elder abuse in the home environment, Eastman (1989) has identified the following types of maltreatment:

(1) Physical violence (as defined earlier in this chapter);
(2) Threats of physical violence;
(3) Sexual abuse, including rape and pornography;
(4) Neglect, such as locking an elderly relative in a room, refusing to provide meals and refusing material or emotional support;
(5) Abandonment—either to hospital, residential care or the street;
(6) Psychological abuse, including intimidation, humiliation and the threat of abandonment;
(7) Exploitation, such as financial abuse of the elderly person's resources for the personal gain of the caregiver.

Eastman (1989) goes on to give a case example:

> Mrs Roberts, an 89-year-old woman, was often seen by the home-help to be struck by her daughter. Not infrequently the home-help found her client sitting in the kitchen with a pair of rubber gloves pushed into her mouth.

However, abuse of elderly relatives most frequently manifests itself in neglect (Steinmetz, 1978): for example, tying an elderly person who needs constant watching onto a bed or chair in order to complete the housework or shopping, or the excessive use of sleeping medication and alcohol in order to make the person more manageable. It is important to recognize that this type of neglect may not be intended necessarily to harm the elderly person. There is a lack of knowledge about how to care for the elderly, and in some cases abuse is not intentional. In the United States, Block (1983) showed that the caregivers used a wide range of means to control their elderly relatives; 40% screamed or yelled, 6% used physical restraint, 6% force-fed or used medication, 6% threatened to send them to a nursing home, 4% threatened physical force and 3% used physical force. US police reports have found that 62.7% of all assaults against elderly people are committed by the caregiving relative other than the spouse (Baltimore Police Department, 1978).

THE EXTENT OF ELDER ABUSE

It is clear why there are difficulties in assessing the prevalence of elder abuse. Elderly people are not involved in social networks such as schooling or employment. They are, on average, even more isolated from the mainstream of society than younger adults. Victims are also unwilling to report maltreatment. Only one in four known cases of abuse are reported by the victims themselves (Legal Research and Services for the Elderly, 1979).

According to Gelles and Cornell (1985), there are several reasons why the elderly are reluctant to report their abuse. They may be too embarrassed to admit to having raised a child capable of such behaviour (assuming that a son or daughter is involved). They may also assume the blame for the abuser's behaviour, a trait that is also common in wife- and child-abuse victims. Often the love for the abuser is stronger than the desire to leave. Despite these difficulties, it is estimated that 7% of the elderly US population are abused

(Pierce and Trotta, 1986). Indeed, Press (1979) has reported that at least 500 000 elderly persons aged 65 or over who live with younger members of their families are physically abused each year in the United States. Block and Sinnott (1979) place the figure closer to one million victims annually. Although there are no reliable estimates for the UK, both Renvoize (1978) and Freeman (1979) suggest that 'granny bashing', as they call it, may be increasing as a result of the rise in numbers of elderly dependent individuals in UK society. This is especially true for very elderly people (i.e. aged 75 or over), many of whom are mentally infirm and/or physically disabled (see Browne, 1984). The economic and social burden of caring for these old people has fallen increasingly on the relatives, with more than 50% living with their immediate families (DHSS, 1978). The stress of increased caregiving responsibility within the family and the resulting problems, such as relatives resenting the unwanted intrusion into their lives of 'granny sitting', places a heavy strain on family relationships (Renvoize, 1978). Indeed, in a study of 50 adults who had parents living with them, 75% reported a variety of familial difficulties due to their parents ageing (Simos, 1976). Pierce and Trotta (1986) report that it is this stress, associated with caring for the elderly relative, which is the precipitating factor for violence in the majority of cases (63%).

CAUSES OF VIOLENCE AGAINST ELDERLY RELATIVES

The causes of elder abuse are similar to wife abuse in that they are multifactorial. Bolton and Bolton (1987, pp. 38–9) have demonstrated that most of the situational and structural stressors associated with spouse abuse are relevant also to elder abuse. In addition, psychopathological explanations, such as psychiatric illness and alcoholism, have been associated with elder abuse (Brennan, 1977; Falcioni, 1982; Douglas and Hickey, 1983). Furthermore, social learning explanations of elder abuse have been suggested where the carer has experienced abuse as a child, especially if it was at the hands of the now-aged parent (Rathbone-McCuan, 1980; Anderson, 1981; Steinmetz, 1983). The irony is that violence may be revisited upon the perpetrator by previous victims, due to the intergenerational transmissions of aggressive responses to stress and frustration.

Indeed, there is evidence for this reversed cycle of violence. Children treated violently have been estimated to have a one in two chance of becoming abusive towards their parents, while those who had non-violent childhood experiences have a one in 400 probability of parent abuse (US Congress Select Committee on Aging, 1981). Gelles and Cornell (1985, p. 104) state that '. . . the abuser is typically identified as being female, middle aged and usually the offspring of the abused'. However, the abuser may also be an in-law or even a grandchild (Steinmetz, 1983).

The dependent status of an elderly relative in the family has led to elder abuse being highly associated with child abuse (see Bolton and Bolton, 1987). However, there are some distinct differences.

The knowledge that children gradually become increasingly less dependent as they grow older can be a source of relief to their parents. The care of the elderly contrasts sharply with this: as they grow older they are likely to become more demanding and more dependent (Galbraith and Davison, 1985). The elderly person may be extremely difficult to handle, but more often the stress and frustration is related to the caregivers' unwillingness to devote themselves entirely to that person. This happens frequently where a daughter feels acute distress at having to look after an aged parent, when perhaps for the first time since her own children have grown up, she is seeking self-fulfilment as a woman beyond the family boundaries.

The family needs external resources such as 'day centres' and 'home-helps' to alleviate the intense care of an elderly relative for a number of hours each day. Together with a secure and supportive spouse relationship (itself a buffer to stress, see Figure 6.1), the possibility of elder abuse will be considerably reduced.

PREVENTION AND TREATMENT

Primary Preventions of Fundamental Change

Recent overviews of the causes and consequences of elder abuse (Kosberg, 1983; Douglas, 1983; Zdorkowski and Galbraith, 1985) suggest that primary interventions should be concerned with the maintaining of rights, safety and health of elderly individuals, and the reformulation of 'ageist' attitudes in our society. Furthermore, Giordano and Giordano (1984) assert that changes in health and social policy could reduce elder abuse.

At present, services to the elderly focus on those who live alone without family support and those in institutions. It is now necessary to acknowledge the family's contribution to care of the elderly and to provide services that support and enhance their role. Such services include home nursing, day and residential care as a respite for the caregivers. The provision of these services is increasingly important with the demographic changes in population (see Selby and Schechter, 1982).

Secondary Prevention of Prediction and Identification

Elderly people who have undergone abuse are often admitted to hospital with physical injuries which are attributed to falls. Such injuries are treated without suspicion. Thus there is a real need for screening to identify elderly people that are potentially or actually victims of abuse (Rathbone-McCuan and Voyles, 1982).

Case histories which describe elderly abuse appear to associate 16 factors with the problem (Eastman, 1984, 1989). These are listed in Table 6.5. Eastman (1989) claims that an accumulation of these factors can provide a useful guideline to evaluating families at risk of elder abuse.

Table 6.5   Factors associated with elder abuse (Eastman, 1989)

(1)   Physical and/or mental dependency on a 'key member of the family'—the caregiver.
(2)   Poor or negative communication between the elderly dependant and caregiver.
(3)   The caregiver is responsible for the support of 'another' member of the family (e.g. husband, dependant, child, etc.).
(4)   The caregiver makes repeated visits to the general practitioner.
(5)   Frequent periods of hospitalization of the elderly dependant, history of falls, facial bruising.
(6)   Vague explanations given by either the caregiver or elderly dependant.
(7)   Cramped living conditions.
(8)   The elderly dependant has cared for the caregiver in the past (role reversal).
(9)   The presence of a triggering behaviour or condition of the elderly dependant (e.g. incontinence, spitting). The 'trigger' can be almost anything that produces a sense of anger or rage in the caregiver.
(10)   Low self-esteem of the caregiver.
(11)   The dependency of the elderly person is perceived by the caregiver as 'childlike'.
(12)   The caregiver is experiencing multiple stress (e.g. marital conflict, financial problems, etc.).
(13)   The caregiver has a history of mental ill health.
(14)   Unemployment of either caregiver or significant other in the family.
(15)   Drinking problems of either caregiver or dependant.
(16)   Poor or inadequate social health provision.

Assessment procedures

There are only a few assessment procedures specifically designed to evaluate the potential of elder abuse (e.g. Ferguson and Beck, 1983). In addition, techniques such as the Communication Skills Test would be useful in assessing the elderly person's relationship with the caregiver. However, it is most important to assess the mental ability of the elderly relative (Bolton and Bolton, 1987), as impairment severely affects the quality and quantity of social interaction to and from caregivers (Armstrong-Esther and Browne, 1986).

Tertiary Preventions of Treatment and Control

The most frequent form of tertiary intervention is the removal of the elderly relative from the family and family counselling, although a high proportion of elder abuse is 'ignored' by the police and social services and goes unreported (Eastman, 1989).

A pioneering venture has been the establishment of a refuge in Liverpool to support elderly victims of violent assault (Melville, 1987). Nevertheless, the psychological treatment of elder abuse is still in its infancy. Family therapies have concentrated on educational issues about elderly care rather than therapeutic issues. It has been suggested that the main problem in elder maltreatment is not abuse but neglect, which is a result of not knowing how to cope emotionally or functionally with a dependent elderly relative (Steinmetz, 1984). Therefore families must be trained for these responsibilities (Hooyman, 1983; Bolton and Bolton, 1987). The research into anger control has yet to be applied to elder abuse, but it certainly has implications, as many relatives claim that their elderly dependants 'deliberately' provoke them (Eastman, 1989).

CONCLUSION

In summary, elder abuse is strongly associated with stress and frustration of the caregiver, particularly those stressors brought about by the elderly person's increasing age and continual presence at home. In violent families, battered wives and their abusive husbands (and vice versa) are under considerable stress from multiple sources. At the same time, they are deficient in coping skills that might buffer the impact of these stresses, which, in turn, promotes violent control of the social and physical environment. The motives behind marital rape may be slightly different, but this also demonstrates power and anger on the part of the husband, which may be a result of stressful problems associated with his own sexuality.

Family violence should be viewed as a whole, and not merely as the sum of its individual categories. This will help us to understand the intergenerational pattern of family violence and render it less resistant to attempts at intervention. At present, family violence is protected by the societal norms which support the sanctity and privacy of the family and is shrouded in fear and secrecy. Rather than condemn all violent acts, the law and social policy attempts to discriminate between socially acceptable 'normal' violence and unacceptable 'abusive' violence. This has confounded most attempts to deal with this pervading problem.

One clear distinction can be made between elder abuse and neglect and spouse violence. Stopping elder abuse must involve the promotion of safe dependence for elderly relatives, whereas stopping spouse abuse must entail the promotion of safe independence for women.

References

Abidin, R. (1983). *Manual of the Parenting Stress Index (PSI)*, Charlottesville, VA: Psychology Press.

Anderson, C. L. (1981). Abuse and neglect among the elderly. *Journal of Gerontological Nursing*, **7**(2), 283–94.

Archer, J., and Browne, K. D. (1989a). Concepts and approaches to the study of aggression. In J. Archer and K. D. Browne (eds), *Human Aggression: Naturalistic Approaches*, London: Routledge.

Archer, J., and Browne, K. D. (1989b). Naturalistic approaches and the future of aggression research. In J. Archer and K. D. Browne (eds), *Human Aggression: Naturalistic Approaches*, London: Routledge.

Arias, I., and O'Leary, K. (1984). Factors for moderating the intergenerational transmission of marital aggression. *Proceedings of the 18th Annual Convention of the Association for Advancement of Behaviour Therapy*, Philadelphia (cited in Arias *et al.*, 1987).

Arias, I., Samios, M., and O'Leary, K. (1987). Prevalence and correlates of physical aggression during courtship. *Journal of Interpersonal Violence,* **2**(1), 82–90.

Armstrong-Esther, C. A., and Browne, K. D. (1986). The effect of mental impairment on nurse–patient interaction in the elderly. *Journal of Advanced Nursing,* **11**, 379–87.

Ashby, J., and Pizzey, E. (1974). *Women's Aid and the Problem of Battered Women,* London: Chiswick Women's Aid.

Ball, M. (1977). Issues of violence in the family casework. *Social Casework,* **58**, 3–12.

Ball-Rokeach, S. J. (1980). Normative and deviant violence from a conflict perspective. *Social Problems,* **28**(1), 45–62.

Baltimore Police Department (1978). *Report on Assaults Against Elderly People* (cited in Block, 1983; Gelles, 1987a).

Bandura, A. (1973). *Aggression: A Social Learning Analysis,* Englewood Cliffs, NJ: Prentice-Hall.

Barling, J., O'Leary, K., Joumiles, E., Vivian, D., and McEwen, K. (1987). Factor similarity of the conflict tactics scales across samples, spouses and sites: issues and implications. *Journal of Family Violence,* **2**(1), 37–54.

Barling, J., and Rosenbaum, A. (1986). Work stressors and wife abuse. *Journal of Applied Psychology,* **71**, 346–8.

Bayles, J. A. (1978). Violence, alcohol problems and other problems in disintegrating families. *Journal of Studies on Alcohol,* **39**(3), 551–3.

Beech, R. (1985). *Staying Together: A Practical Way to Make Your Relationship Succeed and Grow,* Chichester: Wiley.

Berk, R. A., and Newton, P. J. (1985). Does arrest really deter wife battery? An effort to replicate the findings of the Minneapolis spouse abuse experiment. *American Scoiological Review,* **50**, 253–62.

Berk, R. A., Newton, P., and Berk, S. (1986). What a difference a day makes: an experimental study of the impact of shelters to battered women. *Journal of Marriage and the Family,* **48**(3), 481–90.

Bernard, J., and Bernard, M. (1984). The abusive male seeking treatment: Jekyll and Hyde. *Journal of Applied Family and Child Studies,* **33**(4), 543–7.

Bernard, M., and Bernard, J. (1983). Violent intimacy: the family as a model for love relationships. *Family Relations,* **32**, 283–6.

Binney, V., Harkell, J., and Nixon, J. (1981). *Leaving Violent Men,* London: National Women's Aid Federation.

Bland, R., and Orn, H. (1986). Family violence and psychiatric disorder. *Canadian Journal of Psychiatry,* **31** (March), 129–37.

Block, M. R. (1983). Special problems and vulnerability of elderly women. In J. I. Kosberg (ed.), *Abuse and Mistreatment of the Elderly,* Boston, MA: CSG.

Block, M. R., and Sinnott, J. (1979). *Battered Elder Syndrome: An Exploratory Study,* College Park: University of Maryland Center on Aging (cited in Gelles and Cornell, 1985; Gelles, 1987a).

Bolton, F. G., and Bolton, S. R. (1987). *Working with Violent Families: A Guide for Clinical and Legal Practitioners,* Beverly Hills, CA: Sage.

Borkowski, M., Murch, M., and Walker, V. (1983). *Marital Violence,* London: Tavistock.

Boss, P. (1988). *Family Stress Management,* Beverly Hills, CA: Sage.

Brand, P. A., and Kidd, A. H. (1986). Frequency of physical aggression in heterosexual and female homosexual dyads. *Psychological Reports,* **59**, 1309–13.

Brennan, K. W. (1977). 'Granny bashing.' *Nursing Mirror,* 22 December.

Browne, K. D. (1984). Confusion in the elderly. *Nursing,* **2**(24), 698–705.

Browne, K. D. (1986). Methods and approaches to the study of parenting. In W. Sluckin and M. Herbert (eds), *Parental Behaviour,* Oxford: Blackwell, pp. 344–73.

Browne, K. D. (1989). The naturalistic context of family violence and child abuse. In J. Archer and K. Browne (eds), *Human Aggression: Naturalistic Approaches,* London: Routledge.

Browne, K. D., and Saqi, S. (1987). Parent–child interaction in child abusing families: possible causes and consequences. In P. Maher (ed.), *Child Abuse: An Educational Perspective*, Oxford: Blackwell, pp. 77–103.

Browne, K. D., and Saqi, S. (1988). Approaches to screening families' high risk for child abuse. In K. D. Browne, C. Davies and P. Stratton (eds), *Early Prediction and Prevention of Child Abuse*, Chichester: Wiley.

Browning, J., and Dutton, D. (1986). Assessment of wife assault with the Conflict Tactics Scales: using couple data to quantify the differential responding effect. *Journal of Marriage and Family*, **48**, 375–9.

Capara, G., Cinanni, V., D'Imperio, G., Passerini, S., Renzi, P., and Travaglia, G. (1985). Indicators of impulsive aggression: present status of research on irritability and emotional susceptibility scales. *Personality and Individual Differences*, **6**(6), 665–74.

Carlson, B.E. (1977). Battered women and their assailants. *Social Work*, **22**, 455–60.

Carroll, J. C. (1977). The intergenerational transmission of family violence: the long term effects of aggressive behaviour. *Aggressive Behaviour*, **3**, 289–99.

Cate, R. M., Henton, J. M., Koval, J., Christopher, F., and Lloyd, S. (1982). Premarital abuse: a social psychological perspective. *Journal of Family Issues*, **3**, 79–90.

Cloke, C. (1983). *Old Age Abuse in the Domestic Setting: A Review*, England: Age Concern. (Cited in Eastman, 1989.)

Coleman, K. H. (1980). Conjugal violence: what 33 men report. *Journal of Marital and Family Therapy*, **6**, 207–13.

Curtis, L. (1974). Criminal violence. In *National Patterns and Behaviour*, Lexington, MA: Lexington Books.

Davies, L. V. (1984). Beliefs of service providers about abused women and abusing men. *Social Work*, **29**(3), 230–6.

Davis, L. V., and Carlson, B. E. (1987). Observation of spouse abuse: what happens to the children?. *Journal of Interpersonal Violence*, **2**(3), 320–45.

De Maris, A. (1987). The efficacy of a spouse abuse model in accounting for courtship violence. *Journal of Family Issues*, **8**(3), 291–305.

Deal, J. E., and Wampler, J. E. (1986). Dating violence: the primacy of previous experience. *Journal of Social and Personal Relationships*, **3**, 457–71.

Department of Health and Social Security, UK (1978). *Elderly at Home*, London: HMSO.

Deschner, J. P., and McNeil, J. S. (1986). Results of anger control training for battering couples. *Journal of Family Violence*, **1**(2), 111–20.

Dietz, C. A., and Craft, J. L. (1980). Family dynamics of incest: a new perspective. *Social Casework*, **61**, 602–9.

Dobash, R. E., and Dobash, R. P. (1979). *Violence Against Wives: A Case Against Patriarchy*, London: Open Books.

Dobash, R. E., and Dobash, R. P. (1987). Violence towards wives. In J. Orford (ed.), *Coping with Disorders in the Family*, Surrey: Guildford Press, pp. 169–93.

Dobash, R. E., Dobash, R. F., Cavanagh, K., and Wilson, M. (1978). Wifebeating: the victims speak. *Victimology*, **2**(3/4), 608–22.

Dobash, R. E., Dobash, R. P., and Cavanagh, K. (1985). The contact between battered women and social and medical agencies. In J. Pahl (ed.), *Private Violence and Public Policy*, London: Routledge and Kegan Paul.

Douglas, R. L. (1983). Domestic neglect and abuse of the elderly: implication for research and services. *Family Relations*, **32**, 395–402.

Douglas, R. L., and Hickey, (1983). Domestic neglect and abuse of the elderly: research findings and a systems perspective for service delivery planning. In J. I. Kosberg (ed.), *Abuse and Maltreatment of the Elderly: Causes and Interventions*, Boston, MA: J. Wright.

Dutton, D. G. (1987). The criminal justice response to wife assault. *Law and Human Behaviour*, **11**(3), 189–206.

Eastman, M. (1984). *Old Age Abuse*, England: Age Concern.

Eastman, M. (1989). Old age abuse. In J. Archer and K. D. Browne (eds), *Human Aggression: Naturalistic Approaches*, London: Routledge.

Edleson, J. L. (1984). Working with men who batter. *Social Work*, **29**(3), 237–42.

Edleson, J. L., Eisikovits, Z., and Guttmann, E. (1985a). Men who batter women. *Journal of Family Issues*, **6**(2), 229–47.

Edleson, J. L., Miller, D. M., Stone, G. W., and Chapman, D. G. (1985b). Group treatment for men who batter. *Social Work Research and Abstracts*, **21**(3), 18–21.

Edmunds, G., and Kendrick, D. C. (1980). *The Measurement of Human Aggressiveness*, Chichester: Ellis Horwood (Wiley).

Ewing, C. P. (1987). *Battered Women who Kill: Psychological Self-defense as Legal Justification*, Lexington, MA: Lexington Books.

Fagen, J. A., Stewart, D. K., and Hansen, K. V. (1983). Violent men or violent husbands? In D. Finkelhor, R. Gelles, M. Straus and G. Hotaling (eds), *The Dark Side of the Family: Current Family Violence Research*, Beverly Hills, CA: Sage, pp. 49–67.

Falcioni, D. (1982). Assessing the abused elderly. *Journal of Gerontological Nursing*, **8**(4), 208–12.

Faulk, M. (1974). Men who assault their wives. *Medicine, Science and Law*, **14**, 180–3 (cited in Roy, 1977, pp. 119–25).

Ferguson, D., and Beck, C. (1983). Half tool for assessment of elder abuse. *Geriatric Nurse* (Sept.–Oct.), 301–4.

Fergusson, D., Horwood, L., Kershaw, K., and Shannon, F. (1986). Factors associated with reports of wife assault in New Zealand. *Journal of Marriage and the Family*, **48**(2), 407–12.

Filsinger, E. (1983). *Marriage and Family Assessment: A Sourcebook for Family Therapy*, Beverly Hills, CA: Sage.

Fincham, F. D., and Bradbury, T. N. (1988). The impact of attributions in marriage: empirical and conceptual formulations. *British Journal of Clinical Psychology*, **27**, 77–90.

Finkelhor, D., and Hotaling, D. (1988). *Stopping Family Violence*, Beverly Hills, CA: Sage.

Finkelhor, D., and Yllo, K. (1982). Forced sex in marriage: a preliminary report. *Crime and Delinquency*, **28**, 459–78.

Finkelhor, D., and Yllo, K. (1985). *License to Rape: Sexual Abuse of Wives*, New York: Holt Rinehart and Winston.

Finn, J. (1985). The stresses and coping behaviours of battered women. *Social Casework*, **66**, 341–9.

Finn, J. (1986). The relationship between sex role attitudes and attitudes supporting marital violence. *Sex Roles*, **14**(5/6), 235–44.

Floyd, F. J., and Markman, H. J. (1984). An economical observational measure of couples' communication skill. *Journal of Consulting and Clinical Psychology*, **52**, 97–103.

Floyd, F. J., O'Farrell, T. J., and Goldberg, M. (1987). Comparison of marital observational measures: the Marital Interaction Coding System and the Communication Skills Test. *Journal of Consulting and Clinical Psychology*, **55**(3), 423–9.

Freeman, M. D. (1979). *Violence in the Home*, Farnborough, Hampshire: Saxon House, p. 237.

Galbraith, M. W., and Davison, D. C. (1985). Stress and elderly abuse. *Focus on Learning*, **11**(1), 87–92.

Gayford, J. J. (1975). Wife battering: a preliminary survey of 100 cases. *British Medical Journal*, **25**(1), 94–7.

Gayford, J. J. (1976). Ten types of battered wives. *The Welfare Officer*, **25**, 5–9.

Gelles, R. J. (1973). Child abuse as psychopathology: a sociological critique and reformulation. *American Journal of Orthopsychiatry*, **43**, 611–21.

Gelles, R. J. (1981). The myth of the battered husband. In R. Walsh and O. Procs (eds), *Marriage and Family, 81.82*, Guildford, Surrey: Dustkin.

Gelles, R. J. (1983). An exchange/social control theory. In D. Finkelhor, R. Gelles, M. Straus and G. Hotaling (eds), *The Dark Side of the Family: Current Family Violence Research*, Beverly Hills, CA: Sage.

Gelles, R. J. (1987a). *Family Violence*, 2nd edition, Beverly Hills, CA: Sage (Library of Social Research No. 84).

Gelles, R. J. (1987b). *The Violent Home*, 2nd edition, Beverly Hills, CA: Sage (Library of Social Research No. 13).

Gelles, R. J., and Cornell, C. P. (1985). *Intimate Violence in Families*, Beverly Hills, CA: Sage.

Gelles, R. J., and Straus, M. A. (1979). Determinants of violence in the family: toward a theoretical integration. In W. B. Burr, R. Hill, F. I. Nye and I. L. Reiss (eds), *Contemporary Theories About the Family*, Volume 1, New York: Free Press, pp. 549–81.

Gerson, L. W. (1978). Alcohol-related acts of violence. *Journal of Studies on Alcohol,* **39**(7), 1294–6.

Gil, D. (1978). Societal violence in families. In J. M. Eekelaar and S. N. Katz (eds), *Family Violence*, Toronto: Butterworths, pp. 14–33.

Giles-Sims, J. (1983). *Wife-beating: A Systems Theory Approach*, New York: Guilford.

Giles-Sims, J. (1985). A longitudinal study of battered children and battered wives. *Journal of Applied Family and Child Studies*, **34**(2), 205–10.

Giordano, N. H., and Giordano, J. A. (1984). Elder abuse: a review of the literature. *Social Work*, **29**(3), 232–7.

Goldstein, A. P. (1983). Behaviour modification approaches to aggression prevention and control. In *Prevention and Control of Aggression: Principles, Practices and Research*, The Centre for Research on Aggression (eds), Syracuse University, New York: Pergamon Press, pp. 156–209.

Goldstein, D. (1983). Spouse abuse. In *Prevention and Control of Aggression: Principles, Practices and Research*, The Centre for Research on Aggression (eds), Syracuse University, New York: Pergamon, pp. 37–65.

Goldstein, D., and Rosenbaum, A. (1985). An evaluation of the self esteem of maritally violent men: family relations. *Journal of Applied and Family and Child Studies*, **34**(3), 425–8.

Goldstein, J. H. (1986). *Aggression and Crimes of Violence*, 2nd edition, Oxford: Oxford University Press.

Gondolf, E. W. (1987). Evaluating programs for men who batter: problems and prospects. *Journal of Family Violence*, **2**(1), 95–108.

Goode, W. J. (1974). Force and violence in the family. In S. K. Steinmetz and M. A. Straus (eds), *Violence in the Family*, New York: Harper and Row, pp. 25–43.

Gully, K. J., and Dengerink, H. A. (1983). The dyadic interaction of persons with violent and non-violent histories. *Aggressive Behaviour*, **9**(1), 13–20.

Hall, R. (1985). *Ask Any Woman*, Bristol: Falling Wall Press.

Hall, R., and Ryan, L. (1984). Therapy with men who are violent to their spouses. *Australian Journal of Family Therapy*, **4**, 281–2.

Hanks, S. E., and Rosenbaum, C. P. (1978). Battered women: study of women who live with violent, alcohol-abusing men. *American Journal of Orthospychiatry*, **47**, 291–306.

Hanmer, J. (1977). Community action, women's aid and the Women's Liberation Movement. In M. Mayo (ed.), *Women in the Community*, London: Routledge and Kegan Paul, pp. 91–108.

Hanmer, J. (1978). Violence and the social control of women. In G. Littlejohn (ed.), *Power and State*, London: Croom Helm.

Hanneke, C. R., and Shields, N. A. (1985). Marital rape: implications for the helping professions. *Social Casework*, **66** (October).

Haskey, J. (1982). The proportion of marriages ending in divorce. *Population Trends,* **27**, London: HMSO.

Helton, A. (1986). The pregnant battered female. *Response to the Victimisation of Women and Children,* **(1)**, 22–3.

Hendricks-Matthews, M. (1982). The battered woman: Is she ready for help? *Social Casework,* **63**, 131–7.

Henton, J. M., Cate, R., Koval, J., Lloyd, S., and Christopher, S. (1983). Romance and violence in dating relationships. *Journal of Family Issues,* **4**, 467–82.

Hooyman, N. R. (1983). Abuse and neglect: community interventions. In J. I. Kosberg (ed.), *Abuse and Maltreatment of the Elderly,* Boston, MA: J. Wright.

Horley, S. (1986). Wife battering: police must act. *Social Work Today,* **17**(39), 22.

Hudson, W., and McIntosh, S. (1981). The assessment of spouse abuse: two quantifiable dimensions. *Journal of Marriage and Family,* **42**, 873–85.

Hughes, H. M., and Barad, J. (1983). Psychology functioning of children in a battered women's shelter: a preliminary investigation. *American Journal of Orthopsychiatry,* **53**(3), 525–31.

Jacob, T. (1987). *Family Interaction and Psychopathology: Theories, Method and Findings,* New York: Plenum.

Jaffe, P., Wolfe, D., Telford, A., and Austin, G. (1986). The impact of police charges in incidents of wife abuse. *Journal of Family Violence,* **1**(1), 37–50.

Jaffe, P., Wolfe, D., Wilson, S., and Zak, L. (1986). Similarities in behaviour and social maladjustment among child victims and witnesses to family violence. *American Journal of Orthopsychiatry,* **56**, 142–6.

Johnson, N. (ed.) (1985). Marital violence. *Sociological Review Monograph,* **31**, London: Routledge and Kegan Paul.

Johnson, T. F., and O'Brien, J. G. (1985). *Elder Neglect and Abuse: An Annotated Bibliography,* New York: Greenwood Press.

Kalmuss, D. (1984). The intergenerational transmission of marital aggression. *Journal of Marriage and the Family,* **46**, 11–19.

Kosberg, J. I. (ed.) (1983). *Abuse and Maltreatment of the Elderly: Causes and Interventions,* Littleton, MA: J. Wright.

Legal Research and Services for the Elderly (1979). Elderly abuse in Massachusetts: a survey of professionals and paraprofessionals. Boston, MA: mimeo (cited in Gelles and Cornell, 1985; Gelles, 1987a).

Levine, E. M. (1986). Sociocultural causes of family violence: a theoretical comment. *Journal of Family Violence,* **1**(1), 3–12.

Levine, E. M., and Kanin, E. J. (1987). Sexual violence among dates and acquaintances: trends and their implications for marriage and family. *Journal of Family Violence,* **2**(1), 55–65.

Levine, M. B. (1975). Interparental violence and its effects on the children: a study of families in general practice. *Medical Science and Law,* **15**, 172–6.

Levinger, G. (1966). Sources of marital dissatisfaction among applicants for divorce. *American Journal of Orthopsychiatry,* **26**, 803–97.

Levinson, D. (1985). On wife-beating and interventions. *Current Anthropology,* **26**(5), 665–6.

Lewis, B. Y. (1987). Psychosocial factors related to wife abuse. *Journal of Family Violence,* **2**(1), 1–10.

London, J. (1978). Images of violence against women. *Victimology,* **2**, 510–24.

Lystad, M. H. (1975). Violence at home: a review of the literature. *American Journal of Orthopsychiatry,* **45**(5), 328–45.

McClintock, F. H. (1978). Criminological aspects of family violence. In J. P. Martin (ed.), *Violence in the Family,* Chichester: Wiley.

McCubbin, H. I., and Patterson, J. M. (1983). Stress: the family inventory of life events and change. In E. Filsinger (ed.), *Marriage and Family Assessment,* Beverly Hills, CA: Sage, pp. 275–98.

Makepeace, J. M. (1981). Courtship violence among college students. *Family Relations*, **30**(1), 97–102.

Makepeace, J. M. (1983). Life events-stress and courtship violence. *Family Relations*, **32**(1), 101–9.

Marsden, D. (1978). Sociological perspectives on family violence. In J. P. Martin (ed.), *Violence in the Family*, Chichester: Wiley, pp. 103–34.

Martin, D. (1976). *Battered Wives*, New York: Pocket Books.

Mazur, A. (1983). Physiology, dominance and aggression in humans. In *Prevention and Control of Aggression: Principles, Practices and Research*, The Centre for Research on Aggression (eds), Syracuse University, New York: Pergamon Press, pp. 145–55.

Meichenbaum, D. (1985). *Stress Innoculation Training*, Oxford: Pergamon Press.

Melville, J. (1987). Helping victims survive. *New Society*, **82**(1297), 18–19, 6 November.

Merrick, J., and Michelsen, N. (1985). Child at risk: child abuse in Denmark. *International Journal of Rehabilitation Research*, **8**(2), 181–8.

Milner, J. S., and Gold, R. G. (1986). Screening spouse abusers for child abuse potential. *Journal of Clinical Psychology*, **42**(1), 169–72.

Moore, D. M. (1979). An overview of the problem. In D. M. Moore (ed.), *Battered Women*, Beverly Hills, CA: Sage, pp. 7–32.

Neidig, P. H., Friedman, D. H., and Collins, B. S. (1986). Attitudinal characteristics of males who have engaged in spouse abuse. *Journal of Family Violence*, **1**(3), 223–33.

Novaco, R. W. (1978). Anger and coping with stress. In J. P. Foreyt, D. P. Rathjen and D. P. Rathjen (eds), *Cognitive Behavior Therapy*, New York: Penguin Books.

O'Brien, J. (1971). Violence in divorce-prone families. *Journal of Marriage and the Family*, **33**, 692–8.

O'Keefe, N. K., Brockopp, K., and Chew, E. (1986). Teen dating violence. *Social Work*, **31**(6), 465–8.

O'Leary, K. D., Fincham, F. D., and Turkewitz, H. (1983). Assessment of positive feelings toward spouse. *Journal of Consulting and Clinical Psychology*, **15**, 949–51.

Orkow, B. (1985). Implementation of a family stress checklist. *Child Abuse and Neglect*, **9**(13), 405–10.

Pagelow, M. D. (1979). Research on women battering. In J. B. Flemming (ed.), *Stopping Wife Abuse*, New York: Anchor Books, pp. 334–49.

Pagelow, M. D. (1982). *Woman Battering: Victims and Their Experiences*, Beverly Hills, CA: Sage.

Pagelow, M. D. (1984). *Family Violence*, New York: Greenwood Press.

Pahl, J. (1978). *A Refuge for Battered Women*, London: HMSO.

Pahl, J. (1985). Violent husbands and abused wives: a longitudinal study. In J. Pahl (ed.), *Private Violence and Public Policy*, London: Routledge and Kegan Paul, pp. 23–94.

Patterson, G. R. (1976). The aggressive child: victim and architect of a coercive system. In L. A. Hamerlynck, E. J. Mash and L. C. Handy (eds), *Behaviour Modification and Families*, New York: Brunner/Mazel.

Persky, H., Smith, K. D., and Basu, G. K. (1971). Relation of psychological measures of aggression and hostility to testosterone production in man. *Psychosomatic Medicine*, **33**, 265–77.

Pierce, R. L., and Trotta, R. (1986). Abused parents: a hidden family problem. *Journal of Family Violence*, **1**(1), 99–110.

Pillemer, K. A., and Wolf, S. (1986). *Elder Abuse: Conflict in the Family*, New York: Auburn House.

Pizzey, E. (1974). *Scream Quietly or the Neighbours Will Hear*, Harmondsworth: Penguin Books.

Pleck, E., Pleck, J., Grossman, M., and Bart, P. (1978). The battered data syndrome: a comment on Steinmetz's article. *Victimology*, **2**(3/4), 680–3.

Press, R. (1979). Battered grandparents: hidden family problem. *Christian Science*

Monitor, 9 (cited in Pierce and Trotta, 1986).

Purdy, F., and Nickle, N. (1981). Practice principles for working with groups of men who batter. *Social Work with Groups*, **4**, 111–22.

Quinn, M. J., and Tomita, S. K. (1986). *Elder Abuse and Neglect: Causes, Diagnosis, and Intervention Strategies*, New York, Springer.

Rathbone-McCuan, E. (1980). Elderly victims of family violence and neglect. *Social Casework*, **61**, 296–304.

Rathbone-McCuan, E., and Voyles, B. (1982). Case detection of abused elderly parents. *American Journal of Psychiatry*, **139**(2), 189–92.

Renvoize, J. (1978). *Web of Violence: A Study of Family Violence*, Harmondsworth: Pelican Books, pp. 128–42.

Roberts, A. R. (1987). Psychosocial characteristics of batterers: a study of 234 men charged with domestic violence offenses. *Journal of Family Violence*, **2**(1), 81–94.

Roscoe, B., and Benaske, N. (1985). Courtship violence experienced by abused wives: similarities in patterns of abuse. *Journal of Applied Family Child Studies*, **34**(3), 419–24.

Rose, P., and Marshall, L. (1985). Gender differences: effects of stress on expressed or received abuse. *Proceedings of the 93rd Annual Convention of the American Psychological Association*, Los Angeles (cited in Arias *et al.*, 1987).

Rosenbaum, A., and O'Leary, D. (1981). Marital violence: characteristics of abusive couples. *Journal of Consulting and Clinical Psychology*, **49**, 63–71.

Roy, M. (1977). A survey of 150 cases. In M. Roy (ed.), *Battered Women: A Psychosociological Study of Domestic Violence*, New York: Van Nostrand Reinhold.

Roy, M. (1982). *The Abusive Partner*, New York: Van Nostrand Reinhold.

Russell, D. (1982). *Rape in Marriage*, New York: Macmillan.

Rutter, M. (1985). Aggression and the family. *Acta Paedopsychiatrica*, **6**, 11–25.

Saunders, D. (1986). When battered women use violence: husband abuse or self-defense? *Violence and Victims*, **1**(1), 47–60.

Selby, P., and Schechter, M. (1982). *Ageing 2000: a Challenge for Society*, Boston, MA: MTP.

Select Committee Report (1975). *Violence in Marriage* (HCP,553,II), London: HMSO.

Simos, G. (1976). Adult children and their aging parents. In J. Davenport and J. A. Davenport (eds), *Social Services and the Aged*, Washington, DC: University Press.

Star, B. (1980). Patterns of family violence. *Social Casework*, **61** (June), 339–46.

Steinfeld, G. J. (1986). Spouse abuse: clinical implications of research on the control of aggression. *Family Violence*, **1**(2), 197–208.

Steinmetz, S. K. (1977a). *The Cycle of Violence: Assertive, Aggressive and Abusive Family Interaction*, New York: Praeger.

Steinmetz, S. K. (1977b). The battered husband syndrome. *Victimology*, **2**(3/4), 499–509.

Steinmetz, S. K. (1978). Battered parents. *Society*, **15**(5), 54–5.

Steinmetz, S. K. (1983). Dependency stress and violence between middle-aged caregivers and their elderly relatives. In J. I. Koberg (ed.), *Abuse and Maltreatment of the Elderly*, Boston, MA: J. Wright.

Steinmetz, S. K. (1988). *Duty Bound: Elder Abuse and Family Care*, Beverly Hills, CA: Sage (Library of Social Research, Vol. 166).

Straus, M. A. (1978). Wife-beating: how common and why? *Victimology*, **2**(3/4), 443–58.

Straus, M. A. (1979). Measuring intrafamily conflict and violence: the conflict tactics scales. *Journal of Marriage and the Family*, **41**, 75–86.

Straus, M. A. (1980). A sociological perspective on causes of family violence. In M. R. Green (ed.), *Violence and the Family*, New York: Bould & Westview, pp. 7–13.

Straus, M. A., Gelles, R. J., and Steinmetz, S. K. (1980). *Behind Closed Doors: Violence in the American Family*. New York: Anchor Press.

Truesdell, D., McNeil, J., and Deschner, J. (1986). Incidence of wife abuse in incestuous families. *Social Work*, **31**(2), 138–40.

Truninger, E. (1971). Marital violence: the legal solutions. *Hastings Law Review*, **23**, 259–76.

US Congress Select Committee on Aging (1981). US House of Representatives. *Elder Abuse: An Examination of a Hidden Problem*, Washington, DC: US Printing Office, Committee Publication No. 97, p. 270.

Valentine, D., and Cash, T. (1986). A definitional discussion of elder maltreatment. *Journal of Gerontological Social Work*, **9**(3), 17–28.

Van Hasselt, V. B., Morrison, R. L., and Bellack, A. S. (1985). Alcohol use in wife abusers and their spouses. *Addictive Behaviours*, **10**, 127–35.

Van Hasselt, V. B., Morrison, R. L., Bellack, A. S., and Hersen, M. (1987). *Families in Trouble: Handbook of Family Violence*, New York: Plenum

Walker, L. E. (1979). *The Battered Woman*, New York: Harper and Row.

Walker, L. E., and Browne, A. (1985). Gender and victimization by intimates. *Journal of Personality*, **53**, 179–95.

Wardell, L., Gillespie, D., and Leffler, A. (1983). Science and violence against wives. In D. Finkelhor., R. Gelles, M. Straus and G. Hotaling (eds.), *The Dark Side of the Family: Current Family Violence Research*, Beverly Hills, CA: Sage, pp. 69–84.

Weiss, R. L., Hops, H., and Patterson, G. R. (1973). A framework for conceptualizing marital conflicts: a technology for altering it, some data for evaluating it. In L. A. Hamerlynck, L. C. Handy and E. J. Mash (eds), *Behavior Change: Methodology, Concepts, and Practice*, Champaign, IL: Research Press, pp. 309–42.

Weiss, R. L., and Summers, K. J. (1983). Marital interaction coding system III. In E. Filsinger, E. (ed.), *Marriage and Family Assessment: A Sourcebook for Family Therapy*, Beverly Hills, CA: Sage, pp. 85–116.

Weissberg, M. (1983). *Dangerous Secrets: Maladaptive Responses to Stress*, New York: W. N. Norton.

Weitzman, J., and Dreen, K. (1982). Wife beating: a view of the marital dyad. *Social Casework*, **63**, 259–65.

Whipple, V. (1985). The use of reality therapy with battered women in domestic violence shelters. *Journal of Reality Therapy*, **5**, 22–7.

Wilson, W., and Durrenberger, R. (1982). Comparison of rape and attempted rape victims. *Psychological Reports*, **50**, 198.

Zdorkowski, R. T., and Galbraith, M. W. (1985). An inductive approach to the investigation of elder abuse. *Ageing and Society*, **5**(4), 413–29.

7

The Physical Abuse of Children

NEIL FRUDE
Department of Psychology, University College, Cardiff, UK

It is now over 25 years since Henry Kempe and his colleagues wrote their classic paper identifying 'the battered child syndrome' (Kempe *et al.*, 1962), and since that time a large amount of research has been conducted to establish the nature of the problem and ways in which child abuse can be predicted, prevented and treated. The extreme behaviour which causes serious injury to the child is rare, and even in abusive families is likely to occur only once or a few times during the child's life. Thus an adequate explanation of the phenomenon of physical abuse is unlikely to focus on stable characteristics such as the parent's personality or social situation, which remain relatively constant over many months or even years. Such characteristics may be associated with an increased risk of injury, but they need to be integrated into a model which ultimately focuses on the abuse *incident*.

The purpose of this chapter is to explore reasons why such incidents occur and to suggest why they have a higher probability in some families than in others. Physical methods of discipline are used in most homes (Gelles, 1979) and the average child is subjected to literally thousands of hits during the period of development. Yet only a few children would be said to be at high risk for abuse. Although there is a degree of probability that almost any child will be injured as a result of a serious parental attack, it is clear that some children are far more at risk than others (Reid *et al.*, 1982). Although there is undoubtedly an element of randomness determining which children eventually suffer injury, certain factors appear to systematically affect the probability that injury will occur. In recent years much more has become known about these factors, and this chapter will review the evidence and examine how they relate to the specific event of child abuse.

In summary, the argument to be presented takes the following form. There is a certain probability that any parent might abuse his or her child, but this

Clinical Approaches to Violence. Edited by K. Howells and C. R. Hollin
© 1989 John Wiley & Sons.

is generally very low. The probability is greatly increased, however, if harsh aggression is frequently directed towards the child. 'Customary high aggression' signals a relatively high probability that the child will one day be injured. The likelihood of serious injury is related not only to the frequency but also to the form of aggression generally used. Thus if punches to the head are customary, the danger of serious injury will be much greater than if customary attacks take the form of slaps to the buttocks.

Taking a further step back in the probability chain, it is possible to identify certain factors which increase the probability of such 'customary high-level agression'. In particular, this seems to be associated with a frequent occurrence of serious disciplinary encounters. If a parent frequently tries, with low success, to control a child's behaviour, such situations may escalate in seriousness so that aggression frequently results.

A further step in the analysis involves examining the antecedents of frequent and difficult disciplinary encounters. A number of factors within the parent–child relationship can be identified as leading to the frequent use of harsh disciplinary practices. Some of these factors involve aspects of the child's behaviour, some involve the parent's general parenting style, and some focus specifically on the style of parent–child interaction during disciplinary encounters. Briefly, the evidence to be presented suggests that the risk of frequent and harsh discipline being used is increased if the child presents more behaviour difficulties, and is more aggressive and less compliant, if the parents are critical, 'blame oriented' and unskilled in child management, and if a distant, unloving and mutually aggressive relationship develops between the parent and child.

This analysis traces the probability chain from the event to be explained back through a series of antecedents. An alternative to such a 'retrospective' presentation of the causal analysis is to trace the chain 'in prospect'. Such an analysis would begin by identifying certain aspects of the parent–child relationship which appear likely to lead to disciplinary problems. It would then consider how such problems might escalate in seriousness and lead to the customary use of dangerous aggression. The analysis might end at this stage, with the final conclusion that if serious aggression takes place frequently there will be a high probability that injury will eventually occur. Alternatively, further analysis could be provided in an attempt to explain why, on a particular day and at a particular time, the extreme and 'particular' event of abuse took place. Such a prospective analysis constitutes the theme for this chapter.

THE PARENT–CHILD RELATIONSHIP

It has become clear that many aspects of parent–child interaction differ in abusing (or 'high risk-for-abuse' families) and non-abusing families (Schindler and Arkowitz, 1986). Comparisons of interaction styles in the two groups indicate significant differences over a wide range of characteristics. Before reviewing the evidence for such differences a number of general points should be noted. One is that abusing (or 'high-risk') families are selected as an 'extreme' group in order to examine potential differences in 'high contrast'.

Results from this method of comparison may tend to reinforce the idea that abusive families are of a special 'type', whereas it is more likely that such families will tend to occupy positions towards one extreme of a continuum. The group comparison method also tends to obscure the fact that different families within either group are likely to differ considerably on any of the characteristics studied. A significant difference between groups does not imply that there is no overlap between the groups on any particular characteristic.

There are also limits to the degree that any characteristic which differentiates the groups can be said to be predictive of abuse. Many families that display the interactive styles which characterize abusive families may not themselves be abusive. Finally, it must be acknowledged that comparison studies of the type generally undertaken in the abuse field are able to identify only associations between variables. Although there is a natural tendency to conclude that such variables play a causal role in precipitating abuse, for many of the characteristics it is highly plausible to suggest that the particular style of parent–child interaction may have developed as a *result* of abusive, 'quasi-abusive' or 'pre-abusive' actions. It is likely that certain interaction difficulties resulting from previous abusive behaviour may act as causal antecedents for future abusive acts. Most of the studies so far undertaken in this area are able to provide only synchronic accounts of what are undoubtedly long narrative affairs.

The parent brings to the relationship with the child a personal history, a personality, a set of attitudes and expectations and a current lifestyle. The child, too, brings many individual characteristics. The relationship which develops between them, however, emerges in a highly dynamic and interactive way, and each is constantly changing as a result of the other's behaviour. To a large degree, the parenting of any parent reflects the child who is parented. However, the behaviour of the child who is parented largely reflects the parenting which he or she has experienced. However, although the behaviour which occurs between parent and child is essentially interactive, it is often more meaningful to consider certain aspects of such behaviour in terms of parent factors and child factors. This is convenient because it tends to reflect the observer's view of the behavioural topography ('who does what'), but it should not be understood to imply any particular pattern of causal antecedents. A particular aspect of a parent's current parenting style may reflect the child's behaviour more than it reflects the parent's 'original' parental tendencies. Also, the child's behaviour may reflect parenting more than it reflects any 'independent' behavioural tendency.

PARENT CHARACTERISTICS

Absence of Warmth and Positive Responding

The impression gained both from interview studies with parents and from observational studies is that the overall atmosphere in such families often lacks warmth. For example, Reid (1983) found that observers who watched abusive parents interacting with their children judged that these parents enjoyed their children significantly less than non-abusive parents. Many abusive parents show few positive behaviours towards the child. Various studies reviewed by Kelly (1983) indicate that such parents exhibit low rates of positive behaviours such as showing physical affection and praising good behaviour. Fontana and Robison (1984) found that abusing mothers spent less time looking at their children and focused less attention on them, and Starr (1980) stated that abusive parents touched their children less often than controls. Burgess and Richardson (1984) and Starr (1980) noted a low rate of general verbal interchanges, and Bousha and Twentyman (1984) found that abusive mothers expressed approval of their children less often. Reid (1983) found that abusive parents reported significantly less playful teasing and less humour in their interactions with the child than did non-abusive parents.

Non-contingent and Negative Responses

It thus seems that abusive parents tend to exhibit a general low level of child-directed or child-responsive behaviour. In addition, many studies indicate that the behaviour which parents do direct towards the child is often inappropriate and negative in tone. Burgess and Conger (1978) found that whereas abusive mothers displayed 40% fewer positive behaviours (including 'affection' and 'supportive comments'), they displayed an average 60% higher rate of negative actions (e.g. complaints and threats), compared to non-abusive mothers. They found that abusive mothers made significantly more disapproving comments and expressed more dislikes about their child. Fontana and Robison (1984) found that when abusive parents engage in lively interactions they tend to bombard the child with questions, demands and orders, and ignore the child's own initiatives. These authors suggest that such behaviour indicates that these mothers are unable to view the child as a separate being, and take little account of the child's own desires and feelings in their attempts to control the child's behaviour.

Lack of Empathy and Negative Bias

A lack of empathy by abusing parents has also been revealed by the research findings of Letourneau (1981) and of Fraiberg et al. (1975), who suggest that the low empathy may be a consequence of the abusive parent's own history of being abused as a child. Lack of empathy or insight may be one reason why abusive parents often fail to respond positively to their children, but another reason may be a definite bias against, and dislike of, the child. There is now good evidence that many abusing parents do have such a negative bias in their perceptions and attributions of their children's behaviour (e.g. Lorber et al., 1982; Mash et al., 1983). It seems that many aspects of the child's behaviour are disapproved of, and that many are experienced as aversive. It appears that abusive parents may have both a specific dislike for the abused child and a general aversive tendency towards many of the behaviours which all children exhibit. The view that there may be a specific bias against the abused child is supported by the results of a study by Herrenkohl and Herrenkohl (1979). They measured abusing parents' attitudes towards 295 abused children and their 284 non-abused siblings, and found that the abused children were seen more negatively than the siblings and were described by the parents in mostly negative terms.

Aversion to Child Behaviours

On the other hand, several other studies suggest that many abusing parents may also have a very generalized aversion to a wide range of normal child behaviours. A number of studies have shown that abusing parents tend to become physiologically aroused and stressed when viewing videotapes of even quite innocuous child and infant behaviour. In an early study of this type, Disbrow et al. (1977) compared the responses of abusing, neglecting and normal parents to videotapes of positive, neutral and negative family interactions. Physiological assessment showed that whereas the heart rate of non-abusing parents varied with the type of action they were observing, abusing and neglecting parents demonstrated little variation and were generally more aroused throughout the whole session.

Similarly, Frodi and Lamb (1980) showed videotapes of infants crying and smiling while monitoring physiological responses, and then asked the women to describe their feelings. They found that abusive mothers tended to respond somewhat aversively not only to the crying but also to the smiling infants, and that these mothers often described their reaction to crying infants in terms of anger and annoyance. In another study, Wolfe et al. (1983) asked abusive and non-abusive parents to rate the stressfulness of a number of scenes of child behaviour. These workers, too, found that abusive parents responded with relatively high levels of arousal not only to stressful scenes but also to those scenes which had been included as 'non-stressful'.

Criteria for Judging Behaviour as 'Bad'

There is now abundant evidence from research studies to support the view that abusive parents fail to discriminate accurately between positive and negative child behaviours. For example, Wood-Shuman and Cone (1986) showed abusive, at-risk and control mothers videotapes of children aged from 6 months to 7 years in various situations (e.g. child refusing a command, child crying, child refusing to go to bed, child playing quietly). The results indicated that abusive mothers tended to rate even innocuous child behaviour as negative. The authors described the mothers as 'blame oriented', and suggested that having been abused oneself might lead to an inappropriate classification of behaviours as 'good' and 'bad', with 'bad' being used to label a very wide category of behaviours. They further suggested that mothers who were relatively isolated had few opportunities for learning how to classify behaviours, and to acquire normal expectations of the child.

Wolfe et al. (1983) also found that abusive parents judged a broad range of child behaviours to be 'bad'—'thus increasing the number of child behaviours that might set the occasion for aversive responding'. Wahler and Dumas (1984) showed videotapes of child behaviour to mothers who were experiencing child-management problems and found that they tended to rate as 'problematic' certain behaviours which trained observers saw as innocuous. Thus the mothers who reported management problems seemed to be responding to a wider range of child behaviour as 'calling for disciplinary intervention'.

Thus abusing parents appear not to discriminate accurately between positive and negative child behaviours but, rather, to react to a broad range of child behaviours as though they were negative. This is evident both in their physiological responses (many child behaviours seem to act as aversive stimuli) and in their cognitive processing (they judge many innocuous behaviours to be 'bad'). As a result of these twin processes, a large number of actions of the child are likely to be seen as calling for disciplinary intervention.

Unrealistic Expectations and Standards

One reason why abusive parents may judge their own child's behaviour to be 'bad' or negative may be that they have inappropriately high standards and an unrealistic appraisal of developmental norms. Sometimes, for example, such parents have somewhat bizarre notions about how clean, or tidy or obedient children generally are, and judge their own child's 'normal' behaviour as exceptional and blameworthy. Research shows that abusing parents tend to have extremely high expectations of their children in terms of both their obedience and their achievement levels.

Steele and Pollock (1968) suggested that abusive parents make excessive demands on their infants and expect them to perform tasks which are beyond the ability of the child and beyond their level of comprehension. In their study they found major differences between the abusive and control group parents in their level of expectations of the child's behaviour. Abusive parents had unrealistically high standards and inappropriate judgements of the age-related capabilities of children. Thus behaviours which were in fact age-appropriate for the child tended to be judged by these parents as 'regressive'. Several more recent studies have also shown abusing mothers to have unrealistic expectations of the child and to apply standards of neatness, cleanliness, good manners, etc. which are unrealistically high (e.g. Azar et al., 1984; Rosenberg and Repucci, 1983; Twentyman and Plotkin, 1982).

Stable, Internal Attributions

When a child is judged to be doing something 'naughty' or 'bad', the emotional impact and the parent's response to the misdemeanour will largely reflect assumptions about *why* the child is misbehaving. Parents differ considerably in making such attributions. Golub (1984) found that abusive mothers were more likely to see misbehaviour as caused by stable factors that would continue to cause problems throughout the child's development. They were also more likely to see the child as misbehaving intentionally, and as acting in order to harass the parent. Call (1984) provides examples of how ordinary child behaviours may be interpreted by parents in negative ways. Using the phrase 'the semantics of crying', he describes how the meaning attributed to cries reflects the parents' mythology, and their projections of motives, wishes and feelings. He suggests that thumbsucking is often interpreted by the parent as a sign of unacceptable immaturity, that normal biting responses may be seen as symptoms of hostile aggression and that the turning away from the breast or bottle may be regarded as an act of defiant disobedience. In an early analysis of abuse, Steele (1970) had similarly suggested that distorted perceptions of the meaning of a cry sometimes elicit aggressive assaults, with the crying infant seen as greedy, poorly behaved, defiant or morally corrupt.

These tendencies towards viewing normal, innocuous and age-appropriate behaviours as deviant, aversive and regressive will all tend to increase the number of occasions on which the parent believes that discipline is needed. They will also tend to increase anger and the harshness of the punishment given to the child; this is especially the case for perceived intentionality (Golub, 1984).

CHILD BEHAVIOUR

Clearly, abusing parents often experience their children in negative ways. However, although there is a good deal of evidence that many such parents have a somewhat distorted view of the child, it cannot simply be assumed that their negative experiences result entirely from their own perceptual 'biases'. There is a need to consider whether the behaviour of children who are abused is 'objectively' less appealing, more aversive or more 'naughty' than that of other children. An examination of the relevant evidence does in fact indicate that many such children frequently behave in ways which are disturbed and disturbing. While it is certainly possible that some of this disturbance results from a history of parental mishandling and abuse, this fact may be of little relevance when attempting to explain the parent's response. We do not need to establish why such children exhibit disturbed behaviour to note that the abusive parent's characterization of the child may have a veridical basis. Another way of asserting that the causal aspect is not highly pertinent here would be to say that the significance of the child's disturbed behaviour, for the parent, is likely to lie in its manifestation rather than in its aetiology.

Developmental Difficulties

A number of difficulties and behavioural styles exhibited by certain children seem likely to prevent ideal parent–child interaction, and many of these have been positively identified as risk factors in child abuse. Some babies settle comfortably into the arms of the caregiver, whereas others are awkward or 'floppy'. Some babies are more socially responsible (and thus 'rewarding') than others, and some are more easily soothed. It would seem likely that the parent's response to the comfortable, responsible and easily soothed baby would be more positive than to the floppy, unresponsive and 'unsoothable' infant. Such factors have been suggested as important in the context of child abuse. Heinicke (1984), for example, describes differences in 'infant soothability' as being especially relevant.

At-risk infants have a tendency to be less healthy than other children, and have more illnesses in the first year of life (Martin, 1979). They also show decreased muscle tone and significant developmental delays in sensory motor skills (Oates et al., 1979; Schilling and Schinke, 1984).

Behavioural Symptoms

Martin and Beezley (1977) found that older abused children exhibited a number of behavioural symptoms, including tantrums, enuresis, opposition, compulsivity, hypervigilance and pseudo-mature behaviour. Perry and Doran (1983) reported that abused children were more cautious, shy and anti-social. Mental and physical handicap have long been established as important risk factors for abuse (Friedrich and Boriskin, 1976; Starr et al., 1984). On the basis of their review of studies on the behavioural styles of young abused children, Main and Goldwyn (1984) concluded that such children showed an aversive unsympathetic response to the distress of others, and a tendency to isolate themselves. Bousha and Twentyman (1984) found that abused children were less compliant.

The child who is not 'ideal' on objective measures of medical or psychological health is likely not to be seen as 'ideal', and may not provide optimal rewards for the parent. By virtue of their illness, handicap or temperament, such children may not invite or return affection, and they are likely to make extra care demands involving the parents' time, effort and money. The parents may feel less proud of the child than of a 'perfect' child, and the difficulties experienced in dealing with the special difficulties may lead to anxiety, depression, guilt, frustration and anger. As a consequence of the child's problem, the parents may suffer from relative social isolation and their self-esteem may be reduced. Some parents respond to such difficulties by investing extra energy and developing a high positive regard for the child, but many will find it difficult to develop an intense loving response to their 'imperfect' offspring.

Children's Aggression

There is likely to be a special difficulty in responding well to a child who is aggressive and who appears to be hostile towards the caregiver. Once again it is worth noting that, in attempting to explain the parent's 'here and now' response to the aggressive child, the cause of the aggression is largely irrelevant, and it may well be that much of the aggression observed in abused children is the result of their frustration, parental mishandling and modelling.

A high level of aggressiveness would appear to be a dominant characteristic of many abused children. This is evident in parents' reports of their children's behaviour in survey studies and in observations conducted both in clinics and in the home. Patterson (1982) reviewed studies showing that aversive behaviour is reliably higher in abused children, and Main and Goldwyn (1984) concluded from their analysis of studies of young (1–3-year-old) abused children that they had a general difficulty with the control of aggression. Burgess and Conger (1977) found more fighting and conflict among siblings for abused than for non-abused children, and Straus (1983) also showed that abused children exhibited a high degree of aggression towards siblings. Of the children in his sample who were frequently abused by the parents, 76% repeatedly and severely assaulted a sibling during the year studied (compared to 15% of those whose parents used no physical punishment or violence).

Reid et al. (1981) found that youngsters in high risk for abuse families displayed higher rates of both highly aversive behaviours (such as hitting and threatening others) and mildly obnoxious ones (whining and teasing). Correlational analyses show that the more aversive the behaviour shown by the child, the greater the likelihood that the parents would show high rates of aversive behaviour (Reid et al., 1982). Reid (1986, p.243) acknowledges that there is a problem of assigning a causal direction to this finding but draws attention to the implication that 'the more aversive the child, the higher the risk of abusive behaviour by the parent'.

George and Main (1979) found that in a play situation abused children more often hit, slapped and kicked their peers. They also assaulted or threatened to assault their caregivers four times as frequently as controls. Such behaviour could often be described as 'harassment'—an out-of-context behaviour aimed at the discomfiture of the victim. The battered children were seen to harass their caregivers eight times more often than controls, and they were also found to be markedly more avoidant of the friendly overtures of both peers and caregivers. Whereas many of the control children showed sadness, concern or empathy when they observed the distress of a peer, none of the abused infants ever showed any concern or sadness when a peer was distressed. Instead, the abused children tended to respond with disturbed behaviour patterns—fear, anger, physical abuse or a 'puzzling diffuse anger'. Thus in some instances peer distress triggered an aggressive and malicious response.

Children who avoided the mother when she returned to the room after a period of absence tended to show sudden 'inexplicable' bouts of angry behaviour and to attack (or threaten to attack) the mother. Such children, labelled 'mother avoidant', were also found to be avoidant of the friendly overtures of other adults, and Sroufe (1983) reported that such children are often hostile and isolated at school, lack empathy and tend to respond to peer distress maliciously.

Children who are highly aggressive, whatever the origin of this characteristic, would seem especially likely to attract an aggressive response from a parent. For one thing, there is the tendency of behavioural reciprocity—people tend to behave towards another person as that person has behaved towards them; friendliness tends to elicit friendliness and hostility to elicit hostility. There is a tendency to meet force with force. A child's aggression is likely to be seen as calling for a strong, immediate disciplinary action. Also, the child's use of aggression may be interpreted by a parent as justifying an aggressive reprisal.

PARENT–CHILD INTERACTION

It is clear that the rare event of abuse, the discrete incident which leads directly to the injury of a child, is often not an aberrant behaviour which takes place in the context of an otherwise 'normal' parent–child relationship. Relationships between abusing parents and their children are often chronically and seriously disturbed. Although we may isolate, for the purposes of analysis, certain features of this relationship that seem to be the 'parent's contribution' and those that seem to be the 'child's contribution', it is more appropriate to stress the reciprocal and interactive nature of the problem. Gaensbauer et al. (1980) speak of a 'lack of sensitive and contingent reciprocity between mother and infant'. Although it is undeniable that the behaviour of the infant and child is largely shaped by the behaviour of the parents, the notion that each child begins life as a passive tabula rasa has long been discarded. Children are individuals, and their distinct characters have profoundly different effects on their parents.

If we were to attempt to trace the origins of the difficulties in the relationships between abused children and their parents as revealed in these various studies we would need to consider the biological characteristics of the infants, the early life of the parents and the recent and contemporary lifestyle of each parent. Thomas et al. (1970) and others have well documented the fact that there are reliable individual differences in the behaviour of neonates, and Schaffer (1977) and others have shown that such differences have profound effects on the behaviour of the caregiver. Thus the infant acts as a stimulus for the parents' behaviour as well as responding to parental actions. On the other hand, some of the biological factors which help to shape the parent–child relationship will also owe their origin to that relationship. Thus stress on the child may produce somatic symptoms such as psychogenic vomiting and asthma.

Aspects of the parents' contemporary lifestyle and their own childhood history also affect their behaviour (and, thereby, the child's response). Belsky (1987) noted a consistent finding across several research studies indicating that individuals in happier marriages, and those with a supportive network of family and friends, tend to provide more nurturant and less punitive care. Belsky and Isabella (1985) found that predictions about how men and women adjusted to parenthood could be made from both the husbands' and wives' self-reports of their own childhood history.

Main and Weston (1982) found that a mother's apparent rejection by her own mother in childhood was strongly correlated with her own rejection of her infant, and these authors conclude that adverse experiences in childhood may affect cognitive processes in such a way that the mother's rejection of her own children is made more likely. These authors also found, in line with the interactional view, that a mother's rejection is related to the degree to which the infant avoids her following brief separations. They suggest that the mother's rejecting behaviour may lead to the development of a child syndrome of avoidance, hostility and lack of feeling for others, and that such behaviour by the child is likely to further antagonize the mother.

There is clearly a complex story to be told about the antecedents of poor parent–child relationships, but the main concern here is not to consider these antecedents but rather their consequences. If the quality of the relationship is poor then one effect of this may be to create special problems when parent and child are in conflict, and when the parent attempts to control and discipline the child. If the general relationship is poor, if parent and child have little liking for, and little understanding of each other, then such occasions are likely to be fraught with difficulty. The discipline issue is evidently of special importance, for many serious aggressive and abusive incidents arise in the context of disciplinary confrontations.

DISCIPLINE

It is to be expected that disciplinary confrontations will be more frequent and more hostile in families in which the parent–child relationships are poor. Such a relationship will not necessarily produce aggressive and abusive behaviour, but it is likely to increase the frequency of disciplinary confrontations, and these may escalate so that aggressive attacks become relatively common, with a consequent increase in the probability that an injurious incident will occur.

Many of the features which have been shown to characterize the poor parent–child relationship that holds in abusive families will have a special bearing on how disciplinary confrontations are generated and how they progress. Children in such relationships are likely to be more difficult and less compliant than other children. Where the parent–child relationship is poor, the child is likely to be more unsettled, more attention seeking and more aggressive, and his or her behaviour may therefore be more problematic. The parents will be likely to find many aspects of the child's behaviour aversive, and will regard a wider range of behaviours as 'bad' or 'regressive'. They are also likely to blame the child and to make uncharitable attributions about why he or she has 'behaved badly'.

As a result, the parents may frequently see the child's actions as calling for disciplinary action, and there is in fact good evidence of an increased frequency of disciplinary encounters in abusive families. Reid *et al.* (1981), for example, found that parents in high risk for abuse families reported more discipline problems on a daily basis.

ESCALATION OF DISCIPLINARY ENCOUNTERS

Disciplinary Skills

Not only do abusive families engage more frequently in disciplinary encounters but these tend to last longer and to escalate in severity. Again there are a number of contributory factors. It seems that abusive parents tend to be less skilled in discipline management, that abused children are less compliant and less easily controlled, and that a norm of harshness develops in the parents' punishment style.

Reid *et al.* (1981) found that abusive mothers were less successful in terminating the problem behaviour of their children by normal disciplinary means. These authors suggest that this lack of success tends to undermine the abusive mother's confidence that she is able to control the child. The resulting uncertainty then has adverse effects on the development and performance of disciplining skills. In a review of relevant studies, Kelly (1983) also concludes that abusive parents tend to display high rates of ineffective behaviour (for example, failing to notice the child's good behaviour, frequently threatening punishment and issuing many unclear and inconsistent commands). Further evidence of low management skills has been provided by a number of other workers, including Kadushin and Martin (1981) and Herrenkohl *et al.* (1983). Effective discipline involves not only responding to undesirable behaviours but also positively reinforcing good behaviour, and especially compliance. Schindler and Arkowitz (1986) reported that abusive mothers in their sample reinforced compliance significantly less often than controls.

Children are often attention-seeking, and will act in any way that brings social recognition. Thus even 'negative attention' (shouting, threatening, hitting, etc.) may reinforce and strengthen the behaviour it is intended to stop (Miller, 1980; Patterson, 1982), especially if the child receives little other positive attention. Descriptions of abusive families provide evidence that many of these parents do inadvertently reinforce their children's continued misbehaviour (Kelly, 1983).

To some extent, parents develop discipline skills as a result of trial and error. They learn how to control the child by witnessing how he or she responds to various forms of punishment, threat and goading. Thus disciplinary skills are developed during interactions with the child and may reflect the child's response patterns as well as parent behaviours. It has been suggested that abused children may be especially attention-seeking, that they are relatively immune to positive goading and that they are generally low in compliance (Bousha and Twentyman, 1984; Schindler and Arkowitz, 1986). Such children, therefore, may be especially poor in 'training' their parents in effective disciplinary skills.

Parental Anger

The problem with discipline may be amplified by the fact that abusive parents tend to respond more aversively to a disciplinary failure than would other parents facing a similar problem. Reid (1983) asked abusive and non-abusive parents to complete 'discipline report forms' each day. These reports included information about the most significant disciplinary confrontation of the day, and about how much anger had been experienced. Parents in the abusive group reported feeling significantly more angry during a typical discipline confrontation. Abusive parents' increased anger in response to child misbehaviour has also been reported by Frodi and Lamb (1980) and Altemeir *et al.* (1982).

Some of the factors which might help to explain why these parents become more angry have already been identified. They find many child behaviours aversive, for example, and they tend to blame the child inappropriately. However, many of them also face difficulties in other areas of their lives which may also increase their general level of hostility and bitterness. Patterson (1982) showed that depression and other emotional problems decrease the extent to which parents are able to handle discipline problems, and Schinke et al. (1986) point to the role of stress as a trigger for anger and interpersonal violence. These authors also draw attention to the fact that the important stresses which affect day-to-day behaviour are not just the major life events such as bereavement or divorce but also the 'hassles' of everyday life. Some such hassles will stem from the child's behaviour, but some will originate in other areas. If stress and anger are produced by such hassles the child may become the target for the resulting anger. Many case studies of abusive behaviour testify to the importance of such an effect. In a study reported by Scott et al. (1982), for example, careful interviews revealed that most instances of a mother's violent behaviour towards her child occurred when she was angry following heated disagreements with her boyfriend. Wahler (1980) found an increase in troubled parenting on those days when mothers had few (or difficult) extrafamilial interactions. The role of marital conflict in precipitating abuse has been identified by, among others, Reid et al. (1981) and Straus (1980).

It is not surprising that the degree of anger felt by the parent is found to be predictive of the severity of the punishment meted out to the child. Golub (1984) found that the degree of anger reported after child misbehaviour was highly correlated with harshness of the parental response, and Engfer and Schneewind (1982) also found that 'anger-proneness' was predictive of harsh parental punishment.

Harsh Punishment Methods

A large body of evidence supports the view that abusive parents tend to use harsh punishment methods in the normal course of disciplining. Reid (1978) and Patterson (1982) have both reviewed relevant behavioural observation studies, and have drawn the conclusion that the rate of aggressive behaviour is reliably higher in mothers in abusive families (compared with those from non-abusive ones). Among the research reports indicating high rates of aggressive interchanges in child abusive families are those of Burgess and Conger (1978), Reid et al. (1981), Reid (1986), Sandgrund et al. (1975), Bousha and Twentyman (1984) and Lahey et al. (1984).

Reid (1986) reports that abusive mothers are between three and four times as likely to engage in aversive interchanges with their children and, given an aversive interchange, the likelihood that an abusive parent will engage in quasi-abusive child-directed behaviour is five times that of the non-distressed parent. Reid draws attention to the fact that the great majority of aversive episodes are very brief. In his own study, aversive behaviour by mothers usually consisted of a single aversive maternal behaviour, with over 90% of the episodes lasting 11 seconds or less. He did find, however, that the episodes involving abusive mothers tended to last significantly longer than those involving non-abusive mothers.

Why should some parents develop harsh styles of discipline? One relevant factor is the parent's attitude to child control. Several studies have suggested that abusive parents tend to believe that strong discipline is necessary to control a child, and parents who express a positive attitude towards strong punishment also tend to report using stronger types of punishment in the day-to-day disciplining of their children (Frude and Goss, 1979). Studies of the 'desensitizing' effects of exposure to violence (Berkowitz, 1962) suggest that those who are exposed to aggression by parents in their own childhood tend to develop a high personal tolerance of violence. Herrenkohl *et al.* (1983) found that parents who were abused as children and who grew up in stressed families tended to use severe methods of discipline.

The main reason why some parents use harsh disciplinary measures, however, may relate to their history of attempts to discipline the child. Most disciplinary acts are attempts to curtail ongoing behaviour which the parent finds aversive or judges to be 'naughty'—they are attempts to control the immediate situation. If the child stops behaving badly in response to a request or a reprimand then the use of that strategy for bringing about control will be reinforced, and that form of action will tend to be used again. If an action is ineffective, however, then the parent may progress to a harsher means of attempting control, and escalation may continue until an effective action is found. Parents will differ in the rate at which they ascend the 'harshness' hierarchy and in how far they are prepared to go, but the level will also be largely determined by the response of the child. Children differ in their compliance, their sensitivity to different forms of punishment and the speed with which they habituate to mildly aversive disciplinary acts. There may be a tendency to acclimatize to particular forms of punishment. Thus whereas a shout may bring about control on the first occasion, it may prove insufficient later on. Also, because abusive parents are *generally* more punitive, their children may habituate to low-level punitive controls more rapidly, thereby increasing the risk of escalation (Kelly, 1983).

The process by which violence is shaped by the rewards and punishments which follow behaviours has been well described by Patterson (1982). He speaks of a 'coercive' family cycle in which both the parents and the child engage in escalating rates of aversive behaviour towards one another. According to Patterson's Coercion Theory, inconsistent punishment and positive reinforcement for anti-social behaviours will tend to produce an escalation of hostility, and in such a situation, Patterson suggests, both parties will make hostile attributions concerning the other's malevolent intent. The parents' hostility may act as a stimulus to further child misbehaviour, rather than an effective control, and the situation may then become that of a vicious circle which spirals into extreme violence.

Thus certain types of difficult parent–child relationships tend to produce frequent and harsh disciplinary encounters which may become violent. Some of these encounters will escalate to become truly aggressive attacks by the parent on the child. We will therefore turn to examine the particularities of abusive incidents.

DISCIPLINE AND ABUSE

There is now a degree of consensus that abusive behaviour tends to arise in the context of disciplinary encounters. Schindler and Arkowitz (1986) suggest that abusive behaviour is triggered by a series of non-compliant behaviours by the child which frustrate the parent. Physical abusiveness, they suggest, is a coercive attempt to induce compliance, and results from the parents' frustration and an awareness that other attempts at control have proved ineffective. Kelly (1983) also reviewed the relevant evidence, and concluded that child abuse is usually a consequence of a parents' overly harsh and violent approach to child management. Parents who rely on physically punitive controls will, he maintains, have a high probability of injuring the child in the course of discipline. Reid (1986, p.247) drew a similar conclusion, again making much of the probability argument: 'For a parent who reports spanking his or her child on the average of once every three days . . . who makes a practice of using threats in his or her attempts to control the behaviour of the children, it is simply a matter of time before a discipline confrontation will escalate into violence.'

Kadushin and Martin (1981) similarly focus on disciplinary encounters, and describe many instances in which disciplinary encounters had led, through 'chains of escalating coercions to injurious attacks on the child. They found that a large proportion of abusive parents reported that the intent of the attack had been instrumental—an attempt to control the child—and that these parents often regarded their behaviour as a legitimate use of force.

THE AGGRESSIVE/ABUSIVE INCIDENT

So far, we have reviewed factors that may be considered as increasing the risk that an aggressive (or an abusive) attack will be launched on the child. However, a poor parent–child relationship, and harsh disciplinary measures, although they may be considered as 'necessary conditions' for abuse occurring are clearly not 'sufficient conditions'. It has been argued elsewhere (Frude, 1980) that any full understanding of the nature of abuse must include a detailed analysis of the abusive incident itself. A model put forward by the author (Frude, 1980) offers a framework for understanding child-abuse incidents. The model is based on a simple five-stage analysis of aggression (Figure 7.1). This

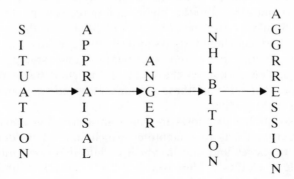

Figure 7.1

is a model of hostile aggression. The distinction is commonly made between hostile and instrumental aggression, but few cases of child abuse are primarily instrumental in nature (Frude and Roberts, 1980).

Briefly, the model can be described in the following way. Aggression incidents are commonly triggered by situational events which are judged by the potential aggressor in such a way that anger results. This anger is then expressed as aggressive behaviour unless there are inhibitions against such aggression.

Following this model, we can see that abusive incidents will be more likely to occur where there are frequent situational triggers (e.g. an infant's prolonged crying or aggressive actions by the child), where the parent tends to judge the child's behaviour as being 'deliberate' or 'bad', where they react with high anger, where they have few inhibitions against acting in a physically aggressive way towards the child and where the type of aggression they engage in is of a serious or dangerous type.

It is clear that much of the evidence reviewed above has implications for one or other of the stages in the model. We will now focus directly on those aspects which are relevant to specific incidents in which the child is attacked.

Situation

In almost all cases of child abuse the attack is triggered by some action of the child. Parents do not attack the passive, sleeping child. Typically, the trigger is prolonged crying or screaming, in the case of babies, or, for older children, some act of defiance or 'naughtiness'. A number of the home observational studies reviewed above found that parents who physically abuse their children experience more misbehaviour from their children than do those who report no problems with child management. At-risk children are more aggressive, less compliant and seek attention through negative behaviours.

Kadushin and Martin (1981) provide a detailed analysis of the process of child abuse. The results of their study with 66 families lead the authors to conclude that the behaviour of children and adolescents contributes to, precipitates and, in some cases, 'causes' abuse: 'In every instance, the chain of interactions which finally culminated in physical abuse begins with some behaviour manifested by the child and perceived by the parent as aversive'(p.148). Similarly, Herrenkohl et al. (1983) studied the records of 328 abusive families, and concluded that physical abuse is associated with the child's behaviour at the time—refusals, fighting and arguing, dangerous behaviour, inconveniences due to the child or the child being perceived as spoiled. They add that most of these circumstances are not unusual in the normal course of child-rearing.

Terr (1970) also quoted examples in which an attack had apparently been precipitated by extreme acts of naughtiness (including an incident in which clothes were cut to pieces and one in which a child defecated into a laundry basket full of clean clothes). Thomson et al. (1971) also found that most abusive incidents are 'provoked' by the child. They mention crying, wetting, refusing to eat and such acts of naughtiness as lying and stealing. Several other authors have also provided evidence that most abuse incidents begin as attempts to control misbehaviours (Mastria *et al.*, 1979; Wolfe and Sandler, 1981; Wolfe *et al.*, 1982).

The presence of a situational trigger is indicated in aggressive incidents at all levels of seriousness. Thus in a survey of non-abusing mothers, Frude and Goss (1979) reported that anger incidents were always associated with some environmental trigger. None of the mothers in this survey reported feeling aggressive towards the child 'for no reason'. In a study of fatal abuse incidents (Scott, 1973), each of 29 imprisoned fathers claimed that his attack on the child had been precipitated by some especially annoying behaviour by that child.

There is, then, a great deal of consensus about the importance of specific trigger events in provoking the abuse incident. If such an event is indeed a 'necessary condition' for abuse occurring then it would follow that preventing the trigger from occurring would prevent the abuse. However, the event which triggers aggression is often of a type so common, and so 'ordinary', that it would be unrealistic to imagine that such triggers could be avoided or eliminated altogether.

Appraisal

The way in which a situation is judged is a major determinant of its emotional impact. A judgement that a baby is screaming 'deliberately', for example, will typically cause much more anger than the view that the baby is crying because of pain. The above review showed that abusive parents' general appraisal style when judging the behaviour of the child tends to be negative. They see many behaviours as 'bad', they are 'blame oriented', they attribute deliberate and malevolent intentions to behaviours and they have unrealistic expectations about young children's capabilites. In addition, they experience many child behaviours as aversive. These tendencies are evident in case reports of specific abuse incidents. Thus one abusive mother told the NSPCC (Baher *et al.*, 1976): 'I couldn't stand to hear a child scream, it went right through me.' Others reported feeling physically nauseous when they saw their child eating messily. One mother, disturbed by her baby's crying during her favourite soap opera on television, felt that the child was 'deliberately' interrupting the programme. In an example from another study, a baby's 'look' was inappropriately interpreted: 'He looks at me as if to say "Just you try and feed me"' (Brandon, 1976). Another mother reported: 'When he cried all the time, it meant he didn't love me, so I hit him' (Steele and Pollock, 1968).

Anger

The tendency to appraise situations negatively will often lead to an angry response. For this reason alone we might expect abusive parents to become more angry than others faced with the same situation. However, there is also evidence that they may have a tendency to be quick-tempered and to flare up when faced with difficulties (Reid, 1983). An angry response to one event may lower the threshold for anger to recur, and anger can accumulate. Case evidence indicates that abuse often occurs on an especially difficult day, when a sequence of events has left the parent in a highly aroused state. An example of this is found in Steele and Pollock's (1968) case of 'Larry':

> After losing his job, Larry told his wife; she immediately walked out on him, leaving him alone with the baby. When the baby started to cry, Larry was unable to find the feeding bottle. Looking everywhere, with the cries of the hungry baby becoming louder and louder, Larry became totally frustrated. Finally, unable to satisfy the baby's hunger, his temper finally exploded and Larry beat the child severely.

Abuse incidents are frequently associated with situations in which the anger threshold is noticeably lowered. Thus in cases of extreme marital tension, pre-menstrual stress and extreme tiredness, abuse appears to be more likely. Case reports suggest that such factors are indeed associated with abuse incidents.

Inhibition

Not all anger is expressed as open aggression. Most people are able to control the aggressive impulse when they feel angry. However, in a review of the characteristics of abusing parents, Parke and Collmer (1975) concluded that one of the most striking and consistent of findings was the general difficulty such parents had in controlling aggression. This, they claimed, is often a general characteristic extending beyond the particular abuse incident.

A low level of inhibition against hitting a child dangerously may stem from particular attitudes about the need for strong discipline. Abusing parents often attempt to justify their use of strong physical punishment by insisting that it is necessary to maintain proper control over the child. They may express the fear that, without strong discipline, the child may 'run amok' or become 'spoilt'. Thus the attitudes of such parents towards discipline may be in line with their habitual use of smacking and their occasional use of abusive methods. If an incident has been triggered by an aggressive action by the child, the parent may feel that 'aggression deserves to be met with aggression'. If they have a history of having been beaten themselves as children, and are relatively isolated from other parents, they may have a false idea of punishment norms. Inhibitions against beating the child may also be lowered by the parent's lack of empathy or sympathy for the hurt the child suffers.

Since abusive parents frequently use highly aggressive behaviour towards the child they become desensitized to such action—their inhibitions are reduced through a habituation-like process. Such a process of escalation has been extensively documented by Patterson, and is also evident in many first-hand reports by parents:

> The first time I hit her it was only a small blow and I cried all the rest of the day. I swore to myself I'd never lift a finger to her again. But it was only a few days after when she drove me mad with her crying and I hit her even harder. It sort of escalated, I hit her a bit harder each time (Renvoize, 1978).

Aggression

Abusive parents tend to use 'dangerous levels' of aggression and dangerous methods. They may model methods on those they experienced themselves in childhood (Gelles, 1979). The level of their aggressive behaviour may also have been shaped by earlier responses of the child, and the level may thus have escalated over time. In a behavioural observation study, Reid *et al.* (1981) found that abusive parents engage in many more *serious* aversive acts towards the child. The high-risk mothers hit their children four times as frequently as non-abusive ones and issued substantially more threats. Overall, both parents in the abusive families exhibited ten times the rate of aversive behaviour towards their children than did non-abusive parents. Reid *et al.* (1982) found that parents who express their anger more openly, as evidenced by yelling, disapproval, humiliation etc., are also likely to demonstrate either quasi- or full-blown abusive behaviours towards their youngsters. In an interview study of the 'normal' punishment styles in child-abusive families, Reid (1983) asked parents how many times they punished their chidren and what types of punishment they employed. The excess of physical discipline reported by abusive parents, compared to controls, was accounted for by their extensive use of the more serious and abusive forms of physical force. Thus observation and self-report data concur in indicating a relationship between child abuse and aversive behaviour by parents on a day-to-day basis.

The precise form of aggression used is very important—it may be a matter of life and death. Several factors seem to influence which form of aggression is used. One of these is *habits*. It seems that parents develop general habits with regard to the method of discipline, and that these are often merely exaggerated in extreme circumstances. Those who habitually use verbal forms may escalate to more extreme ones. Those who slap may slap more harshly. Those who use a stick for the more ritual disciplining may use this later as a deadly weapon. There is some suggestion (Gelles, 1979) that a parent will often use as the preferred means of discipline the method which controlled them in childhood. Several other factors help to shape the form of aggression. Some are 'instrumental' (aggression with a purpose), some represent the execution of a previously made verbal threat and some abusive aggression appears to be symbolic.

Habitual

Parents develop their own forms of aggression. Often these have been shaped by previous responses of the child. Parents find out by a process of trial and error what form of punishment 'works'. In an extreme state the normal type of punishment may be used, but in a more extreme form. Thus if slapping is the normal physical punishment a particularly hard slap may be used in the abuse situation.

Instrumental

Abusive acts are often instrumental in nature (an attempt to stifle a child's screams, for example, or a forceful attempt to feed a child), and may take a dangerous form. A pillow may be held against the face of a screaming child. One mother reported (Baher *et al.*, 1976): 'I put my hand over his mouth to shut him up and suddenly I realized that he'd stopped breathing and was quite limp.' A child who won't eat may be force-fed, a spoon being used as a feeding instrument-cum-weapon, producing broken teeth and bleeding gums.

Threat execution

Verbal threats, even of a bizarre variety, may be used as warnings of dire punishments, and sometimes these threats may be acted upon literally in extreme circumstances. Thus a mother who had threatened to throw her child into a hot oven (presumably, meaning this initially as an empty threat) did just this when extremely provoked (Renvoize, 1974).

Symbolic

Some actions seem to have a symbolic content. Young (1964) reported a case in which pepper was rubbed into the genitals of a little girl who had been 'touching herself'.

Retaliatory

If the child has engaged in some aggressive response towards the parent then the parent may use the same kind of response in retaliation. Epstein (1988) reports the following account by a mother: 'He bit me so I bit him back . . . if he hits me I hit him back . . . he pulled my hair so I pulled it back.'

Opportunist

Sometimes the punishment is meted out with whatever means is to hand, and sometimes the presence of a potentially dangerous weapon can have disastrous consequences. Thus Renvoize (1974) reported a case in which a mother was severely angered by her child while she was ironing. When her anger moved her to act aggressively towards the child she used the hot iron which was to hand and badly burned the child.

IMPLICATIONS FOR TREATMENT

The model developed above has clear implications for the prevention and treatment of physical child abuse. It implies that the problem is multifactorial and heterogeneous, and this suggests that it would be inappropriate to treat all at-risk families in the same way. There is an initial need, therefore, to consider the specific factors within the family which contribute to the high risk.

The model suggests that in many abusive families there are longer-term difficulties with the parent–child relationship, and that if these were to be resolved the risk of abuse would decrease. Several approaches to therapy might prove useful in enriching the parent–child relationship, including family-based and behavioural therapies. The parent could be taught, for example, to monitor his or her level of positive interaction and to increase the frequency with which he or she encourages and praises the child (an excellent overview of behavioural approaches to intervention with abuse-prone families has been provided by Kelly, 1983).

A parent who was found to have an aberrant view of child development (with unrealistic performance expectations, for example) could be provided with a more reasonable and accurate view of the norms for child behaviour through an educational programme. Discussing behaviours with the therapist or with other parents should give parents with special problems a better insight into their children's behaviour, and expose them to alternative interpretations of such behaviour. Other parents, or the therapist, might therefore provide a model of a friendly, close parenting style with a positive and realistic response to children.

Practical steps might also be suggested for reducing the stress of child-care. Skills in handling the child (with sleeping difficulties, or feeding problems, for example) could be taught. With suitable praise for good parenting, the mother or father would be likely to develop a pride in their parenting. The overall stress on the parent might also be decreased by reducing social isolation, and by helping with housing, economic and marital stresses. Parenting stresses could also be reduced by the provision of direct aid through drop-in centres, residential facilities and day-care.

So far, the measures suggested focus on improving the skills of parenting and the satisfaction to be derived from being a parent. The aim is to improve the quality of the parent–child interaction, which is seen as a background to the special difficulties which might produce an abusive attack. Other forms of intervention might be targeted more specifically on such problems.

In order to help with disciplinary situations a number of issues can be addressed in therapy. In cases where a parent finds specific child behaviours highly annoying (or aversive), desensitization or relaxation training might prove effective. Discussion between parents or between parents and the therapist can help to promote a more reasonable categorization of behaviours as 'good' and 'bad'. The effect of these interventions should be to reduce the frequency of disciplinary encounters. Other intervention strategies would focus on increasing the parent's skills in making discipline more effective, so that such encounters are less harsh, less prolonged and less likely to escalate into full-blown abuse. Approaches which focus on such goals are likely to promote consistency in discipline, and to teach specific skills such as the use of 'time out' and the effective employment of attention and attention withdrawal.

Interventions which focus on disciplinary encounters may attempt to change parents' pro-punishmnent attitudes and to deal with any fear that failing to punish a transgression severely will 'spoil' the child. Parents may be told that the frequent use of physical punishment has several disadvantages, having only a temporary effect on behaviour but a detrimental effect on the home atmosphere. Parents could also be made aware of the danger that frequent hitting might also promote a later dangerous escalation.

Finally, the model suggests that injurious abuse might be prevented by therapeutic intervention which is aimed directly at changing the parent's behaviour when there is immediate danger of abuse. The parent could be taught 'emergency tactics' for dealing with such an event. In terms of the incident model advanced above, it can be seen that there are several stages at which such a tactic might prove effective. At the *situation* stage the parent might cope by avoidance (for example, leaving the room in which the child is misbehaving) or by controlling the child's behaviour in some non-abusive manner. At the *appraisal* stage, the parents might use imagery or self-statements to 'defuse' the situational trigger. Thus parents faced with screaming babies may say repeatedly to themselves: 'He is not doing this deliberately; he doesn't understand; all babies behave this way sometimes.' At the *anger* stage there are a number of strategies for promoting self-control (many of which have been documented by Novaco, 1975). These include relaxation, self-distraction, deep breathing, the use of pleasant imagery and directing aggression harmlessly towards inanimate objects.

Inhibitions against expressing anger in an explosive form can be strengthened by calling to mind the dangers of aggression, for either the self (for example, legal action, the child being taken away, or later feelings of guilt) or for the victim. A therapist might inform the parent of the dangers of various forms of abusive action (for example, severely shaking the child may produce diffuse brain damage), so that the parent can use this information to inhibit particular types of behaviour. At-risk parents could also be taught to avoid the use of self-statements which attempt to justify the use of harsh aggression towards the child. Thus if such self-statements as 'he deserves this' or 'he's asked for it' are commonly used by the parent they may be suitable targets for modification. Although the strategies listed here are likely to be effective when part of formal therapy, there is evidence that many parents do use such strategies, with good effect, when they find themselves involved in incidents which might endanger the child (Frude and Goss, 1979).

CONCLUSIONS

Although there is a certain probability that any parent might abuse his or her child this is generally very low. The probability increases substantially if the relationship between the parent and child is poor. A poor relationship is likely to stem partly from parent characteristics, partly from characteristics of the child and partly from specific difficulties in the relationship which develops between parent and child. These difficulties give rise to disciplinary problems, with frequent clashes which tend to escalate in severity. The level of aggression tends to escalate and is likely to result, eventually, in an attack which causes serious injury to the child.

While only a small proportion of interactions between abusive parents and their children are openly hostile, such responses are found much more frequently in the day-to-day interaction between abusive parents and their children than between other parents and their children. Such aggression is evident in both verbal and physical responses. The abusive parents' aggressive responses to their children tend to be more frequent, and stronger, and tend to last longer than those of other parents. These aggressive responses can be seen in terms of responses to situational triggers, the response being amplified by a negative style of appraisal, high anger and low inhibitions against using strong physical methods of discipline and control.

Results obtained from studies that compare groups of abusive and non-abusive families reveal many statistical differences between them. This does not mean, however, that there is no overlap between groups in the levels shown by individuals on the characteristics studied. The results obtained generally reflect quantitative rather than qualitative differences. Thus Main and Goldwyn (1986) caution that abusive parents and children should not be considered 'a breed apart' from parents and children within non-abusive samples, and that entirely new mechanisms need not be brought into consideration with abusive populations. Similarly, Belsky (1987) concludes that 'child abuse and neglect should not be regarded as distinct entities but rather as cases of parenting gone awry which are lawfully related to relationship processes in nondysfunctional families'. Straus (1983, p.231) also emphasized that the same factors are involved in child abuse and 'ordinary physical punishment'—'violence is violence, irrespective of the severity of the attack'.

Thus rather than conceiving of abusive families as a group possessing a set of distinguishing characteristics it is more accurate to regard them as ranged along a continuum of abuse risk. The characteristics reviewed above, therefore, should be regarded as factors associated with the abuse-risk dimension. Even those who can be identified as very high in terms of abuse risk may not actually become involved in an injurious episode, while some of those who do may well have been rated low for abuse risk in terms of those characteristics which distinguish between abusive and non-abusive populations.

References

Altemeir, W.A., O'Connor, S., Vietze, P., Sandler, H., and Sherrod, K. (1982). Antecedents of child abuse. *The Journal of Pediatrics*, **100**, 823–9.

Azar, S., Robinson, D., Hekimian, E., and Twentyman, C.T. (1984). Unrealistic expectations and problem-solving ability in maltreating and comparison mothers. *Journal of Consulting and Clinical Psychology*, **52**, 687–91.

Baher, E., Hyman, C., Jones, C., Jones R., Kerr, A., and Mitchell, R. (1976). *At Risk: An Account of the Work of the Battered Child Research Department, NSPCC*, London: Routledge and Kegan Paul.

Belsky, J. (1987). Child maltreatment and the emergent family system. Paper presented at Conference of the Society for Reproductive and Infant Psychology, Leicester, March.

Belsky, J., and Isabella, R.A. (1985). Marital and parent–child relationships in family of origin and marital change following the birth of a baby: a retrospective analysis. *Child Development*, **56**, 361–75.

Berkowitz, L. (1962). *Aggression: A Social Psychological Analysis*, New York: McGraw-Hill.

Bousha, D.M., and Twentyman, C.T. (1984). Mother–child interactional style in abuse, neglect and control groups: naturalistic observations in the home. *Journal of Abnormal Psychology*, **93**, 106–14.

Brandon, S. (1976). Physical violence in the family: an overview. In M. Borland (ed.), *Violence in the Family*, Manchester: Manchester University Press.

Burgess, R.L., and Conger, R.D. (1977). Family interaction patterns related to child abuse and neglect: some preliminary findings. *Child Abuse and Neglect*, **1**, 269–77.

Burgess, R.L., and Conger, R.D. (1978). Family interaction in abusive, neglectful and normal families. *Child Development*, **49**, 1163–73.

Burgess, R., and Richardson, R. (1984). Coercive interpersonal contingencies as a determinant of child maltreatment. In R.F. Dangel and R.A. Polster (eds), *Parent Training: Foundations of Research and Practice*, New York: Guilford Press.

Call, J.D. (1984). Child abuse and neglect in infancy: sources of hostility within the parent–infant dyad and disorders of attachment in infancy. *Child Abuse and Neglect*, **8**, 185–202.

Disbrow, M.A., Doerr, H., and Caulfield, C. (1977). Measures to predict child abuse. Paper presented at the Biennial Meeting of the Society for Research in Child Development, San Francisco, March.

Engfer, A., and Schneewind, K.D. (1982). Causes and consequences of harsh parental punishment: an empirical investigation in a representative sample of 570 German families. *Child Abuse and Neglect*, **6**, 129–39.

Epstein, C. (1988). *Observational Study of Mother–Infant Dyads*, Unpublished PhD thesis, Brunel University.

Fontana, V.J., and Robison, E. (1984). Observing child abuse. *Journal of Pediatrics*, **105**, 655–60.

Frailberg, S., Adelson, E., and Shapiro, V. (1975). Ghosts in the nursery: a psychoanalytic approach to the problems of impaired mother–infant relationships. *Journal of the American Academy of Child Psychiatry*, **14**, 387–421.

Friedrich, W.N., and Boriskin, J.A. (1976). The role of the child in abuse. *American Journal of Orthopsychiatry*, **46**, 580–90.

Frodi, A.M., and Lamb, M.E. (1980). Child abusers' responses to infant smiles and cries. *Child Development*, **51**, 238–41.

Frodi, A.M., and Smetana, J. (1984). Abused, neglected and nonmaltreated preschoolers' ability to discriminate emotions in others: the effects of IQ. *Child Abuse and Neglect*, **8**, 459–65.

Frude, N.J. (1980). Child abuse as aggression. In N. Frude (ed.), *Psychological Approaches to Child Abuse*, London: Batsford.

Frude, N.J., and Goss, A. (1979) Parental anger: a general population survey. *Child Abuse and Neglect*, **3**, 331–3.

Frude, N.J. and Roberts, W. (1980). *Occasions of Violence: Unit 4 of Open University Course P253*, Milton Keynes: Open University Press.

Gaensbauer, T.J., Mrazek, D.A., and Harmon, R.J. (1980). Emotional expression in abused and neglected infants. In N.J. Frude (ed.), *Psychological Approaches to Child Abuse*, London: Batsford.

Gelles, R.J. (1973). Child abuse as psychopathology: a sociological critique and reformulation. *American Journal of Orthopsychiatry*, **43**, 611–21.

Gelles, R.J.(1979). *Family Violence*, Beverly Hills, CA: Sage.

George, C., and Main, M. (1979). Social interactions of young abused children: approach, avoidance and aggression. *Child Development*, **50**, 306–18.

Golub, J.S. (1984). Abusive and nonabusive parents' perceptions of their children's behaviour: an attributional analysis. Unpublished PhD Dissertation, University of Los Angeles, California.

Golub, J.S., Espinosa, M., Damon, L., and Card, J. (1987). A videotape education program for abusive parents. *Child Abuse and Neglect*, **11**, 255–65.

Halperin, S.M. (1983). Family perceptions of abused children and their siblings. *Child Abuse and Neglect*, **7**, 107–15.

Heinicke, C.M. (1984). The role of pre-birth parent characteristics in early family development. *Child Abuse and Neglect*, **8**, 169–81.

Herrenkohl, E.C., and Herrenkohl, R. (1979). A comparison of abused children and their non-abused siblings. *Journal of the Academy of Child Psychiatry*, **18**, 260–9.

Herrenkohl, R., and Herrenkohl, E.C., and Egolf, B.P. (1983). Circumstances surrounding the occurrence of child maltreatment. *Journal of Consulting and Clinical Psychology*, **51**, 424–31.

Herrenkohl, E.C., Herrenkohl, R.C., and Toedter, L.J. (1983). Perspectives on the intergenerational transmission of abuse. In D. Finkelhor, R.J. Gelles, G.T. Hotaling and M.A. Straus (eds), *The Dark Side of the Family*, Beverly Hills, CA: Sage.

Kadushin, A., and Martin, J.A. (1981). *Child Abuse: An Interactional Event*, New York: Columbia University Press.

Kelly, J.A. (1983). *Treating Child-abusive Families: Intervention based on Skills-training Principles*, New York: Plenum.

Kempe, C.H., Silverman, F.N., Steele, B.B., Droegemueller, W., and Silver, H.K. (1962). The battered child syndrome. *Journal of the American Medical Association*, **181**, 17–24.

Kirkham, M.A., Schinke, S.P., Schilling, R.F., Meltzer, N.J., and Norelius, K.L. (1986). Cognitive–behavioural skills, social supports and child abuse potential among mothers of handicapped children. *Journal of Family Violence*, **1**, 235–45.

Lahey, B.B., Conger, R.D., Atkeson, B.M., and Treiber, F.A. (1984). Parenting behaviour and emotional status of physically abusive mothers. *Journal of Consulting and Clinical Psychology*, **52**, 1062–71.

Letourneau, C. (1981). Empathy and stress: how they affect parental aggression. *Social Work*, **26**, 383–9.

Lorber, R., Reid, J.B., Felton, D., and Caesar, R. (1982). Behavioural tracking skills of child abuse parents and their relationships to famiy violence. Paper presented to Association for the Advancement of Behaviour Therapy, Los Angeles, California.

Main, M., and Goldwyn, R. (1984). Predicting rejection of her infant from mother's representation of her own experience: implications for the abused–abusing intergenerational cycle. *Child Abuse and Neglect*, **8**, 203–17.

Main, M., and Weston, D. (1982). Avoidance of the attachment figure in infancy. In C.M. Parkes, and J. Stevenson-Hinde (eds), *The Place of Attachment in Human Behaviour*, New York: Basic Books.

Martin, H.P. (1979). *Treatment for Abused and Neglected Children*, DHEW Publications (OHDS) 79–30199, Washington, DC, August.

Martin, H.P. (1984). Intervention with infants at risk for abuse or neglect. *Child Abuse and Neglect*, **8**, 255–60.

Martin, H.P., and Beezley, P. (1977). Behavioural observation of abused children. *Developmental Medicine and Child Neurology*, **19**, 373–87.

Mash, E.J., Johnson, C., and Kovitz, K. (1983). A comparison of the mother–child interactions of physically abused and non-abused children during play and task situations. *Journal of Clinical Child Psychology*, **12**, 337–46.

Mastria, E.O., Mastria, M.A., and Harkins, J.C. (1979). Treatment of child abuse by behavioural intervention: a case report. *Child Welfare*, **58**, 253–61.

Miller, K.L. (1980). *Principles of Everyday Behaviour Analysis*, 2nd edition, Monterey, CA: Brooks/Cole.

Novaco, R. (1975). *Anger Control: The Development and Evaluation of an Experimental Treatment*, Lexington, MA: D.C. Heath/Solidus/Lexington Books.

Oates, R.K., Davis, A.A., Ryan, M.G., and Stewart, L.F. (1979). Risk factors associated with child abuse. *Child Abuse and Neglect*, **3**, 547–54.

Parke, R.D., and Collmer, C.W. (1975). Child abuse: an interdisciplinary analysis. In E.M. Hetherington (ed.), *Review of Child Research and Development*, Volume 5, Chicago: University of Chicago Press.

Patterson, G.R. (1974). Retraining of aggressive boys by their parents: multiple settings, treatments and criteria. *Journal of Clinical and Consulting Psychology*, **42**, 471–81.

Patterson, G.R. (1982). *Coercive Family Process*, Eugene, OR: Castalia.

Patterson, G.R., Chamberlain, P., and Reid, J.B. (1982). A comparative evaluation of parent training procedures. *Behaviour Therapy*, **13**, 638–50.

Patterson, G.R., and Reid, J.B. (1973). Intervention in families of aggressive boys: a replication study. *Behaviour Research and Therapy*, **11**, 383–94.

Perry, M.A., and Doran, L.D. (1983). Developmental and behavioural characteristics of the physically abused child. *Journal of Clinical Child Psychology*, **12**, 320–4.

Reid, J.B. (ed.) (1978). *A Social Learning Approach to Family Intervention*, Volume II: *Observation in Home Settings*, Eugene, OR: Castalia.

Reid, J.B. (1983). *Final Report: Child Abuse: Developmental Factors and Treatment*, Grant No. 7 ROI MH37938, NIMH, USPHS.

Reid, J.B. (1986). Social interactional patterns in families of abused and non-abused children. In C. Zahn-Waxler, E.M. Cummings and R. Ianotti (eds), *Altruism and Aggression: Biological and Social Origins*, Cambridge: Cambridge University Press.

Reid, J.B., Patterson, G.R., and Lorber, R. (1982). The abused child: victim, instigator or innocent bystander? In D.J. Bernstein (ed.), *Response Structure and Organization*, Lincoln: University of Nebraska Press.

Reid, J.B., Taplin, P.S., and Lorber, R. (1981). An interactional approach to the treatment of abusive families. In R. Stuart (ed.), *Violent Behaviour: Social Learning Approaches to Prediction, Management and Treatment*, New York: Brunner/Mazel.

Renvoize, J. (1974). *Children in Danger*, London: Routledge and Kegan Paul.

Renvoize, J. (1978). *Web of Violence*, London: Routledge and Kegan Paul.

Rosenberg, M.S., and Repucci, N.D. (1983). Abusive mothers: perceptions of their own and their children's behaviour. *Journal of Consulting and Clinical Psychology*, **51**, 674–82.

Sandgrund, R.W., Gaines, R.W., and Green, A.H. (1983). Child abuse and mental retardation: a problem of cause and effect. *Journal of Mental Deficiency*, **19**, 327–30.

Schaffer, H.R. (1977). *Studies in Mother–Infant Interaction*, London: Academic Press.

Schilling, R.F., and Schinke, S.P. (1984). Maltreatment and mental retardation. In J.M. Berg (ed.), *Perspective and Progress in Mental Retardation*, Volume I, Baltimore, MD: University Park Press.

Schindler, F., and Arkowitz, H. (1986). The assessment of mother–child interactions in physically abusive and nonabusive families. *Journal of Family Violence*, **1**, 247–57.

Schinke, S.P., Schilling, R.F., Barth, R.P., Gilchrist, L.D., and Maxwell, J.S. (1986). Stress-management intervention to prevent family violence. *Journal of Family Violence*, **1**, 13–26.

Scott, P.D. (1973). Parents who kill their children. *Medicine, Science and the Law*, **13**, 120–6.

Scott, W.O.N., Baer, G., Christoff, K., and Kelly, J.A. (1982). Skills training for a child abusive parent: a controlled case study. Unpublished manuscript, Mississippi Medical Center.

Slade, B.B., Steward, M.S., Morrison, T.L., and Abramowitz, S.I. (1984). Loss of control, persistence and use of contingency information in physically abused children. *Child Abuse and Neglect*, **8**, 447–57.

Sroufe, L.A. (1983). Infant–caregiver attachment and patterns of adaptation in preschool: the roots of maladaptation and competence. In M. Perlmutter (ed.), *Minnesota Symposium on Child Psychology*, Volume 16, Hillsdale, NJ: Lawrence Erlbaum Associates.

Starr, R.H. (1980). Towards prevention of child abuse. In S. Harel (ed.), *The At-risk Infant*, Amsterdam: Excerpta Medica.

Starr, R.H., Dietrich, K.N., Fischoff, J., Ceresnie, S., and Zweier, D. (1984). The contribution of handicapping conditions to child abuse. *Topics in Early Childhood and Special Education*, **4**, 55–69.

Steele, B.B. (1970). Parental abuse of infants and small children. In E.J. Anthony and T. Benedeck (eds), *Parenthood: Its Psychology and Psychopathology*, Boston, MA: Little, Brown.

Steele, B.B., and Pollock, D. (1968). A psychiatric study of parents who abuse small children. In C.H. Kempe and R.E. Helfer (eds), *The Battered Child*, Chicago: Chicago University Press.

Straus, M.A. (1980). Social stress and marital violence in a national sample of American families. In F. Wright, C. Bain, and R.W. Rieber (eds), *Forensic Psychology and Psychiatry: Annals of the New York Academy of Science*, p.347.

Straus, M.A. (1983). Ordinary violence, child abuse and wife beating: what do they have in common? In D. Finkelhor, R.J. Gelles, G.T. Hotaling and M.A. Straus (eds) *The Dark Side of the Family*. Beverly Hills, CA: Sage.

Terr, L. (1970). A family study of child abuse. *American Journal of Psychiatry*, **127**, 125–31.

Thomas, A., Chess, S., and Birch, H.G. (1970). The origin of personality. *Scientific American*, **223**, 102–9.

Thomson, E.M., Paget, N.W., Bates, D.W., Mesch, M., and Putnam, T.I. (1971). *Child Abuse: A Community Challenge*, New York: Henry Stewart and Children's Aid and Society for the Prevention of Cruelty to Children.

Twentyman, C.T., and Plotkin, R.C. (1982). Unrealistic expectations of parents who maltreat their children: an educational deficit that pertains to child development. *Journal of Clinical Psychology*, **38**, 497–503.

Wahler, R.G. (1980). The insular mother: her problem in parent–child treatment. *Journal of Applied Behaviour Analysis*, **13**, 159–70.

Wahler, R.G., and Dumas, J. (1984). Changing the observational coding styles of insular and noninsular mothers: a step towards maintenance of parent training effects. In R.F. Dangel and R.A. Polster (eds), *Parent Training: Foundations of Research and Practice*, New York: Guilford Press.

Wolfe, D.A., Fairbank, J.A., Kelly, J.A., and Bradlyn, A.S. (1983). Child abusive parents' physiological responses to stressful and non-stressful behaviour in children. *Behavioural Assessment*, **5**, 363–71.

Wolfe, D.A., and Sandler, J. (1981). Training abusive parents in effective child management. *Behaviour Modification*, **5**, 320–35.

Wolfe, D.A., St Lawrence, J., Graves, K., Brehony, K., Bradlyn, D., and Kelly, J.A. (1982). Intensive behavioural parent training for a child abusive mother. *Behaviour Therapy*, **13**, 438–51.

Wood-Shuman, S., and Cone, J.W. (1986). Differences in abusive, at-risk for abuse, and control mothers' descriptions of normal child behaviour. *Child Abuse and Neglect*, **10**, 397–405.

Young, L. (1964). *Wednesday's Child: A Study of Child Neglect and Abuse*, New York: McGraw-Hill.

8

Aggressive and Violent Children (The Use of Triadic Interventions)

MARTIN HERBERT
Department of Psychology, University of Leicester, UK

INTRODUCTION

There are many different definitions of aggression, most of them betraying assumptions about its nature and origins. In the case of violence the term implies extremes of aggression to some theorists and carries emotive overtones. According to Lorenz (1966), aggression is an instinct—an atavistic but autonomous impulse—to be tamed, exorcised or sublimated in the child as soon as possible. Aggression, and its particularly anti-social manifestations (violence), are explained in terms of the vicissitudes of innate or inborn tendencies and the control systems which evolve to cope with them. Learning theorists, in contrast, point to the fact that as progress is made up the evolutionary scale living creatures depend increasingly less on reflex or instinctual patterns of behaviour and more on experience and learning; hence the many variations in human behaviour, and the optimism about the possibilites of change. Aggressiveness, in this view, is a learned habit or appetite.

These issues of definition and attribution have been described and critically reviewed by many, notably Bandura (1973), Hersov and Berger (1978) and Tedeschi *et al.* (1970). They lead one to conclude that aggression is a generic term for a variety of complicated and many-sided phenomena which include (for example) aggressive actions (behaviour); so-called 'states of mind' such as rage; anger or hostility (subjective feelings); aggressive drives, inclinations, thoughts and intentions (motivations), and conditions under which aggressive behaviours are likely to occur (environmental stimulation). Reference to aggression may be admiring ('he's an aggressive batsman') or pejorative (these aggressive teenage hooligans').

Clinical Approaches to Violence. Edited by K. Howells and C. R. Hollin
© 1989 John Wiley & Sons.

A Definition

For the practical purposes of this chapter aggressive behaviour refers to socially unacceptable ways of behaving which may result in psychological or physical injury to another person or in damage to property. The term *destructive* is applied to children who destroy, damage or attempt to damage an object. *Disruptiveness* is applied to interference with another person so that he or she is prevented from continuing some ongoing activity or caused displeasure. *Physical attack* is a term applied to an actual or attempted assault on someone of sufficient intensity potentially (or actually) to inflict pain. *Verbal abuse* occurs when children scream or talk loudly enough for this to be unpleasant to another person if carried on for a sufficient time, with sufficient intensity, or when the content of their speech is abusive.

A Social Learning Approach

The social learning approach (the one adopted by the author) treats childhood aggression as a learned event that takes place usually in a social context, and that produces *injurious and destructive effects* as well as *social labelling* processes (i.e. the social judgements that lead people to name certain acts as 'aggressive' or 'violent').

Although biological factors do influence aggressive behaviour, children are assumed not to be born with the ability to perform the *specific* complex acts of aggression; this ability must be acquired through learning, either by direct experience or by observing the behaviour of other people (Bandura, 1973). While new forms of aggressive behaviour can be shaped by selective reinforcement of successive approximations to it, much complex behaviour is acquired by watching the behaviour of exemplary models. These may be people the child observes in his or her everyday life, or they may be symbolic models that he or she reads about or observes on television or in films.

Previous Learning Experience

There is a confidently expressed consensus that aggressive behaviour in children can be related to long-term attitudes and child-rearing practices. To summarize the findings (see Herbert, 1987b), parental permissiveness of aggression is said to increase the child's tendency to behave aggressively. More precisely, a combination of lax discipline combined with hostile attitudes in the parents produces very aggressive and poorly controlled behaviour in the offspring. The lax parent is one who gives in to children, acceding to their demands, indulging them, allowing them a great deal of freedom, being submissive and inconsistent, and, in extreme cases, neglecting and deserting them. Parents with hostile attitudes are mainly unaccepting and disapproving of children: they fail to give affection, understanding or explanations to children, and tend to use a lot of physical punishment, but not give reasons when they do exert their authority— something applied erratically and unpredictably, not to mention arbitrarily. Over a long period of time this combination produces rebellious, irresponsible and aggressive children: they tend to be disorderly in the classroom, lacking in sustained concentration and irregular in their working habits.

Modelling

The evidence suggests that children model their behaviour on that of their parents. Bandura and Walters (1959) compared families of adolescents who exhibited repetitive anti-social behaviour with those of boys who were neither markedly aggressive nor passive. It was found that the families differed in the extent to which they trained their sons to be aggressive through precept and example. Parents of the non-aggressive boys did not condone aggression to settle dispute, whereas those of the aggressive boys repeatedly modelled and reinforced combative attitudes and behaviour.

Reinforcement

There is convincing evidence (see Bandura, 1973) of the importance of reinforcement in shaping up and maintaining aggressive behaviour. The major effect of direct experience is to select and shape aggressive behaviour through its rewarding or punishing consequences. Aggressive responses which are followed by reinforcing consequences tend to be retained and strengthened, while those that are unrewarded or punished tend to be discarded. Direct external reinforcement may be of a positive kind involving the presentation of rewards such as tangible resources, attention, approval or social status.

Several theorists (Tedeschi et al., 1970; Patterson, 1982) have looked at aggression in terms of the concept of coercive power. There is fairly good agreement in the clinical literature (see Feshbach, 1970) that there are two major types of aggressive response: (1) hostile or angry aggression, in which the only objective of the angry individual is to harm another person by inflicting some injury; and (2) instrumental aggression, in which the occurrence of harm or injury to another person is only incidental to the individual's aim of achieving some other goal. Bandura (1973) points out that hostile aggression is also instrumental, except that the actions are used to produce injurious outcomes rather than to gain status, power, resources or some other goal. In either case, the 'aggressor' exercises coercive power against another person. Coercive power involves the use of aversive stimuli, threats and punishments to gain compliance, and can be used offensively to take something away from another person. It can also be used defensively to avoid doing something. Patterson (1982) has developed the concept of 'coercive' families to describe events in which parents, caregivers or other people, interacting with the child, become involved in supplying reinforcers for aggressive behaviours. He postulates negative reinforcement as a mechanism to strengthen the behaviour of the aggressor and, in some instances, of the victim as well. It is also hypothesized that some exchanges become extended, and that when this occurs there is likely to be an escalation in the intensity of the painful stimuli. Theorizing of this kind has come into its own in the assessment and treatment of child abuse in the context of violent families (Herbert, 1988).

It is assumed that family systems which permit behaviour control by the use of pain are quite likely to produce children who exhibit high rates of noxious actions. Patterson (1982) observes that *negative reinforcement* is most likely to operate in certain closed social systems where the child must learn to cope with aversive stimuli. In such a family, for example, children's aggressive behaviour will be supported by both positive and negative reinforcement. Their hitting terminates much of the aversive stimulation. In addition, as many as a quarter to a third of their coercive behaviours are likely to receive positive reinforcement for deviant behaviour as well.

Patterson (1982) lists the following possibilities for the child's failure to substitute more adaptive, more mature behaviours for his primitive coercive repertoire:

(1) The parents might neglect to condition pro-social skills (e.g. they seldom reinforce the use of language or other self-help skills);
(2) They might provide rich schedules of positive reinforcement for coercive behaviours;
(3) They might allow siblings to increase the frequency of aversive stimuli which are terminated when the target child uses coercive behaviours;
(4) They may use punishment inconsistently for coercive behaviours; and/or
(5) They may use weak-conditioned punishers as consequences for coercion.

CURRENT ('Here-and-Now') INFLUENCES

Aggressive actions tend to occur at certain times, in certain settings, towards certain objects or individuals and in response to certain forms of provocation; children rarely show aggression in blind, indiscriminate ways. People become aggressive at certain times because of current conditions and influences. There are two categories of contemporary influence to consider in planning treatment: contemporary circumstances which *instigate* aggression (i.e. physical or verbal attacks, deprivation, frustration, conflict and exposure to aggressive models) or *maintain* aggression (i.e. direct, vicarious and self-reinforcement).

The interactions between parents and child go a long way (as we have seen) towards shaping aggressive behaviour because of the reinforcing consequences inherent in their behaviour. Children are likely to generalize what they learn about the *utility* and *benefits* of aggression to other situations. In these circumstances they have to put to the test the consequences of being aggressive. For example, they may try being aggressive because it produced results with siblings or with the peer group in the playground at school. Of course, aggressive behaviour which has been acquired may not be performed, either because appropriate instigating conditions do not occur or because the consequences of aggressive acts are likely to be unrewarding or unpleasant.

Among the most common instigating conditions for aggression are various forms of aversive experience, such as physical assaults, verbal threats or insults and any frustrating conditions which prevent the child from getting what it wants (Bandura, 1973). Although such aversive experiences do sometimes generate aggression, this is not always the case; the anger they evoke may be accompanied by other alternative responses. Various incentives (as we have seen) may also act as instigators of aggressive behaviour. Here, the instigation is the *pull* of expected reward rather than the *push* of aversive experience. Thus aggressive and alternative responses are selected for performance on the basis of their anticipated consequences.

The probable nature of these consequences is conveyed to the child by means of various informational cues or discriminative stimuli. For instance, he or she might be told that acceptance into a gang depends on the successful performance of a certain aggressive act, or the presence of a weak potential victim may facilitate aggression, whereas a stronger victim might be conducive to an alternative response.

Exemplary models also influence the performance of previously learned aggressive responses. In the first place, models who behave aggressively may be emulated by children. Conversely, aggression can be reduced in observers by exposure to models who behave in a non-aggressive way in the face of provocation.

The Triadic Model of Intervention

Here, then, are the basic principles that underly the methods we use at the Centre for Behavioural Work with Families (formerly the Child Treatment Research Unit). It is difficult to select what to include in a relatively brief chapter about many years' work with aggressive (conduct-disordered) children in their natural environments—mainly 'own home' or residential-care settings. Natural environment interventions, in contrast to clinic-based treatment, seek to utilize the ongoing and intensive influence of those in closest everyday contact with the child in attempting to modify deviant behaviour and teach new skills and behavioural repertoires. The triadic model, as it is called, reduces the problem of generalizing improvements from the consulting room to the outside world. The issue of temporal generalization, however, remains a difficult technical problem; nevertheless, parents and teachers—as primary mediators of change—are *in situ* most of the time, and are in a position to apply contingencies in a variety of situations and over the 'long haul' required so often in treating anti-social, aggressive children.

Assessment

The conceptual framework for our work with families (Herbert, 1987a) is rooted in a social learning approach. The assessment phase can be divided into 13 steps (Figures 8.1 and 8.2).

During the initial interview with the child and *both* parents (a crucial therapeutic configuration we have found in families where there are two parents) we explain who we are and how we work. It is the Centre's policy

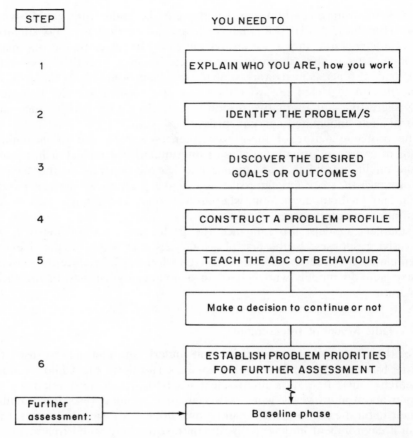

Figure 8.1 Assessment steps for the initial screening interviews. (From Herbert, 1987a, with permission)

to raise some of the major issues generated by a triadic behavioural approach: the concept of a genuine therapeutic partnership; our desire to share our knowledge and thinking with the parents, to take into account their own expertise based on long-standing knowledge of the child; and also to communicate the commitment we have to look at the ethical implications of any plans to institute changes within the family. There is a technical pay-off in sharing information; i.e. a reduction in the number of drop-outs from treatment (Baekeland and Lundwall, 1975). There may, however, be other crucial variables in the style of training (e.g. didactic versus a participant approach) which influence drop-out rates.

Parents—in individual treatment or parent-training groups—frequently tell us at debriefing interviews that this informataion and the 'insights' they gain from a more rigorous definition (and tracking) of anti-social *and* pro-social behaviour mark the beginning of change in their interactions with their child and (for some) a growing sense of competence. The baseline period is seldom

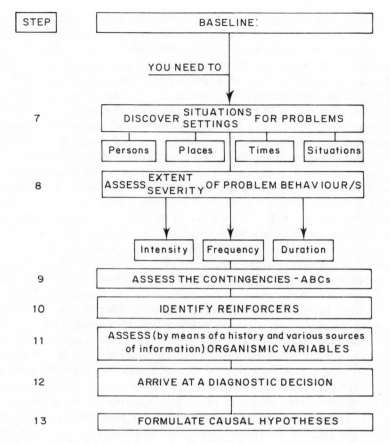

Figure 8.2 Further assessment. (From Herbert, 1987a, with permission)

therapeutically inert. In initiating baseline work our preliminary task is to specify precisely *what* the allegedly maladaptive behaviours are, defining them in terms of their frequency, intensity, number and duration. The analysis is very much (but not exclusively) focused on a functional analysis—what is called the 'ABC' sequence.

An analysis is made (by ourselves and the parents) of environmental conditions (and physical factors) leading up to and immediately preceding the occurrence of the aggressive (and usually associated) non-compliant behaviours and those that follow the performance of such behaviour. In this way we try to discover the antecedent stimuli (A) and consequenes (C) which serve as eliciting or discriminative stimuli and thus trigger and maintain problem behaviour (B) in terms of learning and behavioural principles which will be understandable to the family.

The earlier literature on behaviour modification—as it applied to children's conduct disorders—reflected a relative neglect of antecedent events. In their preoccupation with consequences of behaviour and, hence, operant procedures in the past, practitioners sometimes overlooked environmental controlling stimuli and the possibilities of ameliorating and restructuring the child's environment. The more recent parent-training research has done much to correct this omission (see Ollendick and Cerny, 1981; Topping, 1986).

It is helpful to observe what behaviours the parents model (consciously or unconsciously) for the child to imitate or the confusing or weak verbal signals (instructions) they give. There are other factors to be taken into account (for example, parents' attributions and child-rearing and disciplinary ideologies), but there is insufficient space here to elaborate (see Herbert, 1988).

Effectual individual programmes depend upon a thorough behavioural analysis leading to a formulation which includes specification of the child's aggressive behaviour, the parents' rules and roles, plus hypotheses about the contemporary factors that influence its instigation and maintenance and an appraisal of the resources available for its treatment. (See the case illustration at the end of the chapter.) On the basis of this formulation the goals of the intervention are chosen and the treatment plan is drawn up. If an intervention is considered to be justified and viable, then its goals are likely to be specified within the general framework of the prevention or reduction of aggressive behaviour and the promotion of more acceptable alternatives. It is useful in family work to negotiate a contract which specifies goals and behavioural objectives that are mutually agreeable to the child, the adults caring for him or her, and perhaps other people or agencies (social services or a court of law). The treatment plan provides the therapist with a strategy of intervention, but his or her personal ingenuity and experience are the main resources for its implementation. The treatment phase falls into five steps (see Figure 8.3).

Once we have arrived at a formulation of the problem a detailed plan is made with the parents for the intervention, which *they* initiate. It is vital to warn them, if one is not to lose credibility, that the child is likely to get worse before he or she gets better—the 'extinction burst'. Some children are expert at producing target behaviour criterion confusion or slippage. An *intensive input* at the beginning of a programme (providing prompts, cues, moral support, modelling, etc.) is undoubtedly crucial in facilitating the work. We work basically with a family system: the child is viewed as part of a complex network of interacting social systems, any aspect of which may have a bearing on his or her aggressive behaviour.

The communication negotiation, compromise and formulation of agreements implicit in working contracts make family discussions an important feature of our work. It is helpful, as children get older, to hold family meetings in order to settle differences or decide important family concerns, such as discipline, rules, pocket money or bedtime.

Parents and significant others are trained (sometimes in group settings) in different attention-provision; also how to give instructions and use reinforcement effectively, and family members are encouraged to negotiate compromises and to bring about positive changes in ways other than by sheer coercion. This type of work can also involve communication training.

The Intervention

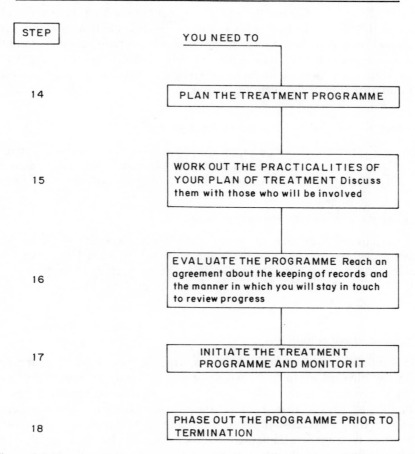

Figure 8.3 Treatment: how to proceed. (From Herbert, 1987a, with permission)

Therapeutic methods

The methods elaborated at the Centre (Herbert, 1987a,b) involve a multifaceted package depending for its final constituents on the behavioural and social assessment. It might involve developmental and/or personal counselling. Variations in family values and attitudes and individual differences in children require the flexibility of *individualized* programmes; thus techniques are *not* applied in a cookbook fashion.

Antecedent Control

There are several methods for reducing aggression based on a modification of the antecedent side of the ABC 'equation'.

Stimulus change: reducing discriminative stimuli for aggression

The absence of, say, the mother in the play room may be a cue for the eldest child that threatening or hitting his younger brother is likely to gain him certain advantages (e.g. the best toys). In other words, certain stimulus conditions provide signals to the child that aggressive behaviour is likely to have rewarding consequences for him. Treatment programmes can be planned to reduce discriminative stimuli for such aggression.

Providing models for non-aggressive behaviour

Acceptable alternatives to aggression may be enhanced by exposing youngsters to prestigious or influential individuals who manifest such alternative behaviours, especially when they are instrumental in obtaining rewards for these models.

Reducing the exposure to aggressive models

We have already seen that there is evidence that exposure to other people behaving aggressively may facilitate the imitation of such behaviour by the observer. An attempt to reduce the exposure of a child to such aggressive models (e.g. parents' behaviour) is likely to decrease the likelihood of him or her behaving similarly.

Reducing aversive stimuli

Violent reactions may be instigated by a large variety of aversive stimuli: by conflct, by physical assaults, by words of a threatening or humiliating nature and by deprivation of the child's proper care, rights and opportunities. It is reasonable to expect that a reduction of such aversive stimuli might be accompanied by a decrease in aggression. One technique is to *resolve conflicts* before they flare up into violence. Another involves the defusing of aversive stimuli by diminishing their power to arouse anger in the child. This can be achieved by using desensitization procedures.

Desensitization

Desensitization, desensitization with cognitive relaxation and desensitization in the absence of relaxation training are therapeutic procedures. O'Donnell and Worell (1973) provide examples of the effectiveness of all three procedures applied in order to reduce anger.

Self-instruction

A technique that has proved invaluable with hyperactive, aggressive (impulsive) children is self-instruction training—the development of children's skills in guiding their own performance by the use of self-suggestion, comments, praise and other directives. With older children and adolescents we tend to use more cognitively orientated methods (see Herbert 1987a, b), including self-control training (assertion and relaxation training, role-play, behaviour rehearsal).

Problem-solving skill training and social skill training are particularly valuable (see Hollin and Trower, 1986), as aggression is often a 'deficit' disorder as well as a problem of 'excess'. These methods are elaborated later.

Cognitive change (with regard to antecedent events)

The performance of aggressive behaviour and its alternatives may be determined by the child's thought processes as well as his or her external environment. For example, the instigation of aggression may be influenced by antecedent cognitive events such as aversive thoughts (e.g. remembering a past grudge), being aware of the probable consequences of aggressive actions or being capable of solving problems mentally instead of 'lashing out' reflexly.

The youngster's search for various possible courses of action in the face of provocation and frustration can be made more flexible by attention to the thinking processes that precede, accompany and follow violent actions. A skill that hostile children sometimes lack is the ability to *identify the precursors* (labelling) to an aggressive outburst, so that they can bring into play more adaptive solutions to their problems (see case illustration).

Modifying a child's cognitions concerning an unpleasant experience might reduce its probability of triggering violent behaviour. To take an example, if the incident of another child knocking over the potential aggressor is redefined as an accident rather than an attack, there may be less risk of a pugnacious reaction.

The influence of pleasant or aversive consequences on a child's actions are enhanced by his or her awareness of these consequences. Thus increasing a child's consciousness of the penalties contingent upon aggressive behaviour may reduce its performance. This information is used to show the child the relationships between his or her behaviour and its controlling conditions.

Conflict resolution ('settling differences')

Conflict situations can be defined as interpersonal situations in which the youth and authority figure (e.g. a parent or teacher) have opposing desires (Kifer *et al.*, 1974). Young people often make inappropriate responses to conflict situations (such as fighting, withdrawing, tantrums or destructive behaviour); an escalation of the conflict may bring them into contact with clinics, courts and other agencies. Negotiation could sometimes defuse these situations and produce more acceptable consequences for both parties.

There are two broad approaches to conflict resolution: arbitration or mediation of specific conflicts, and modification of communication processes (see Herbert, 1988). Behavioural contracting is the most common example of the arbitration approach, and involves the therapist in the role of a mediator or arbitrator who facilitates mutual agreements between opposing parties about reciprocal exchanges of specific behaviours and reinforcers (see Kirschenbaum and Flanery, 1983).

Verbal instructions, practice and feedback are the major techniques used to modify communication processes. Kifer *et al.* (1974) describe attempts to modify communication processes. Their emphasis was entirely on learning new adaptive behaviours rather than eliminating problem behaviours, and the techniques were primarily educational rather than therapeutic.

There is sound evidence (to be reviewed) that procedures based on selective reinforcement can reduce aggressive behaviour. In some studies aggressive behaviour is consistently ignored; in others it is ignored while a competing pattern of pro-social conduct is rewarded. In other cases pro-social behaviour is positively reinforced, but aggression is punished by removing the child from the scene (time out).

Outcome Control

Extinction of aggressive behaviour

It should be possible to extinguish aggressive behaviour by discontinuing its reinforcing consequences if they can be identified:

(1) Planned ignoring may be utilized; and/or
(2) Time out and response cost.

Planned ignoring, time out and response cost have been systematically applied in programmes designed to provide stimulus conditions which signal to the child that his or her aggressive behaviour will not only fail to have rewarding consequences but, indeed, will result in punitive consequences. The provision of such discriminative stimuli may bring aggression under control while more acceptable alternative behaviour is being acquired.

Punishment

Aversive consequences (punishments) are another contemporary influence on the performance of aggressive behaviour and a contentious issue in any treatment repertoire.In general, punishment tends to decrease aggression but the effects are complex and often paradoxical.

Modifying self-perceptions/reinforcers

Given the low self-esteem and underachievement commonly found in aggressive, conduct-disordered youngsters, in planning an intervention it is worth bearing in mind potent sources of reinforcement for aggressive behaviour—the aggressors themselves. To some extent, children regulate their actions by self-produced consequences. They tend to repeat behaviour which has given them feelings of satisfaction and worth.. Conversely, they tend to refrain from behaviour that produces self-criticism or other forms of self-devaluation.

Irrational beliefs about oneself may be acquired through the remarks and teaching of other people or may be self-generated. These fictional reinforcement contingencies can be even more powerful than *real* external reinforcing conditions. Faulty self-reinforcement can occur when children hold unrealistically high standards for themselves and remain chronically dissatisfied with their achievements. Such low self-efficacy expectations may lead the child to stop trying to succeed, since success seems impossible. Alternatively, some people have overgenerous standards and are satisfied with nearly any form of their own behaviour whether selfish, gauche, heartless or insensitive. Self-standards are learned from others through modelling and through direct reinforcement (Bandura, 1977).

Skills Training

Children often lack (due to a variety of social deprivation experiences) skills to choose between alternative courses of action in person-to-person situations, and, in addition, the actions ('solutions') which they can take, plus some means of choosing between those they do have. Alternatively, they are locked into narrow, rigid and perhaps self-destructive modes of action, aggression being a classical example. Thus the therapeutic aim is to increase the person's (child or caregiver) repertoire of possible actions in person-to-person situations, making his or her relationships with others both more constructive and more creative.

Baseline (pretreatment) assessment is commonly derived from the client's performance of social behaviours on role-play tests. Direct observation in naturalistic settings, sociometric devices and a variety of self-report instruments are also made use of in assessment.

The problem-solving model

The assumption here is that some children fail to fully develop proficiency (or lose it) due to lack of opportunity to practise or use social skills. It is crucial to unravel the situational factors in social deficit problems (e.g. the complicated social situations), to analyse them and to generate alternative solutions to the self-defeating strategies so far adopted. Those adopting a cognitive-social learning model view effective social functioning as being dependent upon the client's

(1) Knowledge of specific interpersonal actions and how they fit into different kinds of person-to-person situations;
(2) Ability to convert knowledge of social nuances into the skilled performance of social actions in various interactive contexts; and
(3) Ability to evaluate skilful and unskilful behaviour accurately and to adjust one's behaviour accordingly.

Bornstein *et al.* (1980) examined the effectiveness of social skills training with four highly aggressive children who were inpatients in a psychiatric setting.

The children who ranged in age from 8 to 12 years, were observed to manifest extreme levels of aggression with their peers and were unable to express frustration and disappointment in an appropriate manner. More specifically, the children were found to exhibit a low rate of eye contact, an inability to make appropriate requests of others and a high degree of hostile tone in their responses. These specific responses were measured on a series of role-play scenes.

Following pretreatment assessment, the children received three half-hour sessions of social skills training for each of the three targeted deficits observed in the role-play assessment. Training was first applied to eye contact, then to hostile tone and finally to appropriate requests. Training consisted of instructions, feedback, modelling, behavioural rehearsal and reinforcement. The therapist presented one of the interpersonal scenes and instructed the child on appropriate behaviour; the child performed the response; the therapist provided feedback and reinforcement; a confederate modelled the appropriate response; the therapist provided feedback, reinforcement and new instructions to the child; the child rehearsed the response for several trials until the criteria for the targeted response had been reached. Upon satisfactory performance, training proceeded in a similar way to new interpersonal situations. Throughout training, the children were assessed on the role-play scenes approximately three times per week.

Elder, *et al.* (1979) conducted a study with four highly aggressive, adolescent psychiatric patients but extended the test of generalization to untrained role-play scenes, natural settings and ward behaviour. Training was conducted in a group and in an on-ward classroom. Further, training was conducted four days per week for approximately 45 minutes per day for a total of 14 sessions. Hence, training was extended; it was conducted in groups in a natural setting; and an attempt was made to assess generalizaton from a number of perspectives. Training proceeded in a standard way and included instructions, feedback, modelling, behavioural rehearsal and reinforcement.

Results of Bornstein *et al.*'s investigation indicated that positive effects of training were achieved for each target behaviour for each child. However, the changes noted in training did not generalize consistently to other settings. Thus although the findings indicate that social skills training altered specific responses in specific role-play situations, the training did not generalize consistently to untrained prompts or to more natural situations. Still, the results of this study indicate that social skills training may be useful with aggressive children.

Elder *et al.*'s study indicated that social skills training was highly effective, and that all three targeted social skills were acquired by each of the adolescents. Generalization of the trained skills was evident in the untrained scenes and in the ward setting. The adolescents were observed to make fewer interruptions, to employ more appropriate responses to negative situations and to make more appropriate requests of others. Furthermore, these changes in social skills were associated with ward changes.

The problem-solving model

Life is full of crises, problems and decisions, but many children do not have the appropriate problem-solving skills to manage them. Much of what we think of as problematic behaviour in a client can be viewed as the consequence of ineffective behaviour and thinking. The individual is unable to resolve certain dilemmas in his or her life; the unproductive attempts to do so have adverse effects such as anxiety and depression, not to mention the creation of additional problems such as confrontations and interpersonal conflict—often leading to aggression.

There is evidence that the performance of aggressive acts is influenced by cognitive *problem-solving processes* (Herbert, 1987b, 1988). The processes which often precede and guide subsequent overt behaviour are as follows:

(1) Being able to recognize problematic situations when they occur;
(2) Making an attempt to resist the temptation to act impulsively or to do nothing to deal with the situation;
(3) Defining the situation in concrete or operational terms and then formulating the major issues to be coped with;
(4) Generating a number of possible responses which might be pursued in this situation;
(5) Deciding on the course(s) of action most likely to result in positive consequences; and
(6) Finally, acting upon the final decision and verifying the effectiveness of the behaviour in resolving the problematic situation.

For professionals, the way to decode the child's sometimes incomprehensible actions is to ask themselves about the child's *perception* of the circumstances *and* what he or she is trying to 'achieve'—seen from the child's point of view (see Herbert, 1988). What is the payoff? Their 'solutions' may produce immediate benefits which, for that reason, are difficult to discard even though they involved unacceptable or self-defeating actions. Does the 'tunnel vision' of their subjectivity (personal involvement), perhaps their inexperience and immaturity, stop them from seeing how self-defeating their chosen course of action is over the longer term?

The emphasis is very much (but not exclusively) on *how* the person thinks; the goal in therapy of training is to generate a way of thinking (this applied to parents as well)—a way of using their beliefs and values in decision making relative to problems that arise.

Spivack and his colleagues (1971) have defined a number of differing interpersonal cognitive problem-solving skills. They suggest a series of skills rather than a single unitary ability. The significance of each of these abilities in determining the degree of social adjustment is said to differ as a function of age. These skills include:

(1) *Problem-sensitivity*, which is the ability to be aware of problems which arise out of social interactions and a sensitivity to the kinds of social situations out of which interpersonal difficulties may arise. It also involves

the ability to examine relationships with others in the here and now.

(2) *Alternative solution thinking.* A close parallel to this is brainstorming. The key feature is the ability to generate a wide variety of potential solutions to the problem.

(3) *Means–ends thinking* reflects the ability to articulate the step-by-step means necessary to carry out the solution to a given interpersonal problem. The skill encompasses the ability to recognize obstacles, the social consequences deriving from these solutions and that interpersonal problem-solving takes time.

(4) *Consequential thinking* involves the consequence of social acts as it affects self and others, and includes the ability to generate alternative consequences to potential problem solutions before acting.

(5) *Causal thinking* reflects the degree of appreciation of social and personal motivation and involves the realization that how one felt and acted may have been influenced by (and, in turn, may have influenced) how others felt and acted.

To facilitate the problem-solving process in children they require help in identifying their aggressive behaviour and recognizing the conditions which provoke and maintain it. The problem situation is analysed, broken down into its component parts and (hopefully) represented in a way most likely to lead to a solution. A number of procedures are available for this purpose and include self-recording by the child of his or her hostile activities, together with their observations of the circumstances in which they occurred and their consequences. This information is used to show the child the relationship between his or her behaviour and its controlling conditions.

DISCUSSION

There is little doubt that parents—in individual treatment or parent-training groups—can be taught to use behavioural methods with their children and that for aggressive problems (and other disorders) they are effective (see Ollendick and Cerny, 1981; and Topping, 1986, for a critical review). As with the history of systematic desensitization, the main thrust of research is to discover the active therapeutic expedients in what are usually multi-element treatment packages and the refinements which facilitate parent training. It must be admitted, however, that experience in both natural and residential homes tells us that behavioural work with aggressive, conduct-disordered children has some limitations. In the very nature of the families of many aggressive, pre-delinquent or delinquent young people, co-operation will not always be forthcoming from parents or caregivers. Implementation of treatment programmes may require very lengthy casework just to get to the point of a useful assessment, let alone to the consistency and application required of a challenging and tiring programme. The problem of temporal generalization is particularly acute with caregivers whose commitment is half-hearted. Results to date are sufficiently encouraging for us to err on the side of optimism rather than pessimism. Such guarded optimism arises from what we know of the 'natural history' of conduct disorders.

It is difficult to provide a base rate for aggressive conduct problems because of difficulties of definition and a paucity of longitudinal evidence. However, unlike the development of fears and many other problems of childhood, there is not the same tendency for the conduct problems to be transitory. Early aggression—when intense and high in frequency—must be taken seriously. Writers like Robins (1966) suggest that, by aged 7 or 8, the child with *extreme* anti-social aggressive patterns of behaviour is at quite considerable risk of continuing on into adolescence and indeed adulthood, with serious deviancy of one kind or another. Lefkowitz *et al.* (1977) followed a group of New York children from ages 8 to 19; their study has a particular focus on the persistence of aggression. Aggression was much less common in girls than in boys, but in both sexes, children who were highly aggressive at age 8 tended also to be unduly aggressive at 19 (correlations of 0.38 for boys and 0.47 for girls). In West and Farrington's study of London boys, substantial continuity was again shown (Farrington, 1978). Of the youths rated most aggressive at 8–10 years, 59% were in the most aggressive group at 12–14 years (compared with 29% of the remaining boys) and 40% were so at 16–18 years (compared with 27% of the remainder). The boys who were severely aggressive at 8–10 years were especially likely to become violent delinquents (14% versus 4.5%). The same study demonstrated the very considerable extent to which troublesome, difficult and aggressive behaviour in young boys was associated with later juvenile delinquency.

In our own studies (e.g. Herbert and Iwaniec, 1981) we have found that a substantial number of children seem temperamentally predisposed to develop difficult, unsocial behaviour. Early learning is shaped in such a way that the range of coercive tactics (crying, screaming, wilful tantrums, non-compliance) which are common to all young children are not relinquished in this kind of child as he or she grows older, because of the way in which potent behaviour has been mismanaged. The possibilites for doing productive *preventive* (as well as remedial) work are very real and encouraging. After all, most parents, with little or no training (and parenting is, in large part, a skill) rear their children into broadly pro-social, norm-abiding adults (with the help of other socializing agents). It is a minority who flounder. Fortunately, there seems to be a fair amount of latitude in learning conditions for the child with an intact central nervous system, healthy body and a relatively unvolcanic temperament. For them, parental inconsistency, double-binds, unclear rules, etc. seem no more than a minor hindrance in the business of growing up.

For others, predisposed to problem formation (particularly non-compliance and aggression) by handicaps, temperamental lability or learning deficits a more predictable and persistent learning environment becomes essential. The demand characteristics of such children—the high-rate, high-intensity behaviours of a coercive kind so often associated with handicap—sadly (and too often) shape an environment which is fraught, unpredictable, unpersevering and sometimes dangerously abusive (Frude, 1980).

The case of Freddie B. (Herbert, 1987b; quoted with permission), aged 9 years, 4 months, illustrates some of the points made in this chapter, in particular the successful use of cognitive and self-control training. Here was a child who was disrupting his home by bouts of aggressive behaviour. This was a crisis intervention, because there was a distinct possibility of his being taken into care. His parents could not cope with him because (they claimed) he was out of control at times. The assessment was made on the basis of visits to Freddie's home, a school visit to his school (for the blind), some 60 miles from his home village, and outings with him to a swimming pool.

Freddie presented an intensely aggressive 'picture' on the first two visits. If we had made an assessment in generalized global terms based on this session it would have been highly misleading. A colleague saw Freddie initially, and he attacked her physically and then made himself bleed by putting his fist through a glass door. The author paid the second visit and was met by obscenities. These died away when Freddie was taken for a drive in a car. Indeed, after this truculent and physically and verbally violent beginning, Freddie came over as a friendly and articulate boy. Despite his near-complete blindness, he could get around (e.g. in the swimming pool) with remarkable ease and agility. He was robust, vigorous and powerful. We gradually developed a warm and affectionate relationship. Freddie tended (probably out of loyalty to his parents) to be reserved about some of his worries at home and at school, but, in almost imperceptible stages, he opened up about these.

He lived in a terraced house with his mother (a woman of 45 with a serious heart condition) and his father (a man of 64, near retirement). Although he had no siblings, a girl of his age, Alice, lived a few doors away, was very much like a sister to him and seemed as much at home in his house as he was.

Some of the refinements of a leisurely assessment had to be curtailed as the case was an emergency one. The parents were at their wits' end, and were arguing about whether or not to have Freddie at the weekends because of his difficult behaviour and its adverse effect on Mrs B's deteriorating health. The parents were threatening to 'walk out' in relation to each other and in relation to Freddie. Social Services were involved in the case.

An assessment of Freddie's difficult behaviour suggested that it was highly specific to a refusal to return in the school bus to his school for the blind, on a Sunday afternoon. His behaviour leading up to, and particularly at, the point of being asked to go to the bus waiting outside his home consisted of what the parents called 'spasms'. These involved an escalation from grumbling, threatening his parents with words, fists or a stick, to kicking the cat or the door, or throwing his toy cars or the radio at the parents themselves. An analysis of his behaviour showed that these tantrums were not so much frequent as frighteningly intense. Freddie would roar like a bull, adding to a very formidable scene. The parents were certainly daunted. The impending arrival of the bus to take Freddie back to school was the invariable (and main) trigger.

There were minor (i.e. milder) tantrums on a Saturday morning if Freddie was thwarted while playing with his friend, and again on Saturday evening at about bedtime, when his parents were reading at a time of night when Freddie's radio programme had finished. In the case of these situations, the antecedents were either that Freddie was bored, frustrated or thwarted (e.g. did not wish to go to bed). The analysis of the consequences of these sequences of difficult behaviour suggested that the parents were inconsistent and ineffectual. Freddie would generally get his own way if he had a tantrum. The exception, interestingly, involved his major problem. No matter how violent he was, he was made to return to school and (with the help of the driver) forced onto the bus.

It soon became clear from attempts to work out the broad outlines of a management programme with Mr and Mrs B that practical difficulties would make for a doubtful outcome. It was decided to concentrate mainly on Freddie, helping him to learn self-control strategies. He took to the programme with remarkable enthusiasm. The therapeutic sessions were conducted in the context of swimming outings; the boy was only available at weekends and his home was unsuitable for quiet discussion or for rehearsing the exercises. Mrs B tended to interrupt and to interfere with the training.

Several observations were made of the family at home and of Freddie's behaviour at school. A consideration of his physical constitution and his home situation, together with the weekly separations that his way of life involved, led to the conclusion that despite the violent episodes—which were fairly specific—Freddie had really made an extraordinary adjustment to life. In a sense, his outbursts (although regrettable and requiring moderation) were wholly proportionate to the life problems he had to solve. He certainly did not appear to be an emotionally disturbed child. The following themes were the ones which had a bearing on this conclusion:

(1) He was a premature baby and the birth was an anoxic one. He was in and out of hospital as a hydrocephalic baby and had a valve fitted at 4 months. In 1971 his vision deteriorated as a result of intracranial pressure. He had an operation and a new valve was fitted. Freddie had epilepsy during his third year of life. He also suffered other vicissitudes in his formative years, including many separations from his mother while in hospital himself and when she was in hospital for psychiatric treatment.

(2) His birth was unwelcome as the parents were unmarried and, indeed according to Mrs B, she saw Freddie's disabilities as a punishment by God for her wrongdoing. She said she still bore a heavy sense of guilt that she was living with Mr B in an unmmarried state, and this was made worse at weekends when Freddie pestered her about his sight, asking for it back and appealing to her to take him to other doctors. He sometimes said that he hated God for making him blind.

(3) Freddie's early separation experiences may well have sensitized him to overreact to the Sunday separation; he hated going back to school. He said to me that he wished that he could be at home all the time with his mother and father, like other children.

(4) Freddie was refusing to accept his blindness; his teacher told the author that he had always overestimated the amount of residual sight that he

actually possessed. It became apparent that he was frightened of losing what vision he retained and, from the way his mother talked about his reluctance to return to school, it seemed that the school represented the world of the blind (something he rejected), while his home village represented that of the sighted (with whom he identified himself).

(5) In addition to these considerations, going back to school made Freddie insecure because he had been made to feel responsible for his mother's illness; it had been strongly suggested that his behaviour would be the 'death of her'. He understood that she had a serious heart condition, and he confided that he was worried about whether she would be there when he got back. This insecurity was exacerbated by the frequent threats (in the past) by both parents that they would leave him or each other if he did not behave.

(6) The mother had not been a very good model of the sort of pacific behaviour she required of Freddie. He asked me (at one stage) if I would teach his mother self-control, as she had thrown a chair at his father.

The object of therapy was conceptualized in terms of assisting Freddie to identify and focus his aggressive behaviour and to recognize the antecedent and outcome conditions which controlled it. A broader aim was to discuss with Freddie his perception of himself as 'sighted', and his rejection of everything to do with the blind—the special school, learning Braille, etc. An effort was made to identify his strengths and possibilities (e.g. his swimming skill and musical appreciation).

The first phase was a baseline assessment to indicate how Freddie behaved when no self-control measures were applied. Freddie was taken through a diary of events kept by his mother during three weekends and asked to comment on his behaviour, his feelings and the situations in which they arose.

Next, an attempt was made to increase his awareness of his feelings and maladaptive behaviours. This involved discussions in which we labelled the external and internal stimuli (situations and feelings) which led to his violent outbursts. It also involved training him to monitor and 'talk out' his feelings in role-played evocations of the 'return-to-school' situation. Later this was conducted in the 'real-life' situation (with the therapist present). 'Techniques' to help self-control such as 'playing turtle' and 'counting to ten' and formulae such as 'think first, act later' were role-played for various situations at home and school in which he became angry. His reactions were rehearsed with him. During this phase, Freddie's performance at weekends was discussed with him on the following weekend (based on his mother's recording and later on a self-rating). Parents were advised how to make life easier for Freddie by not threatening to put him into care, to separate or to become ill as a result of 'bad' behaviour. Little was achieved in this aspect of the work with Mr and Mrs B.

A good deal was accomplished in making his weekends less 'claustrophobic'. Where previously he had been cooped up indoors, outings were arranged. Freddie and the therapist discussed several issues such as Mrs B's illness,

Freddie's sight, school, and so on. The positive aspects of school were emphasized (aided by the teacher). Despite the absence of any real co-operation from the parents, Freddie's violent behaviour diminished in intensity within two weeks of beginning the self-control programme. There were only two setbacks over the period of over a year (once when Mrs B had a serious heart attack and another when Freddie's valve was blocked for a short period). Freddie's violent tantrums at home reduced completely within eight weekends of beginning treatment.

References

Baekeland, F., and Lundwall, L. (1975). Dropping out of treatment: critical review. *Psychological Bulletin*, **82**, 738–83.

Bandura, A. (1973). *Aggression: A Social Learning Analysis*, Englewood Cliffs, NJ: Prentice-Hall.

Bandura, A. (1977). *Social Learning Theory*, Englewood Cliffs, NJ: Prentice-Hall.

Bandura, A., and Walters, R.H. (1959). *Adolescent Aggression*, New York: Ronald Press.

Bornstein, M.R., Bellack, A.S., and Hersen, M. (1980). Social skills training for highly aggressive children. *Behaviour Modification*, **4**, 173–86.

Elder, J.P., Edelstein, B.A., and Narick, M.M. (1979). Adolescent psychiatric patients: modifying aggressive behaviour with social skills training. *Behavior Modification*, **3**, 161–78.

Farrington, D.P. (1978). The family background of aggressive youths. In L.R. Hersov and M. Berger (eds), *Aggression and Anti-social Behaviour in Childhood and Adolescence*, Oxford: Pergamon Press.

Farrington, D.P. (1979). Delinquent behaviour modification in the natural environment *British Journal of Criminology*, **19**, 353–72.

Feshbach, S. (1970). Aggression. In P.H. Mussen (ed.), *Carmichael's Manual of Child Psychology*, Chichester: Wiley.

Frude, N. (ed.) (1980). *Psychological Approaches to Child Abuse*, London: Batsford.

Herbert, M. (1987a). *Behavioural Treatment of Children with Problems: A Practice Manual* 2nd revised edition, London: Academic Press.

Herbert, M. (1987b). *Conduct Disorders of Childhood and Adolescence: A Social Learning Perspective*, Chichester: Wiley.

Herbert, M. (1988). *Working with Children and Their Families*, London: British Psychological Society/Routledge.

Herbert, M., and Iwaniec, D. (1981). Behavioural psychotherapy in natural homesettings: an empirical study applied to conduct disorders and incontinent children. *Behavioural Psychotherapy*, **9**, 55–76.

Hersov, L.R., and Berger, M. (eds) (1978). *Aggression and Anti-social Behaviour in Childhood and Adolescence*. Oxford: Pergamon Press.

Hollin, C.R., and Trower, P. (eds) (1986). *Handbook of Social Skills Training*. Volume 1, *Applications Across the Life Span*, Oxford: Pergamon Press.

Kifer, R.E., Lewis, M.A., Green, D.R., and Phillips, E.L. (1974). Training predelinquent youths and their parents to negotiate conflict situations. *Journal of Applied Behavior Analysis*, **7**, 357–64.

Kirschenbaum, D.S., and Flanery, R.C. (1983). Behavioral contracting: outcomes and elements. *Progress in Behavior Modification*, **15**, 217–75.

Lefkowitz, M.M., Eron, L.D., Walder, L.O., and Heussman, L.R. (1977). *Growing to be Violent*, Oxford: Pergamon Press.

Lorenz, K.Z. (1966). *On Aggression*, New York: Harcourt, Brace and World.

O'Donnell, C.R., and Worell, L. (1973). Motor and cognitive relaxation in the desensitization of anger. *Behaviour Research and Therapy*, **11**, 473–81.

Ollendick, T.H., and Cerny, J.A. (1981). *Clinical Behaviour Therapy with Children*, New York: Plenum.

Patterson, G.R. (1982). *Coercive Family Process*. Eugene, OR: Castalia.

Robins, L.N. (1966). *Deviant Children Grown-up*, Baltimore, MD: Williams & Wilkins.

Spivack, G., Platt, J.J., and Shure, M.B. (1971). *The Problem-solving Approach to Adjustment*. San Francisco, CA: Jossey-Bass.

Tedeschi, J.T., Smith, R.B., and Brown, R.C. (1970). A reinterpretation of research on aggression. *Psychological Bulletin*, **77**, 301.

Topping, K.J. (1986). *Parents as Educators: Training Parents to Teach Their Children*, London: Croom Helm.

9

Sexual Violence

W.L. MARSHALL

and

H.E. BARBAREE
Department of Psychology, Queen's University, Kingston, Ontario, Canada

Sexual violence may refer to a variety of behaviors, depending on who is defining the term, and there are some who see all sexual relations where there is a power imbalance as coercive. However, for the purposes of this chapter we will restrict our consideration to those behaviors which involve explicit sexual elements and either an unwilling partner or one who is incapable of giving consent (e.g. a child). Since there is very little evidence bearing on any of these classes of behavior except rape, child molestation and genital exhibitionism, we will limit our discussion to these offenses. Of course, not all these behaviors involve physical violence, not even all rapes, although, even in exhibitionism, the victim may experience the act as violence directed toward her; indeed, a frightened response by the victim typically enhances the pleasure an exhibitionist experiences when offending.

Among incarcerated offenders, Christie *et al.* (1979) and Marshall and Christie, (1981) found that 71% of rapists and 58% of child molesters physically abused their victims in excess of the forcefulness necessary to secure their sexual goals with an unco-operative victim. Of our outpatient child molesters, some 25% had used similar gratuitous violence (Marshall, 1982). Since our recent data with child molesters (Barbaree and Marshall, 1986) appears to reveal in many of these men a progression from the first offense onwards in both the level of force and violence enacted against the victim and the level of sexual intrusiveness (a progression from fondling to intercourse), it seems reasonable to consider all child molesters as either presently or potentially violent. While none would argue with our classifying rapists as violent offenders, some may have problems with describing exhibitionists as violent. However, as we noted, many of them do seem to derive pleasure from frightening their

Clinical Approaches to Violence. Edited by K. Howells and C. R. Hollin
© 1989 John Wiley & Sons.

victims and, in any case, clinical experience indicates that most sex offenders, although only apprehended for a particular offense (e.g. rape, exhibitionist or child molestation), have often committed several other types of offenses. Abel *et al.* (1985) have documented this multiple-paraphilia feature of sexual offenders, showing that 50.6% of rapists had molested children, 29.2% had exposed themselves, 20.2% had engaged in voyeurism and 12.4% were also frotteurs. Similarly, of the child molesters, 16.8% had also raped an adult female, 29.7% had exposed themselves, 13.8% were voyeurs and 8.6% were frotteurs.

The sexual assault of an adult female by an adult male may range from uninvited sexual touching to rape, and similarly the sexual molestation of children may range from fondling the genitals to actual or attempted penile penetration of the vagina or anus of an immature partner. Exhibitionism takes many forms, but we will only be concerned with males who deliberately expose their genitals to unwilling adult females. Those men who expose exclusively to children rarely limit their behaviors to exposing, so they are more accurately described as child molesters. Legal prohibitions embrace all of the above behaviors under various labels across different legal jurisdictions, so that using offense convictions as a basis for classification presents problems. We will count as examples of sexual violence all instances of coercive sexual behaviors involving an unwilling partner, although we recognize there are boundary offenses which may be difficult to classify.

Rapists, of course, are not all equally violent (Groth and Birnbaum, 1979; Prentky *et al.*, 1985; Rada, 1978), but even the least aggressive are forceful to some degree (Gibbens *et al.*, 1977). Indeed, one of the problems facing theorists, researchers and clinicians in this area concerns the very fact that sexual violence ranges all the way from implied threats, through overt threats with a weapon, to forceful and even sadistic behaviors.

A number of classification systems which have been developed for rapists assume that the offenders can be categorized according to either their inferred motivation, or the behavior displayed during their offenses or a combination of these two (Cohen *et al.*, 1971; Gebhard *et al.*, 1965; Guttmacher and Weihofen, 1952). Other systems classify rapists according to the social roles exemplified by their offense behavior (Amir, 1971), or according to clinical criteria (Rada, 1978), or by virtue of a complex and wide range of features (Prentky *et al.*, 1985). In all these systems the clear implication is that a rapist, so classified, will always remain in his specific category (i.e. retain his idiosyncratic features) so long as he continues to rape. Even behavioral models, which suggests that rape is an acquired behavior (Abel *et al.*, 1976; Laws, 1986), posit that once a rapist develops his particular deviance he remains essentially unchanged unless persuaded by treatment or incarceration to give up his offensive habits. We have data on child molesters (Marshall *et al.*, 1987a; Marshall *et al.*, 1986a) which suggests that repetitive practice of their deviant acts produces progressive changes in the behavior of many of these men which reveals an increasing degree of sexual intrusiveness and more violence and sadism over time. Of course, if sexual violence is a learned behavior it follows that the degree of violence and its associated behaviors should reveal a similar learned progression. In the history of individual use of pornography there is often revealed a progressively changing appetite for more and more eccentric and unacceptable behaviors (Marshall, 1985a; Zillman, 1986), and this appears to be paralleled in the changes displayed over time in the repeated enactments of sexual offenses, although in both cases this progressive change is not manifest by all men.

THEORIES OF CAUSATION

Since information relevant to the etiology of exhibitionism is quite limited relative to that available on rapists and child molesters, we will restrict our focus here to the latter two groups.

Situational Theories

Classificatory systems of sexual offenders frequently imply etiological explanations of the behaviors, but there are also some explicit theories of the cause of sexual violence. Theories concerning the cause of sexual violence focus on different temporal points in the emergence of the behavior and may hold the offender or the victim to be wholly or partly responsible. Theories which attribute responsibility to the victim (e.g. in rape, see Amir, 1972, or Goode, 1969; and in child molestation see Bowman, 1951, or Revitch and Weiss, 1962) are essentially situational theories in which features of the behavior of the victim and momentary misinterpretations by the offender are said to be causal. Indeed, the latter notion entered British law by a ruling of the Law Lords (*DPP* v. *Morgan* (1975), reported in Coote and Gill, 1975), which allowed that if a man honestly thought the woman was consenting, no matter what her behavior indicated to the contrary, he was to be found innocent of a criminal offense. During the same year a similar ruling was made by the California Supreme Court (Schwendinger and Schwendinger, 1983). The empirical data, however, do not support such an interpretation of rape (Geller, 1977; Hursch, 1977; Quinsey, 1986), and in a detailed analysis of our case records on 109 child molesters we could find very little to support the idea that the children had invited sexual contact by the adult, at least on the initial occasion of sexual interaction (Marshall and Barbaree, 1986). Many of the offenders told us that the children were provocative or actually seductive, but the available evidence contradicted this, and after treatment most of these men had changed their minds about their interpretation of the children's behavior.

Other situational theories concern the influence of alcohol or other intoxicants, momentary but overwhelming sexual arousal, temporary insanity or anger. Remarkably few sex offenders are psychotic, so this will not serve as a general explanation, and even in those cases where the offender is psychotic it must be explained why the psychosis expressed itself in sexual violence in this man, since very few insane people engage in sexual assaults.

In fact, this seems to be a common problem for all of these situational accounts of sexual assault. Why is it that this intoxicated man raped a woman or molested a child when other intoxicated men in similar circumstances did not? Why did this angry man sexually attack when others did not? Why did this highly aroused man not simply masturbate? These situational factors are certainly relevant, there being ample evidence that they are associated with sexual assault (Groth and Birnbaum, 1979; Knight et al., 1983), but on their own they will not serve as explanatory theories. As we hope to show, situational factors need to be accommodated within a more comprehensive account which will illustrate why some men respond to such transitory experiences by acting in a sexually aggressive way.

Feminist Analyses

Feminist theories of sexual assault have taken various forms, but it seems to be the delight of some critics of such theories to set up an extreme version of feminist interpretations in order to readily dismiss all such perspectives. Almost invariably, these reviewers cite Brownmiller's (1975) claim that rape is 'nothing more or less than a conscious process of intimidation by which all men keep all women in a state of fear' as the quintessential feminist position and then summarily dismiss all similar analyses as patently absurd. Such a response ignores many important and valuable aspects of Brownmiller's own analysis of rape, but, most importantly, fails to come to grips with the valuable contributions which feminist writers have made to the public's awareness of the extent of these problems and to the awareness of researchers to neglected but important features of sexual abuse.

In fact, feminist views of rape express a diversity of theoretical underpinnings. For example, Russell (1975) relies on psychoanalytic concepts such as marked insecurities among rapists regarding their masculinity, displacement of economic frustrations and exaggerated genital orientations in these men. Clark and Lewis (1977), on the other hand, construe rape within an opportunity structure theory which essentially claims that women possess a desired commodity (i.e. female sexuality) which they hoard and miserly dispense. According to this view, it is this control over a sought-after commodity which lies at the base of misogyny and rape. A more recent feminist analysis (Herman, in press) involves an analogy between repetitive sexual offending and addictive processes. This view is in harmony with recent attempts to apply relapse prevention strategies developed for addictive behaviors (Marlatt, 1982) to sexual offenders (Pithers et al., 1983), although these two approaches appear to have been developed independently. Recent data support the value of relapse-prevention strategies in the treatment of rapists and child molesters (Pithers et al., in press), although these data can only be considered to be tentative.

Despite the diversity of views expressed in feminist analyses of sexual violence, these theorists agree on a number of issues, and on these issues they have successfully (and almost exclusively) raised the awareness of the public as well as that of researchers and clinicians. In the first place, as noted above, feminists have made the public and research-funding agencies more fully aware of the extent and nature of sexual abuse. In this regard they have been far more effortful and successful than have traditionally minded researchers and clinicians.

Feminists also point to the political function of sexual violence, which, as Brownmiller (1975) notes, serves to facilitate the oppression of women whether or not one accepts her claim that this is a conscious process. Similarly, feminists see coercive sexuality as an exaggeration (albeit a crude one) of prevailing norms exemplifying the eroticization of male dominance and female submission (Herman, in press). In this respect, their analyses have served to draw attention to the socio-cultural attitudes and beliefs which help create a world in which women and children are highly vulnerable to sexual abuse and harassment, and in which the behavior of females and children is often circumscribed by fear of sexual attack. Certainly, it has been almost entirely due to feminist analyses of socio-cultural structures and socialization processes that we now recognize these influences as important to any comprehensive theory of rape or child molestation.

Psychoanalytic Perspectives

Psychoanalytic theories often suggest that sexual violence against adult females stems from a hatred of women which is said to have arisen from unfortunate childhood experiences (Moore, 1969: Stoller, 1975, 1977). Groth has been one of the foremost advocates of this view. He declares that rape is a pseudosexual act which serves primarily non-sexual needs: 'Rape is always and foremost an aggressive act . . . [it] is, in fact, the use of sexuality to express . . . issues of power and anger' (Groth and Birnbaum, 1979, pp. 12–13). We have certainly found that gratuitous violence (Christie et al., 1979) and deliberate humiliation (Marshall and Darke, 1982) are prominent features of rape, but the evidence concerning hostility toward women in general is not so clear. We found significantly greater evidence of hostility toward women among rapists than among other offenders (Marshall et al., 1984), but Stermac and Quinsey (1986) did not. Similarly, we have demonstrated that anger disinhibits sexual arousal to rape scenes in non-rapist males (Yates et al., 1984), but there have been no such studies of rapists.

The evidence, nevertheless, does appear to be consistent with the view that aggression, power and the intent to humiliate play an important part in sexual violence against women, and this is further supported by cross-cultural observations indicating that negative attitudes toward women predict high frequencies of rape (Chagnon, 1977; Sanday, 1981). The latter data suggest that widespread hostile attitudes toward women may be encouraged by a socio-cultural context in which women are without economic or political power and where they are generally treated in a violent and disrespectful way. Unfortunately, hostility arising from experiences in childhood (or, indeed, anger arising from any source) may be readily directed within such a society toward women. The question remains, however, why it is that most males who experience anger, even within a society where the attitudes are negative toward women, do not rape.

Groth has also developed a theory of child molesters (Groth and Birnbaum, 1978) within which these men can be classified as one of two types:

(1) The fixated offender whose psychosexual development was arrested in childhood, and as a consequence he prefers the company of children and
(2) The regressed offender who engages in sex with children when his adult relations become unsatisfying or stressful.

Again, the claim is made that what appears to be a sexual act is not:

> Child Molestation is the sexual expression of non-sexual needs and unresolved life issues. Pedophilia goes beyond sexual need and is, ultimately, a pseudo-sexual act (Groth *et al.*, 1982, p.137).

No doubt the sexual molestation of children is multiply determined and likely satisfies many needs, but to call explicit sexual behaviors, including rape as well as child abuse, 'pseudo-sexual' is to deny sexual motivation altogether. Clearly, there are sexual elements involved in both types of abuse, and Groth does not deny this. He asserts, however, that the sexual behaviors in these assaults are instrumental in achieving other more primary goals related to power and control. This position almost amounts to a denial of the sexual component, and some followers of Groth have explicitly made this claim (Frude, 1982). As Finklehor (1984) points out, all sexual behavior involves non-sexual motivation. Indeed, Neubeck (1974) lists 14 categories of needs which may be met by sexual activity, of which only one is explicitly sexual. Even if we are reluctant to agree with Neubeck's clinical inferences regarding specific categories of needs, very few would disagree with the claim that sexual behavior serves many non-sexual needs. Should we accordingly conclude that all sexual behavior is masquerading as sexual, and is best described as 'pseudo-sexual'? As we will see, many child molesters are strongly sexually aroused by children, and many rapists masturbate to fantasies of raping a woman, so the sexual component of these acts cannot be summarily dismissed. In any case, an unfortunately significant proportion of non-rapist men are hostile toward women (Burt, 1980) and yet do not rape, and many men feel powerless and are unsatisfied with their adult sexual partner and yet they do not molest children. A more multifaceted account of the problem seems necessary.

Behavioral Theories

Behaviorally oriented researchers have, over the years, developed increasingly more comprehensive accounts of sexual abuse, but at the heart of most of these theories is the notion that sexual attractions underly the behaviors, and that these sexual attractions have been acquired via classical conditioning processes. McGuire *et al.* (1965) were the first to articulate such a theory. They proposed that all sexual preferences are entrenched by pairing fantasies depicting particular acts or partners with sexual arousal induced by masturbation. According to classical conditioning theory, such pairing will endow previously neutral stimuli with strong sexual valence, and, according to McGuire *et al.*, this will ultimately result in the person acting according to these acquired preferences. In McGuire *et al.*'s view, the scene which is fantasized derives from an initial actual sexual experience, and they see this primary experience as critical to the later development of sexual preferences. Abel and Blanchard (1974) describe McGuire *et al.*'s paper as 'an outstanding theoretical model', and Laws (1986) has incorporated classical conditioning processes into a more complex learning-based account of sexual abuse.

In each of these conditioning theories a crucial factor in the chain of events leading to deviant sexual acts is the formation of a strong sexual attraction to these deviant acts. As we have seen, this is said to result from the repeated pairing, during masturbation, of fantasies involving the deviant act and sexual arousal. Sexual arousal to deviant stimuli should, therefore, be manifest at laboratory evaluations of sexual preferences. Unfortunately, however, substantial numbers of men who engage in deviant sexual behavior fail to display deviant sexual preferences when tested. In particular, the majority of incest offenders, even those who have engaged in quite persistent and instrusive sexual interactions with female children in their care, show quite normal sexual preferences (Barbaree and Marshall, 1986; Quinsey *et al.*, 1979). The same appears to be true for a significant number of non-familial child molesters (Barbaree and Marshall, 1986; Marshall *et al.*, 1987a), rapists (Marshall *et al.*, 1986b), and exhibitionists (Marshall *et al.*, 1987c). Thus even if a conditioning account can explain the etiology of the deviant behavior of some sexual offenders, it does not seem applicable to a substantial proportion of them.

As evidence in support of the classical conditioning model, Evans's (1968, 1970) treatment research with exhibitionists is typically cited. He found that those exhibitionists who failed to profit from aversive therapy had used deviant masturbatory fantasies prior to treatment, whereas those for whom treatment was successful had not masturbated to deviant fantasies prior to treatment. These data seem to more readily contradict rather than confirm the classical conditioning theory. First, such a theory cannot account for the emergence of the exhibitionistic behavior in those men with no history of using exhibitionistic fantasies during masturbation (i.e. those who were successfully treated). Secondly, the treatment procedure employed aversive classical conditioning, which surely should have more readily eliminated exhibitionism in those who acquired the tendency by classical conditioning (i.e. those who masturbated to deviant fantasies) than in those who apparently engaged in their problematic behaviors in the absence of classically conditioned sexual preferences for exhibiting (i.e. those who did not use deviant masturbatory fantasies). Furthermore, in a study of exhibitionists which we have recently completed (Marshall *et al.*, 1987c), only 17% reported entertaining exhibitionistic fantasies during masturbation, and not one of these men said that this was their preferred fantasy (i.e. they said they only used such fantasies occasionally).

Finally, there is the problem of why these offenders engaged in their initial deviant experience and at what age they had this initial experience. It appears to be assumed in these theories that the initial experience was adventitious and occurred in childhood. While this makes sense, it runs immediately into the problem of why it is that so few men who have childhood sexual experiences with other children subsequently develop fixated deviant masturbatory fantasies (involving either exposing behaviors or children as sexual partners) which, in turn, lead to deviant acts. It also seems extremely unlikely that rapists experienced raping another person when they were children. Clearly, other factors must influence the course of these events.

A Comprehensive Behavioral Perspective

Recently Marshall and Barbaree (1984) elaborated a more complex but still essentially a learning-based view of the development of sexual aggression toward adults, and this model lends itself to a more encompassing version which would include child molestation. This theory attempts to integrate biological endowment, childhood experiences and the influence of the socio-cultural environment with both situational factors such as transitory states (e.g. anger, intoxication, etc.) and particular circumstances (e.g. easy access to a victim or temporary lack of constraints, as in the case of a soldier during war).

The genotype provides the human male with a relatively undirected sexual drive (Kinsey *et al.*, 1948). The sexual phenotype is a result of the channeling of sexual behavior according to society's rules. To say that males are endowed with the capacity to rape women or molest children is perhaps as trite as noting that all humans are capable of murder, but it does seem necessary to note that the capacity to sexually aggress is an inherent part of the human male's potential. This does not, however, align our theory with socio-biological accounts of aggression which all too often read like justifications for assaultive behavior (Hamburg, 1973; Popp and DeVore, 1979) and do not encourage attempts to prevent such offensive acts. Furthermore, socio-biological explanations of sexual assault (see Quinsey, 1984, for an example of such a theory) necessarily involve the claim that such behaviors were once (and still are under certain conditions) an advantageous male reproductive strategy. Whether this is true or not, it is irrelevant to a determination of why men rape in Western industrialized societies, since issues of reproductive advantage surely never enter the motivational considerations of a sentient modern rapist.

There seem to be two features of the shared biological inheritance of males which are relevant to these issues and which may have had evolutionary relevance in the distant past. First, the neural and hormonal mediators subserving sex and aggression are near enough identical to make their distinct expression and self-perceived independence a difficult task for the developing male (Marshall and Barbaree, 1984). Quinsey (1984) takes this structural proximity and biochemical identity as grounds for saying that human males will readily learn to aggress in a sexual way. We see in this juxtaposition quite the reverse; that is, human males are faced with the task of learning to inhibit aggression in a sexual context, a task which is very likely maximally difficult at puberty, when the sex steroid system increases its functioning fourfold (Sizonenko, 1978).

The second biological feature which seems relevant is the relatively unspecified direction of the inborn sexual drive. No doubt there are clear benefits for the survival of species who characteristically seek opposite-sexed partners, but it is unlikely that even this direction of sex drive is well formed in the absence of experience. Children frequently engage in sex play with other children of either gender, when given the opportunity. If these early experiences serve as the basis for subsequent masturbatory fantasies which entrench sexual preferences, as McGuire et al. (1965) would have us believe, then the miracle is that the majority of men prefer adult females. The flaws in McGuire's view notwithstanding, it is clear that the shift in the age of partners, which must occur throughout development for an appropriate adult orientation to finally emerge, appears to be quite a remarkable feat, particularly when rather sudden intense desires are provoked during puberty.

Human males, then, appear to be faced with two quite difficult learning tasks: (1) to inhibit aggression in a sexual context; and (2) to continually change the age of desired sexual partners throughout development. If we observe other mammals it is apparent that the absence of highly structured social rules permit somewhat indiscriminate attempts at mating with physically immature conspecifics as well as with unreceptive partners, although we should be careful not to impute aggressive features to these behaviors. Similarly, we have demonstrated that the responses of normal human males to rape cues can readily be disinhibited. Our consenting and forced-sex cues are identical in terms of the types of sexual behaviors described and in the temporal location of these behaviors; they differ only in terms of the female's consent or lack of it and the male's forcefulness. Typically, normal males display strong arousal to the consenting cues while the cues of non-consent and force, added to the ongoing sexual elements, markedly inhibits their arousal. However, when we intoxicated these men (Barbaree et al., 1983), or had them angered by a female (Yates et al., 1984), their arousal to the sexual elements in the rape scenes was significantly disinhibited. Other researchers have demonstrated additional factors which similarly disinhibit the arousal of normal males to rape scenes (Malamuth, 1984; Quinsey et al., 1981). Responses to sexual aggression are, therefore, under rather weak control of learned inhibitory constraints.

Given that males are faced with the difficult task of learning inhibitory controls, we must consider why it is that some do and some do not. Our attention will be given to those who do not, with the implication that the reciprocal factors will facilitate the acquisition of controls so that disinhibition will not readily occur.

In terms of their childhood experiences, rapists and child molesters appear to be remarkably similar to other criminals. Their parents provide poor models and engage in parenting practices which involve severe and inconsistent discipline, the fathers are typically aggressive, drunken and often in trouble with the law, and sexual abuse of the child or his or her siblings is not uncommon (Gebhard et al., 1965; Langevin et al., 1985; Rada, 1978). Such family circumstances lead, not surprisingly, to delinquency in these boys, and Knight *et al.* (1983) have shown that such anti-social behavior in boys increases the likelihood that they will commit rape as adults.

As a result of these experiences we would not expect these boys to develop much concern for the needs and rights of others; we would expect them to be self-centered, to not learn to constrain their aggression, and because aggressive delinquency tends to isolate these boys (Achenbach, 1982), we would expect them to have poor social skills. This lack of social skill may be critical to a teenage and adult inability to achieve satisfying appropriate relations with peer-aged females. Again, Knight *et al.* (1983) found that childhood and early teenage social incompetence was also a strong predictor of adult sexual deviance, particularly the tendency to rape.

Exposure to these types of parental styles clearly ill prepares the growing boy to acquire the constraints and skills necessary to function appropriately in adult sexual relations. Similarly prevailing socio-cultural attitudes may make the acquisition of constraints more difficult in boys who have had such poor parenting. Cross-cultural studies reveal that those societies which accept and encourage interpersonal violence, which are male-dominated and whose members hold negative views of women all have far higher rates of forceful sexuality than do societies which do not have these features (Chagnon, 1977; Otterbein, 1979; Sanday, 1981). In such societies children are likewise seen as the property of males to do with as they wish. The United States, which has the highest per capita rates of rape and child molestation among Western societies, also appears to accept and even admire violence (Leyton, 1986; Marshall, 1986), and certainly a large proportion of its adult males hold negative views of women (Briere *et al.*, 1981; Burt, 1980).

Pornography, even in its most 'hard-core' versions, is widely available in the United States and yet the sentiments expressed in much of these materials is essentially negative toward women, and implies (if not clearly states) that a woman's role in sex is to serve male needs and that women really enjoy being raped even if they appear to resist. The research literature is replete with the harmful effects of exposure to violent pornography in the sense that it changes the attitudes and sexual responses of non-rapist males in the direction of those of rapists (Donnerstein, 1984; Malamuth, 1981). Given that instructions indicating that it is acceptable to display arousal to rape, disinhibit the arousal of normal males to forced-sex scenarios (Quinsey *et al.*, 1981), it should not be surprising that exposure to rape pornography subsequently disinhibits arousal to rape (Malamuth, 1981). Since rape pornography is sold as 'entertainment', this may be construed by some consumers to indicate that arousal to such scenes is acceptable. Also there is evidence that some rapists and child molesters use pornography to incite themselves to commit offenses (Marshall, in press, a). Of course, not all sex offenders use pornography and not all non-offenders are negatively influenced by exposure to such materials, but this does not deny that some males (presumably, in particular, those exposed to the poor parenting described above) are vulnerable to its influences (Marshall, in press, b). Those who are vulnerable apparently find the messages in pornography to be persuasive, perhaps because the acceptance of such messages confers a sense of power which is otherwise lacking in these males. The important point to note here about the possible influence of pornography and the associated socio-cultural attitudes is that our perceptions are shaped by experience. It is not claimed here that the cultural environment in the United States is so overwhelmingly negative as to corrupt all the males in that society. Clearly, this is not true. Each person perceives the socio-cultural mosaic selectively, and focuses on those features which encourage views and behaviors congruent with the desires and attitudes shaped in that person by their previous experience. It is in this sense that we must conceptualize the influence of all environmental factors.

An additional (and perhaps related) feature concerns the molestation of boys by adults. Generally, child molesters report higher frequencies of such molestation in their childhood than do men who have not offended against children (Seghorn et al., in press; Quinsey, 1986), and frequently these molestations are accompanied by the deliberate exposure of the child to pornography, presumably as an attempt by the offender to arouse the boy's sexual interest (Marshall, in press, a). No doubt the combination of exposure to pornography, an adult modelling child molestation and the boy's own sexual arousal in this context provide a basis for future sexual fantasies which may entrench an attraction to deviant sexual behaviors.

Thus males who are ill prepared by their childhood experiences to counter negative socio-cultural influences fail to fully develop constraints against sexual aggression. This does not mean, however, that all such men will enact these offensive behaviors; it requires particular proximal circumstances to elicit such propensities. As noted earlier, we have demonstrated that alcohol intoxication and anger disinhibit the arousal to rape of normal males, and it is clear that many rapists and child molesters are intoxicated or angered immediately prior to and often during their sexual attacks (Christie et al., 1979). The prolonged experience of stress also seems to reduce the capacity of some males to inhibit tendencies to sexual aggression (Gebhard et al., 1965; Mohr et al., 1964), as does prior sexual arousal (Malamuth et al., 1980). No doubt there are other states which similarly disinhibit men. Perceived anonymity appears to be one such state, although there is no clear evidence on the issue except that more than 30% of non-rapists indicate some likelihood they would rape *if they knew they could get away with it* (Malamuth, 1981)! It is important to note that these disinhibiting factors, if strong enough, persistent enough and in combination, may overwhelm even well-entrenched social constraints, but our theory posits that the majority of offenses will be committed by men whose experience has not provided them with strong inhibitions against sexual aggression.

Similarly, certain ways of construing the behavior of women and children may allow men to set aside any developed controls. For example, child molesters have repeatedly told us that their victims were provocative if not downright seductive, despite the quite clear evidence to the contrary. One recent patient, when he saw an 8-year old girl sit opposite him with her feet up on the sofa, thereby revealing her crotch to his view, saw this as a deliberate attempt on the part of the child to have him touch her sexually. He maintained this perspective, despite the fact that the child's attention was clearly absorbed by the television show she was watching and that the girl's mother was present in the room. Likewise, many child molesters and rapists appear to believe that their assaults do no harm to the victims and may even be beneficial. Of course, all these cognitive distortions are self-serving, and no doubt grown out of the offender's need to rationalize his behavior. Nevertheless, they do allow the offenders to set aside whatever constraints they have developed against sexual molestation.

Opportune circumstances provide the final link in this chain of events which trigger an overt sexual attack. When males gather together, exclusive of females, this tends to promote at least transitory attitudes negative to women and approving of aggression, and to encourage definitions of masculinity in terms of sexual prowess. Amir (1971) describes these circumstances as preceding group rapes, but he suggests that rapes will not result from these circumstances unless the males are already aggressive and harbor negative attitudes toward women, and unless at least their leader is intoxicated. Having ready access to a woman or a child, particularly one who may be unlikely to report them, obviously does not encourage a male whose controls are poorly developed to restrain his sexually aggressive urges. Since the majority of rapes and child molestations are planned (Amir, 1971; Geller, 1977; Quinsey, 1986), it is clear that offenders frequently set up the circumstances which facilitate abuse, including deliberately intoxicating themselves and priming themselves by viewing ponrography (Marshall, in press, a,b).

Once a man has taken the initial step of sexually attacking a woman or a child, subsequent offenses may be less vigorously resisted, particularly if the offender does not suffer any consequences. This lowered resistance may result from the desensitization to threat which occurs when the deviant act goes unpunished, and from the rewarding effects of subsequent sexual fantasies of the act. Actually, the issue of desensitization appears to be particularly important. In another context, Zillman (1986) has demonstrated that exposure to pornography desensitizes viewers and reduces their prior abhorrence of various eccentric sexual behaviors. Barbaree and Marshall (1986) have suggested that their data are consistent with the view that, over the course of repeated offending, child molesters, apparently through a similar process of desensitization, progressively lose their inhibitions toward intrusive sex with their victims (i.e. they seem to progress from fondling to oral–genital sex to intercourse) and toward their use of coercive tactics. Abel *et al.* (1975) reported a similar progression in a sadistic rapist.

Those experiential and momentarily disinhibiting factors so salient to the initial offense may be somewhat less relevant to continual offending over many years; at least the strength of the necessary disinhibitors would be markedly reduced and the simple habit strength of repeatedly rewarded and non-punished behaviors would be expected to be most crucial to the maintenance of the deviant tendencies.

ASSESSMENT METHODS

Given our theoretical outline of the causes of sexual assaults, and particularly that aspect of the theory concerning the persistence of such behaviors, we are in a position to specify what needs to be assessed in these men in order to both provide information regarding the future likelihood of offending and to design and evaluate treatment. Concurrent with the development of our theory we have, as a product of our research and our understanding of the research of others, continually expanded the areas of functioning we assess and treat.

Sexual Behavior

We assess two aspects of sexual behavior in these offenders: deviant sexual preferences and broader features of their general sexual functioning. Although the range of features assessed has progressively expanded over the years, deviant sexual preferences have, from the outset, been primary targets.

Deviant sexual preferences

Freund (1965, 1967a, b) was the first to report the assessment of the sexual preferences of child molesters, and this work, plus Freund's (1961) earlier report concerning the laboratory diagnosis of homosexuality, served as the basis for all subsequent research on the evaluation of deviant sexual proclivities in various paraphilias. For a more complete description of these assessment procedures, and for an indication of how to set up such a laboratory, the reader is referred to Earls and Marshall (1983) and Laws and Osborne (1983). The validity of these assessments is attested to by their capacity to differentiate males with known differences in their sexual preferences, ranging from homosexuals (McConaghy, 1982) and fetishists and transvestites (Marks and Gelder, 1967), to exhibitionists (Langevin et al., 1979), child molesters (Freund, 1965, 1967a) and rapists (Abel et al., 1977). There is also some evidence bearing on the reliability of these measures (Eccles et al., in press; Farkas et al., 1979)., and they have been shown to be responsive indices of changes with treatment (Marshall, 1973; Quinsey et al., 1976).

Freund's procedure involves the direct measurement of the male's erectile response to the presentation of stimuli relevant to the deviation under consideration. For example, when assessing men who have molested young girls, Freund presents stimuli which depict females ranging in age from pre-schoolers to adults. The results of his research demonstrated that, as a group, men who molest other people's children prefer children over adults as sexual partners; that is, these men display stronger erectile responses to children than they do to adults. Non-deviant males showed a preference for adults. Quinsey and his colleagues have essentially replicated Freund's findings (Quinsey et al., 1975; Quinsey et al., 1979), but they have also demonstrated that, as a group, incest offenders appear to sexually prefer adults rather than children.

Marshall et al. (1986a) found similar group differences between non-offenders

Table 9.1 Sexual preference profiles for age of target females

Group	Child	Child–adult	Profile shape Non-discriminating	Teen–adult	Adult
Non-familial child molesters	35[a]	12.5	15	25	12.5
Incest offenders	0	5	40	15	40
Non-offenders	0	0	18	14	68

[a] Percentage of each group.

and offenders, and among familial and non-familial offenders who had molested girls. However, subsequent analyses of the individual data (Barbaree and Marshall, 1986) revealed quite a different picture. We were able to classify each individual's erectile response pattern over the various ages of the females depicted in our stimuli (color slides of naked females aged 3 through 24 years in two-year age steps), into one of five profile shapes:

(1) A clear preference for children with little arousal to adults (the 'Child' profile);
(2) A preference for children and adults with low arousal to pubescent females (the 'Child–adult' profile);
(3) A non-discriminating pattern displaying moderate arousal to females of all ages;
(4) A clear preference for teenage and adult females with little arousal to children (the 'Teen–adult' profile); and
(5) A clear preference for adults (the 'Adult' profile).

Table 9.1 indicates the percentage of each group displaying each preference profile. This type of analysis is clearly more valuable in the clinical description of individual cases, and provides far more information about the obvious heterogeneity of child molesters than do the usual reports of group data.

In both the studies reported above we also extended our appraisal of preferences to include an examination of the offenders' responding to various sexual acts with children. We found that those child molesters who obtained a 'Child' profile in the age preference assessment displayed greater arousal to descriptions of intercourse with a child than they did to fondling or oral–genital sex. Furthermore, the arousal of these same offenders was not at all inhibited by the addition to an ongoing account of sex between an adult male and a female child of descriptions which indicated that the child was upset and resisting, and that the man was using force and violence to get his way. Subjects displaying all other age profiles (i.e. those who had a 'Child–adult', a non-discriminating profile, a 'Teen–adult' or an 'Adult' profile) were progressively less aroused as the described sexual acts became more intrusive, and as the child resisted and the offender engaged in more coercive acts. Those child molesters who revealed the 'Child' profile had far more victims ($\overline{X} = 9$) than the remaining offenders ($\overline{X} = 2.2$), and their offense history revealed greater use of forcefulness and more intrusive sexual acts than did the histories of the other offenders. These men are clearly the most dangerous child molesters, and they also appear to be the ones most likely to recidivate if untreated (Barbaree and Marshall, 1987).

Recently we completed similar studies of men who had molested boys (Marshall *et al.*, 1987a). Although our analyses of these data are not yet complete, we have been able to classify these offenders into those whose responses to adults reveal a homosexual or a heterosexual orientation. Somewhat surprisingly, only one third of these men were classified as homosexual on the basis of our laboratory tests, and most of them reported that their homosexuality was unknown to friends and family; most of these homosexuals were married, although they reported that their sexual relations with their wives were unsatisfactory and infrequent. These homosexual men had targeted boys who were older ($\overline{X} = 12.4$ years) than those targeted by the heterosexuals ($\overline{X} = 7.3$ years).

Clearly, then, the assessment of sexual preferences is essential in the description of child molesters. However, it is clear that not all of these men reveal deviant interests at assessment, and, indeed, we have found that approximately one fifth of the child molesters and one third of the incest offenders attending our clinic show such low responding to all of the stimuli presented in assessment that we cannot use this type of data as a basis for formulating and assessing treatment, nor for generating a prognosis. In our assessment of rapists, using these methods we have come to gloomier conclusions regarding the value of erectile measures.

Early researchers (Abel *et al.*, 1977; Barbaree *et al.*, 1979; Quinsey *et al.*, 1981), working with small numbers of offenders and controls, obtained results indicating that normal males were highly aroused by consenting sex between adults but were progressively inhibited by (i.e. displayed progressively lower arousal to) scenes identical in sexual content but involving a non-consenting female accompanied by increases in forcefulness exercised by the male. In these early studies rapists did not display this inhibition to non-consent and force. However, Baxter *et al.* (1986) subsequently evaluated larger samples of rapists ($N = 60$) and non-rapists ($N = 41$), and found that the rapists were, indeed, significantly inhibited by non-consent and force, just as the non-rapists were. In fact, the only difference we observed between the rapists and the non-rapists was that the latter group showed enhanced arousal to the consenting scenes at a second testing occasion, whereas the rapists remained unchanged. Just what this odd difference means we are not at all sure at present.

Our recent findings of similar inhibition processes in normals and rapists in response to the rape scenarios are quite unlike the earlier reports, and there are several reasons why this may have happened. First, simply increasing the size of the sample may have provided sufficient power to discern differences in responding among the rapists between consenting and non-consenting scenes.

However, this seems unlikely, since Quinsey *et al.* (1984) actually found that rapists responded *more* to the non-consenting than to the consenting scenes. It is very likely that the groups in the earlier studies sampled an eccentric and unusually dangerous segment of the rapist population, partly on account of the nature of the setting (Abel's clinic is nationally renowned in the United States, and may very well have attracted the worst offenders from around the country; Quinsey's studies were conducted in a secure hospital for the criminally insane; and we were initially referred the most dangerous offenders). Some researchers have suggested to us that our results derive from the fact that we do not use sufficiently provocative materials, and that if we instructed the rapists to suppress their arousal they would appear more deviant. Marshall *et al.* (1986b) recently reported the assessment of 99 rapists (a sample quite independent of the Baxter *et al.*, 1986, subjects), who were assessed using both audiotaped descriptions (much like those used in the Baxter *et al.* study) and Abel *et al.*'s (1981) videotaped scenes. In addition, these rapists were assessed under instructions to allow themselves to become aroused and under instructions to suppress their arousal. Although the different instructions and modes of presenting the stimuli produced varying overall levels of arousal, the rapists demonstrated, under all conditions, very clear inhibition to the elements of non-consent and force.

Despite these findings, it is essential to assess these preferences with rapists, since some of them, notably the sadists, appear to have aberrant arousal patterns (Langevin *et al.*, 1985; Quinsey *et al.*, 1984). Nevertheless, such assessments will not be as fruitful with rapists as they are with child molesters. In any case, whether or not any specific patient reveals deviant sexual preferences at laboratory assessment, his skills in other areas of sexual functioning will have to be evaluated.

While other researchers (Cox and Daitzman, 1980; Langevin *et al.*, 1979) have described exhibitionists as being aroused by depictions of exhibiting behaviors, Marshall *et al.* (1987b) have found no group differences between these offenders and matched non-offender controls in their responses to exhibitionistic scenes. In fact, only 21% of our patients displayed more than 20% of a full erection to the exhibitionistic scenes. The maximum arousal displayed by any of these men to these scenes, relative to their arousal to appropriate sex scenes, was 60% and this level of relative arousal was only apparent in 12% of the offenders. Erectile evaluations of exhibitionists, then, as with the rapists, are, at best, of equivocal value.

Sexual functioning

Contrary to the expectations of some theorists (see Langevin, 1985; Quinsey, 1984, for a discussion of such theories), many men who rape women or sexually abuse children have ongoing sexual relations with an adult female partner (Christie *et al.*, 1979). However, the sexual aspect of these relationships is frequently deemed unsatisfactory by the offender, either on account of low frequency, a sense of unfulfilment or because of the presence of sexual dysfunctions. On the latter point, Burgess and her colleagues (Burgess and Holmstrom, 1974, 1976; Groth and Burgess, 1977) have found that rape victims frequently report that their attackers had erectile or ejaculatory problems during the offense. A number of our patients have described their typical sexual relations with consenting partners as involving little in the way of pre-coital preparatory behaviors, and, indeed, they often express prudish attitudes toward the usual range of non-coitus sexual practices (Record, 1977) and are quite naive about sex in general. Their aim in consenting sexual relations with adult partners appears to be to attain orgasm as quickly as possible, with little in the way of affectionate interactions and with little concern for mutual satisfaction. The needs which sexual behavior satisfies are extensive, and clearly involve more than simply sexual release (Neubeck, 1974; Schimel, 1974). However, the majority of sexual assaulters seem to be quite unaware of these other motives; perhaps this is why they cannot account for their persistent experience of dissatisfaction with their sexual relations, since they pay little attention to these other features of sexual interchanges.

Methods to assess these aspects of sexual functioning are' not remarkably sophisticated, and we have had to rely on self-reports and structured interviews which, where possible, include the offender's adult partner. We have developed two questionnaires: the Sexual Knowledge Questionnaire, which not only describes the information base of the patient but also his prudishness; and the Sexual Relations Questionnaire. In addition, the Sexual Incident Report has been developed by us as a structured interview guide to assess the patient's sexual, fantasy and offense history. We have found that gathering this information from an interview increases the accuracy of the information, because the loosely structured responses from the patient allow the interviewer to pursue more detailed descriptions of events and fantasies and also because it permits the interviewer to cross-check the descriptions by raising the issues on several occasions.

Social Incompetence

Most sexual offenders appear to be inept in one or more areas of social functioning, although it may be true that, as a group, rapists do not appear to be deficient in conversational skills (Segal and Marshall, 1985a, b; Stermac and Quinsey, 1986). Child molesters, however, are more generally inept (Segal and Marshall, 1985a, b) and both groups are poor at predicting their own social performance (Segal and Marshall, 1986).

The range of social functioning which we assess includes: conversational skills; empathy; assertiveness; social anxiety; relationship skills and marital adjustment; anger control; social problem solving; and social self-esteem. We use several self-report measures including: the Social Self-esteem Inventory (Lawson et al., 1979); the Social Response Inventory (Keltner et al., 1981); the Social Avoidance and Distress Scale and the Fear of Negative Evaluations Scale (Watson and Friend, 1969); the Locke and Wallace Marital Adjustment Scale (Locke and Wallace, 1957); and an Empathy Scale which we have derived from the work of Andrews (1983). In addition, we have patients role-play a variety of social interactions which we videotape and subsequently rate for conversational skill and anxiety and for problem-solving skills. Relatively unstructured interviews with the clients, of course, provide extensive information relevant to all these issues as they do on all other facets of the evaluation. In particular, within the context of our interviews we attempt to infer the patient's competence in financial management, job search-and-secure skills and their use of leisure time.

We assess the various aspects of social competence partly because we see them as etiologically significant, but primarily because we consider them to be crucial to the maintenance of their offensive behaviors. If a man is socially incompetent this will not only serve to reduce the probability that he will be able to form satisfying and acceptable relations with adult partners, but such incompetence will cause severe stress in his life, and stress increases the likelihood of all manner of dysfunctional and anti-social behaviors (Dohrenwend and Dohrenwend, 1974). Similarly, we consider the attitudes and beliefs of these men serve to maintain their offensive behaviors.

Faulty Cognitions

Negative attitudes toward women characterize the belief systems of rapists (Hegeman and Meikle, 1980), and child molesters hold a variety of attitudes and beliefs about sex with children which serve to continue their offensive behaviors (Abel *et al.*, 1984; Stermac and Segal, 1987). The prudishness of rapists, noted above, may be related to their negative views, since Burt (1980) has shown that sexual conservatism leads to a ready acceptance of myths about rape which essentially hold the woman to be responsible and which typically attribute to the victim a desire to be raped. Child molesters all too often believe that their sexual interactions with children are educational or in other ways beneficial to the child (e.g. they claim to give physical affection to emotionally deprived children), despite clear evidence to the contrary. In addition, child molesters see children as sexually provocative, and they believe children enjoy sexual encounters with adults. Similarly, exhibitionists frequently consider they are providing education or sexual titillation to their victims.

We have developed two approaches to the assessment of these attitudes and distorted cognitions: role-played responses to scenarios involving either adult females or children; and self-report measures. The self-reports include the Attitudes toward Women Scale (Spence *et al.*, 1973); our development of Abel's Distorted Cognitions Scale (Abel *et al.*, 1984), which taps beliefs about sex with children; and the Buss–Durkee Hostility Inventory (Buss and Durkee, 1957). Again, the role-plays are videotaped and later scored for the presence and degree of distortions (or non-conventional views) evident in the man's responses.

Process of Assessment

We assess offenders typically for two purposes: (1) to assist in the determination of the future likelihood of repeated offending, and in estimating the patient's amenability to treatment; and (2) to evaluate the effectiveness of treatment. Our confidence in estimating future offending has recently been increased by Maletzky's (1987) large-scale follow-up study of treated offenders, in which he was able to identify features which predicted poorer outcome, and by our own long-term recidivism data on untreated child molesters, which likewise produced predictive factors (Barbaree and Marshall, 1987). Our own data and those of Maletzky also provide a basis for estimating who is likely to respond well to treatment. In terms of future offending in both the treated and untreated child molesters, if the man attempted intercourse with his victims he has a poor prognosis, and this proved to be the most powerful predictor we discerned. This is somewhat unfortunate, since it is a static factor, and whatever is associated with such a propensity (and we have not found anything yet), it is apparently not as readily changed by treatment as are other features of these offenders.

As far as evaluating treatment is concerned, our assessments are conducted prior to treatment and at various points thereafter. This is meant to provide an immediate evalution of the effects of treatment as well as determining whether changing these features of the offenders is related to the cessation of their offensive behaviors. In terms of the latter, we follow up patients through official police records (which document all charges and convictions throughout the whole of North America), as well as through informal sources such as Children's Aid Societies' records and unofficial information kept in local police files. Unfortunately, the reports of patients and their families have proved to be marked underestimates of recidivism compared with official police records, and these in turn indicate a far lower re-offense rate than do our informal sources (Marshall and Barbaree, 1987; in press). Similarly, our data reveal that follow-up evaluations conducted less than four years after treatment discharge will underestimate recidivism rates.

FORMULATION OF THE INDIVIDUAL CASE

To illustrate the formulation of a case we will describe one particular patient we assessed and treated some time ago, but the reader should not infer that this man is a 'typical' offender except in respect of some of his features. There is, in fact, no such person as a 'typical' offender. The process of data collection and formulation of a prognosis and treatment plan illustrated with this man is, however, typical.

Mr H, a 33-year-old caucasian male, was referred to our clinic from the local psychiatric hospital for treatment of aberrant sexual behavior. He was divorced six years prior to referral, apparently because of his repeated convictions for exhibitionism and voyeurism. Despite his frequent convictions, he had spent little time in jail and had been gainfully employed with very few periods of unemployment in his adult life. Indeed, even after release from 10 months in jail, he had a job within one week. He was also careful with his money and had a reasonably substantial bank balance, owned his own car and was planning to purchase a house if treatment was successful. His intelligence was assessed as above-average (Raven's Progressive Matrices IQ equivalent = 118) and he had a high-school diploma graduating from Grade 13. He had no problems with alcohol or other drug use and no history of violence outside of a sexual context.

He described having begun peeping and exposing at approximately age 12, and he said he had engaged in these behaviors on a weekly basis almost continuously since then. This high rate of offending was reflected in over 30 charges for various crimes related to these behaviors (e.g. indecent acts, loitering with intent, etc.). Four years prior to attending our clinic, his offensive behaviors had begun to extend to more aggressive and intrusive acts. Initially, this showed itself in aggressive remarks to his exposure victims, and then on two occasions he chased after these women and indecently assaulted one of them. He also entered the tents of three different females while they slept at a camping site, although he touched only the last of these women. Finally, he committed a very aggressive offense, for which he was convicted and received a two-year jail sentence, of which he served 10 months. On this particular occasion he offered a ride home in his car to a 24-year-old female acquaintance. Instead of driving her home, however, he took her to a secluded area, where he forced her to strip naked and made her engage in various sexual acts with him.

Considering the aggressive and humiliating features of his behaviors with this unfortunate woman (e.g. he inserted a screwdriver into her vagina and he urinated on her), the court took a remarkably lenient view in sentencing him and the Parole Board subsequently took the same position, perhaps in both instances because he presented as a well-dressed, shy, quiet man who appeared as anything but dangerous in his demeanor. In these judgements the authorities were mistaken, since he recommenced exposing two weeks after release, and within six months he had molested two female children (aged 9 and 11 years) and one retarded 18-year-old woman; he attempted vaginal and anal intercourse with the 11-year-old girl. Although he was reported for all three offenses, he was only charged with the assault on the 18-year-old, and this charge was later dismissed, although he admitted to us that he had committed all three crimes. Shortly before attending our clinic, this man had tried to get the 13-year-old daughter of a female friend to perform fellatio on him, but she refused and told her mother, who directed our patient to get professional help or she would press charges. On our advice, the mother reported the offense, but neither the woman nor her daughter were willing to appear as witnesses, so no charge was laid.

Our assessments revealed several features of this man which were in need of change. Although he was reasonably skilled in brief conversations and had satisfactory skills at problem solving, he was quite unassertive. He characteristically won friends by excessive gift-giving and by his eager willingness to do almost anything for people. All too often this led to him being taken advantage of, with consequent costs to his self-esteem; these times of very low self-esteem coincided with higher frequencies of sexual offending. Associated with this, he seemed unable to accept the responsibilities entailed in relationships, even though he desired the benefits to himself which resulted from having a sexual partner. Even the everyday responsibilities of relationships (e.g. assisting in household management, sharing shopping, etc.) were experienced as burdensome and aversive by him. When pressures were placed on him to meet these responsibilties, he characteristically reacted by offending.

In addition, he displayed multiple deviations during our erectile assessments. He was aroused by female children (as well as adults), by adult males, by scenes of forceful sex with females of all ages and by descriptions of peeping and exhibiting. Multiple paraphilias in sex offenders are not uncommon (Abel et al., 1985) but it is usually too time consuming to assess every possible deviation; in this case we did so·because these themes were clearly evident in his offense history and because he told us they were exciting to him. Although he engaged in various sexual acts, including consenting sex with age-appropriate partners, he reported that all of these were only marginally and transitorily satisfying to him. He said he was driven to engage in high rates of sexual activity of whatever kind he could secure, including masturbation or impersonal sex with other males in public washrooms if no other alternative partner was available. He said he thought that, sooner or later, he would discover a sexual partner who would give him a sense of fulfilment, although he could not say just what this would entail. Given this high drive, he was referred for an evaluation of his hormonal functioning but, somewhat surprisingly, he was found to be within normal limits on all aspects assayed, and therefore anti-androgen therapy did not seem called for.

This man had given no consideration to the possible harmful effects on his victims, despite seeming able to empathize effectively in other circumstances. His cognitions regarding harm were, therefore, simply undeveloped, but no doubt he had avoided considering these issues in order to avoid the experience of guilt and remorse. He did, however, see children as seductive, he believed that at least some women enjoyed being raped and he did not consider peeping or exposing to be offensive; in fact, he seemed somewhat annoyed with the women who had reported him for these offenses. However, in general, he did not harbour hostile feelings toward women.

The data from our assessments were discussed with the patient and we used these discussions and the remainder of our interviews to test our hypotheses derived from these evaluations. Our assessments and interviews revealed the following strengths in this man: above-average intelligence and good educational attainment; good conversationalist and good social problem-solver; no drug or alcohol problems; little or no hostility to females; generally good empathic skills; a good worker with a good employment record and financial security;

normal hormonal functioning; and a desire to secure more than physical gratification from sexual relations. His deficits included: unassertiveness; low self-esteem; inability to accept the responsibilities of relationships; high sex drive manifest in excessively frequent sexual acts, including appropriate and inappropriate behaviors; deviant sexual interests in children, peeping, exhibiting and forceful sex associated with aberrant fantasizing when masturbating and impersonal sex with males; and, finally, distorted cognitions about the role and desires of the victims of his offenses and an undeveloped notion of the harm his acts may have caused.

Our formulation of this and other cases is primarily aimed at articulating a prognosis and treatment plan. Not surprisingly, we concluded that the prognosis would be poor in the absence of treatment. The fact that he had attempted intercourse with one of his child victims, that he had strong arousal to forced sex with both adult and child females and that he had enacted sexual violence against a female led us to conclude that not only was he at very high risk to re-offend, he was also a potential danger to future victims. This conclusion is partly derived from clinical experience and common sense but also from data on our untreated offenders. However, since he expressed a determination to overcome his problems, and since he understood quite clearly that this would require considerable effort on his part over an extended period of time, we thought he was a good candidate for treatment. His other strengths also encouraged this positive outlook on likely treatment benefits.

In terms of a formulation concerning the etiology and maintenance of any individual's problem behaviors we are always somewhat cautious. This patient did come from a background in which his father was alcoholic and violent, although he did not seem to have acquired similar general aggressive tendencies; no doubt this was due to the very positive influence of his mother, whose love and support offset to some extent the negative influence of his father. However, our patient had always tried to impress his father but was quite unsuccessful, and this seemed to be largely responsible for his low self-esteem. Also, he noted that he was afraid of a commitment to a relationship, since he had observed such dreadful effects of this on his mother and this appeared to be the basis for his inability to accept responsibilities. We believe that his low self-esteem, unassertiveness and poor relationships were all functionally related, and led him to attempt, through sex, to demonstrate to himself that he was powerful and masculine. In addition, sex came to provide momentary satisfaction when the experience of satisfaction was otherwise remarkably uncommon in his life. Also, he realized he was searching for something more in sex but was unsure what it was. Our guess was that it was something to do with intimacy and acceptance (see Marshall et al., 1987b, for a discussion of the relevance of these issues). Since his striving for satisfaction was partially but not completely fulfilled in sex, this led to an increase in the frequency of sexual acts and to an extension of these beyond those usually deemed acceptable, in pursuit of these elusive goals. Perhaps an accidental opportunity (although he could not recall his first offense) to expose or peep started him on a deviant course, although it may have been the result of the gradual modification of masturbatory fantasies as consensual themes became satiated.

TREATMENT METHODS AND ISSUES

In an important sense, treatment of the individual is an extension of the process of testing the hypotheses generated in our formulation of the case. The same is true for our group outcome appraisals, which are not only aimed at determining effective treatment components but also serve to evaluate our overall theoretical account of the problem. First, we will deal with the more general issues concerning the description and evaluation of treatment methods, and then we will extend the formulation of the individual case described in the previous section to the implementation and outcome of treatment with him.

Before describing the elements of our program we wish to make a few preliminary remarks about the evaluation of treatment in general. Most treatment outcome studies reported in the literature describe processes by which patients are selected for treatment, and some of these involve a quite thorough screening of potential candidates. Although the precise bases for selection are rarely made explicit, it is clear that the aim is to choose only those patients who are thought to be best suited to the program. From a practical point of view, this appears to be quite sensible, but there are at least three objections which can be raised against this strategy. First, we do not know in advance just who might benefit from any particular program, and if we carefully select patients we will have necessarily narrowed the variance in the possible predictors, consequently eliminating the possibility of relating patient features to outcome. Second, in this selection process it is very likely that those patients chosen for treatment will also be those deemed most likely to succeed in the absence of treatment. Thus a very successful outcome evaluation (i.e. a low recidivism rate after treatment) may mislead us into thinking that it is the treatment program which has produced this, when it may simply be a product of the thorough selection process. Finally, adopting such a policy of carefully selecting for treatment only those patients whom it is thought will benefit from the program does nothing to help us learn how to deal with the more problematic offenders. Accordingly, we accept into treatment all patients who are willing, and we attempt to persuade all those offenders whom we assess that they are in need of treatment and that we can help them. If someone does not take advantage of our offer it is not on account of any attempt on our part to exclude them.

In addition to the selection issue, another concern regarding treatment evaluation is the need to distinguish long-term outcome (i.e. changes in the actual offensive behaviors) from an estimate of changes in those features of patients which are targeted in treatment (the 'within-treatment' changes). These latter features are those deemed necessary to change in order to reduce offending. In our program these are the features which we have described in the assessment section, namely: sexual behaviors, social competence and faulty cognitions. We need to determine whether or not treatment processes do in fact induce changes in these features of patients, and whether or not such changes are related to outcome. Few treatment programs, for any problem, distinguish within-treatment changes from long-term behavioral change, much less relate the former to outcome.

We will not discuss non-behavioral treatment programs except to mention that other forms of psychological treatment have not been demonstrated, in sound methodological appraisals, to be effective (Barbaree and Marshall, in press). However, this is not to say these approaches are ineffective but rather to note that there is simply no convincing evidence of their efficacy. Physical procedures, on the other hand, do seem to be effective, although many of the studies supporting their value also leave a lot to be desired methodologically. Bradford (1985) has provided an excellent review of this literature and the reader is referred to his article for a more extensive account of the evidence. While physical castration and stereotaxic neurosurgical procedures may reduce aberrant sexual behavior, they are unlikely to be adopted as treatment methods in all but the rarest cases. Chemical agents such as cyproterone acetate and medroxyprogesterone acetate have been (and will, no doubt, continue to be) used as effective treatment methods. Even here, however, since these agents on their own do nothing to correct the many problems in these men which are functionally related to their offensive behavior, hormonal agents will most effectively be employed in combination with behavioral methods, and perhaps even then only in those cases where hormonal aberrations are present.

A Behavioral Treatment Program

Since 1970 we have developed our program and evaluated limited aspects of it. For instance, it was first described by Marshall (1971) as the application of behavioral strategies to modify the deviant sexual interests and enhance the restricted social functioning of a man who molested both girls and boys. This was later expanded to an inpatient program for child molesters located in a psychiatric hospital (Marshall and McKnight, 1975) and to a program for rapists and child molesters incarcerated in a penitentiary (Marshall and Williams, 1975; Marshall et al., 1976;. McCaldon and Marshall, 1977), and finally it was extended to an outpatient program for a mixed group of sexual deviates and offenders (Marshall, 1973, 1974). While these evaluations all served useful purposes in extending our understanding of the value of our treatment components and the patients with whom they might be maximally useful, such appraisals did not meet the criteria required of a thorough evaluation, since they did not involve more than a few subjects, the patients were not homogeneous groups, the programs were limited in scope, the instruments for measuring changes were very limited and the period of follow-up assessment was quite short. However, recently Marshall and Barbaree (in press) have made a first attempt at estimating the value of the outpatient program which we have operated for the past several years restricting our analyses to familial and non-familial child molesters. This evaluation is also limited by the fact that it was not a systematic planned investigation (therefore there is no controlled allocation of subjects to groups nor is there an assessment of the contribution of the different components), and there were only limited aspects of the measurement of change available (only erectile measures of sexual preferences). Perhaps most importantly, however, the program evolved in form and content over the 11 years of the collection of data. Although the latter aspect reduces the strictly scientific merit of the study, it would be poor clinical practice not to change a program in the face of expanding knowledge.

In describing our present program we will focus on the three areas of dysfunction which we have already identified: deviant sexuality, social incompetence and attitudinal/cognitive problems. However, the reader should not take these descriptions to mean that all offenders suffer from defects in each and all of these areas. Just as we observe in other complex human problems, there is a significant degree of individuality in both the nature and expression of difficulties, and we have already seen this in our formulation of the individual case. However, these idiosyncracies usually take the form of varying degrees of aberration within limited areas of dysfunction, and it is rare to have to look beyond the areas we have identified to describe and modify behaviors so that control over sexual offending is achieved. Nevertheless, treatment is always individualized within the constraints of the overall design of the program. Thus in reducing deviant sexual interest, variations on the procedures may be employed, depending both on features of the individual patient as well as on his response to the usual procedures. Similarly, in enhancing social skills and modifying attitudes and beliefs the specific content of training procedures will, to some extent, be individually determined, although most of the social and attitudinal change procedures are conducted within a group context which limits the degree of individualization.

Early behavior therapists believed that altering deviant sexual preferences was all that was needed to eliminate deviant behavior (Evans, 1968), but recently these programs have been expanded to include more general aspects of sexual, social and cognitive functioning (Abel et al., 1985; Annon and Robinson, 1985; Marshall et al., 1983).

The modification of sexual preferences

The goal here is to normalize the preferences of those patients who display aberrant patterns at the pre-treatment physiological assessments. Two separate although not independent targets are identified: (1) reduction of sexual arousal to deviant acts or inappropriate partners; and (2) enhancement or establishment of arousal to appropriate partners and acts. We use a combination of procedures to achieve these two goals, including aversive therapy, masturbatory reconditioning and satiation, covert sensitization and a self-administered procedure for reducing spontaneous urges. Throughout this component of treatment we repeatedly elaborate a model of deviant sexual behavior which emphasizes the role in maintaining aberrant behavior, of sexual thoughts, images or fantasies involving children, forceful sex or genital exhibiting. Accordingly, our procedures in this component focus on eliminating these thoughts and replacing them with thoughts of appropriate partners and behaviors.

Aversive therapy may take a variety of forms (Marshall, 1985b), but the procedural features which all these variations have in common is the pairing of the presently attractive but unacceptable stimuli or behaviors (in the present case, child molestation, rape or exhibiting) with an unpleasant experience. Repeated associations of the presently attractive behaviors/stimuli with these unpleasant experiences is meant to diminish the attractiveness of the behavior/ stimulus complex.

We typically use as the aversive event a moderately unpleasant electric shock delivered to the calf-muscle of the patient. However, electric currents are not always suitable, and care in selecting the appropriate aversive stimulus is important. We have had a few patients who do not seem to find even quite intensive electric currents at all aversive; for these patients alternative stimuli such as foul odors (Laws *et al.*, 1978; Maletzky, 1987) may be suitable, particularly for those patients for whom the odors of children are a particularly attractive feature.

In electric aversive therapy the events to be paired with the aversive stimulus can be either stimuli which are thought to elicit the deviant act (e.g. pictures of children) or some simulation of the actual deviant acts themselves. Abel *et al.* (1970) had subjects fantasize their deviant acts and then they were shocked. In this procedure it may be advantageous to move the model locus of the shocks backward in the sequences over treatment sessions until the initial thoughts of seeking out a child for sex are punished (Marshall, 1973). Quinsey *et al.* (1980) presented deviant stimuli to their patients while measuring their erectile responses. When the erectile responses to the deviant stimuli were over a certain percentage of a full erection a red light was activated and a shock was delivered; over sessions, the criterion for the signal and shock presentation was lowered, until finally responding to the deviant stimuli was negligible.

Any one of these procedures or a much simpler method which follows a classical conditioning paradigm may be utilized. In this latter procedure we simply present colored slides depicting the deviant act or stimulus and pair these with shock. The classical conditioning procedure lends itself well to the treatment of child molesters, whereas one of the other two are more useful for rapists and exhibitionists.

Patients typically attend two sessions of aversive therapy per week for three weeks and then two additional sessions over a subsequent two weeks. Each aversive therapy segment in each session lasts approximately 25 minutes and involves approximately 30 pairings of deviant stimuli and shocks. Offset of the deviant stimulus and the shock is followed by the onset of an appropriate stimulus which typically depicts consensual sex with an adult female. This is meant to provide a brief respite from the aversive sequence, but there are also theoretical reasons for supposing that the pairing of this escape from an aversive sequence with the appropriate stimuli might endow the appropriate stimuli with a positive valence (Bellack, 1985).

Marshall (1974) found that office-based electrical aversion techniques do not always generalize to other features of the patient's deviant interests and activities, so we employ three additional procedures to facilitate this generalization. Masturbatory satiation was developed by us (Marshall, 1979; Marshall and

Barbaree, 1978; Marshall and Lippens, 1977) initially as an alternative to aversive therapy but we now use it as a companion technique. Alford *et al.* (1987) have recently provided independent confirmation of the efficacy of this procedure in reducing deviant sexual preferences. Orgasmic reconditioning (Marquis, 1970) or masturbatory reconditioning (Annon, 1973; Davison, 1968) is a procedure designed to enhance arousal to appropriate partners or activities, and it can readily be paired with masturbatory satiation to achieve both our goals at once.

In this combined procedure, which is conducted by the patient away from the therapist's office as a form of home practice, the patient is instructed to masturbate under the circumstances which are usual for him. However, he is to commence masturbating by fantasizing (using visual or other aids, if necessary) appropriate acts with an appropriate partner. If arousal to these images is difficult due to their presently non-provocative nature, the patient is to switch to his preferred deviant images until he is aroused, at which point he switches back to the appropriate image. As soon as orgasm occurs to the appropriate image and a refractory state onsets (see Masters *et al.*, 1985, for a description of this state), the patient is instructed to abstain from masturbating and to immediately verbalize aloud every variation he can think of on his deviant fantasies and acts. He is to continue this verbalizing for at least 20 minutes. The idea here is that pairing arousal (pre-orgasm and orgasm) with appropriate sexually provocative thoughts, while associating the deviant thoughts with a time when the patient is refractory to sexual stimulation, will extinguish the provocativeness of the deviant images and enhance attraction to the appropriate ones. The advantages of this procedure are that it allows frequent practice in a natural setting and employs a practice (i.e. masturbation) which is often held responsible for the development of the deviance in the first place (Laws, 1986; McGuire *et al.*, 1965).

In addition, we teach the patient to recognize the detailed sequence of events which leads him to the sexual molestation of children. For example, for a child molester this sequence might on some occasions be: feeling bored and wishing for excitment; thinking about having sex with a child; drinking some alcohol to reduce inhibitions; seeking out a child; approaching the child and either offering an inducement or coercing the child; and then engaging in sex with the child. It is important to note that these sequences will be unique for each patient, and there will be several such sequences. Such sequence analyses were first proposed by Abel *et al.* (1970) and Marshall (1973) for use in aversive therapy, but Annon and Robinson (1985) have adapted this approach to use as an element in the cognitive treatment component of their comphehensive program. In this respect it is understood that having the patient recognize the sequence which leads to the aberrant behavior will be valuable, but Annon and Robinson also teach their patients impulse control procedures which interrupt the sequence and abort the possibility of the patient offending. We also do this by providing the patient with smelling salts, which he is to carry with him at all times; whenever he recognizes the commencement of a deviant sequence he is to hold the open smelling salts close to his nose and take a rapid deep inhalation (Hunt, 1985). This effectively interrupts the sequence, and the patient then deliberatley initiates an alternative, more appropriate, sequence of thinking and acting which is meant to defuse the threat to offend.

To facilitate the recognition of these sequences we have the patient write out (or we write out with him) several of them. These are on pocket-sized cards with accompanying written descriptions of various possible unpleasant consequences to enacting the offensive behaviors. These possible consequences might take the form of, for example, being caught in the act by the patient's wife, the child's father, the woman's husband or a police officer, with their associated results such as being rejected by his wife, beaten by the father or husband or charged by the officer. In addition, we elaborate consequences concerning the embarrassment associated with being prosecuted and a subsequent term in jail with its associated threat to sexual offenders. The patient is instructed to read each of these cards describing the sequences and the unpleasant results at least three times each day, in a variety of possibly risky situations. This procedure is modelled after covert sensitization, which was originally described by Cautela (1967, 1985) and applied effectively to exhibitionists by Maletzky (1983) and to a child molester by Brownell et al. (1977).

At each session during these attempts to alter deviant sexual preferences the therapist provides instructions about the procedures to be employed as well as a rationale for their use, and he or she checks to ensure that the patient is following the required home practice. These checks require the patient to describe in detail just what it is he has done and in what circumstances he carried out the procedures. Excuses for not having maintained home practice as required are not accepted, and the patient is advised that further failures to adhere to instructions may result in premature discharge, with a record of treatment failure registered. In fact, appropriately setting up the conditions for full participation in therapy from the outset, which involves repeatedly making the patient aware of his own role in acting deviantly and his responsibilty for change, usually ensures co-operation, although the repeated careful checks seem essential to maintaining this co-operation.

Enhancing social competence and modifying attitudinal/cognitive factors

These features are addressed within a group format, where the emphasis is on experiential learning rather than didactic instruction. In this sense, we provide a description of each topic and its relevance to the problem of sexual offending, but we also elicit from each participant his version and experience of the particular topic, which is then followed by group discussion and group problem solving. We do not expect to completely normalize each man on these features by the end of our treatment, but rather we hope to change him sufficiently so that he is equipped to continue the long-term process necessary to prevent future abuse.

We use a male and a female therapist who share the roles and activities, so that we are able thereby to model the kind of male/female relationships which we are encouraging our patients to emulate. However, when an individual is particularly inept we may engage individual role-playing at times, independent of the man's involvement in the group. The groups meet once a week for 3 hours over a six-week period.

Training in conversational skills involves enhancing motor, verbal and perceptual skills relevant to effective interpersonal functioning (McFall, 1982; Morrison and Bellack, 1981), as well as reducing anxiety (Marshall and Segal, in press) and enhancing self-confidence (Marshall and Christie, 1982). Assertiveness training aims at increasing the patients' capacity to express positive and negative feelings and to stand up for their rights (Gambrill, 1985). Social problem solving teaches effective ways of analyzing problems, generating various solutions and evaluating the likely outcome of such solutions (Marchione, 1985).

Each of these training elements is conducted according to the following format:

(1) The patients are assisted in identifying problem situations where they may be awkward, unassertive, aggressive or anxious;
(2) They are given instructions on possible appropriate and less than appropriate responses, including a consideration of the likely outcomes associated with these responses;
(3) The patients are provided by the therapists with modeled examples of these responses;
(4) They are then given the opportunity to try out these responses with another group member acting as a co-subject; and
(5) The group then provides feedback regarding the adequacy of their execution of these responses.

We emphasize the use of specific motor responses, including verbal behaviors, as well as improving overall assertiveness, increasing the precision of the timing of behavior, and directing the patients' attention to the need for reciprocity in conversations (i.e. they must reward and encourage the other person). During the course of these rehearsals the offender is given advice concerning the accurate perception of the other person's feelings, and how he might respond to these. In order to facilitate this we have the offender and his co-subject reverse roles. Anxiety is usually reduced simply by the practice of enacting coping behaviors in the behavior rehearsal, but we also provide brief training in self-relaxation, which the patients are instructed to use as a coping response (McGlynn, 1985).

We also use the group context to teach personal management skills, which cover such things as job search and secure skills, seeking and selecting appropriate accommodation, budgeting skills and the effective use of leisure time. We have begun to evaluate these and other features of Life Skills Training, and our tentative results suggest that we are able to enhance these skills and that these skills are functionally related to better adjustment (Marshall and Turner, 1987).

In addition, the group format permits us to deal with relationship difficulties, including selection of appropriate partners, conflict resolution, effective communication and the development of mutually enjoyable shared activities. Jacobson and Dallas (1981) have shown that these behaviors are required for the full enjoyment of relationships, and that they are best trained in this type of group setting. If relationship skills are severely deficient, and the patient has a partner, we typically refer them to a specialized community service.

We also give instruction on the use of intoxicants and the role intoxication often plays in sexually offensive behavior. Group discussion here centers on ways to control levels of intoxication and behavior when intoxicated, rather than on abstinence. Again, if the man has a severe drug or alcohol problem he is referred to a local agency for specialized treatment.

Within the group context we provide sex education, which aims at expanding knowledge while modifying prudishness and those attitudes which limit the possibility of the mutual enjoyment of sex. These attitudes primarily concern those related to negative and hostile views of women and children noted earlier. We also consider it inappropriate to focus on the technical aspects of anatomy and physiology, or to use the clinical language of professionals, although these are alluded to. Instead, we concentrate on the functional utility and frequency, within the population at large, of a range of sexual behaviors which might enhance the affectionate aspects of relationships and which might be engaged in a way which conveys respect for the other person.

Those attitudes and beliefs identified earlier, which appear to play a role in the maintenance of sexually aberrant behaviors, are modified through both the group process and within individual therapy. In both cases these attitudes and beliefs are challenged and a range of alternative views are discussed in much the way cognitive therapists deal with these issues (Beck, 1976; Beck *et al.*, 1979; Thase, 1985). Patients are given the opportunity to discuss both their own views and the alternatives in interchanges with other patients and with the therapists. Attempts are made to illustrate the consequences, both to themselves and to others, of acting according to these inappropriate perceptions as well as the benefits of acting upon more appropriate views.

Finally, at the last group session with our patients we attempt to alert them to potential high-risk situations which they may encounter in the future, and we give them advice about how they might deal with these potentially threatening circumstances. In these matters we follow the suggestions for relapse prevention derived from Pithers's work (Pithers *et al.*, 1983; in press).

Treatment Outcome

Three reports of outcome relating to comprehensive behavioral programs are available (Abel *et al.*, in press; Maletzky, 1987; Marshall and Barbaree, in press). We note that relying on patient's self-reports to estimate re-offense rates, as Abel does, seems unwise, and that while official police records seem to improve matters (Maletzky relies on these), even these provide underestimates of actual re-offending. In our outcome study (Marshall and Barbaree, in press) we were only able to elicit, at long-term follow-up, replies from 22% of our 117 child molesters. Of the 26 patients who responded, not one reported any recurrence of urges to offend, much less any actual offenses, and yet official police records revealed that four of these men *had actually been convicted of a sex crime*! Clearly, the self-reports of these men on this issue are unreliable. Similarly, we found that the official police records (which in Canada describe all charges, whether dismissed or convicted, recorded by police anywhere in North America) indicate a rate of re-offending which is only 42% of that revealed by the unofficial files of police or children's aid societies. These unofficial files record all possible involvement in crimes of suspected or known offenders, but we extracted only those where there was relatively unequivocal indication of complicity on the part of our ex-patients. Typically, these involved reports from children detailing quite precisely offensive behaviors enacted by our patients but where there was no corroborating evidence (required by Canadian criminal law for a child's evidence) or the child was too young to endure the legal process necessary to convict.

Our outcome data, to be described below, refer to child molesters, but we have similar data for exhibitionists (Marshall *et al.*, 1987a) but none unfortunately for rapists. Davidson (1984), however, reported outcome for rapists from a penitentiary-based treatment program which included psychotherapy components as well as behavioral procedures targeting sexual preferences, interpersonal skills and sexual knowledge. While Davidson's evaluations of long-term outcome (2–5 years' follow-up) indicate that the program was effective for child molesters, treated men who had sexually attacked adults did not differ in subsequent recidivism rates from rapists who were untreated.

Follow-up in our evaluation extended from a minimum of one year to a maximum of 9 years, with a mean of 43 months. Some of the patients were, for a variety of reasons, unable to access treatment, although 53 of these men expressed a desire to enter treatment. These motivated patients, who were unable for reasons beyond their control to attend treatment, served as our untreated control group. This is not a perfect control group but ethical reasons prevented us from deliberately withholding treatment from such potentially threatening offenders who actually sought therapy. Sixty-four patients who similarly desired help were treated, and they, fortunately, did not differ from the untreated group on any demographic or offense history features of relevance.

Table 9.2 describes the outcome for these men categorized by target victim and according to whether or not they engaged in genital–genital contact with their young victims. It is clear that, in the absence of treatment, those men who molest girls (their own daughters or the children of others) are far more at risk to recidivate if they engaged in genital–genital contact. Although treatment greatly reduces recidivism in all groups (even in those who had genital–genital contact), the latter group do not fare as well in treatment. For reasons presently unknown the genital–genital contact variable (or, more accurately for these men, 'genital–anal' contact) does not affect recidivism in

Table 9.2 Recidivism rates in treated and untreated child molesters

Group	Untreated			Treated		
	Genital–genital contact	Non-genital–genital contact	Total	Genital–genital contact	Non-genital–genital contact	Total
Child molesters (female)	83[a]	23	42 (n=19)	30	12	19 (n=27)
Child molesters (male)	49	43	42 (n=12)	14	14	14 (n=14)
Incest offenders (daughters)	27	9	18 (n=22)	18	0	9 (n=23)

[a] Percentages of each subcategory of offenders who recidivated.

those men who molested boys, even though at least as many had engaged in such behaviors.

We have also recently completed an evaluation of this program with exhibitionist outpatients (Marshall and Barbaree, 1987). While treatment significantly reduced recidivism from 69% in the untreated men over a 72-month follow-up period to 55% in the treated patients, treatment benefits for these exhibitionists is not remarkable in clinical terms. We have now modified the program for these offenders to place greater emphasis on covert sensitization, particularly illustrating the sequence leading to the offensive behavior, and on issues relating to assertiveness and taking responsibilities in relationships. So far this appears to be a more effective strategy, but we clearly need long-term follow-up data to confirm its value.

A Treatment Case Study

This is a continuation of the case study described in the assessment section of this chapter. We recall that this man was underassertive, pandered to the wishes of others to the exclusion of his own desires, had low self-esteem and was unable to take responsibility in relationships. He also experienced high sexual drive and had strong deviant arousal to a variety of aberrant acts. In addition, his cognitions were inappropriate regarding the behaviors and desires of his victims, and the consequences for them of his offenses. As we noted earlier, his strengths encouraged us to believe he would be a good candidate for treatment.

At the time we saw this man we did not have sufficient funds to operate the group format, so all of his treatment was conducted on an individual basis in which he co-operated fully. He received electric aversive therapy based on the fantasy sequence which also served as the basis for the covert sensitization card-set. We used this strategy with this man because he had such a diversity of deviant interests, and many of them lent themselves rather better to this format than to the other strategies. He used orgasmic reconditioning and satiation during masturbatory practices, which were very frequent in the initial stages of treatment. He also employed the smelling salts, as he had repeated urges elicited by environmental stimuli. After 12 sessions of aversive therapy (due to the range of deviant interests, it took more sessions than usual to cover all variations), and the accompanying home practices, he was re-assessed, at which time he showed significant changes although his profile had not been fully normalized. We advised him to continue the home practice elements while we commenced our attempts to enhance his social functioning and to alter his distorted cognitions.

We recruited volunteers to serve as role-play partners and initiated procedures aimed at increasing his assertiveness and decreasing his anxiety. We also had him enrol in an assertiveness training program at a local community college, which markedly reduced the load on our resources. This allowed us to concentrate on his other problems. We attempted to enhance his self-confidence by making him identify his personal strengths and repeat to himself descriptions of these positive attributes over and over again during his daily activities. He also followed this repetition with some enjoyable behavior. In addition, he was instructed to engage in esteem-enhancing social interactions which had a high probability of success, and we urged him to increase the range and frequency of his social contacts. We also challenged his distorted beliefs, pointed to their functional disadvantages and offered him more consensually accepted views while indicating their functional utility. Repeated discussions, frequently going over the same issues, seem essential to modifying these well-entrenched self-serving perspectives. We also made him examine in detail his motives for engaging in sex, and we encouraged him to adopt a more functionally valuable understanding of the many motives which sex satisfies. In this respect it was necessary to challenge his somewhat superficial understanding of sexual motivation. Of course, our decision about what motives sex serves is not empirically based and is open to challenge, but it has been our experience that a greater attention to motives other than simple physical gratification helps these offenders gain greater insight into the factors controlling their behavior, and that this, in turn, leads to their experiencing a greater sense of personal control. Finally, he was given relapse-prevention strategies to use in the future. These strategies are a condensed version of those described by Pithers *et al.* (in press) and essentially help the man identify behaviors and situations which put him at risk and provide him with ways to combat temptations when they arise.

This man demonstrated changes at the end of treatment (just short of six months) which indicated that he had succeeded in achieving normalized levels of functioning on all indices, including sexual preferences. We have now followed this man for 3 years and he has been trouble free, except for one occasion of exposing, which was not at all typical of his previous offenses. This relapse occurred five months after treatment and he has been problem free since. He has changed adult sexual partners twice since treatment, but has been settled with the same woman, who has two teenage children, for the past 14 months. He continues to work, and he now discusses his life and future with an enthusiasm and optimism which was not previously evident. Re-testing at two-years follow-up revealed a maintenance of gains on all indices.

CONCLUSIONS

In summary, our comprehensive assessment and treatment program derives from our theoretical perspective of the etiology and maintenance of sexual offending, and the evidence to date is most encouraging. This approach is able to accommodate idiosyncratic features of offenders while at the same time providing a format for group treatment. However, not all offenders profit from this program, and the rapists, exhibitionists and the most sexually intrusive child molesters appear to be the patients who are least responsive. The most pressing need for treatment research, therefore, concerns ways in which we can deal with these most difficult patients.

References

Abel, G.G., Barlow, D.H., Blanchard, E.B., and Guild D. (1977). The components of rapists' sexual arousal. *Archives of General Psychiatry*, **34**, 895–903.

Abel, G.G., Becker, J.V., and Cunningham-Rathner, J. (1984). Complications, consent and cognitions in sex between children and adults. *International Journal of Law and Psychiatry*, **7**, 89–103.

Abel, G.G., and Blanchard, E.B. (1974). The role of fantasy in the treatment of sexual deviation. *Archives of General Psychiatry*, **30**, 467–75.

Abel, G.G., Blanchard, E.B., and Barlow, D.H. (1981). Measurement of sexual arousal in several paraphilias: the effects of stimulus modality, instructional set and stimulus content on the objective. *Behaviour Research and Therapy*, **19**, 25–33.

Abel, G.G., Blanchard, E.B., Barlow, D.H., and Flanagan, B. (1975). A case report of the behavioral treatment of a sadistic rapist. Paper presented at the 9th Annual Convention of the Association for the Advancement of Behavior Therapy, San Francisco, California, December.

Abel, G.G., Blanchard, E.B., and Becker, J.V. (1976). Psychological treatment for rapists. In M. Walker and S. Brodsky (eds), *Sexual Assault*, Lexington, MA: Lexington Books.

Abel, G.G., Levis, D., and Clancy, J. (1970) Aversion therapy applied to a taped sequence of deviant behavior in exhibitionism and other sexual deviation: a preliminary report. *Journal of Behavior Therapy and Experimental Psychiatry*, **1**, 58–66.

Abel, G.G., Mittelman, M.S., and Becker, J.V. (1985). Sexual offenders: results of assessment and recommendations for treatment. In M.H. Ben-Aron, S.J. Hucker and C.D. Webster (eds), *Clinical Criminology: the Assessment and Treatment of Criminal Behavior*, Toronto: M & M Graphics.

Abel, G.G., Mittelman, M.S., Becker, J.V., Rathner, J., and Rouleau, J.L. (in press). Predicting child molesters' response to treatment. *Annals of the New York Academy of Sciences*.

Achenbach, T.M. (1982). *Developmental Psychopathology*, 2nd edition, New York: Wiley

Alford, G.S., Morin, C., Atkins, M., and Schoen, L. (1987). Masturbatory extinction of deviant sexual arousal: a case study. *Behavior Therapy*, **18**, 265–71.

Amir, M. (1971). *Patterns of Forcible Rape*, Chicago: University of Chicago Press.

Amir, M. (1972). The role of the victim in sex offenses. In H.L.P. Resnick and M.E. Wolfgang (eds), *Sexual Behaviors: Social, Clinical, and Legal Aspects*, Boston, MA: Little, Brown.

Andrews, D. (1983). *Scales to Measure Attitudes and Behaviours of Probationers*, Report to Ontario Correctional Services, Toronto.

Annon, J.S. (1973). The therapeutic use of masturbation in the treatment of sexual disorders. In R.D. Rubin, J.P. Brady and J.D. Henderson (eds), *Advances in Behavior Therapy*, Volume 4, New York: Academic Press.

Annon, J.S., and Robinson, C.H. (1985). Sexual deviation. In M. Hersen and A.S. Bellack (eds), *Handbook of Clinical Behavior Therapy with Adults*, New York: Plenum.

Barbaree, H.E. and Marshall, W.L.(1986). An analysis of sexual preference profiles. Paper presented at 2nd Annual Conference on Treating Sexual Offenders, Tampa, Florida, April.

Barbaree, H.E., and Marshall, W.L. (1987). Recidivism in untreated child molesters. Paper presented at 3rd Annual Conference on Treating Sexual Offenders, Newport, Oregon, May.

Barbaree, H.E., Marshall, W.L., and Lanthier, R. (1979). Deviant sexual arousal in rapists. *Behaviour Research and Therapy*, **14**, 215–22.

Barbaree, H.E., Marshall, W.L., Yates, E., and Lightfoot, L. (1983). Alcohol intoxication and deviant sexual arousal in male social drinkers. *Behaviour Research and Therapy*, **21**, 365–73.

Baxter, D.J., Barbaree, H.E., and Marshall, W.L. (1986). Sexual responses to consenting and forced sex in a large sample of rapists and nonrapists. *Behaviour Research and Therapy*, **24**, 513–20.

Beck, A.T. (1976). *Cognitive Therapy and the Emotional Disorders*, New York: University of Pennsylvania Press.

Beck, A.T., Rush, A.J., Shaw, B.F., and Emory, G. (1979). *Cognitive Therapy of Depression*, New York: Guilford Press.

Bellack, A.S. (1985). Aversion relief. In A.S. Bellack and M. Hersen (eds), *Dictionary of Behavior Therapy Techniques*, New York: Pergamon Press.

Bowman, K. (1951). The problem of the sex offender. *American Journal of Psychiatry*, **108**, 250–7.

Bradford, J.M.W. (1985). Organic treatments for the male sexual offender. *Behavioral Sciences and the Law*, **3**, 355–75.

Briere, J., Malamuth, N., and Check, J. (1981). Sexuality and pro-rape beliefs. Paper presented at the 62nd Annual Convention of the Canadian Psychological Association, Toronto, June.

Brownmiller, S. (1975). *Against Our Will: Men, Women and Rape*, New York: Simon and Schuster.

Brownell, K.D., Hayes, S.C., and Barlow, D.H. (1977). Patterns of appropriate and deviant sexual arousal: the behavioral treatment of multiple sexual deviations. *Journal of Consulting and Clinical Psychology*, **45**, 1144–55.

Burgess, A.W., and Holmstrom, L.L. (1974). *Rape: Victims of Crisis*, Bowie, MD: Robert J. Brady Co.

Burgess, A.W., and Holmstrom, L.L. (1976). Rape: its effect on task performance at varying stages in the life cycle. In M.J. Walker and S.L. Brodsky (eds), *Sexual Assault: the Victim and the Rapist*, Lexington, MA: D.C. Heath.

Burt, M.R. (1980). Cultural myths and supports for rape. *Journal of Personality and Social Psychology*, **38**, 217–30.

Buss, A.H., and Durkee, A. (1957). An inventory for assessing different kinds of hostility. *Journal of Consulting Psychology*, **21**, 343–9.

Cautela, J.R. (1967). Covert sensitization. *Psychological Record*, **20**, 459–68.

Cautela, J.R. (1985). Covert sensitization. In A.S. Bellack and M. Hersen (eds), *Dictionary of Behavior Therapy Techniques*, New York: Pergamon Press.

Chagnon, N.A. (1977). *Yanomamo: the Fierce People*, 2nd edition, Toronto: Holt, Rinehart and Winston.

Christie, M.M., Marshall, W.L., and Lanthier, R. (1979). *A Descriptive Study of Incarcerated Rapists and Pedophiles*, Report to the Solicitor General of Canada, Ottawa.

Clark, L.M.G., and Lewis, D.J. (1977). *Rape: the Price of Coercive Sexuality*, Toronto: Women's Educational Press.

Cohen, M.L., Garofalo, R., Boucher, R., and Seghorn, T. (1971). The psychology of rapists. *Seminars in Psychiatry*, **3**, 307–27.

Coote, A., and Gill, T. (1975). *The Rape Controversy*, London: National Council for Civil Liberties.

Cox, D.J., and Daitzman, R.J. (1980). *Exhibitionism: Description, Assessment and Treatment*, New York: Garland STPM Press.

Davidson, P.R. (1984). Behavioral treatment for incarcerated sex offenders: post-release outcome. Paper presented at Conference on Sex Offender Assessment and Treatment, Kingston, Ontario, March.

Davison, G. (1968). Elimination of a sadistic fantasy by a client-controlled counter-conditioning technique: a case study. *Journal of Abnormal Psychology*, **73**, 84–90.

Dohrenwend, B.S., and Dohrenwend, B.D. (1974). *Stressful Life Events: Their Nature and Effects*, New York: Wiley.

Donnerstein, E. (1984). Pornography: its effect on violence against women. In N.M. Malamuth and E. Donnerstein (eds), *Pornography and Sexual Aggression*, Orlando, FLA: Academic Press.

Earls, C.M., and Marshall, W.L. (1983). The current state of technology in the laboratory assessment of sexual arousal patterns. In J.G. Greer and I.R. Stuart (eds), *The Sexual Aggressor: Current Perspectives on Treatment*, New York: Van Nostrand Reinhold.

Eccles, A., Marshall, W.L., and Barbaree, H.E. (in press). The vulnerability of erectile measures to repeated assessments. *Behaviour Research and Therapy*.

Evans, D.R. (1968). Masturbatory fantasy and sexual deviation. *Behaviour Research and Therapy*, **6**, 17–19.

Evans, D.R. (1970). Subjective variables and treatment effects in aversion therapy. *Behaviour Research and Therapy*, **8**, 147–52.

Farkas, G.M., Evans, S.M., Sine, L.F., Eifert, G., Wittlieb, E., and Vogelmann-Sine, S. (1979). Reliability and validity of the mercury-in-rubber strain gauge measure of penile circumference. *Behavior Therapy*, **10**, 555–61.

Finklehor, D. (1984). *Child Sexual Abuse: New Theory and Research*, New York: Free Press.

Freund, K. (1961). Laboratory differential diagnosis of homo- and heterosexuality—an experiment with faking. *Review of Czechoslovak Medicine*, **7**, 20–31.

Freund, K. (1965). Diagnosing heterosexual pedophilia by means of a test for sexual interest. *Behaviour Research and Therapy*, **3**, 137–43.

Freund, K. (1967a). Diagnosing homo- or heterosexuality and erotic age-preference by means of a psychophysiological test. *Behaviour Research and Therapy*, **5**, 209–28.

Freund, K. (1967b). Erotic preference in pedophiolia. *Behaviour Research and Therapy*, **5**, 339–48.

Frude, N. (1982). The sexual nature of sexual abuse. *Child Abuse and Neglect*, **6**, 211–23.

Gambrill, E. (1985). Assertiveness training. In A.S. Bellack and M. Hersen (eds), *Dictionary of Behavior Therapy Techniques*, New York: Pergamon Press.

Gebhard, P.H., Gagnon, J.H., Pomeroy, W.B., and Christenson, C.V. (1965). *Sex Offenders: an Analysis of Types*, New York: Harper and Row.

Geller, S.H. (1977). The sexually assaulted female: innocent victim or temptress? *Canada's Mental Health*, **25**, 26–9.

Gibbens, T.C.N., Way, C., and Soothill, K.L. (1977). Behavioral types of rape. *British Journal of Psychiatry*, **130**, 32–42.

Goode, W.J. (1969). Violence among intimates. In D.J. Mulvihill, M.M. Tumin and L.A. Curtis (eds), *Crimes of Violence*, Washington, DC: United States Government Printing Office.

Groth, N., and Birnbaum, J. (1978). Adult sexual orientation and the attraction to underage persons. *Archives of Sexual Behavior,* **7**, 175–181.

Groth, N., and Birnbaum, J. (1979). *Men who Rape*, New York: Plenum.

Groth, N., and Burgess, A. (1977). Sexual dysfunction during rape. *New England Journal of Medicine*, **297**, 764–6.

Groth, N., Hobson, W., and Gary, T. (1982). The child molester: clinical observations. In J. Conte and D. Shore (eds), *Social Work and Child Sexual Abuse*, New York: Haworth.

Guttmacher, M.S., and Weihofen, H. (1952). *Psychiatry and the Law*, New York: W.W. Norton.

Hamburg, D.A. (1973). An evolutionary and developmental approach to human aggressiveness. *The Psychoanalytic Quarterly*, **42**, 185–200.

Hegeman, N., and Meikle, S. (1980). Motives and attitudes of rapists. *Canadian Journal of Behavioral Science*, **4**, 359–72.

Herman, J.L. (in press). Thinking about sex offenders. *Signs: Journal of Women in Culture and Society*.

Hunt, F.M. (1985). Contingent aromatic ammonia. In A.S. Bellack and M. Hersen (eds), *Dictionary of Behavior Therapy Techniques*, New York: Pergamon Press.

Hursch, C.J. (1977). *The Trouble with Rape*, Chicago, IL: Nelson Hall.

Jacobson, N.S., and Dallas, M. (1981). Helping married couples improve their relationships. In W.E. Craighead, A.E. Kazdin and M.J. Mahoney (eds), *Behavior Modification: Principles, Issues and Applications*, Boston, MA: Houghton Mifflin.

Keltner, A., Marshall, P.G., and Marshall, W.L. (1981). Measurement and correlation of assertiveness and social fear in a prison population. *Corrective and Social Psychiatry*, **27**, 41.

Kinsey, A.C., Pomeroy, W.B., and Martin, C.E. (1948). *Sexual Behavior in the Human Male*, Philadelphia: Saunders.

Knight, R.A., Prentky, R., Schneider, B., and Rosenberg, R. (1983). Linear causal modeling of adaptation and criminal history in sexual offenders. In K. Van Dusen and S. Mednick (eds), *Prospective Studies of Antisocial Behavior*, Boston, MA: Kluwer–Nijhoff.

Langevin, R. (1985). An overview of the paraphilias. In M.H. Ben-Aron, S.J. Hucker and C.D. Webster (eds), *Clinical Criminology: the Assessment and Treatment of Criminal Behavior*, Toronto: M & M Graphics.

Langevin, R., Bain, J., Ben-Aron, M., Coulthard, R., Day, D., Handy, L., Heasman, G., Hucker, S., Purins, J., Roper, V., Russon, A., Webster, C., and Wortzman, G. (1985). Sexual aggression: constructing a predictive equation. In R. Langevin (ed.), *Erotic Preference, Gender Identity, and Aggression in Men: New Research Studies*, Hillsdale, NJ: Lawrence Erlbaum Associates.

Langevin, R., Paitich, D., Ramsey, G., Anderson, C., Pope, S., Pearl, L., and Newman, S. (1979). Experimental studies of the etiology of genital exhibitionism. *Archives of Sexual Behavior*, **8**, 307–31.

Langevin, R., Paitich, D., and Russon, A. (1985). Are rapists sexually anomalous, aggressive, or both? In R. Langevin (ed.), *Erotic Preference, Gender Identity, and Aggression in Men: New Research Studies*, Hillsdale, NJ: Lawrence Erlbaum Associates.

Laws, D.R. (1986). A conditioning theory of sexual offending. Paper presented at the 12th Annual Meeting of the International Academy of Sex Research, Amsterdam, September.

Laws, D.R., Meyer, J., and Holmen, M.L. (1978). Reduction of sadistic sexual arousal by olfactory aversion: a case study. *Behaviour Research and Therapy*, **16**, 281–5.

Laws, D.R., and Osborn, C.A. (1983). How to build and operate a behavioral laboratory to evaluate and treat sexual deviance. In J.G. Greer and I.R. Stuart (eds), *The Sexual Aggressor: Current Perspectives on Treatment*, New York: Van Nostrand Reinhold.

Lawson, J.S., Marshall, W.L., and McGrath, P. (1979). The Social Self-esteem Inventory. *Educational and Psychological Measurement*, **39**, 803–11.

Leyton, E. (1986). *Hunting Humans: the Rise of the Modern Multiple Murderer*, Toronto: McClelland & Stewart.

Locke, H.J., and Wallace, K.M. (1957). Short marital-adjustment and prediction tests: their reliability and validity. *Marriage and Family Living*, **21**, 251–5.

Malamuth, N.M. (1981); Rape fantasies as a function of exposure to violent sexual stimuli. *Archives of Sexual Behavior*, **10**, 33–48.

Malamuth, N.M. (1984). Aggression against women: cultural and individual causes. In N.M. Malamuth and E. Donnerstein (eds), *Pornography and Sexual Aggression*, New York: Academic Press.

Malamuth, N.M., Haber, S., and Feshbach, S. (1980). Testing hypotheses regarding rape: exposure to sexual violence, sex differences, and the 'normality' of rapists. *Journal of Research in Personality*, **14**, 121–37.

Maletzky, B.M. (1983). *The Treatment of the Sexual Offender*, New York: Wiley.

Maletzky, B.M. (1987). Long-term treatment outcome with sex offenders. Paper presented at the 3rd Annual Conference on Treating Sexual Offenders, Newport, Oregon, May.

Marchione, K. (1985). Problem solving training. In A.S. Bellack and M. Hersen (eds), *Dictionary of Behavior Therapy Techniques*, New York: Pergamon Press.

Marks, I.M., and Gelder, M. (1967). Transvestism and fetishism: clinical and psychological changes during faradic aversion. *British Journal of Psychiatry*, **113**, 711–29.

Marlatt, G.A. (1982). Relapse prevention: a self-control program for the treatment of addictive behaviors. In R.B. Stuart (ed.), *Adherence, Compliance, and Generalization in Behavioral Medicine*, New York: Brunner/Mazel.

Marquis, J.N. (1970). Orgasmic reconditioning: changing sexual choice through controlling masturbatory fantasies. *Journal of Behavior Therapy and Experimental Psychiatry*, **1**, 263–71.

Marshall, W.L. (1971). A combined treatment method for certain sexual deviations. *Behaviour Research and Therapy*, **9**, 292–4.

Marshall, W.L. (1973). The modification of sexual fantasies: a combined treatment approach to the reduction of deviant sexual behavior. *Behaviour Research and Therapy*, **11**, 557–64.

Marshall, W.L. (1974). A combined treatment approach to the reduction of multiple fetish-related behaviors. *Journal of Consulting and Clinical Psychology*, **42**, 613–16.

Marshall, W.L. (1979). Satiation therapy: a procedure for reducing deviant sexual arousal. *Journal of Applied Behavioral Analysis*, **12**, 10–22.

Marshall, W.L. (1982). Aggression in child molesters. Paper presented at the 8th International Congress on Law and Psychiatry. Quebec City, June.

Marshall, W.L. (1985a). *The Use of Pornography by Sex Offenders*. Report to the US Attorney General's Commission on Pornography, Washington, DC.

Marshall, W.L. (1985b). Aversive conditioning. In A.S. Bellack and M. Hersen (eds), *Dictionary of Behavior Therapy Techniques*, New York: Pergamon Press.

Marshall, W.L. (1986). Multiple murder: a male crime. *Queen's Quarterly*, **93**, 868–73.

Marshall, W.L. (in press, a). The use of explicit sexual stimuli by rapists, child molesters and nonoffender males. *Journal of Sex Research*.

Marshall, W.L. (in press, b). The use of pornography by sex offenders. In D. Zillman and J. Bryant (eds), *Pornography: Recent Research, Interpretations, and Policy Considerations*, Hillsdale, NJ: Lawrence Erlbaum Associates.

Marshall, W.L., and Barbaree, H.E. (1978). The reduction of deviant arousal. *Criminal Justice and Behavior*, **5**, 294–303.

Marshall, W.L., and Barbaree, H.E. (1984). A behavioral view of rape *International Journal of Law and Psychiatry*, **7**, 51–77.

Marshall, W.L., and Barbaree, H.E. (1986). Changes with treatment in child molesters' views of the provocativeness of their victims. Unpublished manuscript.

Marshall, W.L., and Barbaree, H.E. (1987). Tentative outcome data from a behavioral treatment program for child molesters. Paper presented at the 3rd Annual Conference on Treating Sexual Offenders, Newport, Oregon, May.

Marshall, W.L., and Barbaree, H.E. (in press). An outpatient treatment program for child molesters: description and tentative outcome. *Annals of the New York Academy of Sciences*.

Marshall, W.L., Barbaree, H.E., and Butt, J. (1987a). Sexual offenders against male children: sexual preferences for gender, age of victim and type of behavior. Unpublished manuscript.

Marshall, W.L., Barbaree, H.E., and Christophe, D. (1986a). Sexual offenders against female children: sexual preferences for age of victims and type of behavior. *Canadian Journal of Behavioral Science*, **18**, 424–39.

Marshall, W.L., Barbaree, H.E., Laws, D.R., & Baxter, D. (1986b). Rapists do not have deviant sexual preferences: large scale studies from Canada and California.

Paper presented at the 12th Annual Meeting of the International Academy of Sex Research, Amsterdam, September.

Marshall, W.L., Bates, L., and Ruhl, M. (1984). Hostility in sex offenders. Unpublished manuscript.

Marshall, W.L., Check, J., and Barbaree, H.E. (1987b). The relevance of attachment bonds, intimacy and emotional loneliness for understanding sexual and nonsexual aggression. Unpublished manuscript.

Marshall, W.L., and Christie, M.M. (1981). Pedophilia and aggression. *Criminal Justice and Behavior*, **8**, 145–58.

Marshall, W.L., and Christie, M.M. (1982). The enhancement of social self-esteem. *Canadian Counsellor*, **16**, 82–9.

Marshall, W.L., and Darke, J. (1982). Inferring humiliation as motivation in sexual offenses *Treatment for Sexual Aggressives*, **5**, 1–3.

Marshall, W.L., Earls, C.M., Segal, Z.V., and Darke, J. (1983) A behavioral program for the assessment and treatment of sexual aggressors. In K. Craig and R. McMahon (eds), *Advances in Clinical Behavior Therapy*, New York: Brunner/Mazel.

Marshall, W.L., and Lippens, K. (1977). The clinical value of boredom: a procedure for reducing inappropriate sexual interests. *Journal of Nervous and Mental Diseases*, **165**, 283–7.

Marshall, W.L., and McKnight, R.D. (1975). An integrated treatment program for sexual offenders. *Canadian Psychiatric Association Journal*, **20**, 133–8.

Marshall, W.L., Payne, K., and Barbaree, H.E. (1987c). Erectile responses to exposing behavior in exhibitionists and normals. Unpublished manuscript.

Marshall, W.L., and Segal, Z. (in press). Behavior therapy. In G.C. Last and M. Hersen (eds), *Handbook of Anxiety Disorders*, New York: Pergamon Press.

Marshall, W.L., and Turner, B. (1987). *An Evaluation of Life Skills Training for Penitentiary Inmates*. Report to the Solicitor General of Canada, Ottawa.

Marshall, W.L., and Williams, S. (1975). A behavioral approach to the modification of rape. *Quarterly Bulletin of the British Association for Behavioral Psychotherapy*, **4**, 78.

Marshall, W.L., Williams, S., and Christie, M.M. (1976). The rapist: a review of treatment. Paper presented at the Symposium on Rape, Brown University/Butler Hospital Series, Providence, Rhode Island, October.

Masters, W.H., Johnson, V.E., and Kolodny, R.C. (1985). *Human Sexuality*, 2nd edition, Boston, MA: Little, Brown.

McCaldon, R.J., and Marshall, W.L. (1977). Conjoint treatment of incarcerated sex offenders. Paper presented at the Annual Meeting of the Ontario Psychiatric Association, Toronto, January.

McConaghy, N. (1982). Sexual deviation. In A.S. Bellack, M. Hersen and A.E. Kazdin (eds), *International Handbook of Behavior Modification and Therapy*, New York: Plenum.

McFall, R.M. (1982). A review and reformulation of the concept of social skills. *Behavioral Assessment*, **4**, 1–33.

McGlynn, F.D. (1985). Cue-controlled relaxation. In A.S. Bellack and M. Hersen (eds), *Dictionary of Behavior Therapy Techniques*, New York: Pergamon Press.

McGuire, R.J., Carlisle, J.M., and Young, B.G. (1965). Sexual deviations as conditioned behaviour. *Behaviour Research and Therapy*, **2**, 185–90.

Mohr, J.W., Turner, R.E., and Jerry, M.B. (1964). *Pedophilia and Exhibitionism*, Toronto: University of Toronto Press.

Moore, J.E. (1969). Problematic sexual behavior. In C.B. Broderick and J. Bernard (eds), *The Individual, Sex, and Society*, Baltimore, MD: Johns Hopkins University Press.

Morrison, R.L., and Bellack, A.S. (1981). The role of social perception in social skill. *Behaviour Therapy*, **12**, 69–79.

Neubeck, G. (1974). The myriad motives for sex. In L. Gross (ed.), *Sexual Behavior: Current Issues*, New York: Spectrum.

Otterbein, K.F. (1979). A cross-cultural study of rape. *Aggressive Behavior*, **5**, 425–35.

Pithers, W.D., Kashima, K.M., Cumming, G.F., and Beal, L.S. (in press.) Sexual aggression: breaking the addictive process. In A. Salter (ed.), *Treatment of Child Sexual Abuse*, New York: Lexington Press.

Pithers, W.D., Marques, J.K., Gibat, C.C., and Marlatt, G.A. (1983). Relapse prevention with sexual aggressives: a self-control model of treatment and maintenance of change. In J.G. Greer and I.B. Stuart (eds), *The Sexual Aggressor: Current Perspectives on Treatment*, New York: Van Nostrand Reinhold.

Popp, J., and DeVore, I. (1979). Aggressive competition and social dominance theory: synopsis. In D.A. Hamburg and E.R. McCown (eds), *The Great Apes*, Reading, MA: Benjamin/Cummings.

Prentky, R., Cohen, M., and Seghorn, T. (1985). Development of a rational taxonomy for the classification of rapists: the Massachusetts Treatment Centre system. *Bulletin of the American Academy of Psychiatry and the Law*, **13**, 39–70.

Quinsey, V.L. (1984). Sexual aggression: studies of offenders against women. In D. Weistub (ed.), *Law and Mental Health: International Perspectives*, Volume 1, New York: Pergamon Press.

Quinsey, V.L. (1986). Sexual aggression: studies of offenders against children. In D. Weistub (ed.), *Law and Mental Health: International Perspectives*, Volume 2, New York: Pergamon Press.

Quinsey, V.L., Bergersen, S.G., and Steinman, C.M. (1976). Changes in physiological and verbal responses of child molesters during aversion therapy. *Canadian Journal of Behavioral Science*, **8**, 202–12.

Quinsey, V.L., Chaplin, T.C., and Carrigan, W.F. (1979). Sexual preferences among incestuous and nonincestuous child molesters. *Behavior Therapy*, **10**, 562–5.

Quinsey, V.L., Chaplin, T.C., and Carrigan, W.F. (1980). Biofeedback and signalled punishment in the modification of inappropriate sexual age preferences. *Behavior Therapy*, **11**, 567–76.

Quinsey, V.L., Chaplin, T.C., and Upfold, D. (1984). Sexual arousal to nonsexual violence and sadomasochistic themes among rapists and non-sex offenders. *Journal of Consulting and Clinical Psychology*, **52**, 651–7.

Quinsey, V.L., Chaplin, T.C., and Varney, G. (1981). A comparison of rapists' and non-sex offenders' sexual preferences for mutually consenting sex, rape, and physical abuse of women. *Behavioral Assessment*, **3**, 127–35.

Quinsey, V.L., Steinman, C.M., Bergersen, S.G., and Holmes, T.F. (1975). Penile circumferences, skin conductance, and ranking responses of child molesters and 'normals' to sexual and nonsexual stimuli. *Behavior Therapy*, **6**, 213–19.

Rada, R.T. (1978). *Clinical Aspects of the Rapist*, New York: GruneαStratton.

Record, S.A. (1977). *Personality, Sexual Attitudes and Behavior of Sex Offenders*, Unpublished doctoral dissertation, Queen's University, Kingston, Ontario.

Revitch, E., and Weiss, R.B. (1962). The pedophiliac offender. *Diseases of the Nervous System*, **23**, 73–8.

Russell, D.E.H. (1975). *The Politics of Rape: the Victim's Perspective*, New York: Stein & Day.

Sanday, P.R. (1981). The socio-cultural context of rape: a cross-cultural study. *The Journal of Social Issues*, **37**, 5–27.

Schimel, J.L. (1974). Self-esteem and sex. In L. Gross (ed.), *Sexual Behavior: Current Issues*, New York: Spectrum.

Schwendinger, J.R., and Schwendinger, H. (1983). *Rape and Inequality*, Beverly Hills, CA: Sage.

Segal, Z.V., and Marshall, W.L. (1985a). Heterosexual social skills in a population of rapists and child molesters. *Journal of Consulting and Clinical Psychology*, **53**, 55–63.

Segal, Z.V., and Marshall, W.L. (1985b). Self-report and behavioral assertion in two groups of sexual offenders. *Journal of Behavior Therapy and Experimental Psychiatry*, **16**, 223–9.

Segal, Z.V., and Marshall, W.L. (1986). Discrepancies between self-efficacy predictions and actual performance in a population of rapists and child molesters. *Cognitive Therapy and Research*, **10**, 363–76.

Seghorn, T.K., Boucher, R.J., and Prentky, R.A. (in press). Childhood sexual abuse in the lives of sexually aggressive offenders. *Journal of the American Academy of Child Psychiatry*.

Sizonenko, P.C. (1978). Endrocrinology in preadolescents and adolescents. *American Journal of Diseases of Children*, **132**, 704–12.

Spence, J.T. Helmreich, R., and Stapp, J. (1973). A short version of the Attitudes toward Women Scale (AWS). *Bulletin of the Psychonomic Society*, **2**, 219–20.

Stermac, L.E., and Quinsey, V.L. (1986). Social competence among rapists. *Behavioral Assessment*, **8**, 171–85.

Stermac, L.E., and Segal, Z.V. (1987). Condoning or condemning adult sexual contact with children: a criterion group based analysis. Unpublished manuscript, Clarke Institute of Psychiatry, Toronto.

Stoller, R.J. (1975). *Perversion: the Erotic Form of Hatred*, New York: Pantheon Books.

Stoller, R.J. (1977). Sexual deviations. In F. Beach (ed.), *Human Sexuality in Four Perspectives*, Baltimore, MD: Johns Hopkins University Press.

Thase, M.E. (1985). Cognitive therapy. In A.S. Bellack and M. Hersen (eds), *Dictionary of Behavior Therapy Techniques*, New York: Pergamon Press.

Watson, P., and Friend, R. (1969). Measurement of socio-evaluative anxiety. *Journal of Consulting and Clinical Psychology*, **33**, 448–57.

Yates, E., Barbaree, H.E.., and Marshall, W.L. (1984). Anger and deviant sexual arousal. *Behavior Therapy*, **15**, 287–94.

Zillman, D. (1986). Effects of prolonged consumption of pornography. Paper presented to the US Surgeon General's Workshop on Pornography and Public Health, Arlington, Virginia, June.

Part 3
Institutional and Professional Contexts

10

Violence in Institutions for Young Offenders and Disturbed Adolescents

Malcolm R. Gentry and Eugene B. Ostapiuk
*South Warwickshire District Health Authority and Glenthorne Youth
Treatment Centre, UK*

NATURE OF THE PROBLEM

Violence to staff, whether in the Health Service, Prison Service, Personal
Social Services or the Social Security system is becoming an increasingly
pressing problem. This is supported by a commonly held view that violence
apears to be a sign of the times in which we live. Despite the fact that serious
violent incidents are only infrequently reported and tragedies are few, less
extreme examples are more numerous and should be regarded as serious
(DHSS, 1986). Witness to this fact has been the rapid expansion of initiatives
(some government inspired), conferences and publications aimed at addressing
the presenting problem of violence in everyday life. This concern with defining,
in the first instance, the extent of the problem cuts across different professional
boundaries and working contexts. It highlights at the same time the difficulty
in making adequate provision for coping with the phenomenon of violence
before assessing its extent and context. Most researchers confirm that serious
violence is not a regular occurrence (Strong, 1973; Fottrell, 1980), but also
suggest that official records do not fully represent the extent of the problem.
Since there is no requirement to keep records of violent incidents it is no
surprise that records are not available or, where available, are incomplete or
inaccurate (Weiner and Crosby, 1987). They often confirm the obvious, that
violence occurs in environments where it might reasonably be expected: locked
intensive-care wards of psychiatric hospitals (Hodgkinson *et al.*, 1984),
community release programmes for psychiatric patients (Sharron, 1985), in the

*The views expressed in this chapter are those of the authors alone and not of their employing
agencies.

context of field social work (Rowett, 1986) and local authority care establishments (Leeds Department of Social Services, 1985). There is less available
evidence from establishments offering care, containment or treatment of young
offenders/disturbed adolescents. The work of Millham *et al.* (1976) and Cawson
and Martell (1979) represents most of what is known about the nature of
violence and its frequency in provisions, both open and secure, for young
people with behavioural problems.

ISSUES AND CONCERNS

Setting aside any difficulties in assessing the extent of the problem which
violence represents in the workplace, several authors have touched on equally
important, related issues needing urgent address. Among those are questions
of adequacy of resources to combat violence; staff training and education;
support for victims of violence; and the need for secure provision in order to
contain some violent individuals. Sharron (1985), discussing violence against
social workers, has argued that the lack of sufficient resources of the right
kind, made available at the right time, has compounded difficulties in effective
containment of the problem. Others have argued that increasing staffing levels
and using security in the form of locked doors can make a positive contribution
to client care, and may ultimately prove the most effective means of managing
violent and disturbed clients (Cobb and Gossop, 1976). Robinson (1987),
looking at the role of education for nurses in relation to the prevention and
management of violent behaviour by patients, concluded that basic training
does not always provide carers with an adequate base of skill and knowledge
for diffusing violent incidents. Infantino and Musingo (1985) have shown that
additional preventative training can make a difference. They examined the
impact of staff training in aggression control on the incidence of patient assaults
on staff and of assault-related injuries. Their findings support the case that
trained staff can signficantly reduce potentially violent situations and reduce
the frequency of resulting injuries when compared to untrained staff. Although
violent behaviour of clients may be considered an occupational health hazard
of care professionals, organizations and managements have often ignored the
plight of the victimized employee. Engel and Marsh (1986) found that
professional staff who have been assaulted often resist seeing themselves as
victims, despite reporting feelings and reactions typical of other victims. The
authors suggest that they need help in dealing with emotional trauma, and
they describe a victim-assistance programme designed to meet this need.

A number of researchers have argued that attempts to deal with violence to
staff in the workplace needs to be set in the context of an overall framework
designed to help managements and employees examine the problems in their
own organization. Poyner and Warne (1986) describe a simple diagrammatic
framework for representing assaults on staff. Their purpose is to help establish
all the relevant information needed to understand how assaults can happen
and also make it easier to consider possible ways of preventing them. They
offer suggestions on how some aspects of this process should be managed, and

who should be responsible for dealing with the problem of violence to staff within an organization. Brown *et al.* (1986) have similarly attempted to provide an overall perspective designed to help social work staff avoid becoming the victims of violence, and respond appropriately in situations where violence is offered. Drawing on their own research, other studies and a wide range of examples from practice, they show that physical precaution training programmes and management strategies are most likely to reduce the risks that are an inevitable part of the social work task.

THE RESIDENTIAL-CARE EXPERIENCE

Despite the view that standards of behaviour in residential establishments for young people have been deteriorating in recent times with a consequent rise in levels of disturbance and violence, the true picture is difficult to unravel from documentary evidence alone. Indeed Millham *et al.* (1978) have suggested that staff anxiety about violence is unrelated to the actual incidence of aggression or the numbers of violent young people in institutions; rather, it tends to reflect individual staff fears and insecurities. Others, while pointing to the fact that staff behaviour may often be responsible for provoking violent responses in young people, have argued that the preponderance of adolescents in residential care has faced staff with new difficulties (Morgan-Klein, 1985). Morgan-Klein has shown that problems of achieving independence and related problems of unemployment and shortage of housing for young people causes considerable anxiety for both young people and staff, often resulting in conflict. Such conflict need not necessarily result in violence, although staff may feel that the threat of violence is there. Perhaps the central issue underlining the problem of violence in institutions for young people is that of control. Berry (1975) has argued that the haphazard nature of control in the residential sector mainly arises because staff are poorly trained, and often fail to understand that any control approach is influenced not just by their own skill and resilience but also by the context in which it takes place.

It seems that the overwhelming conclusion from available literature is that staff must be aware of the theoretical assumptions underlying their management of conflict and consistently translate this theory into practice.

The remainder of this chapter describes a framework of practice which has been developed at Glenthorne Youth Treatment Centre. This Centre is provided by the Department of Health and Social Security in the UK for the long-term care, control, treatment and education of boys and girls, aged between 10 and 18 years, who are severely disturbed and disruptive and who may have committed serious offences.

FROM PROBLEM TO POLICY

In formulating a policy for the management of violence three main factors need to be taken into account; the characteristics of the organization/institution, the theoretical model on which the therapeutic practices are based and external policy constraints.

The *characteristics of an organization* set the limits within which a policy will actually be operated. In any residential establishment the design of the building has a substantial influence on the behaviour of both staff and residents. An obvious feature in this context is the capacity to section off an area in which a violent incident occurs and the provision of individual secure rooms where someone can be contained. More generally, interior design and decoration can convey to residents something about the staff expectation of disruptive behaviour, (e.g. fixed furniture and plastic cutlery). They can also directly affect the levels of potential environment stressors. For example, noise level is affected by the type of floor surface and wall coverings: inappropriate lighting and temperature can cause irritability (Health Services Advisory Committee, 1987). Consideration should also be given to provision of personal space to ensure that residents do not feel overcrowded and forced to live in a situation which does not allow them sufficient distance from other residents behaving in a disruptive and threatening manner.

There are a number of important issues concerning staffing. An appropriate staff ratio is essential to maintain confidence and morale among staff. This also conveys to residents that there is sufficient control within the organization. At Glenthorne, each living unit accommodates up to 10 youngsters who are cared for by a staff team of 12 groupworkers, a Unit Leader and his or her deputy.

The quality of staff will determine what tasks can be expected of them. All groupworkers at Glenthorne are qualified as residential child-care officers, teachers or nurses, and each unit team receives a good level of psychology and social work input. The expectations which senior management have of the unit teams are therefore very high, and these are made clear to staff. Each team is expected to produce a good level of care and to achieve specific treatment goals with each youngster. In addition, each team is expected to develop its overall care and treatment programme and not become complacent.

Staff training should achieve the goals of making clear the objectives of the organization and the expectations of staff and ensuring that staff have the necessary skills to perform effectively. In addition to in-service training, Glenthorne has developed a Diploma Course in Applied Social Learning Theory with the University of Leicester, to which groupworkers are seconded every year.

The adoption of a single *theoretical approach* is necessary in an organization in which the primary agents of treatment are care workers who must work together as a team. There has been an increase in the development of the multidisciplinary approach to the treatment of people with psychological problems, on the basis that no single profession can provide a comprehensive service. While there are clearly advantages in such professional collaboration, it is sometimes difficult to reconcile different perspectives, with the result that there is an absence of an overall philosophy.

The social learning approach which has been adopted at Glenthorne comes within the broad area of behavioural psychology. The main focus of attention is observable behaviour, and the purpose of treatment is to achieve some definite behavioural change. Assessment is mainly concerned with current behaviour and the environmental factors which contribute to its occurrence, although past influences are also examined in order to determine how particular behaviour patterns have developed. Behavioural approaches are based on the hypothesis that much of a person's behaviour is learned, maintained and regulated by the effects of environmental consequences of that behaviour to the individual. The social learning approach supports the further proposition that there is a reciprocal influence between individuals and their environment. Thus people are not regarded either as being like weathervanes, totally at the mercy of environmental influences, or as if they existed in a social vacuum in which such influences do not operate.

Social learning theorists maintain that there are four main types of learning which are important processes in human behaviour: classical, operant, cognitive and observational. This is distinct from more radical behavioural approaches, and reflects the development of behavioural theory over the last twenty years (Mischel, 1973; Bandura, 1973, 1977). This perspective does not exclude the importance of other important influences on behaviour which are of a different kind (e.g. genetic, organic). For example, there are specific mechanisms in the brain which have been shown to be associated with aggressive behaviour in both humans and animals (Avis, 1974). Biological factors which influence the development of aggressive behaviour in children are also acknowledged, but the ability to perform specific acts must be acquired either by observation of other people (Bandura, 1965, 1973) or by direct experience, i.e. through the process of learning. The maintenance of aggressive behaviour is very largely dependent on its consequences in that aggressive behaviour which is rewarded will tend to recur and aggressive behaviour which is either not rewarded or punished will diminish.

The adoption of a behavioural approach as the main component of treatment implies the acceptance of individual/environmental interaction as being the most promising area for consideration in order to achieve a long-term change in an individual's behaviour. A specific example of the difference between behavioural and some other approaches which is often noted is the role of insight (Herbert, 1978; Yelloly, 1972). Insight certainly can produce change in attitude and behaviour, but behaviour therapists do not regard it as being a primary means of achieving thereapeutic goals. Rather, there is evidence that insight which seems apparent from what a person says during the course of therapy frequently follows rather than precedes behavioural changes (Cautela, 1965; Yelloly, 1972). Within this framework some behaviourists (Owens and Walter, 1980) have claimed that behavioural psychotherapy is possible, i.e. behaviour change brought about by appropriate verbal guidance concerning environmental factors. Thus it is accepted that instruction and counselling are valid methods of producing behaviour change in the absence of manipulation of reinforcement/punishment, which operant behaviourists would regard as essential.

External policy considerations are no less important in shaping the ethos and practice of child care in an institution. The Child Care Act 1980 and Secure

Accommodation (No.2) Regulations (1983) (specifically, the criteria for placement of a child in a single separation room) made it clear that certain practices which had previously gone unquestioned were now unacceptable. It became necessary to provide official justification for certain courses of action and meet specific criteria in order not only to detain a young person in security but also to use the obvious physical aspects of security (i.e. locking a child in a room) to contain violent and aggressive behaviour.

Such external guidelines prompted Glenthorne to re-examine its existing practice in an attempt to comply with the spirit and the letter of the law. The Centre's policy on handling violent incidents, in line with the DHSS circular on management of violent hospital patients (DHSS 1976), had to be clarified. As a result, the Centre's earlier rejection of medication as a means of control was reaffirmed. Time out was carefully defined and its application tightly prescribed (e.g. it was to be seen as an individualized and carefully considered consequence rather than a standard penalty for disruptive, non-compliant behaviour). It was further emphasized that time out (a treatment procedure) should not be operated in separation rooms designated for the purpose of containing a violent person (a management/control procedure).

These were only some of the issues addressed in an attempt to achieve a balance between narrow compliance with regulations, on the one hand, and, on the other, a flexible and responsive system that recognized individual differences in violent responses. The internal policy which was developed at Glenthorne resulted from careful consideration of these three main areas. The following brief extract will help to put the latter description of procedures into context.

> Violent behaviour is often the main reason for a youngster being placed in a YTC. In the process of modifying this type of behaviour and helping youngsters to achieve self-control and learn acceptable alternative behaviours, staff must expect to receive much of the angry and aggressive responses which the youngster has learned elsewhere. However, there are limits to the level of abuse which staff can reasonably be expected to tolerate while treatment is being carried out. There are two basic principles:
>
> a. For the safety of everyone in Glenthorne it must be made clear to youngsters that physical assault is no more acceptable within the Centre than outside.
> b. Response by staff to a serious incident must be immediate and uncompromising. It is therefore essential that response options are clearly understood in order to minimize the risk of injury.

The type of intervention by staff in a particular incident should be the least restrictive on the aggressor, necessary to achieve a safe outcome. On one hand, it may be enough to talk to the youngster in a firm and patient manner until tension has dissipated. A more serious situation may involve the use of physical restraint and the placement of the youngster in a locked secure room.·

FROM POLICY TO PROCEDURES

It is important to make a distinction between two types of management:

(1) Containment refers to the immediate response of staff to either a potential or an actual incident of violence where the main objective is to limit the amount of harm done. It is necessary to have a set of procedures which clearly specify what measures may be taken and the criteria which should be applied.
(2) Treatment refers to the long-term goal of enabling a youngster to replace violent reactions with alternative behaviours. Achieving this goal requires staff who are skilled in the application of therapeutic techniques.

Containment

Containment and control of violent incidents as they occur is the prerequisite for the successful, longer-term treatment of young persons with aggressive tendencies. Institutional and management needs for control and, initially at least, compliance with prerequisites for the smooth functioning of an organization are important factors to be taken into account when establishing a coherent policy for managing violence. This need for clearly stated boundaries implies that young persons must experience firm external control from the day they are admitted to the Centre. The amount of external control applied and the rate at which it is gradually released depends not only upon the characteristics of the client and the severity of the client's presenting problem (these issues will be discussed in the section on treatment) but also upon official guidelines concerning placement of persons in secure conditions (i.e. Child Care Act 1980; Secure Accommodation (No.2) Regulations (1983) and in-house regulations and codes of practice.

The process of containment should begin with an awareness by staff of signs of tension. This may be limited to a single individual or be evident in an overall atmosphere which appears to involve everybody. When tension has been identified then a decision has to be made whether to do anything, and what form any action should take. It is important to intervene early, before tension becomes translated into aggression. This might take the form of taking a youngster to one side and attempting to discover the cause of the tension with a view to helping to sort out the problem. When this low-key intervention is not possible or proves unsuccessful, verbal aggression and threatening behaviour may follow. The staff will now be required to use assertive skills and impose themselves on the situation. Key skills here will include self-control (not showing anxiety or fear) and control of the youngster. This directive, controlling intervention is in contrast to problem-solving approaches, and yet the two styles are best used in a flexible way during a difficult incident. If staff behaviour is conceptualized in terms of using these two approaches then a

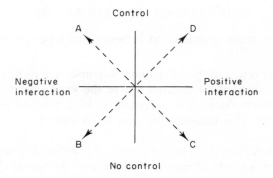

Figure 10.1 Intervention styles in violent situations

diagrammatic representation can be made, as shown in Figure 10.1.

In this figure, position A represents staff behaviour which has the effect of controlling a situation in a manner which is perceived very negatively by the youngster involved. For example, the youngster might be physically overpowered and threatened with sanctions without any attempt being made to balance any necessary control with counselling as appropriate. Position B is the worst combination, in which a negative interaction is combined with lack of overall control of the situation. This might involve a member of staff appearing frightened and shouting instructions and threats to a youngster who continues to behave violently towards another resident. Position C combines an attempt at positive interaction with a youngster without the necessary control being applied. This would include a situation in which a member of staff persisted in attempting to deal with a youngster's problem while at the same time being on the receiving end of a torrent of abuse and intimidation. Position D represents the ideal combination of control and positive interaction from the youngster's point of view. While the main emphasis is on appropriate control in order to ensure safety, attention is also paid to engaging the youngster in a constructive dialogue to reduce the level of tension and find a way forward out of the situation.

When violence is actually taking place then it is necessary to use physical restraint to prevent further injury. At Glenthorne, this is routinely followed by placing a youngster in a Separation Room, which is specifically designed to contain someone safely. A youngster should remain in this confined situation for as brief a period of time as possible, i.e. release should occur as soon as the criteria for isolation are no longer met. Isolation represents one of the clearest examples of the importance of making a distinction between containment and treatment in the overall management of violence. Failure to make this distinction can result in the confinement facility being abused under the guise of 'treatment'. For example, confinement might be described as time out, which is a treatment procedure used as a consequence of a wide variety of behaviours. This could result in a youngster being confined in isolation for relatively minor misbehaviour (e.g. being persistently cheeky to staff).

All incidents of aggressive behaviour should be recorded in a form which encourages accurate reporting. It is expecting a lot of staff who have been through a difficult incident to sit down and write an account in a completely unstructured way. A specific incident form should be available which is designed to aid recall and reporting and which is also useful as a basis for subsequent discussion. There is considerable variation in the specific types of forms that are used to record incidents. An example is shown in Figure 10.2, which contains the most important elements of a structured incident report. Consistent with the social learning model there are three sections; Incident (Behaviour), Antecedents, Consequences. Other sections could usefully be added (e.g. a youngster's own account of the incident or how the member of staff directly involved was treated afterwards).

This type of record is essential for staff to be able to analyse incidents and to learn from them. Discussion can then take place about whether anything should have been done differently or whether agreed procedures were implemented or need to be adapted.

The last stage to consider is consolidation. A youngster should be encouraged to discuss what has happened and to accept the immediate and possible long-term consequences (e.g. restriction of privileges and consideration of such behaviour at a future review of general progress). Staff involved in a serious incident should have the opportunity to have their own needs considered. It is not uncommon for staff to report feelings of guilt that they 'allowed a situation to get out of hand', even if they acted quite properly. Other feelings most commonly expressed are fear, anger, resentment and confusion. These feelings may be dealt with adequately by talking to colleagues, and an effective staff team will encourage expression of emotion and be able to cope with this. Staff who do not work in a supportive atmosphere run the risk of 'bottling up' their feelings and suffering stress. In a study on the effects of disruptive behaviour on schoolteachers it was found that teachers often felt unsupported and unable to get help (Dunham, 1977). This was largely due to the fear that they would be regarded as incompetent and unsuitable for the work. A general debriefing involving all staff is useful, so that there is an opportunity to learn from an incident and also for staff not directly involved to air their feelings about what has happened and how it has been handled. An important procedure following incidents is for the line manager to make a point of talking to staff directly involved to assess the effect of the incident and to offer appropriate support. This is particularly important for the relatively less-experienced staff, who may have received useful support from colleagues but remain uncertain of the 'official' view of their conduct. It is also good practice to repeat this process after a day or two, when other feelings may begin to emerge. The containment of incidents is a process that requires a high degree of skill; practical training is essential for all staff who are at risk of having to deal with violent behaviour. It appears generally to be the case that staff working in the care field are inadequately trained in this area. Millham and his colleagues (1976) concluded that lack of staff training was a major factor in problems in controlling children in Community Homes. In the recent review of five health

THE INCIDENT

Where and at what time did the incident occur?

....

What did the client say and do?

....

How did the client appear?

(a)   Physical state

(b)   Psychological state (confused, angry etc.)

....

Who else was directly involved (clients and staff)?

What did they do?

....

How did the incident end?

....

ANTECEDENTS

What was happening immediately before the incident?

....

What particular event(s) triggered the incident?

....

CONSEQUENCES

What happened to the client afterwards?

....

What happened to other clients directly involved afterwards?

....

What did the member(s) of staff directly involved do afterwards?

....

Figure 10.2 Outline of incident report

authorities it was found that only 12% of staff working with a variety of client groups had received any form of relevant training (Health Services Advisory Committee, 1987).

Treatment

Persistent violent behaviour will result in a youngster effectively marking time and making little progress through the Centre. It is essential that youngsters are consistently rewarded for good behaviour and either not rewarded or punished for unacceptable behaviour. This simple statement of good practice cannot be achieved in an institution unless an organized system of observation and recording is maintained together with an effective contingency-management programme. This system has been described elsewhere (Ostapiuk and Westwood, 1986). On the admission unit the youngsters live within a strict regimen in which there is a high level of external control by staff. As youngsters progress through the Centre they are gradually encouraged to monitor their own behaviour and maintain a good level of socially acceptable behaviour without external restraints being imposed by staff. This shift of control is shown in Figure 10.3, and is crucial to the broad aim of treatment, which is to enable youngsters to develop sufficient self-control and self-management to return to the community and live in a socially acceptable way. The treatment process involves the following stages:

Assessment

Incidents of violent behaviour committed by a youngster both at the Centre and prior to admission are recorded and described in detail. Contributing factors to the violent incidents (Antecedents), the exact nature of the incidents (Behaviour) and what happened afterwards (Consequences) are recorded. Particular attention is paid to the frequency, intensity and duration of violent incidents over a period of time. All the assessment information is examined and an overall functional analysis produced in which an attempt is made to explain and make sense of an individual youngster's pattern of behaviour.

Selection of target behaviours

The results of the assessment are discussed with the youngster concerned who will be encouraged to make a commitment to reducing/eliminating the occurrence of violent behaviour and to cooperate in a plan of treatment to

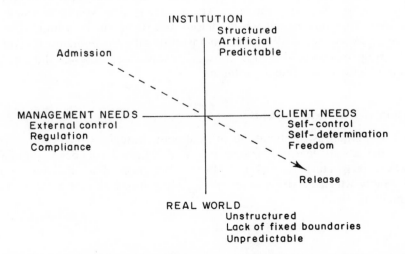

Figure 10.3 Long-term goals in the management of violence. Reproduced by permission of The British Psychological Society

achieve this goal. Most youngsters are unsure about their desire to change or their ability to do so. The combination of observing other youngsters making progress through the Centre by behaving well and individual counselling aimed at increasing motivation to change usually results in youngsters taking an active part in their treatment. (See Miller, 1983, for a discussion of motivational interviewing.) Since the main aim of treatment is the development of self-control by youngsters themselves, targets are usually described in terms of developing alternative patterns of behaviour to violence which will have the same function. A youngster who experiences a build-up of physical tension very quickly in response to mild provocation and who releases this tension in an aggressive manner would be encouraged to develop other ways of reducing this tension in a non-violent way. For another youngster the main target might be persistent aggressive thoughts which result in him or her becoming increasingly tense over a period of time and eventually directing aggression towards an innocent victim. Feldman (1977) has drawn attention to the selection of treatment goals which primarily benefit an institution and do not reflect either the reason for an individual's admission or future placement. For example, emphasis may be placed on compliance with the routine of the institution and on being a 'model inmate', which does not prepare someone for return to the community. Further, while it is more constructive to encourage achievement in educational and occupational activities, undue emphasis on these areas can result in lack of attention being paid to more important areas.

The distinction between under- and overcontrolled individuals is a useful one in this context (Megargee, 1966). An undercontrolled person will tend to exhibit aggressive behaviour in response to relatively minor provocation, and therefore will do so quite frequently. Consequently, the problem is quite obvious and is not likely to be overlooked in discussions about treatment. By contrast, an overcontrolled person will behave aggessively less frequently but it will usually be quite intense. An overcontrolled youngster may have committed a serious assault which caused him or her to be admitted but not behave aggressively at all within an institutional environment. It would be quite wrong to ignore this area simply because the youngster did not cause any immediate management problems.

Selection of treatment methods

There are numerous combinations of treatment strategies which can be applied within the social learning framework and which have been summarized elsewhere (e.g. Herbert, 1981). A brief description of an individual case is given below which illustrates both the general approach and some particular treatment methods.

Case Study

Mark was a 17-year-old who had a history of minor assaults against boys of similar age. These were, typically, sudden outbursts during which he used his fists and then ran away. Sometimes he had himself been injured during the fights. He was generally described as having a quick temper but usually calmed down quite soon. He got angry when prevented from doing what he wanted, when he wanted. He was particularly sensitive to comments about his family, who lived in a poor inner-city area and who were well known to the local police and social services. He said that when he got angry he could not think clearly and felt physically very tense. After an outburst he felt more relaxed but often regretted what he had done. Most of his peers were wary of him and he appeared to enjoy being regarded as someone not to cross. He was of average intelligence.

A very simple functional analysis identified three important antecedents to Mark's violent behaviour: frustration in doing what he wanted immediately; sensitivity to negative comments about his family; and a high level of emotional arousal with a very quick build-up.

His violence was limited to using his fists, and a detailed record of outbursts within the Centre described the other relevant variables (frequency, duration, etc.). The consequences of his violence were: release of physical tension; occasional regret; occasional physical injury; reinforcement of a tough self-image due to the reaction of some of his peers; and negative consequences within the regimen of the Centre.

Commitment to treatment was only achieved after three months of individual counselling, during which Mark stopped saying that he was only 'serving time' and began to discuss the short- and long-term negative consequences of his violent behaviour. Three treatment targets were then identified and agreed with Mark:

(1) Improving his ability to deal with conflict situations. It was evident from discussions with Mark that even when he was calm he was unable to assert himself with another youngster or member of staff in an appropriate way. He had not developed the ability to put forward his own point of view appropriately in a non-threatening manner. This goal was successfully achieved in role-play situations as part of an individual assertiveness training programme.

(2) Reducing the quick and intense anger which he experienced. When the first target had been achieved, Mark began to use his new skills in actual situations outside the training sessions. There were still a number of occasions when he became so angry that he was unable to apply these skills. He no longer used violence but would storm out of the difficult situation and leave matters unresolved. After much discussion it was decided to teach him a self-instruction strategy, which would effectively enable him to 'talk himself out of his anger' and remain calm enough to use his assertive skills. He was taught to be aware of the physical signs of angry arousal and to implement this strategy as soon as possible. Briefly, Mark chose a few statements from a list given to him which had most meaning for him, (e.g. 'I have handled worse situations than this'). Mark was very pleased with the progress that he made and began to talk

about 'beating his anger' and 'being in control'. These were clear signs that the shift in control from external institutional constraints, which had been so prevalent in his early days at the Centre, to self-control was taking place.

(3) Reducing his sensitivity to comments about his family. This was achieved by means of a process of desensitization in individual sessions, during which he was exposed to negative comments about his family made by a member of staff. This was carried out using a simple five-point hierarchy of increasingly distasteful comments for Mark, working through the list from the mildest to the strongest. He also developed appropriate responses to such comments, which allowed him to feel that he had not simply stood back and allowed his family to be criticized.

OBJECTIVES OF PROCEDURES

In the course of staff discussion about the relative merit of different management options the objectives are not always clear. A staff discussion is itself a complex social interaction in which many different factors determine the outcome. When such a group is affected by the emotional impact of dealing with persistent violence then it becomes difficult to remain objective. In her study on children's homes, Berry (1975) reported that staff often rationalized their methods of treatment in terms of a child's needs when they were mainly reacting to their own pressures. Managers and professional advisers can help to keep a staff team on a rational path. One simple technique involves the use of a Needs–Intervention Grid to focus attention on the reasons for making decisions about future actions (Cameron, et al., 1984). The grid comprises a list of needs/interests of everyone involved together with a list of possible interventions. These two lists are used to form a matrix, as shown in Figure 10.4. This technique encourages everyone's needs to be considered and makes it less likely that irrelevant or inappropriate options are adopted.

SERVICE MONITORING

Although the routine use of incident reports is essential for the reasons already outlined, the type of form which has been presented (Figure 10.2) is not sufficient to provide a more global view. Service issues can only be properly addressed if accurate aggregate information is available: for example, the change in the frequency of particular types of incidents in a particular unit over a certain period or the amount of violence to which a member of staff is typically exposed during a working week. The simple addition of a section on the incident form which categorizes incidents takes a minimum amount of time to complete and provides potentially very useful information. For example, the following categories were used in a recent research study carried out in Strathclyde (Strathclyde Regional Council, 1986). Staff were requested to endorse only the most serious aspect of a particular incident: verbal aggression/

State problem		Possible interventions															
		(A)	(B)	(C)	(D)	(E)	(F)	(G)	(H)	(I)	(J)	(K)	(L)	(M)	(N)	(O)	etc
Persons	**Needs/interests**																
(1) Client																	
(2)																	
(3)																	
(4)																	
(5)																	
(6)																	
(7)																	
(8)																	
etc.																	

Using the grid:
1. State problem in top left-hand box as clearly as possible.
2. List in the first column—headed 'Persons'—people who are or who might be involved in some way with the problem: for example, client, relative, other clients, staff, unit manager, service management, etc.
3. Write against each of the above persons (that is, client, relative, etc.) what, in your view, their needs/interests are in this situation (for example, client needs attention; family needs to get some sleep at night; staff need not to have to clear up broken glass; service manager needs to stop staff complaining about the client).
4. List possible interventions in boxes along the top (for example, give medication; lock doors; transfer to alternative placement; call in 'expert'; refer problem to unit manager; change client management; modify environment; change behaviour of others; discuss problem with client, etc.).
5. Ask yourself, for each person, whether each intervention meets their needs and place a tick, cross, or question mark in the appropriate boxes.
   √ = yes
   × = no
   ? = not sure (use sparingly)

Figure 10.4 Needs – interventions grid

threat; throwing of damaging objects; physical posturing/challenging; verbal/emotional abuse; physical violence; or physical violence with a weapon.

This type of categorization allows for a quick analysis of the type of violence which is occurring. A clearly defined list on the incident form also cues staff to the type of behaviour which they should be recording. This is an important issue, because staff members can vary considerably in their tolerance of aggressive behaviour and their tendency to complete a formal report. The inclusion of non-physical violence is also important. Bute (1979) has pointed out that the threat of violence may be a greater problem for staff than actual assault, because it happens much more frequently.

The practical use of service monitoring is illustrated by some of the findings reported in the Strathclyde study. Information was collected from a variety of establishments over a period of two months. It was found that 30 incidents of violence (including verbal as well as physical violence) had occurred in eight children's homes. Analysis showed that in half the incidents the main antecedent seemed to be a child not doing as he or she was told. It is possible that staff training and discussion would result in improved interactions in child/staff conflict situations, and identify the need to introduce a behavioural management system which would help to depersonalize such conflicts.

Procedures for managing violent behaviour need to be reviewed periodically to take account of changing situations and to encourage the introduction of new initiatives. Such a review could usefully consider the following checklist as a basis for monitoring the service:

> Do we know whether violence is a problem for the staff?
> Is there a structured recording system?
> Do we evaluate data from incident records?
> Have all staff received training in containment of incidents?
> Have relevant staff received training in treatment of clients who exhibit violent behaviour?
> Do all staff have a copy of our policy towards violent behaviour?
> Do all staff have a copy of procedural guidelines?
> Is there a support system for staff?
> Are any changes required in current procedures or staff training as a result of evaluating data?

Prevention of violence must be considered a key function of management. In searching for solutions management must look not only at the potentially violent person but also at the needs of staff and the setting in which they meet. The risk of violence must be considered when decisions are made concerning a broad range of areas: building design, staffing levels, job design, working practices, communications, training and occupational health. In designing an effective prevention package an organization must consider those factors which influence an assailant towards violence and which make particular staff more vulnerable to violence as well as situations which might foster violence. The ultimate aim should be to design a system which offers not only specific countermeasures but also an overall strategy, which includes identification of the problem, data collection, effective preventative measures, implementation procedures and, in every case, detailed monitoring.

References

Avis, H. (1974). The neuropharmacology of aggression. *Psychological Bulletin*, **81**, 47–63.

Bandura, A. (1965). Behavioural modification through modelling procedures. In L. Krasner and L. P. Ullman (eds), *Research in Behaviour Modifications*, New York: Holt, Rinehart and Winston.

Bandura, A. (1969). *Principles of Behaviour Modification*, New York: Holt, Rinehart and Winston.

Bandura, A. (1973). *Aggression: A Social Learning Analysis*, Englewood Cliffs, NJ: Prentice-Hall.

Bandura, A. (1977). *Self-efficacy: towards a unifying theory of behavioural change. Psychological Review*, **84**, 191–215.

Berry, J. (1975). *Daily Experience in Residential Life*, London: Routledge and Kegan Paul.

Brown, R., Bute, S., and Ford, P. (1986). *Social Workers at Risk*, London: Macmillan.

Bute, S. (1979). Guidelines for coping with violence by clients. *Social Work Today*, December.

Cameron, R., Bailey, M., and Wallis, J. (1984). Difficult and disruptive behaviour: 1. Reconciling needs of clients and staff. *Mental Handicap*, **12**, 45–97.

Cautela, J. (1965). Desensitisation and insight. *Behaviour Research and Therapy*, **3**, 59–64.

Cawson, P., and Martell, M. (1979). *Children Referred to Closed Units*, Research Report No.5, London: HMSO.

Cobb, J. P., and Gossop, M. R. (1976). Locked doors in the management of disturbed psychiatric patients. *Journal of Advanced Nursing*, **6**, 469–80.

DHSS (1976). *The Management of Violent or Potentially Violent Hospital Patients*, Health Circular (11), Health Services Management.

DHSS (1980). *Child Care Act 1980*, London: HMSO.

DHSS (1983). *Secure Accommodation (No.2) Regulations (1983)*, London: HMSO.

DHSS (1986). Conference on Violence to Staff, Church House, Westminster, December.

Dunham, J. (1977). The effects of disruptive behaviour on teachers. *Educational Review*, **3**, 151–7.

Engel, F., and Marsh, S. (1986). Helping the employee victim of violence in hospitals. *Hospital and Community Psychiatry*, **2**, 159–62.

Feldman, P. (1977). *Criminal Behaviour: A Psychological Analysis*, Chichester: Wiley.

Fottrell, E. (1980). A study of violent behaviour among patients in psychiatric hospitals. *British Journal of Psychiatry*, **136**, 216–21.

Health Services Advisory Committee (1987). *Violence to Staff in the Health Services*, Health and Safety Commission.

Herbert, M. (1978). *Conduct Disorders of Childhood and Adolescence: A Behavioural Approach to Assessment and Treatment*, Chichester: Wiley.

Herbert, M. (1981). *Behavioural Treatment of Problem Children: A Practice Manual*, London: Academic Press.

Hodgkinson, P., Hillis, T., and Russell, D. (1984). Assaults on staff in a psychiatric hospital. *Nursing Times*, **16**, 44–6.

Infantino, J., and Musingo, S. Y. (1985). Assaults and injuries among staff with and without training in aggression control techniques. *Hospital and Community Psychiatry*, **12**, 1312–14.

Leeds Department of Social Services (1985). Report of the working group on conflict and aggression.

Megargee, E. (1966). Undercontrolled and overcontrolled personality types in extreme antisocial aggression. *Psychological Monograph*, **80**, 5, 1–29.

Miller, W. (1983). Motivational interviewing with problem drinkers. *Behavioural Psychotherapy*, **11**, 147–72.

Millham, S. (1977). Violence in residential child care establishments. *Concern*, **25**, 27–9.

Millham, S., Bullock, R., and Hosie, K. (1976). On violence in Community Homes. In N. Tutt (ed.), *Violence*, London: HMSO.

Millham, S., Bullock, R., and Hosie, K. (1978). *Locking Up Children: Secure Provision Within the Child Care System*, Farnborough: Saxon House.

Mischel, W. (1973). Toward a cognitive social learning reconceptualisation of personality. *Psychological Review*. **80**, 252–83.

Morgan-Klein, B. (1985). *Where am I Going to Stay? Young People Leaving Residential*

Care in Scotland, Scottish Council for Single Homeless.

Ostapiuk, E., and Westwood, S. (1986). Glenthorne Youth Treatment Centre: Working with adolescents in gradations of security. In C. Hollin and K. Howells (eds), *Clinical Approaches to Criminal Behaviour: Issues in Criminological and Legal Psychology*, No.9, Leicester: British Psychological Society (DCLP).

Owens, G., and Walter, A. J. (1980). Naive behaviourism and behaviour modification. *Bulletin of the British Psychological Society*, **33**, 312–14.

Poyner, B., and Warne, C. (1986). *Violence to Staff: a Basis for Assessment and Prevention*, London: HMSO.

Robinson, S. (1987). *A Study of Some Aspects of the Role and Education of the Nurse in Relation to the Prevention and Management of Violent Behaviour by Mentally Ill Patients*, London: Nursing Education Research Unit.

Rowett, C. (1986). *Violence in the Context of Local Authority Social Work*, Cambridge: Institute of Criminology.

Sharron, H. (1985). When terror is a fact of life. *Social Work Today*, **1**, 8–9.

Strathclyde Regional Council (1986). *Violence to Staff: Policies and Procedures*, a report of the Joint Departmental Trade Union Working Party.

Strong, P. G. (1973). Aggression in the general hospital. *Nursing Times*, **6**, 21–4.

Weiner, R., and Crosby, I. (1987). *Handling Violence and Aggression*, Adolescent Project Training Paper.

Yelloly, M. (1972). The concept of insight. In D. Jehu (ed.), *Behaviour Modification in Social Work*, Chichester: Wiley.

11

Violence in Prisons†

HANS TOCH
State University of New York, USA

We can start to think about the dynamics of prison violence by reviewing the career of an inmate who is very violent in the prison. As this man's story unfolds in official documents, we discover that he assiduously assaults prison staff members, and that his first assault on a correction officer occurs early in his sentence. This incident is described as follows:

> The inmate spit on the wall and stairs while coming off his gallery on the way to the mess hall. A correction officer attempted to counsel him and he struck the officer in the left cheekbone, then dove into the officer and secured a bodyhold on him and attempted to bite him in the neck. The officer slammed the inmate into the bars in an attempt to free himself, also pulled the inmate's hair to get his teeth off his neck. Other inmates came to the officer's aid and pulled the inmate off and restrained him until help arrived.

In retrospect, other officers observe that the inmate 'seemed to indicate that he did not understand' what the officer had told him before he exploded with rage. A staff member who interviews the inmate while he is awaiting disciplinary disposition writes that:

> He pretended at first that he could not speak English. After the third meeting with him he began to carry on a conversation in English. He can communicate in simple phraseology. He is more concerned about his return to school and plumbing class than he is over the possible disposition of the [incident].

The inmate retrospectively suggests that he 'wasn't in a very good mood on that day' and 'thought the officer had said something else to him'. He later explains:

†The research on which this chapter is based was supported by Grant Number R01 MH39573 (The Disturbed and Disruptive Inmate from the Center for Studies of Antisocial and Violent Behavior of the National Institute of Mental Health, US Department of Health and Human Services.

Clinical Approaches to Violence. Edited by K. Howells and C. R. Hollin

I was taking a spoon to the mess hall to eat. The officer took it away from me
and threw it in the garbage. He didn't tell me why.

In the segregation unit the inmate is described as 'very moody', and, as an
example of his moodiness, staff note that 'from time to time he would throw
garbage and other items out of his cell'. Later the inmate's 'moodiness' takes
a turn for the worse, and an officer files a disciplinary report as well as a
psychiatric referral form, noting that:

> The inmate called me over to his cell. He asked me to write the words 'Lucky
> Strike' on a carton of cigarettes as he could not write too well in English. As I
> started the words, the inmate reached through the bars and slapped me across
> the face. I backed away from him and the inmate tried to hit me again. I then
> proceeded up the gallery while the inmate was hollering that I had changed his
> cigarettes.

Three days later the man sets fire to his cell. After his accommodation is
changed, officers find a weapon in the vacated cell consisting of a piece of
wood wrapped in cloth. One month later an officer files a report which reads:

> While letting out the above inmate for the yard, he refused to be pat frisked. I
> told him either to submit to the frisk or return to his cell. He then threw a punch
> at me and hit me under the left eye. [Another officer] grabbed him from behind
> and we wrestled him to the floor.

The two officers involved in this incident require medical attention and must
take compensation leave, but the inmate off-handedly explains that 'I don't
like being told what to do. I was only fighting with the officers.' Three days
later another disgruntled officer records:

> While passing by the inmate's cell to dispense mail to [a neighboring cell] the
> inmate threw a container of urine at myself hitting me in the right shoulder and
> back of the head. I continued on and dispensed the mail. As I was leaving this
> area I again had to pass by the inmate's cell and was hit again by a second cup
> of urine. This one hit me in the back of the head.

A few days later a lower-key incident is recorded. On this occasion, according
to an officer:

> When the inmate finished his shower, he refused to lock in his cell. He said he
> wanted to see a sergeant. I told him to lock in and I would call a sergeant to
> come to see him. He refused this order and continued to loiter on the gallery.
> The sergeant arrived, and then the inmate returned to his cell.

Within three days a more dramatic version of the same incident unfolds in
the hospital building:

> The inmate refused to shower or go back to his cell. He said he wanted a sergeant
> and then attempted to leave the corridor. An officer stayed in the doorway to
> keep him from leaving. The inmate made verbal threats and repeated he would

not move until he had seen a sergeant. He said he wanted to be moved. I gave him three direct orders to return to his cell. Each order was given at a slow count. After the third order I pressed my personal alarm. [Two sergeants and six officers] came to assist. The inmate was put in his cell by force using hands, arms and body to get the inmate to his cell. The inmate tried to resist and attempted to assault the employees involved. After he was returned to his cell he spat in my face.

The next incident occurs two days later. The report reads:

After picking up trays and spoons at supper meal the inmate . . . refused to let me close the plexiglass cover. The inmate was given a direct order to remove his hand from the plexiglass cover but he refused. He stated, 'I want to see the psychiatrist right now.' I told him it was impossible to see the psychiatrist right now. He still refused to remove his hand. At this time I had two trays in my left hand. I set the trays down and called for [another officer] to be a witness that the inmate was refusing a direct order. When the inmate saw I had two hands on the plexiglass cover and was in the process of closing it, he removed his hand. The inmate then spat in my face. He started cursing at me calling me 'a big mother fucker' and 'I will get you some day. You are a crazy son of a bitch. I'm not crazy. You are.' Then the inmate started beating the cell door, shouting statements that were incoherent. After this he beat his chest with his fists stating, 'I am a Puerto Rican and you can't hurt me. Me tough.' He made more verbal threats that he would get me and stated he hoped I slept good tonight because 'some day I'm getting you.'

A report filed several days later in the same location reads:

An officer assigned to observation watch reported that the inmate had covered his light with a paper creating a fire hazard and making it impossible to see into the cell without the aid of a flashlight. A sergeant responded with [two officers]. The inmate refused to remove the object covering his light. The door was opened and when [one of the officers] attempted to remove the paper from the light the inmate punched the officer . . . After the inmate was subdued he was placed on his bed so that the officers could get out of his cell. While backing out of the cell [the inmate] jumped up from his bed and spit at the officers. The door was then closed without further incident.

The next incident also takes place in the observation ward. An officer reports:

When the inmate came out for a shower he immediately assaulted me. I opened the cell door with my left hand and the inmate came out of his cell swinging with both hands. I was able to block the blows but he scratched my neck with his fingernails while swinging. I pushed the inmate against the wall. [Another officer] used a neckhold and I used an armlock to put the inmate on the floor . . . While in this position the inmate said, 'You mother fucker, I will kill you someday because I am doing 26 years and I don't care.' . . . We then picked the inmate off the floor using our hands, and put him back in his cell.

Four days later, in the early morning, another incident report is filed, which notes that:

> The inmate started yelling, throwing his pillow and mattress around, banging on the door and walls, and throwing water from his toilet. A nurse advised [that she proposed] to use medication by injection authorized by the doctor. When the door opened, the inmate refused to lie down and came at the officers. An officer used a shield to push the inmate to the wall. [Three other officers] held the inmate's arms and placed him on his bed. The inmate offered little resistance as the nurse gave him an injection. He was released and the officer left the room. The inmate threw toilet water at the officers [as they were] leaving.

A disciplinary hearing is held covering the last set of incidents. Staff at this juncture are concerned about the possibility that the inmate may need mental health assistance and indicate they would like to see the inmate transferred to another setting where such assistance is available. In a request for transfer, they note:

> The subject is extremely aggressive and hostile toward correctional staff. He is reasonably civil with civilian staff but impulsive and antiauthoritarian toward correction officers. His problem has escalated to where he has [disciplinary] proceedings continuously. He has been evaluated as not psychotic and more of a disciplinary problem by the facility doctors. Conversely his language difficulty contributes to his problems. He also lacks positive attitudes with his peers. There is no psychiatrist available at this facility except for parole board evaluations . . . The inmate is presently retained in a hospital observation unit to avoid bodily harm to himself and staff members.

The institution's physician endorses the recommendation of a transfer, suggesting that the inmate 'would do better in an environment that was psychiatrically oriented'. The inmate's counselor writes that 'the inmate's most pressing personal problem at this point in time is psychiatric in nature . . . No institutional programming for this resident appears appropriate at this point.' A consulting psychiatrist interviews the inmate and records:

> The inmate told me that he was constantly getting in fights with people but justified this by saying the he was always the victim of other people's unpleasantness before he hit out. He said that for the most part his problems were with the corrections officers . . . He strenuously denied being crazy. I could find no evidence of any mental illness today and think from my interview and the information on his file that this man is merely an explosive psychopath. I do not think that any psychiatric treatment is likely to make any difference to his behavior. However, he is so extremely intolerant of any type of frustration he is likely to prove a continual disciplinary problem in this situation and I would concur with the recommendation made by [the physician] for transfer, if and when this can be arranged.

The inmate is eventually sent to a new institution with a note from the segregation counselor, who advises that:

> If the writer may coin a phrase, this subject is suffering from a 'hate the police officers' syndrome . . . His response toward any person that might represent authority is almost pavlovian, in that the stimulus is the sight of the authority figure and the response is hate and aggressiveness . . . He is a prime candidate for a psychotherapeutic community in the event that such a unit is established in

the system. His present attitude is such that he will spend the majority of his remaining period of incarceration in special housing unless he has a very drastic change in attitude.

The man indeed starts by spending several months in the segregation unit of his next prison. Here the first entry records that 'the subject has been suspected of urinating on the floor, and when he talks, he talks in mumbles and frequently to himself.' The next entry notes that:

The subject was placed in a plexiglass covered cell over the weekend because of allegedly spitting at a correction officer. He has been moved to a stripped cell at this time and seems to be behaving rationally.

Two weeks later the segregation counselor writes:

The above subject continues to remain incoherent and incomprehensible at this time. His body appearance and cell are disgraceful at best, and he continues to request that he be transferred to Puerto Rico. He again was advised that this is relatively impossible to do, and he then stated that he would like to go down to population in this facility and participate in the programs. In view of his mental situation it is this interviewer's impression that he will be with me for quite some time.

After the inmate has spent three months in segregation and his deportment has surprisingly improved the counselor requests that the inmate be transferred, and he is sent to another prison, where three months later he receives another long segregation sentence for an incident which is described as follows:

An officer approached the inmate who was washing his clothes in the utility sink and told the inmate to either take his shower or lock in his cell. The inmate stated, 'When I finish washing my clothes I'll take a shower.' The officer again stated his order to the inmate. The inmate left the sink and proceeded toward his cell with the officer following him. The inmate turned quickly, and using his fist struck the officer on the right side of the face. The inmate then grabbed the officer around the neck and started choking him. The officer broke loose and the inmate attempted to strike him again. The officer defended himself, and when the inmate grabbed his coat, the officer pushed the inmate into his cell and locked the door.

After the inmate completes this segregation term he is transferred to a different institution, where he spends several months accumulating a satisfactory work record, but is repeatedly locked up. He finally drops out of programs, claiming that he is taken advantage of by other inmates. He also commits fewer dramatic violations, and this pattern continues at the next prison to which he is sent, where his most salient offence consists of marking his cell walls with a pen, explaining that he 'didn't like the way they looked'. The inmate at this time also refuses to accept mail from his mother, which produces a frantic inquiry, to which the prison warden replies that the inmate

receives counseling and individual therapy from a trained psychologist and seems to be making some progress. He will continue to be seen, and will receive treatment as may be indicated.

Finally the inmate is transferred to a newly established program for victim-prone prisoners 'so that he would have the opportunity of participating in therapy'. The program staff write:

> Since entering the unit the resident has posed certain administrative difficulties. He appears to be of limited intelligence with emotional problems of long standing, as well as having a great deal of difficulty with the English language. The resident for the most part has demonstrated a positive attitude toward program participation. His motivation has been limited by stress from other inmates and a difficulty with the language barrier . . . He has received a number of misbehavior reports since his last parole board appearance. However, in fairness it would be advisable to evaluate the most recent reports. [On one occasion] he was written up for destruction of state property when he cut into his mattress and made a pillow from the stuffing. Destruction of state property cannot be tolerated, but one must understand that for a period of time in the block we did not have enough pillows for all our residents, and the inmate may have requested a pillow and been denied. He admitted to the adjustment committee that he did not have a pillow, and he needed one. [On another occasion] he received a misbehavior report from the recreation leader in our mandatory physical education program for refusing to participate in a floor hockey game. The inmate, according to the report, attempted to explain to the recreation leader that he doesn't know how to play hockey. Several residents have experienced difficulty while participating in some mandatory competitive sports, while in this program. Previously the inmate received a misbehavior report for failure to follow a direct order. This order was given by the correction officer, telling the inmate that he had to go to the gym program when the inmate had informed the officer that he did not wish to go. He has received one other misbehavior report when he interfered with an officer by hollering his cell location in in the presence of other inmates. A brief explanation of these misbehavior reports has been given so that the parole board may be able to see the inmate as an individual of limited intelligence with a definite communication problem who has demonstrated a difficulty following institutional procedures and processes which have resulted in misbehavior reports . . . The inmate has been able to decrease the number of misbehavior reports and decrease the seriousness of those reports.

Actually the man's pattern of difficulties has been tempered, and when he leaves the prison he stands transformed from an incredibly recidivistic assaulter into a clumsy and somewhat volatile individual, who is seen as having nuisance value and who invites pity from staff. It is hard to tell, of course, whether any fundamental change has occurred beyond the fact that after four or five years it has at some level dawned on the man that his pattern is self-destructive, and that the parole board can keep him in prison a good deal longer if he continues brawling with every officer who makes him feel resentful.

The term 'brawling' is used advisedly, because, as this man sees it, his conflicts with officers are 'fights'. In other words, they are disputes which are settled physically, as disputes must be settled among men. This view is partially shared and reinforced by the officers, who repeatedly describe in vivid detail the wrestling holds they deploy to neutralize the man, although they obviously resent his tendency to attack people without warning and the damage he does before one knows what he is about. The man is said to have 'communication problems' and these are reciprocal. Observers do not know when he feels mortally affronted because they no more understand him than he understands the concerns of those around him. The central issue often appears to be that the man feels himself treated like a child, and that his version of *machismo* holds that no man must be ordered about by another man, and that it is demeaning and insulting to be told to do things, particularly when you have explained why you do not wish to do them or would have explained if you could have.

The issue of the man's alleged reactions to uniforms does not necessarily enter the equation because the man sees encounters between himself and officers as personal, and perceives custodial instructions as originating in whims and expressions of disdain or disrespect. When the man feels disdained or disrespected in this way he reacts at the first available opportunity, which makes his behavior unpredictable, because his reaction does not necessarily coincide with the move that originates the offense to which he reacts.

In the first incident, for example, the officer does not know that the inmate is puzzled and enraged because the officer takes the plastic spoon the inmate thinks he will need for his meal. The officer also does not heed the inmate's expression of resentment, which consists of spitting on the floor, and the attack follows when the officer lectures the inmate about prison sanitation rules, which the inmate (who does not understand most of this lecture) perceives as adding insult to injury. In the second incident the officer is similarly oblivious to the fact that the inmate is enraged because he has ordered one brand of cigarettes and has been mistakenly given another, an act the inmate regards as deliberate and contemptuous.

When the inmate must rely on officers to obtain what he needs (or thinks he needs) such as cigarettes, contact with a sergeant or a psychiatrist, or permission to wash his clothes, he feels that this dependency is in itself demeaning. Thus when his requests are not immediately responded to, the humiliation becomes more serious, because not only has he had to ask for something but also those who have compromised his manliness by making him a mendicant now deny his requests, to show him who is in charge. He also sees himself receiving the same arbitrary and demeaning messages when officers present him with forced-choice situations (such as 'submit to the frisk or return to your cell') which do not include the option (go to the yard for recreation) that he elects to exercise. Since the inmate feels that officers make unacceptable demands and he knows that his own verbal skills are deficient, he usually concludes that there is nothing further to be said, a fight ensues and his subjection by (occasionally overwhelming) force reinforces his perspective. The fact that he keeps losing these fights because he is badly outnumbered has no bearing on the principle involved, which is that a man must fight when he must fight, and that it is better to fight and lose than to permit oneself to be belittled and emasculated by being ordered about like a child, having legitimate requests denied or having somebody else's will prevail in a contest of will, which denotes childish subservience. To be wrestled into the ground by greatly superior forces is not to be considered unmanly and is not a cause for shame, particularly if one can indicate, by spitting at one's retreating enemy or by otherwise declaring oneself inviolate ('You can't hurt me. Me tough'), that suppression is not tantamount to surrender.

It is true that the man does begin to intuit something of the authority structure of the prison, although it takes a great many months of segregation to get to the juncture where he no longer reacts with rage to what he regards as belittling and rejecting moves of officers. This does not mean, however, that even at this juncture the man accepts or understands the demands the prison makes on him, which include not skipping meals and appearing at work on days when he does not feel like working, or taking showers he feels he does not need.

The man's violations at this stage show fewer refusals to conform, but he has learned to temper his indignation when he is admonished, because he has learned that officers enforce rules rather than invent them to humiliate inmates. This means that a man's honor need not be at stake when he is asked to abide by a prison rule or when he is taken to task for non-conformity.

DEPICTING A VIOLENCE PATTERN

We have reviewed a somewhat redundant career in exhaustive detail to illustrate methodological as well as substantive points. The methodological issue revolves around the specification of the violence pattern, which can be the core of the clinical enterprise when we deal with violent offenders. Kozol *et al.*, (1972) take this position, and have indicated that 'the terms used in standard psychiatric diagnosis are almost totally irrelevant to the determination of dangerousness' (p. 383). These authors also concur that 'of paramount importance is a meticulous description of the actual assault . . . The description of the aggressor in action is often the most valuable single source of information' (p. 384).

With recurrent violent behavior the prime concern must be with *patterned* information, which covers consistencies of perspective and motive across a person's violent incidents (Toch, 1984, 1986). Such consistencies can be situational (phenotypic) or may relate to underlying (phenotypic) dispositions (Allport, 1961). Phenotypic commonalities consist of inventories of the circumstances in which the person aggresses, such as the common characteristics of individuals he selects as victims (Monahan, 1981). Genotypic consistency of necessity underlies phenotypic consistency. It can accommodate situational diversity, but this does not mean that where superficial commonalities exist we need dig no deeper. Incidents in hospitals, for example, often occur at given times of the day, such as in the morning or when staff shifts change (Lion and Reid, 1983). This fact tells us little, however, until we translate time and place into changed levels of environmental impingement, which lead us to infer that some patients feel overstimulated when their environment becomes enriched, making them irritable and over-responsive to trivial demands. We similarly learn little from the fact that our inmate assaults prison guards until we consider the connotations the officers' interventions hold for the inmate, which explain the intensity of the rage reactions with which he responds to seemingly innocuous instructions.

To arrange events in chronological order, as we have done in our example, is helpful on a number of counts:

(1) Temporal patterns often call attention to the effects of environmental changes which contribute to violence or ameliorate pressures to which the person reacts. A prisoner, for example, may discontinue violent reactions when he is segregated (our inmate does not), which suggests that the relative isolation of confinement is paradoxically beneficial in his case (Suedfeld, 1980a). Another person may be involved in a great deal of violence in an age-homogeneous prison for younger inmates, but may reduce his involvements in a prison that contains an older population, which provides clues to the peer temptations and pressures to which the inmate has reacted.

(2) Chronologies often point to time-bound internal states, such as tensions, fear and anxieties. Disturbed inmates, for example, frequently act out at entry into the prison system or when they face impending release, which mobilizes subsurface anxieties.

(3) Time-bound reductions of aggressivity can also provide clues to the therapeutic impact of serendipitous experiences, which we can only systematically mobilize once we have identified them (Bandura, 1986).

Our case study also shows that motives and dispositions of even patterned offenders can change over time. In our inmate's case, in fact, the change is extreme, involving an attentuation of behavior from recidivistic aggressivity to helpless confusion. Although most changes we encounter are not as significant, improvements over time are nonetheless prevalent. Young prisoners, who are most involved in violence, frequently improve their deportment over the course of their prison terms. Such changes, which at one time were regarded as anticipatory reactions to release from prison (Garabedian 1963), are attributable to varying combinations of the effects of maturation and adaptation to the prison.

PATHOLOGY AND PATTERNED VIOLENCES

Before we address the substance of patterned violence in the prison we must ask to what extent such violence falls under the purview of traditional mental health expertise and of the professionals who exercise it. Our inmate's case points up this issue, in that the inmate had been enthusiastically referred for mental health assistance on numerous occasions but had been consistently adjudged non-disturbed. The only circumstance in which a formal diagnosis was entered involved a psychiatrist who diagnosed the inmate as suffering from an anti-social personality disturbance, which, as defined by American psychiatry (American Psychiatric Association, 1983), is a category that is applicable to the great majority of prison inmates. The diagnosis and its variants (psychopathic or sociopathic personality) is frequently deployed for inmates who have been involved in violence, and some students (e.g. Hare,

1981) view this practice as clinically defensible. However, aggressivity is not among the attributes of the personality disorder as conventionally defined (Cleckley, 1976), which suggests that the diagnosis is an expression of clinical disapproval. Persons diagnosed in this way are also deemed refractory to treatment, which means that the diagnosis discourages, rather than encourages, referrals of the patient for mental health services. (For another perspective on the subject of psychopathy and violence, see Chapter 2.)

Inmates who are emotionally disturbed or who receive mental health services are disproportionately involved in prison infractions (Toch and Adams, 1986). They are also disproportionately involved in violent incidents, given that the correlation between violent infractions and other prison misconduct is high (of the order of 0.5). Although statistics do not suggest a causal link, some patterns of conduct carry no such ambiguity. Some disturbed inmates, for example, display the same cryptic outbursts in the prison as they do in hospitals (see Chapter 12). Such outbursts, which are statistically infrequent, reflect delusional concerns or respond to command hallucinations. Other psychosis-related violence responds to paranoid (conspiracy-centered) concerns, but most violence forms part of 'flight–fight' patterns, in which inmates retreat from reality but sporadically explode. In such cases the link between violence and mental illness is direct, with the former being a product of the latter.

However, in most cases of violence of even disturbed inmates the link, if any, between pathology and violence is less clear, and an unfortunate result of this fact is that violent inmates are often rejected as mental health clients. Disturbed violent inmates can be shuttled between custodial personnel of the prison (who refer them for diagnosis) and mental health personnel (who classify them as management problems and refuse to intervene). In extreme cases such staff interaction entails physically transporting the inmate from prison to mental health settings and back, a practice that is referred to pejoratively as 'bus therapy' (Freeman et al., 1977; Wilson, 1980; Toch, 1982).

DEPLOYING THERAPEUTIC COMMUNITIES

One assumes that defensible mental health service delivery in the prison must include some collaboration between mental health staff and custody personnel in addressing the problems of disruptive inmates. However, it is less clear whether all (or most of) such inmates are to be regarded as emotionally impaired and/or as entitled to mental health services. An affirmative answer is provided, among others, by Vernon Fox (1958), who wrote that 'the types of offenses committed by each individual may be psychiatrically diagnosed according to the area in which the individual finds conformity most difficult', since 'the specific nature of the offenses committed by each individual is partially dependent upon the personality structure of the offender' (p. 324). Fox's connotation of 'diagnosis' includes pathological conditions but obviously transcends them, since Fox would recognize that few violence-involved prisoners formally qualify as emotionally disturbed. Fox's prescription, however, presupposes an extended conception of mental health assistance, which includes mental health staff helping prison workers to understand the violent misbehavior of inmates. What Fox suggests is that we sidetrack recidivistic inmates from the ministrations of the disciplinary punishment process (which has, by definition, failed to modify their conduct) and place such inmates in therapeutic communities, which would 'permit emotional maturation to occur in a controlled environment' (p. 326).

The prescription has a great deal to recommend it, and it has on occasion been implemented (such as at Barlinnie Prison in Glasgow) with considerable success (Boyle, 1977). Among the arguments one can advance for the strategy are that:

(1) The type of inmate who is targeted by the approach has not responded to conventional sanctions, and it therefore makes no sense to subject him to more of the same.

(2) Almost any resocialization experience is infinitely more humane than the prevailing practice of *ad seriatem* solitary confinement (Jackson, 1983).

(3) The stigmatizing connotation of being 'emotionally disturbed' is spared to the clients of such a program.

(4) Therapeutic communities seek to enhance their members' interpersonal competence (Jones, 1953), which, on the face of it, is a non-intrusive contribution to the person's growth and development.

(5) The organization of therapeutic communities requires teaming mental health staff with other personnel (Toch, 1980), which promotes invaluable cross-fertilization. This attribute is particularly useful in prisons, where clinicians often operate in self-contained ghettos. The condition can be inferred, for example, from a survey conducted by the American federal prison system, in which psychologists complained to interviewers that 'they were not being allowed to participate enough in the correctional process', while administrators 'requested more involvement in the overall correctional process through consultation, staff training, and general program development' (Powitzky, 1978).

TREATMENT AND BEHAVIOR MANAGEMENT

Treatment programs that seek to resocialize violence-prone inmates can be accused of serving the ends of the prison rather than those of the prisoners. This charge has been especially addressed to behavior-modification experiments conducted in American adult prisons. An authoritative government monograph has noted that:

> Persons using behavior modification procedures have been particularly criticized for their attempts to deal with rebellious and nonconformist behavior of inmates in penal institutions. Because the behavioral professional is often in the position of assisting in the management of prisoners whose antagonism to authority and rebelliousness have been the catalyst for conflict within the institution, the distinctions among his multiple functions of therapy, management, and rehabili-

tation can become blurred, and his allegiance confused. . . .

Behavior modification programs are intended to give prisoners the opportunity to learn behavior that will give them a chance to lead more successful lives in the world to which they will return, to enjoy some sense of achievement, and to understand and control their own behavior better. . . .

Behavior modification should not be used in an attempt to facilitate institutionalization of the inmate or to make him adjust to inhumane living conditions. Further, no therapist should accept requests for treatment that take the form 'make him "behave"', when the intent of the request is to make the person conform to oppressive conditions (Brown *et al.*, 1975, pp. 16–17).

The ethical problem can be addressed in a number of ways, beyond the essential step of ensuring that program participants be *voluntarily* assigned, at least after they have the opportunity to 'sample' a program (Morris, 1974). One possible option is to avoid modalities which reduce the participation levels of clients, and this excludes the deployment of 'pure' behavior-modification approaches, but not of approaches in which cognitive (insight-centered) and behavioral techniques are combined (Bandura, 1986). High levels of participation can be achieved, for example, if offenders can be enticed to study their own patterns of violence and those of other violent offenders (Toch, 1984).

One 'self-study' model which is applicable to prisons was introduced in an urban police department that had experienced numerous violent confrontations for which some officers were heavily responsible. A group of such violence-prone officers was formed and was assigned the mission of reducing police–citizen violence. The officers designed and implemented a Peer Review Panel, in which each violence-involved officer met with a group of peers to review all his arrests that had resulted in confrontations. The goal was to diagnose the patterned contribution of the officer to his incidents of violence and to evolve alternate approaches which the officer could later rehearse (Toch *et al.*, 1975). Over time, the Review Panel, as a formal unit within its police department, substantially reduced violent incidents involving the police and deployed its graduates as panelists for other officers (Grant *et al.*, 1982).

The police Review Panel took pains to separate itself from the organization's disciplinary-sanctioning process, which assesses complaints by citizens against officers and punishes any officer who is found guilty of misconduct. This dilemma exists in greater measure in the prison, where inmates who commit violent infractions are severely punished, which makes them unavailable for treatment. Two other issues arise in connection with the enactment of sanctions:

(1) The process is offense-centered rather than person-centered, which means that underlying psychological patterns (such as those that one could infer if one reviewed the person's past behavior rather than his last transgression) cannot be considered:

(2) The process also cannot consider the impact of punishment on the offender, including the possible fact that punishment in the past has only made the person's behavior worse;

(3) The process is legalistic and tends to equate fairness with the standardization and inflexibility of sanctions.
(4) The process is concerned with harm that is done rather than with the causes of behavior, and defines the punishment it assigns as a warning to other prisoners who may contemplate comparable malefaction.

The retributive–deterrence framework is not only antithetical to the treatment perspective but also implies that treatment approaches can subvert the order-maintenance goals of the prison, rather than (as charged by critics) straining to subserve them. It is true that if treatment succeeds, the inmate becomes less of a threat to prison staff and/or to other prisoners, but these effects are corollaries of the defensible purpose of treatment, which is to help the person to abandon maladaptive patterns of conduct, which can only be 'tested' in the prison. Treatment also differs from behavior control by being person-centered, sensitively flexible and (if defensible) humane.

The dilemma is mitigated in practice by a number of considerations:

(1) Some influential experts in prison discipline (e.g. Glaser, 1964, 1977) have suggested that punishments can be individualized to take into account the effects of the punishment on the infractor;
(2) Discipline as practiced is invariably more flexible than it is in theory; penalties are, at times, suspended. Segregation stays are shortened in midstream, and lost prison time is restored if behavior improves;
(3) Disciplinary staff have been sensitized to problems of mental illness, and refer inmates to mental health personnel where such personnel are available.
(4) Disciplinary staff find it hard to ignore the recalcitrance of behavior patterns, and do not like conferring sanctions that have failed to modify behavior in the past.

Such considerations make it more acceptable to introduce treatment-oriented interventions, and one can introduce such interventions as options that can be exercised by disciplinary staff themselves when they feel that conventional dispositions are inappropriate. Treatment interventions can either be defined as punishment 'moratoria' (Fox, 1958) or as contractual experiments during which penalties are suspended, subject to reinstatement if the offender rejects treatment or fails to respond to it.

THE RANGE OF PRISON VIOLENCE

Prison violence includes homicides and very serious assaults that are inflicted with a variety of ingenious homemade weapons. The issue of whether the rates of such incidents in the prison are higher or lower than they are in the community is in dispute (Sylvester et al., 1977; Jones, 1976; Bowker, 1980). This question is difficult to resolve, because prisons contain many persons drawn from violence-prone subpopulations, which would have to be replicated through stratification in constituting comparison groups if we wanted to make sensible epidemiological estimates (Toch, 1976).

Putting this issue aside, prisons are unquestionably violent settings, and particularly so where penal institutions contain large proportions of young inmates, who disproportionately account for disruptive behavior (Flanagan, 1983). This fact is unsurprising, since (youthful) age is the best predictor we have of violent behavior anywhere, and of crime in general (Wilson and Herrnstein, 1986; Hirschi and Gottfredson, 1983). (Actually, the best predictor of violent behavior is past violent behavior. A first or solitary violent act is not predictable, but probabilities of violent behavior increase with greater involvement in violence, so that future violence can be extrapolated from recidivistic past violence, with decreased margins for error.) The probabilities of violence are also enhanced where large numbers of prisoners are 'state-raised youths', a term that is used to describe prisoners who have extensive experience of juvenile institutions, where a climate of exploitation and violence is usually prevalent (Irwin, 1970; Bartollas et al., 1976; also see Chapter 13).

Violence levels in prisons are further enhanced by the fact that peer status in the inmate culture (or some segments of this culture) hinges heavily on demonstrated bravery, and low status accrues to those who demonstrate fear. This status hierarchy of the prison invites a 'testing' process, revolving around the willingness to engage in physical combat at the slightest provocation (Sykes, 1958), a norm which is particularly troublesome for inmates who are non-violently non-resilient (Toch, 1975). Moreover, one variant of the testing process involves threatening other inmates—particularly young ones—with the imminence of rape, and rape threats often result in violent incidents, either pre-emptively or as a reinforcement of a threat (Lockwood, 1980). More mundane forms of prison violence can be avoided by the inmate, however, because they result from inmate 'underworld' involvements, such as gambling, loansharking and drug trafficking, which includes organized gang activity.

Prison violence of conventional kinds is almost exclusively confined to male prisons, which does not mean that violence does not occur among female prisoners. Violence in women's prisons, however, is usually non-instrumental, and heavily comprises angry outbursts that occur in reactions to perceived stress situations (Fox, 1982). Female prisoners are also much more apt than male ones to define themselves as emotionally disturbed, and to seek mental health assistance where it is available.

Accurate statistics on prison violence are, unfortunately, hard to come by, because fear of retribution and a premium on non-informing result in under-reporting (Porporino, 1986). Prison systems are also lax in collecting incident statistics, and where such statistics exist, their reliability is often in question. The fact is particularly obvious in the case of self-directed violence, which is prevalent in prisons but only sparsely reflected in official statistics (Toch, 1975). Self-mutilation, however, must be taken very seriously by clinicians, not because it suggests mental illness (which it does not), but because it reflects despair that demands a humane response.

Facts about prison violence which are available in the literature are mostly unhelpful to clinicians. This is so because academic conerns focus on aggregate contextual and background characteristics, which are clinically of marginal relevance. The exception to this rule concerns the well-known finding that violence rates increase with increased social density among young inmates (Megargee, 1977; Nacci et al., 1977). Although 'crowding' itself is an ambiguous concept, the stressors that crowding entails (reduced privacy and increased arousal) have obvious personal impact (Toch, 1977; Suedfeld 1980b). The same point holds with respect to the effects of high inmate turnover rates, which create instability in prison environments (Ellis, 1984; Poporino, 1986).

THE PSYCHODYNAMICS OF PRISON VIOLENCE

In prisons, as in other settings, a small proportion of the population accounts for a large amount of the violence (Porporino, 1986). This draws our attention to personality attributes that predispose persons to behave aggressively, or that enhance the probability that interpersonal encounters will be resolved through uses of physical force.

The psychology of violence has not advanced to the point where a taxonomy of violence-proneness is available, but two themes are candidates for inclusion in such a taxonomy, and a third enters when we consider motives for assaults on staff. The two principal themes are (1) developmental immaturity, impulsivity and egocentricity; and (2) compensatory reactions to low self-esteem. The third theme (to which we have alluded in our case example) relates to issues of autonomy/dependence.

Development Deficits

Reviews of prison incidents suggest that much of the violence in prisons is a manifestation of impulsivity, which denotes ego deficits that center on lax impulse control (Redl and Wineman, 1951, 1952). Another way of characterizing such patterns is that they reflect deficient socialization, which leaves the individual fixated at impulse-ridden and opportunistic stages of personal development (Loevinger, 1976).

The purest impulsivity patterns are those that describe persons who engage in repeated behavior that is designed to satisfy their needs in a direct and primitive way. One source of violence for such persons is that they may encounter others who are similarly oriented, and will resolve their rivalries through physical combat. More violence-promotive is predatory aggression, in which the person regards others as objects of need satisfaction, and uses violence or threats of violence to intimidate, extort, expropriate or bully those susceptible to intimidation, who may also violently resist being victimized.

A third impulsivity pattern involves a susceptibility to reacting with aggression to comparatively minor frustrations (Dollard et al., 1930). When impulsive persons of this kind are disappointed or obstructed in the pursuit of their goals they often become disgruntled and engage in explosive aggression, which consists of expressions of blind anger and rage. A different quality (back-to-the-wall despair) points to stress rather than frustration as a source of aggression. In this pattern the person is apt to feel that situations close in on him; consequently he experiences panic and anxiety, and tends to give way to tantrums that express a sense of helplessness. (Limited verbal skills, as in our example, can be contributors to this pattern.)

One variation of the violent impulsivity issue reflects the 'stimulus-seeking' propensity that has been underlined by Eysenck (1964). This propensity in action can be described as 'Russian roulette' behavior, because the person takes unreasonable risks in the service of short-term goals and excitement, and seemingly does not care that he gets into trouble, or at least does not draw lessons from the fact. Other impulsive offenders, however, are not oblivious to aversive stimuli in the long run. Such persons engage in consistently non-reflective, childlike, self-serving and irresponsible behavior, but eventually discover that their behavior generates unwelcome repercussions they cannot accept. This discovery, unfortunately, often mobilizes unhealthy defenses, and the person indulges in self-pity rather than self-reflection, a reaction which treatment interventions must surface and deal with.

Compensatory Violence

Much violent behavior is designed to cement a person's sense of self-esteem, either by trying to build a reputation or by defending against feelings of low self-esteem through compensatory behavior (Adler, 1927; Toch, 1984). In the most direct manifestation of this pattern the person may use violence to demonstrate toughness or 'manhood' in an attempt to achieve a reputation as an individual to be admired by his peers. We have described this pattern elsewhere (Toch, 1984) as 'self-image demonstrating', and have contrasted it with another pattern, which we call 'self-image defending'. This pattern is somewhat represented in the case we have reviewed, in that the inmate (typical of self-image defenders) tended to feel easily disparaged and affronted, and reacted violently when he thought himself offended or slighted.

Another pattern we have described (reputation defending) is more group-centered. In this type of pattern the person functions as a member of a violence-prone group, and acts with and on behalf of his group and in defense of its values. However, to the extent to which the person meets his group more than half-way, compensatory features may overlap this pattern. Irrespective of group membership, for instance, the person may see himself as a gladiator, and may regard violence as a skill and a preferred way to resolve disputes, which makes him engage in combat readily and casually to resolve interpersonal disputes.   Pattern admixtures involving neuroses are also sometimes encountered. One such pattern involves the use of violence to pre-empt anticipated unpopularity. Such violence occurs where the person expects to be rejected and reacts with provocation and hostility in anticipation of rejection, thereby documenting his assumptions.

Compensatory violence is defended by a wide range of psychological mechanisms, and many of these defenses can make the person uninviting as a client of therapy. Not surprisingly, for instance, some violence-prone individuals who have low self-esteem feel unable to compromise or retreat from rigidly defined positions, and equate this stance with defending their sense of worth.

Autonomy/Dependence

Given the authority structure of prisons, it is not surprising that prisons evoke regressive behavior that is concerned with dependence upon or independence from parental figures, such as persons in authority. For persons who engage in such behavior, as does the inmate whose career we have reviewed, the issue of dependence/autonomy is emotionally charged, because it relates to definitions of adulthood which include emancipation, on the one hand, and loss of support, on the other. This issue is a paradoxical one, and includes patterns in which the person alternates between dependent and violently rebellious behavior, hinging upon whether he feels his needs are met or frustrated.

Other inmates, however, take a very consistent and systematically rebellious, defiant and challenging stance toward persons in authority. Some such inmates are particularly concerned with rejecting personal constraints, such as autonomy constraints that are endemic in the prison. These persons feel that no one has a right to infringe on their own autonomy, and they react angrily to infringements whose rationale they cannot understand or accept (Toch, 1977). Being apprehended and punished can be particularly irksome to such persons, because this experience is reminiscent of childhood (Sykes, 1958).

Although autonomy concerns seem particularly inhospitable to interventions, the impression is unwarranted, because persons who manifest such patterns regard authority figures as significant to them, and therefore establish transferences with comparative ease (Toch, 1981).

A FINAL NOTE

Given the scope of this chapter, we cannot presume to offer programmatic or therapeutic prescriptions, except to note (as we have done) that inmates often mature in prison, and that assistance in accelerating this endeavor is not misplaced. We have also suggested that where misbehavior patterns prove chronic (as on occasion they do), continued disciplinary processing is not an appropriate response.

Beyond these points, we have suggested that violence can be a subject as well as object for treatment. Patterns such as those we have described can help staff make sense of individual violence, but, more to the point, they can help a violent person make sense of his violence, when he is ready and willing to abandon his defenses. The task of working through defenses is difficult and, at first, uninviting, but incentives can be deployed to make it attractive. For one, self-study is more attractive than other experiences that violent inmates customarily encounter in reaction to their behavior. Second, group settings can provide social support in the shape of other offenders who are engaged in comparable self-exploration. Third, behavioral strategies can be evolved that have a short-term payoff as behavior alternatives are rehearsed and found to 'work'. Finally, humane staff can be a powerful incentive, if such staff show personal acceptance, making it clear to the offender that while they reject his past conduct, they respect his capacity for self-understanding, regeneration and eventual reform.

References

Adler, A. (1927). *The Practice and Theory of Individual Psychology*, New York: Harcourt.

Allport, G.W. (1961). *Pattern and Growth in Personality*, New York: Holt, Rinehart and Winston.

American Psychiatric Association (1983). *Diagnostic and Statistical Manual of Mental Disorders*. 3rd edition, Washington, DC.

Bandura, A. (1986). *Social Foundations of Thought and Action: A Social Cognitive Theory*, Englewood Cliffs, NJ: Prentice-Hall.

Bartollas, C., Miller, S., and Dinitz, S. (1976). *Juvenile Victimization: The Institutional Paradox*. New York: Wiley.

Bowker, L.H. (1980). *Prison Victimization*, New York: Elsevier.

Boyle, J. (1977). *A Sense of Freedom*, London: Pan.

Brown, B.S., Wienckowski, L.A., and Stolz, S.B. (1975). *Behavior Modification: Perspective on a Current Issue*. Washington, DC: Department of Health, Welfare and Education.

Cleckley, H. (1976). *The Mask of Sanity*, 5th edition, St Louis, MO: Mosby.

Dollard, J., *et al.* (1930). *Frustration and Aggression*, New Haven CONN: Yale University Press.

Ellis, D. (1984). Crowding and prison violence: integration of research and theory. *Criminal Justice and Behavior*, **11**, 277–308.

Eysenck, H. (1964). *Crime and Personality*, Boston, MA: Houghton Mifflin.

Flanagan, T. (1983). Correlates of institutional misconduct among state prisoners. *Criminology*, **21**, 29–39.

Fox, J.G. (1982). Women in prison: A case study in the social reality of stress. In R. Johnson and H. Toch (eds), *The Pains of Imprisonment*, Beverly Hills, CA: Sage.

Fox, V. (1958). Analysis of prison disciplinary problems. *Journal of Criminal Law, Criminology and Police Science*, **49**, 321–6.

Freeman, R.A., Dinitiz, S., and Conrad, J.P. (1977). A look at the dangerous offender and society's efforts to control him. *American Journal of Correction*, January–February, 25–31.

Garabedian, P.G. (1963). Social roles and processes of socialization in the prison community. *Social Problems*, **11**, 140–52.

Glaser, D. (1964). *The Effectiveness of a Prison and Parole System*, Indianapolis, IND: Bobbs-Merrill.

Glaser, D. (1977). Institutional disciplinary action and the social psychology of disciplinary relationships. In R.M. Carter, D. Glaser and L.T. Wilkins (eds), *Correctional Institutions*, 2nd edition, Philadelphia: Lippencott.

Grant, J.D., Grant, J., and Toch, H. (1982). Police–citizen conflict and the decision to arrest. In J. Konecni and E.B. Ebbeson (eds), *The Criminal Justice System: A Social–Psychological Analysis*, San Francisco, CA: Freeman.

Hare, R.D. (1981). Psychopathy and violence. In J.R. Hays, T.K. Roberts and K.S. Solway (eds), *Violence and the Violent Individual*, New York: Spectrum.

Hirschi, T., and Gottfredson, M. (1983). Age and the explanation of crime. *American Journal of Sociology*, **89**, 522–84.

Irwin, J. (1970). *The Felon*, Englewood Cliffs, NJ: Prentice-Hall.

Jackson, M. (1983). *Prisoners of Isolation: Solitary Confinement in Canada*, Toronto: University of Toronto Press.

Jones, D. (1976). *The Health Risks of Imprisonment*, Lexington, MA: D.C. Heath.

Jones, M. (1953). *The Therapeutic Community: A New Treatment Method in Psychiatry*, New York: Basic Books.

Kozol, H.L., Boucher, R.J., and Garofalo, R.F. (1972). The diagnosis and treatment of dangerousness. *Crime and Delinquency*, **18**, 371–92.

Lion, J.R., and Reid, W.H. (eds) (1983). *Assaults within Psychiatric Facilities*, New York: Grune & Stratton.

Lockwood, D. (1980). *Prison Sexual Violence*, New York: Elsevier.

Loevinger, J. (1976). *Ego Development*, San Francisco, CA: Jossey-Bass.

Megargee, E.I. (1977). The association of population density, reduced space and uncomfortable temperatures with misconduct in a prison community. *American Journal of Community Psychology*, **5**, 289–98.

Monahan, J. (1981). *Predicting Violent Behavior: An Assessment of Clinical Techniques*, Beverly Hills, CA: Sage.

Morris, N. (1974). *The Future of Imprisonment*, Chicago, IL: University of Chicago Press.

Nacci, P.L., Teitelbaum, H.E., and Prather, J. (1977). Population density and inmate misconduct rates in the federal prison system. *Federal Probation*, **41**, 26–31.

Porporino, F.J. (1986). Managing violent individuals in correctional settings. *Journal of Interpersonal Violence*, **1**, 213–37.

Powitzky, R. (1978). Reflections of a federal prison psychologist. *Quarterly Journal of Corrections*, **2**, 7–12.

Redl, F., and Wineman, D. (1951). *Children who Hate: The Disorganization and Breakdowns of Behavior Controls*. New York: Free Press.

Redl, F., and Wineman, D. (1952). *Controls from Within: Techniques for the Treatment of the Aggressive Child*, New York: Free Press.

Suedfeld, P. (1980a). *Restricted Environmental Stimulation: Research and Clinical Applications*. New York: Wiley.

Suedfeld, P. (1980b). Environmental effects on violent behavior in prisons. *International Journal of Offender Therapy and Comparative Criminology*, **24**, 107–16.

Sykes, G. (1958). *The Society of Captives: A Study of a Maximum Security Prison*. Princeton: Princeton University Press.

Sylvester, S., Reed, J., and Nelson, D. (1977). *Prison Homicide*, New York: Spectrum.

Toch, H. (1975). *Men in Crisis: Human Breakdowns in Prison*. Chicago, IL: Aldine.

Toch, H. (1976). *Peacekeeping: Police, Prisons and Violence*. Lexington, MA: D.C. Heath.

Toch, H. (1977). *Living in Prison: The Ecology of Survival*, New York: Free Press.

Toch, H., (ed.) (1980). *Therapeutic Communities in Corrections*, New York: Praeger.

Toch, H. (1981). Psychological treatment of imprisoned offenders. In J.R. Hays, T.K. Roberts, and K.S. Solway (eds), *Violence and the Violent Individual*, New York: Spectrum.

Toch, H. (1982). The disturbed disruptive inmate: where does the bus stop? *Journal of Psychiatry and Law*, **10**, 327–49.

Toch, H. (1984). *Violent Men*, Cambridge, MA: Schenkman.

Toch, H. (1986). True to you, darling, in my fashion: the notion of contingent consistency. In A. Campbell and J.J. Gibbs (eds), *Violent Transactions: The Limits of Personality*, London: Blackwell.

Toch, H., and Adams, K. (1986). Pathology and disruptiveness among prison inmates. *Journal of Research in Crime and Delinquency*, **23**, 7–21.

Toch, H., Grant, J.D., and Galvin, R. (1975). *Agents of Change: A Study in Police Reform*, Cambridge, MA: Schenkman.

Wilson, J.Q., and Herrnstein, R.J. (1986). *Crime and Human Nature*, New York: Simon and Schuster.

Wilson, R. (1980). Who will care for the mad and bad? *Corrections Magazine*, **6**, 5–17.

12

The Nature of Violence in Psychiatric Hospitals

JONQUIL DRINKWATER
Highfield Unit, Warneford Hospital, Oxford, UK

and

GISLI H. GUDJONSSON
Institute of Psychiatry, University of London, UK

INTRODUCTION: IS VIOLENCE A PROBLEM IN PSYCHIATRIC HOSPITALS?

If mental health professionals were asked whether violence is a problem in psychiatric hospitals they would find themselves in a difficult position. What evidence could they use to decide on a response? Over the last 20 years a series of enquiries into violence in British psychiatric hospitals would suggest that there is a problem (e.g. Whittingham Hospital, 1972; Napsbury Hospital, 1973; Brookwood Hospital, 1980; Rampton Hospital, 1980). Additional evidence might come from the report of a UK government committee set up to look at, among other things, violence in psychiatric hospitals (DHSS and Home Office, 1975). This committee thought that the problem was severe enough to recommend the establishment of medium-secure facilities to house psychiatric patients who have a history of violent behaviour. Another source of evidence is the concern expressed by nursing unions over the number of violent incidents they are required to manage in psychiatric hospitals (e.g. Confederation of Health Service Employees, 1977).

However, these sources of evidence are all somewhat indirect. One of the most striking aspects of the study of violence in psychiatric hospitals is that there are no readily available current statistics for the prevalence of violence. COHSE (1977), one of the major British nursing unions, reported only 311 violent assaults on staff in Britain over a 3.5-year period. However, this seems remarkably low, and other UK studies have suggested higher rates. Fottrell

(1980) looked at three British psychiatric settings: Tooting Bec Hospital, Park Prewitt Hospital and the Chiltern Psychiatric Wing. Tooting Bec Hospital is an urban psychiatric hospital with approximately 1100 patients, where 353 violent incidents were recorded in one year. This is equivalent to 6.8 incidents per week throughout the hospital, or an assault rate of 0.3 incidents per patient per year. Park Prewitt Hospital is of similar size but in a rural setting, and had 3.4 incidents per week or an assault rate of 0.15 per patient per year. The Chiltern Psychiatric Wing has 56 beds in a general hospital setting, and had 0.65 incidents per week or an assault rate of 0.6 incidents per patient per year. It can be seen from these figures that there may be an effect on incident rates of the type of hospital catchment area and setting, the highest assault rate being for a general hospital setting and the lowest for a rural psychiatric hospital.

All these hospitals had similar treatment regimens, emphasizing physical treatments such as drugs and ECT. Drinkwater and Feldman (1982) looked at a small urban psychiatric hospital of 105 beds run as a therapeutic community, and found 4.22 violent incidents per week or an assault rate of 2.1 per patient per year. Of these, the most frequent type was assault on another person without a weapon, followed by assault on property, self-harming and finally assault with a weapon. Clearly, there is a need for more detailed statistics on the prevalence of violent incidents in all British psychiatric hospitals. These initial findings suggest high levels of violent incidents, the overall level of violence possibly affected by the type of hospital, its location and the form of treatment undertaken. It is important to note that many problems of violence are caused by relatively few patients who are repeatedly violent rather than by many who are periodically and infrequently assaultive (Depp, 1983; Drinkwater, 1988; Roscoe, 1987). Overall, nursing staff are much more likely to be assaulted than members of many other professions. Fisher (1980) states that the average person in the UK can expect to be assaulted once every 100 years, in contrast to every 9 months for staff who work in some psychiatric hospitals.

Studies in the United States have also suggested high rates of violence, but again it is not easy to obtain very comprehensive statistics. Evenson et al. (1974) looked at the incidents at St Louis State Hospital, and found an overall assault rate of 0.3 per patient per year. This is exactly the figure obtained in an urban psychiatric hospital in Britain (Tooting Bec Hospital, London). Evenson et al. also reviewed the effect of sex, and found a higher assault rate for men of 0.5 per patient per year. A legislative committee found that there were more than 12 000 violent incidents each year in the 28 psychiatric facilities in New York State (1975–6).

Studies of American psychiatrists also suggest high assault rates. Madden et al. (1976) surveyed 115 psychiatrists, and found that 48 (or 42%) had been assaulted. Haffke and Reid (1983) mailed a confidential questionnaire to every psychiatrist in the state of Nebraska and found that 32% of their respondents had been assaulted within the previous year. Part of their survey involved violence against each psychiatrist's staff, and 48% reported that at least one of their staff had been assaulted. One of the assaults reported was the stabbing to death of an aide on a psychiatric ward.

One interesting finding to emerge from the incident studies is that the majority of assaults in psychiatric hospitals did not result in serious injuries (Ekblom, 1970; Fottrell, 1980; Folkard, 1957). This finding was also reported in an American forensic facility (Dietz and Rada, 1983). Of 221 assaults, 30 (or 13%) resulted in serious injury and 132 (or 60%) in no injury at all. Drinkwater (1988) studied the effect of sex and type of ward (i.e. acute, long-stay or disturbed) on the severity of injuries. She looked at five wards differing by either sex or type, and found that there were no significant differences between the wards in the severity of injuries. The majority (88.1%) of incidents on all wards resulted in no injuries. Only 1.2% of incidents across the wards resulted in major injuries (e.g. cuts requiring stitching).

To summarize, there is little information on the current prevalence of violent incidents in psychiatric hospitals. What is available suggests that violence is common, although the majority of incidents do not result in serious injuries. There is a clear need for central collection of statistics by the government's Department of Health and effective use of the information gathered.

The focus of this chapter will be on the clinician assessing violence in the setting of a psychiatric ward. Clearly, individual patient factors are of key importance, and are dealt with elsewhere in this book. This chapter will focus on aspects of the psychiatric ward environment that the clinician needs to assess before determining a suitable intervention at the appropriate level.

The most frequent source of data on environmental factors in psychiatric wards are violent incident studies. These studies have serious methodological problems, which will be outlined before going on to look at some of the research findings in this area. The nature of the psychiatric ward environment will be examined, and some of the aspects of ward management of patients which may foster violence will be considered. Following on from this will be a section on the management of violent incidents, and a discussion of whether to prosecute patients. Finally, the training of nurses to deal with violence will be briefly examined.

METHODOLOGICAL PROBLEMS

The major methodological problem is inconsistent definitions of aggression and violence. This problem is also central to other chapters in this book, so only a very brief discussion will be included here. A survey of the literature reveals a wide range of different definitions, with very little consensus between them. This has resulted in inconsistent and unreliable categorization, which creates difficulties when comparing results from different studies.

Some of the labelling problems have been aptly described by Bandura (1973): 'Variations in defining features arise mainly because some authors describe aggression solely in terms of the behavior, while others include assumptions about the instigators, the emotional concomitants, or the intent of potentially injurious action.' Hence, a central problem is in the distinction between the behaviour and the influences and evaluations of its observers. Bandura (1973) has proposed that some of the factors which determine social labelling of behaviour as aggressive are: the characteristics of the behaviour; the intensity of responses; expression of pain and injury by the recipient; the intentions attributed to the performer; and the characteristics of both the labellers and aggressors (e.g. age or race).

Two key issues have been the elements of 'intent' and 'injury' in definitions. The notion of 'intent' has been a major problem in operationalizing the concept of violence. Intent usually refers to any behaviour which is non-accidental, under the control of the person and that *aims* to hurt the victim. As it is impossible to prove intent it has to be inferred, therefore incorporating intent into a definition is problematic. However, problems also arise when aggression is defined in terms of its outcomes, i.e. aggression is behaviour which *produces* harm. When this definition is used it is not possible to exclude accidents or include occasions on which a person tried to injure but failed (e.g. attempted to shoot someone but missed). Furthermore, there are then problems defining harm, which has been taken to include both physical and psychological harm (Buss, 1971).

Several authors have tried to get around the problems of definition by proposing different categories of aggression (Buss, 1971; Berkowitz, 1965; Feshbach, 1970). Some examples of different categories in the literature include: instrumental and angry aggression; physical and verbal aggression; active and passive aggression; and direct and indirect aggression. Only a few authors have attempted to distinguish between aggression and violence, and this has led to very similar definitions for both terms. For example, Bandura's definition of aggression is: 'Aggression is defined as behavior that results in personal injury . . .' and Haffke and Reid's (1983) definition of violence is 'Violent behavior may be described as an activity that uses force to inflict injury on another . . .'.

It would appear that there is a clear need for consistent and widely accepted definitions of aggression and violence. It is not possible to be sure that the wide range of activities currently defined as aggression or violence should be subsumed under the same label. Aggression and violence are heterogeneous phenomena, and Bandura (1973) has described attempts at defining them as 'an invitation for a stroll through a semantic jungle'.

However, there are other serious methodolgoical problems in this area of research. The major method of data collection has been violent incident studies, which have several problems. First, there is under-reporting of incidents. Lion *et al.* (1981) documented a remarkable degree of under-reporting of incidents in a US State hospital. Most studies have not included checks on reporting using log books or ward handover notes, but have relied on the incident forms being completed. Dietz and Rada (1983) have pointed to evidence that under-detection of incidents is also a problem. In crowded wards staff may be totally unaware that an incident has occurred.

Another methodological problem is that most studies have been based on routine injury forms which are only filled out when an incident results in injury requiring medical attention: a small proportion of the incidents. Very few studies have developed their own incident forms, including a clear definition of violence and detailed analysis of antecedent and consequent events. Furthermore, few studies have described the type of violent behaviour involved, i.e. whether it was an assault on another patient or staff, a suicide attempt or if a weapon was used. Incidents involving damage to property are usually not recorded. Another problem is that several types of assault are often lumped together.

A final problem is the reliability of the information recorded on the form. In some studies senior nurses who may not have seen the incident or been involved completed the forms. Reliance was placed on second-hand information, often compiled some time after the event. Robinson (1972) highlights a further problem encountered when using hospital injury forms. He suggests that two factors which must be considered are hospital and individual staff attitudes towards the reporting of incidents. The hospital's official attitude should be considered in terms of resulting time off and monetary compensation. Staff attitudes will be affected by the hospital's attitude, and staff will tend to report more frequently if it is known that the hospital is sympathetic and that compensation is forthcoming.

ENVIRONMENTAL FACTORS

The factors which will be reviewed in this section include: time of day; day of the week, architectural blind spots; overcrowding; and staffing levels. The method of investigation has been violent incident studies, so the methodological problems described previously should be borne in mind.

Regarding the time of day of assaults, various different times have been suggested as 'peak' throughout the day (Depp, 1983; Dietz and Rada, 1983; Drinkwater et al., 1983; Fottrell, 1980; Ionno, 1983; Quinsey and Varney, 1977). Similarly, various days of the week have been suggested as 'peak' (Depp, 1983; Dietz and Rada, 1983; Ionno, 1983), while other studies have suggested that the day of the week is not related to violence (Dietz, 1981; Quinsey and Varney, 1977). These conflicting results for both the time of day and day of the week suggest that these variables are not significant in themselves, but rather they reflect the effects of other changes in the ward environment on the incidence of violence. One of these may be modelling effects, because Ionno (1983) reported that incidents 'clustered'. At times, three or more assaults would occur within 3–6 hours, and usually the individuals involved in the assaults were different. This clustering of incidents was also discovered by Drinkwater et al. (1983), who found that each ward studied had a higher frequency of one type of assault than any other. This evidence suggests that modelling of one type of assault facilitates the learning and replication of it by other patients.

Another factor which has been investigated is architectural blind spots. These are defined as architectural arrangements which produce blind spots in staff monitoring of patients. Depp (1983) asked staff to identify places from which it was difficult to observe patients. He found that 22% of incidents occurred in places which were out of sight of staff. However, when he investigated in more detail he discovered that in only 18% of cases could the location have been important. This result suggests that architectural blind spots do not play a part, but further evidence is needed.

The issue of the effect of 'overcrowding' on behaviour has been controversial in research on both humans and other species. Several attempts have been made to improve the definition of overcrowding. Stokols (1972) has proposed that one needs to distinguish between population density, which is a measure of individuals per unit of space, and crowding, which is a subjective stress reaction. A high density of people is a necessary but not sufficient condition for 'crowding' to be felt. A second change to the definition has been proposed by Loo (1972). Loo suggested that it is necessary to distinguish between social density, where the number of individuals varies in a given amount of space, and spatial density, where space is varied and the number of individuals remains the same. Mueller (1983) has pointed out that variations in social density are confounded with variations in the number of others present. There is evidence that the number of others present has a strong influence on aggression, such as an audience (Borden and Taylor, 1973).

Turning to the issue of density of human beings, either social or spatial, there has been the suggestion that high density facilitates 'dominant responses', including aggression. Another theory has been that high density produces stimulus overload, which reduces the quality of social interactions. A third mechanism suggested to mediate between high density and aggression is negative affect, especially in males. However, the evidence for all three theories is weak (Freedman, 1975; Baum and Valins, 1977; Matthews et al., 1979). Overall, there is little support for a relationship between overcrowding and aggression. However, there is evidence that overcrowding in prisons leads to increased psychopathology, such as psychiatric symptoms, self-mutilations and suicide (Cox et al., 1984).

Finally, staffing levels have been a contentious issue for nursing unions, who insist that adequate levels are necessary for managing violence (COHSE, 1977). There has also been the suggestion that inadequate staffing levels may facilitate violence (Robinson, 1972; Ekblom, 1970). The literature reveals little evidence that can be brought to bear on this issue. Tardiff (1983) commented that adequate staffing levels are important in the prevention of violence but presented no data. Rogers et al., (1980) made a retrospective study using standardized incident reports in a maximum-security hospital. They investigated, among other factors, the effect of the availability of professional staff. 'Available professionals' were psychologists, 'BA level activity therapists' and social workers, not nurses or psychiatrists. They found that the presence of one or two professional staff was associated with a significant decrease in violent incidents, but this did not hold when three or more were present. Rogers et al. suggested that the presence of professional staff is curvilinearly related to aggressive behaviour. However, this study was seriously flawed because information about the presence or absence of nurses and psychiatrists was not provided.

Depp (1983) compared average nursing staff levels for the shift and day of an incident with staffing levels for the same period over the previous three days. He found a tendency for higher staffing on the shift or day a violent incident occurred. Drinkwater (1988) looked at whether 'adequate' or 'inadequate' numbers of nurses influenced how the staff managed incidents. The nurses themselves determined what an adequate number of nurses would be for their ward. It was found that whether there were 'adequate' or 'inadequate' numbers of nurses on the ward had no effect on the type of assault, the length of time needed to control an incident, the disruptiveness of an incident to the ward, whether physical restraint was used (and if so, by how many people), whether sedation was used or who the victim was (i.e. staff or patient). The only variable which appeared to be related to the number of staff on duty was the severity of injuries, suggesting that at 'inadequate' staffing levels injuries were likely to be more serious. It is not clear why this should be, because the way incidents are managed and the number of people involved was the same at 'adequate' and 'inadequate' staffing levels.

This finding would tend to support the view that appropriate management of violent incidents is more important than the number of staff available to deal with them. In fact the findings in this section on environmental factors associated with aggression would suggest that there are no simple clear-cut related factors such as time of day, overcrowding or staffing levels.

THE NATURE OF THE PSYCHIATRIC WARD ENVIRONMENT

The Provision of Planned Activities

It is important for a clinician to assess the overall context in which violent behaviour is occurring. Clearly, while psychiatric wards vary there is research which suggests there are certain common features. In the United States Aumack (1968) made an observational study on psychiatric wards and included 24 behaviour categories he thought consisted of a continuum from 'inappropriate–disturbed–isolated' behaviour to 'appropriate–task–interactive' behaviour. When some of his categories (which are essentially similar) were combined it emerged that patients spent 54% of their time unoccupied on psychiatric wards, 0.1% asleep and 18% in disturbed behaviour (e.g. 'gesticulating, grimacing and shouting'). On the more positive side they spent 21% task oriented, 5% passively involved (e.g. watching television), 1.5% in social behaviour and 0.1% in self-maintenance (e.g. attention to appearance).

It might be thought that these findings are peculiar to the United States. However, Drinkwater (1988) found a very similar picture in an observational study of five psychiatric wards in a UK hospital. Patients spent 60% of their time either unoccupied or asleep on the ward. Only a very small amount of time was spent in social behaviour (8%), even though there were other patients and staff around continuously. Patients spent another 8% of their time in passive involvement, (e.g. watching television). Almost as much time was spent in disturbed behaviour (5%) as in self-maintenance (6%). Overall, it is clear that both studies suggest that for the largest part of their time patients are unoccupied and not interacting with staff or patients.

Both Aumack (1968a,b) and Drinkwater (1988) went on to ask staff to rate the appropriateness of each behaviour category included in the observational studies. Aumack found that 64% of patients' behaviour in the ward was considered by staff to be inappropriate while Drinkwater found that 65% were rated as inappropriate. This suggests that overall there may be a mismatch between staff attitudes and their daily management performance: they believe that patients should be actively involved in task-oriented and social behaviour, but in practice do little to promote these.

One hypothesis to explain this is that there are very few planned activities generally provided for patients by staff. Broome and Weaver (1980) demonstrated that most of the day for patients on psychiatric wards consisted of 'free time', in which no particular activity was planned. The activities that were provided for patients were off the ward, involving mainly some kind of work activity or occupational therapy. Drinkwater (1988) found that for the majority of patients observed on the ward, 89% of their day consisted of no planned activities, with the planned activities during the other 11% consisting mainly of meals.

The result of this lack of activity is that patients are not provided with a forum for staff–patient interactions, nor are they encouraged to interact with other patients. It is difficult to see how patients in psychiatric hospitals can learn new skills to cope with life in the community, or with their own psychiatric problems, without interaction with care staff. A lack of planned activities must result in a lack of training in new behavioural skills, and a severe lack of reinforcement for any attempt the patient may be making to practise new skills which would be alternatives to violent behaviour. Hence the lack of planned patient activities, and the long stretches of time spent unoccupied, result in an impoverished environment where neither active treatment nor rehabilitation are promoted.

Support for the view that lack of planned activities for patients may actually foster violence comes from the work of Drinkwater (1988). She found that the frequency of violent behaviour was, on average, four times higher during periods without planned activities. In addition, other behaviours 'prohibited' by staff were also higher during unplanned periods (e.g. breaking ward rules or being verbally abusive).

Staff–Patient Interaction

From the preceding section it is clear that there are very low levels of planned activities for patients. The consequence of this is that there are few periods of the day in which staff–patient interaction is encouraged.

The role of staff–patient interaction in violence has been previously reviewed (Drinkwater, 1982). Research suggests that the amount of staff–patient interaction by nurses is affected by rank and the total number of nurses on the ward (Hargreaves, 1969; Kandler et al., 1952). Another finding has been that staff spend more time interacting with each other than with patients (Hargreaves, 1969; Cohler and Shapiro, 1964; Sanson-Fisher et al., 1979; Drinkwater, 1988). The actual amount of time patients spend in interaction with staff has been estimated in two studies, with greatly differing results. Sanson-Fisher et al. (1979) found that patients interact with staff for half of their time, while Drinkwater (1988) found an average of 4.1% at mealtimes and 3.5% at other times.

The relationship of staff–patient interaction to violence is a very interesting area. McGuire et al. (1977) found that a decrease in the amount of staff–patient interaction led to an increase in 'deviance'. It is possible to speculate that if staff interact less with more severely disturbed patients (Brown et al., 1973; Doherty, 1971) then extreme behaviours such as violence may be the most effective way for these patients to gain attention. This hypothesis is strengthened by two pieces of evidence.

Depp (1983) reported that aggressors seek more staff attention than most ward patients. In 92% of violent incidents it was found that either or both the victim and aggressor were considered a 'prominent' part of the ward in that they required higher levels of supervision and/or competed more for staff attention. This suggests that staff attention after violence may be serving as a reinforcer for these patients. The second piece of evidence is that Drinkwater (1988) found that staff attention played a major role in the management strategies used during and after an incident. During an incident staff attention was involved in 31% of the total nursing actions taken and in 46% of actions taken after an incident. Staff attention took many forms including: reasoning with the aggressor; reprimanding him or her; and assigning a 'special' nurse to be with the aggressor all the time. Hence staff attention is certainly present and is therefore a potential reinforcer.

However, there may be another way in which staff–patient interaction is related to violence, and this is through poor communication skills of staff. Toch (1969) looked at the interaction sequence preceding an assault using assault-prone policemen as his subjects. He found that these men were overly authoritative early in an interaction sequence, and in particular that they asserted their authority in inept ways that caused needless humiliation and defiance. As a result, if they were met with non-compliance these staff had to escalate to threats and physical struggles because they had used last resorts as initial moves.

There is evidence that some of those working in psychiatric settings may also have inept communication skills. Brailsford and Stevenson (1973) in a study of nursing attitudes quote nurses as saying that 'authoritative behaviour and attitudes' and 'lack of tact' result in nurses being assaulted. Similarly, Madden et al. (1976) found that 53% of the psychiatrists who had been assaulted felt that they had acted in a provocative way (e.g. confronting a patient with upsetting material). Ruben et al. (1980) studied 37 psychiatrists in California, and found that those who expressed high levels of irritability towards patients, or who showed their feelings verbally or physically when angry, had been assaulted more than their colleagues.

Hence it is possible to speculate that if inept communication skills lead to staff being assaulted this may effectively punish them for trying. Amongst nurses, increased likelihood of assault, lack of discipline for low levels of staff–patient interaction and inadequate training in the management of incidents may result in their learning to avoid interacting with patients. As a result, rather than developing more effective methods of interacting, nurses progressively interact less with patients. Some anecdotal support for this view comes from comments nurses made about why they tend to congregate in the nursing office: 'inexperience or difficulty in relating to patients', 'lack of confidence', 'inadequacy', 'safety in numbers' (Brailsford and Stevenson, 1973).

To summarize, it has been suggested that the clinician needs to assess wider aspects of ward management as well as the management of individual violent incidents. It is suggested that the context of violence on psychiatric wards is one of very low levels of planned patient activities and low levels of staff–patient interaction. Both these factors appear to foster violence. In addition, many other aspects of ward management have also been found to be relevant, and need to be further researched. These include aspects of staff management such as levels of staff involvement in ward activities, provision of clear 'duties' for staff, staff support, staff communication and staff attitudes to violence (Drinkwater, 1988).

THE MANAGEMENT OF VIOLENT INCIDENTS

It is suggested that the management of violent incidents on psychiatric wards is often inconsistent, and involves mainly the use of inappropriate and traditional techniques. In this section evidence will be reviewed that there are problems with the traditional techniques such as seclusion, physical restraint and sedation. This will be followed by evidence on the inconsistent use of management strategies for violence.

Traditional Techniques

The continued use of traditional techniques is important, because there is no trend towards newer, superior techniques and also because of the possible adverse effects of some of the methods still in use.

We begin with physical restraint, which is used routinely in psychiatric hospitals. However, little research has been carried out on its effectivenss, criteria for use and rationale. One problem is that nurses are likely to be unskilled in the use of physical restraint. Bridges et al. (1981) and Brailsford and Stevenson (1973) found that nurses in Britain are given inadequate training in restraint. Conn and Lion (1983) report a similar situation in the United States. This raises serious ethical problems, and Snyder (1983) has pointed out that very violent and combative wrestling during restraining may be unavoidable, particularly when staff are untrained. Whereas staff may consider restraint to be justifiable 'treatment', Snyder comments that patients may, at times, have difficulty in deciding whether it constitutes punishment or actual abuse.

Another problem is that physical restraint may function as a reinforcer for violence. Gudjonsson and Drinkwater (1986) report a case where a patient was put on a time-out programme involving physical restraint if necessary to remove him into the time-out room. It was found that the frequency of his violent behaviour increased after the onset of this programme, and that this was due to the fact that the patient found restraint sexually arousing. It is possible that the low levels of activity and social behaviour previously described on psychiatric wards may result in many other patients finding any form of physical contact rewarding. Furthermore, it has been suggested that 'prohibitive agents' such as nurses using punitive control actually model the aggressive styles of behaviour they are apparently trying to eliminate in others (Bandura, 1973). This modelling instigation leads to an escalation of violence, as the fact that people in authority can justify its use indicates that aggression must be an acceptable means to an end.

Evidence that physical restraint can escalate violence has come from the work of Dietz and Rada (1983). They report that in a US forensic facility most of the injuries associated with violent incidents occurred while the nurses were trying to 'subdue' patients. The accounts of nurses were often found to involve such phrases as 'the patient had to be forcibly subdued' or 'a violent struggle ensued'. In addition, it was found that of 413 'hits' on victims by aggressors, 47% occurred during restraint, thus providing evidence of both unskilled use of physical restraint and its escalating effect on an incident.

It is suggested that at times sedation may also function as a reinforcer of violence. There is evidence that some of the psychoactive drugs can themselves stimulate aggressive behaviour in some patients. Drugs commonly used as emergency medication (particularly the neuroleptics (Liberman et al., 1981) and the minor tranquillizers such as benzodiazepines (Salzman et al., 1974)) have been found to promote violence. It follows that the use of certain kinds of sedative medication during a violent incident may actually cause it to escalate.

Moreover, there is an ethical problem with the use of sedation. Liberman et al. (1981) have pointed out that sedatives are often used to allay staff anxieties rather than because of any need to control the patients. In a study carried out at Camarillo State hospital, patients were observed before and after changing from four-times-a-day administration of medication to a once-a-day regimen. Nurses were concerned that violence would increase and that people would be injured. Results showed that the only observable difference in behaviour was that patients under once-a-day treatment had their eyes open more often. However, even after seeing the data, nursing staff were convinced that violence had increased. As Liberman comments: 'This failure of empirical evaluation to sway staff opinions highlights the tremendous problems posed by staff attitudes, concerns, and anxiety in the rational use of psychopharmacological agents.'

Finally, seclusion is also a frequently used traditional technique for managing violent incidents, and the problems of using seclusion have been reviewed elsewhere (Drinkwater, 1982). Key issues involve the paucity of evidence on its effectiveness, the ethical problems with its use and the lack of a clear theoretical basis. There is considerable confusion about whether seclusion is a punishment technique or not. It would seem that for seclusion to be an effective punishment procedure it would have to involve isolation in a non-reinforcing environment, and the exclusion from normal ward activities would need to be aversive. However, neither of these preconditions are necessarily found in practice.

Furthermore, there is evidence that seclusion can be reinforcing for some patients. Plutchik *et al.* (1978) asked hospital staff to suggest possible changes in the use of seclusion, and discovered that the majority agreed that the seclusion room should be a comfortable, unlocked side room available to patients who would like to be alone for a while. When they asked patients for their ideas about how to change usage, 70% were of the opinion that patients should be free to spend more time in the seclusion room whenever they desired. Wells (1972) found that patients were in fact receiving special attention from members of staff while in seclusion, including regular visits and conversation.

To summarize, there are serious problems with current usage of traditional techniques such as physical restraint, sedation and seclusion. As Boynton noted in the Rampton Hospital Report (DHSS, 1980) some of the traditional punishment techniques used do not appear to decrease violent behaviour but rather to maintain it.

Management of Violent Incidents

One of the major problems with current management of violent incidents is that it is often inconsistent. Depp (1983) has commented: 'While there was no evidence of *intentional* positive reinforcement by patients or staff for violent behaviour, neither was there very much evidence of negative sanctioning.' He found that violent behaviour of similar severity could result in a wide range of management responses, from 'extreme' to no response at all. Furthermore, he discovered that similar incidents resulted in 'highly variable time periods' of seclusion. Drinkwater and Feldman (1982) also found that seclusion was used inconsistently, and that its application covered a range of non-violent as well as violent behaviours. Similarly, Soloff (1979) examined the antecedents to physical restraint and found that violent behaviour accounted for only 40% of cases. The most frequent antecedents were the breaking of a ward rule and refusing medication.

Hence it appears that violent behaviours of similar severity can lead to a wide range of staff responses. Furthermore, seclusion and physical restraint are used for non-violent behaviour. There is also evidence that the management of incidents varies according to factors unrelated to the actual behaviour. Tardiff (1983) studied three control measures: emergency medication, physical restraint and special observation (one-to-one supervision). He found a steady decline in the use of all three measures with increasing age of patients. This did not, however, appear to be directly related to waning strength and hence less danger. Patients in the 35–44 age range, who were presumably still hale and hearty, received physical restraint in only 9% of cases, while patients in the 17–24 age range received it four times as often. This suggests that staff attitudes towards patients of different ages play an important role in the decision to use physical restraint.

In addition, Tardiff found that while patients with non-psychiatric disorders were likely to receive all three control measures, psychotic patients were more likely to receive only emergency medication and one-to-one supervision. Ionno (1983) also reported an effect of diagnosis on the management of violence. Seclusion was used more frequently for psychotic patients and cold wet-packs for non-psychotic ones. As these studies do not report any established criteria for the use of the different techniques it can be concluded that this variable response is mediated by staff attitudes towards the different diagnostic groups. Evidence that staff attitudes can be influential is provided by Depp (1983). He found that the management of incidents depended on how 'pessimistic' staff were about a change in the behaviour of the patient. When staff were 'pessimistic' they relaxed restrictions unless the incident escalated to the point of 'threatening the survival of the ward community'. Depp comments: 'One could then see how pessimism and relaxed constraints would form a vicious circle with each contributing negatively to the care-giving process and positively to the generation of violence.'

The importance of inconsistent management lies in the fact that it almost certainly results in intermittent reinforcement of violent behaviour. For example, Brown and Drinkwater (1984) found that half of the violent incidents in an adolescent assessment and treatment centre were immediately preceded by a staff demand for compliance. Because of inconsistent management, it was found that these demands for compliance were insisted upon afterwards in only 57% of incidents. In other words, through violent behaviour adolescents successfully achieved their aim of avoiding compliance in 43% of the incidents.

The importance of intermittent reinforcement of violent behaviour is that (1) it is a very powerful form of reinforcement and (2) it makes violent behaviour very difficult to eliminate. The management techniques most frequently used to eliminate violence such as physical restraint and seclusion can be construed as attempts at punishment. However, Bandura (1973) examined the effectiveness of punishment and concluded: 'Aggression control through punishment becomes more problematic when aggressive actions are socially or tangibly rewarded, while alternative means of securing desired outcomes are either unavailable, less effective in providing results, or not within the capabilities of the aggressors.' It has already been suggested that alternative means of securing 'desired outcomes' are not taught or reinforced on psychiatric wards. The problems of eliminating intermittently reinforced aggression in these circumstances are clearly demonstrated by the classic research of Deur and Parke (1970). They showed that children who were consistently rewarded for hitting later reduced their behaviour more when it was punished than did children who were treated inconsistently by either being rewarded and punished or rewarded and ignored. Hence children, (or adults) who learn that the benefits of aggression are obtained at the risk of some negative outcome are not easily discouraged from persisting.

It could be suggested that one method of improving consistency is to provide clear guidelines for the management of violent incidents. The British Department of Health and Social Security has produced a set of guidelines (DHSS, 1976). In a review of these and other guidelines Drinkwater (1982) concluded that they are loose and unclear, have not been adequately evaluated, have rather rarely been incorporated into ward management practices in hospitals, are often not available to student nurses at the time when they start to encounter violent incidents and are largely discretionary.

Drinkwater (1988) attempted to determine if the DHSS guidelines are adhered to by nurses, using a large-scale violent incident study. The guidelines contain six 'principles' to guide action, and it was found that none of these were followed consistently. One example of this is that staff are told not to physically restrain alone unless it is 'absolutely essential'. However, it was found on some wards that in as many as 50% of the incidents a nurse restrained a patient alone. Furthermore, it was found that the management of incidents was influenced by factors which are not important, rather than by factors which are. For example, the use of physical restraint was related to the sex of the aggressor (male aggressors were more likely to be restrained) and whether the victim was a patient or staff (aggressors were more likely to be restrained if they attacked staff). However, the use of physical restraint was not related to factors such as the number of people attacked by the aggressor, the type of assault or the severity of the injuries inflicted. In addition, it was found that in a significant number of incidents no action at all was taken by nurses during (8%) or after (9%) an incident.

To summarize, it is suggested that violent behaviour is intermittently reinforced through the inconsistent management of incidents. This makes violent behaviour very difficult to eliminate, especially when using punitive techniques and in a context where patients may not have alternative means of securing their aims. Finally, it is suggested that the DHSS guidelines are not currently adhered to, and do not improve the consistency of management.

PROSECUTING PATIENTS

Prosecution can be seen as a negative consequence of violent behaviour. However, this raises the question of whether it is used as inconsistently as other management techniques in psychiatric settings. There are marked differences of opinion among hospital staff about the prosecution of psychiatric patients who commit illegal acts while on hospital property or assault staff while they are carrying out their duties in the community.

Brand (1986) has reported that no specific policies exist to deal consistently with assaults. Legally, clinical practitioners are not obliged to report to the police offences committed by patients (Finch, 1984). Indeed, professional and ethical guidelines may encourage practitioners not to report criminal offences (Gudjonsson, 1987). A patient who seriously assaults a member of staff may be prosecuted either via the police or privately by the victim or his or her representative (e.g. the regional health authority). The victim can sue for compensation in a civil court when he or she believes that the assailant has sufficient finances to pay for damages. When there is evidence that the patient was mentally disturbed at the time of the assault then a private prosecution for damages is unlikely to succeed. A member of staff who sustains an injury as the result of an assault, or when trying to prevent an injury to someone else, can apply for compensation from the Criminal Injuries Compensation Board. Criminal proceedings will not provide the victim with compensation. Furthermore, if members of staff instigate prosecution via the police they cannot later sue for compensation.

There are a number of reasons why it may be advantageous to report a serious assault on staff to the police. First, it highlights the seriousness of the offence to the patient. There appears to be a tendency among some patients to think that violence is permissible and acceptable. For example, in one case a patient in a regional secure unity punched a nurse and broke her tooth. When the patient was told by the consultant that the offence would be reported to the police the patient replied, 'You can't prosecute me, I'm a patient'.

Another reason to report is to ensure that the offence is properly recorded and investigated by an independent authority. As has been mentioned, violent incidents are often poorly and inconsistently recorded. An independent investigator may help to establish objectively all the antecedents and circumstances of the offence. A further advantage of reporting serious offences to the police is that it is the courts who should decide on the appropriate punishment for criminal offences, not the clinical team. Reporting also enables staff to claim for compensation for personal injuries. Hospital staff who wish to apply for compensation from the Criminal Injuries Compensation Board need to prove that a criminal offence took place. If the assault is not reported to the police this may present difficulties. Finally, reporting can help to maintain staff morale, which, in settings where physical assaults on staff are common, tends to be poor. When staff are repeatedly assaulted without any perceived negative consequences for the patient they may feel inadequately supported and protected.

One critical factor determining whether or not to report an assault to the police and to prosecute is the nature and severity of the offence. Minor assaults (i.e. those not amounting to actual or grievous bodily harm) are unlikely to lead to prosecution by the police. Even in the case of a serious assault, the police are commonly reluctant to prosecute current hospital patients, especially when they are already being detained on a civil or a criminal section and the prosecution is unlikely to alter their current status.

An example of a policy on prosecuting patients is included in the Bethlem Royal and Maudsley Hospital guidelines on the management of violence. This document states that offences by current hospital patients should be reported to the police in accordance with the following guidelines (BRH, 1987):

(1) An incident which involves death or danger to life or serious injury to

another person should be reported to the police as soon as possible by the person in charge of the hospital. Rape should only be reported with the consent of the victim and after her doctor has been consulted.

(2) Serious illegal actions which do not pose immediate danger (e.g. setting minor fires, supplying or selling of drugs, serious threats of injury) should be discussed by the clinical team in charge of the patient as soon as possible after the incident occurs or is discovered. The team should advise the patient's consultant whether the incident should be reported to the police. In cases where the patient is not judged to be mentally responsible for the offence, the decision to report the incident to the police should reflect the seriousness of the incident and the need to protect the rights of any victim.

(3) Minor illegal actions (e.g. personal use of non-prescribed drugs, minor theft, minor damage to hospital property) should not normally be reported to the police, unless (a) the offence, in view of the clinical team, was clearly not the result of the patient's mental illness, and (b) it is clinical policy to report the type of incident that occurred.

Other hospitals may develop different policies. The important point is to have a clear one which is known to both patients and staff and is adhered to consistently. In this way prosecution can be seen as another form of management technique, in addition to the other important reasons outlined above for prosecuting patients.

PRE-QUALIFICATION TRAINING FOR MENTAL HEALTH PROFESSIONALS

It is evident that many hospital staff, and nursing staff in particular, are requested to interact with and manage violent and assaultive patients. In order to improve the management of violent behaviour in psychiatric settings it is necessary to have adequate training for the professionals involved. If staff are not adequately trained they place themselves and their colleagues at risk, increase the likelihood that patients in their care will be violent and can eventually become frightened and demoralized.

The amount of training that nurses are given varies between hospitals and the departments within the hospitals. In a recent survey among staff in a London teaching hospital Roscoe (1987) found that 40% of the staff thought it likely or very likely that they would be assaulted within the next year. About half the total sample reported being unsure about their ability to defuse a potentially violent situation, and 66% lacked confidence in their ability to cope with an assault. Of all respondents to the survey, 53% reported having had no training in the management of violence. Most of the training they had received had been on handling violent incidents using role-playing exercises. Little time was spent on learning how to defuse a potentially violent situation.

When the pattern of assaults was analysed with reference to training exposure it was found that those who had received training in the management of violence were significantly more likely to have been assaulted than those who had not. Those who had received training that focused on prevention rather than on the management of violent incidents were the least likely to have been assaulted. This finding suggests that it is the content of the training which is of critical importance, rather than the training *per se*.

Roscoe (1987) speculates that training on how to manage violent incidents increases self-confidence and makes staff less likely to avoid potentially violent situations. His study indicates that training should be carefully planned and properly evaluated. Furthermore, the research on assaults on other mental health professionals (e.g. Ruben *et al.*, 1980) suggests that, in addition to nurses, all other mental health professionals require training in the management of violence.

CLINICAL IMPLICATIONS

There can be little doubt that violence by patients in psychiatric hospitals is a problem, for a number of reasons. First, the assault rates are generally quite high and seem to be on the increase. This is of major concern to some health authorities (BRH, 1987). Second, frequent violence affects the living environment in psychiatric hospitals for both violent and non-violent patients. Tension remains high and this may foster further violence and psychiatric problems. In general, frequent violence is likely to reduce the quality of the patients' lives while in hospital. Third, frequent violent incidents affect staff morale, their rate of sick leave and turnover. Fourth, although the great majority of violent incidents in psychiatric hospitals do not result in serious physical injury to staff or patients, serious injuries do occur on occasions and their importance should not be underestimated.

The overall question posed by this chapter is whether psychiatric hospitals foster violence. It has been suggested that the nature of the psychiatric ward environment is a key issue. The context of violence on psychiatric wards is one of very low levels of planned patient activities, and low levels and poor quality of staff–patient interaction. Both these factors appear to foster violence. Other aspects of ward management which increase violence include staff-management problems and the current management of violent incidents.

It has been suggested that there are serious problems with the use of traditional techniques such as physical restraint, sedation and seclusion. There is evidence that these techniques can escalate incidents and function as reinforcers. Furthermore, violent behaviour is intermittently reinforced by the inconsistent use of management techniques, including the ultimate use of prosecution. This makes violent behaviour very difficult to eliminate. All these factors taken together provide strong evidence that aspects of ward management in psychiatric hospitals foster violence.

The next question is what action the clinician can take. To begin with the management of violent incidents, there are a number of steps that can be taken to prevent incidents occurring in the first place, and to manage them when they do occur. Proper training for staff in the prevention of violence as well as its management seems particularly important. Just training staff in how to manage incidents may increase violence, as staff become more prepared to apply techniques such as physical restraint, rather than attempt to alleviate the tension that often precedes the onset of violence. In addition to training and education it is important to have a clear operational policy about how violent incidents should be managed, monitored, reported and, when appropriate, prosecuted.

Moving on to other areas for the clinician, this chapter has suggested a framework in which to plan an assessment and intervention on psychiatric wards. Clearly, there are also implications for clinical research. An intervention can be made at any level, from an individual treatment programme to a ward-management change. A few of the issues which deserve increased clinical attention are considered below.

First, on the matter of training staff to plan and implement a programme of activities for patients, Broome and Weaver (1980) successfully increased planned activities for patients and, as a result, substantially increased both social and appropriate task-oriented behaviour. Unfortunately their planned activities were off the ward, but a similar programme could be undertaken on it. It would be interesting to evaluate the effect of increased planned activities on the frequency of violent incidents.

Staff-patient interaction is also an interesting area. An intervention could take the form of training in staff–patient interaction of appropriate content and quality. Another possibility is to increase the overall level of staff–patient interactions. However, McGuire et al. (1977) found that the frequency of staff–patient interactions was very resistant to change. Factors examined included changes to ward policy, nursing staff, patients and the physical environment. Hence devising a successful intervention would be no easy task.

Another area for an intervention is in the management of violent incidents. There is scope for research to evaluate and improve traditional techniques, and also to develop new methods for assessing and managing incidents. A key question is how to prevent violence being intermittently reinforced by inconsistent management of incidents. Clearly, there is a need for clinical research into methods of improving the consistency of staff-management practices. Guidelines alone do not appear to provide the solution. However, as part of a comprehensive training programme they may be more effective.

These are only a few of the clinical areas which warrant further consideration and research. The study of violence in psychiatric hospitals is still at an early stage, and it is to be hoped that this interesting field will attract the attention it deserves.

References

Aumack, L. (1968a). The Patient Activity Checklist: an instrument and an approach for measuring behavior. *Journal of Clinical Psychology*, **25**, 134–7.

Aumack, L. (1968b). *Manual for the Patient Activity Checklist*, Veterans' Administration Hospital, Danville, Illinois, Technical Report No. 68–2.

Bandura, A. (1973). *Aggression: A Social Learning Analysis*, Englewood Cliffs, NJ: Prentice-Hall.

Baum, A., and Valins, S. (1977). *The Social Psychology of Crowding: Studies of the Effects of Residential Group Size*, Hillsdale, NJ: Lawrence Erlbaum Associates.

Berkowitz, L. (1965). The concept of aggressive drive: some additional considerations. In L. Berkowitz (ed.,) *Advances in Experimental Social Psychology*, Volume 2, New York: Academic Press.

Borden, R.J., and Taylor, S.P. (1973). The social instigation and control of physical aggression. *Journal of Applied Social Psychology*, **3**, 354–61.

Brailsford, D.S., and Stevenson, J. (1973). Factors related to violent and unpredictable behavior in psychiatric hospitals. *Nursing Times*, 18 January, 9–11.

Brand, J. (1986). A fair cop. *Maudsley and Bethlem Gazette*, **33**, 24–5.

BRH (1987). *Management of Violence*, Policy document, The Bethlem Royal Hospital and Maudsley Hospital SHA.

Bridges, W., Dunn, P., and Speight, I. (1981). The provision of post-basic education in psychiatric nursing. *Nursing Times*, 23 December. Broome, A.K., and Weaver, S.M. (1980). The generalization of new behaviours and maintenance of programme contingencies in a chronic locked ward. *British Journal of Medical Psychology*, **53**, 37–46.

Brown, B., and Drinkwater, J.M. (1984). A method of recording violent episodes in residential care using behavioural analysis. *Orchard Lodge Studies of Deviance*, **4**, 185–200.

Brown, J.S., Wooldridge, P.J., and Van Brugen, Y. (1973) Interpersonal relations among psychiatric patients: the determinants of social attractiveness. *Journal of Health and Social Behavior*, **14**, 51–60.

Buss, A.H. (1971). Aggession pays. In J.L. Singer (ed.), *The Control of Aggression and Violence*, New York: Academic Press, pp. 7–18.

Confederation of Health Service Employees (1977). *The Management of Violent or Potentially Violent Patients*.

Conn, L.M., and Lion, J.R. (1983). Assaults in a university hospital. In J.R. Lion and W.H. Reid (eds), *Assaults within Psychiatric Facilities*, New York: Grune & Stratton.

Cox, J., and Shapiro, L. (1964). Avoidance patterns in staff–patient interaction on a chronic schizophrenic treatment ward. *Psychiatry*, **27**, 377–88.

Cox, V.C., Paulus, P.B., and McCain, G. (1984). Prison crowding research. The relevance of prison housing standards and a general approach regarding crowding phenomena. *American Psychologist*, **39**, 1148–60.

Depp, F.C. (1983). Assault in a public mental hospital. In J.R. Lion and W.H. Reid (eds), *Assaults within Psychiatric Facilities*, New York: Grune & Stratton.

Deur, J.L., and Parke, R.D. (1970). Effects of inconsistent punishment on aggression in children. *Developmental Psychology*, **2**, 403–11.

DHSS (February 1973). *Report of the Committee of Inquiry into Whittingham Hospital* (Chairman: Sir Robert Payne) Cmnd. No. 4861. London: HMSO.

DHSS (1973). *Report of the Professional Investigation into Medical and Nursing Practices on Certain Wards at Napsbury Hospital, Nr St Albans* (Chairman Mr R.R. Romford, CBE), London: HMSO

DHSS Health Services Management (March 1976). *The Management of Violent or Potentially Violent Hospital patients*, Health Circular, HC (76) 11.

DHSS (November 1980). *Report of the Review of Rampton Hospital* (Chairman: Mr Boynton, QC) Cmnd. No. 8073, London: HMSO.

DHSS and Home Office (1975). *Report of the Committee on Mentally Abnormal Offenders* (Chairman: Lord Butler), Cmnd. No. 6244, London: HMSO.

Dietz, P.E. (1981). Threats or blows? Observations on the distinction between assault and battery. *Int. J. Law Psychiatry*, **4**, 401–16.

Dietz, P.E., and Rada, R.T. (1983). Interpersonal violence in forensic facilities. In J.R. Lion and W.H. Reid (eds), *Assaults within Psychiatric Facilities*, New York: Grune & Stratton.

Doherty, E.G. (1971). Social attraction and choice among psychiatric patients and staff: a review. *Journal of Health and Social Behaviour*, **12**, 279–90.

Drinkwater, J.D. (1982). Violence in psychiatric hospitals. In M.P. Feldman (ed.), *Developments in the Study of Criminal Behaviour*, Volume 2, *Violence*, New York: Wiley.

Drinkwater, J., and Feldman, P. (1982). Violence in practice: a preliminary study of British psychiatric hospitals. Unpublished manuscript.

Drinkwater, J., Kirkpatrick, A., and Feldman, M.P. (1983). Violent behaviour in psychiatric hospitals. Paper presented to the Annual Conference of the British Psychological Society, York.

Drinkwater, J.M. (1988). *An Investigation of Psychiatric Ward Management and Violence*, PhD thesis, University of

Ekblom, B. (1970). *Acts of Violence by Patients in Mental Hospitals*, Stockholm: Laromedelsforlagen.

Evenson, R.C., Sletten, I.W., Altman, H., and Brown, M.L. (1974). Disturbing behavior: a study of incident reports. *Psychiatric Quarterly*, **48**, 266–75.

Feshbach, S. (1970). Aggression. In P.H. Mussen (ed.), *Carmichael's Manual of Child Psychology*, Volume 2, New York: Wiley.

Finch, J.D. (1986). *Aspects of Law Affecting the Paramedical Professions*, London: Faber.

Fisher, N. (1988). The fear of assault. *The Bethlem and Maudsley Gazette*, Spring issue, London: The Bethlem and Maudsley Hospital Health Authority.

Folkard, M.S. (1957). A sociological contribution to the understanding of aggression and its treatment. *Netherne Monographs*, **1**, Netherne Hospital.

Fottrell, E. (1980). A study of violent behaviour among patients in psychiatric hospitals. *British Journal of Psychiatry*, **136**, 216–21.

Freedman, J.L. (1975). *Crowding and Human Behavior*, San Francisco, CA: Freeman.

Gudjonsson, G. (1987). The BPS Survey and its implications. In G. Gudjonsson and J. Drinkwater (eds), *Psychological Evidence in Court*, Issues in Criminological and Legal Psychology, **11**, 6–11, Leicester British Psychological Society.

Gudjonsson, G.H., and Drinkwater, J. (1986). Intervention techniques for violent behaviour. *Issues in Criminological and Legal Psychology*, **9**, 38–48, Leicester: British Psychological Society.

Haffken, E.A., and Reid, W.H. (1983). Violence against mental health personnel in Nebraska. In J.R. Lion and W.H. Reid (eds), *Assaults within Psychiatric Facilities*, New York: Grune & Stratton.

Hargreaves, W.A. (1969). Rate of interaction between nursing staff and psychiatric patients. *Nursing Research*, **18**, 418–25.

Ionno, J.A. (1983). A prospective study of assaultive behaviour in female psychiatric inpatients. In J.R. Lion and W.H. Reid (eds), *Assaults within Psychiatric Facilities*, New York: Grune & Stratton.

Kandler, H., Behymer, A.F., Kegeles, S.S., and Boyd, R.W. (1952). A study of nurse–patient interaction in a mental hospital. *American Journal of Nursing*, **52**, 1100–3.

Liberman, R.P., Marshall, B.D., and Burke, K.L. (1981). Drug and environmental interventions for aggressive psychiatric patients. In R.S. Stuart (ed.), *Violent Behaviour*, New York: Brunner/Mazel.

Lion, J.R., Snyder, W., and Merrill, G.L. (1981). Under-reporting of assaults on staff in state hospitals. *Hospital Community Psychiatry*, **32**, 497–8.

Loo, C. (1972). The effects of spatial density on the social behaviour of children. *Journal of Applied Social Psychology*, **4**, 372–81.

Madden, D.J., Lion, J.R., and Penna, M. (1976). Assaults on psychiatrists by patients. *American Journal of Psychiatry*, **133**, 422–5.

Matthews, R., Paulus, P., and Baron, R.A. (1979). Physical aggression after being crowded. *Journal of Nonverbal Behaviour*, **4**, 5–17.

McGuire, M.T., Fairbanks, L.A., Cole, S.R., Sbordone, R., Silvers, F.M., Richards, M., and Akers, J. (1977). Ethological study of four psychiatric wards: behavior changes associated with new staff and patients. *Journal of Psychiatric Research*, **13**, 211–24.

Mueller, C.W. (1983). Environmental stressors and aggressive behavior. In R.G. Geen and E.L. Donnerstein (eds), *Aggression: Theoretical and Empirical Reviews*, New York: Academic Press.

Plutchik, R., Karasu, T.B., Conte, H.R., Siegel, B., and Jerrett, I. (1978). Toward a rationale for the seclusion process. *Journal of Nervous and Mental Disease*, **166**, 571–9.

Quinsey, V.L., and Varney, G.W. (1977). Characteristics of assaults and assaulters in a maximum security psychiatric unit. *Crime and Justice*, **5**, 212–20.

Robinson, I.D. (1972). Accidents to nursing staff in a psychiatric hospital. *New Zealand Medical Journal*, **75**, 347.

Rogers, R., Ciula, B., and Cavanaugh, J.L. (1980). Aggressive and socially disruptive behaviour among maximum security psychiatric patients. *Psychological Reports*, **46**, 291–4.

Roscoe, J. (1987). Survey on the incidence and nature of violence occurring in the joint hospital. *Report of the Working Party*, London: Bethlem Royal Hospital.

Ruben, I., Wolkon, G., and Yamamoto, J. (1980). Physical attacks on psychiatric residents of patients. *Journal of Nervous and Mental Disease*, **188**, 243–5.

Salzman, C., Kochansky, G.E., and Shader, R.F. (1974). Chlordiazepoxide-induced hostility in a small group setting. *Archives of General Psychiatry*, **31**, 401–5.

Sanson-Fisher, R.W., Poole, A.D., Small, G.A., and Fleming, I.R. (1979). Data acquisition in real time — an improved system for naturalistic observations. *Behavior Therapy*, **10**, 543–54.

Snyder, W. (1983). Administrative monitoring of assaultive patients and staff. In J.R. Lion and W.H. Reid (eds), *Assaults within Psychiatric Facilities*, New York: Grune & Stratton.

Soloff, P.H. (1979). Physical restraint and the nonpsychotic patient: clinical and legal perspectives. *Journal of Clinical Psychiatry*, **40**, 302–5.

Stokols, D. (1972). On the distinction between density and crowding: some implications for further research. *Psychological Review*, **79**, 275–77.

Surrey Area Health Authority (1980). *Report of the Committee of Inquiry into Standards of Patient Care at Brookwood Hospital*, Kingston: SAHA.

Tardiff, J. (1983). A survey of assault by chronic patients in a state hospital system. In J.R. Lion and W.H. Reid (eds), *Assaults within Psychiatric Facilities*, New York: Grune & Stratton.

Toch, H. (1969). *Violent Men*, Chicago, IL: Aldine.

Wells, D.A. (1972). The use of seclusion on a university hospital psychiatric floor. *Archives of General Psychiatry*, **26**, 410–13.

Editors' Note

The following chapter differs from the others in a number of important respects. Whereas the other chapters in the book have focused on the perpetrators of violence, Dr Davies considers what professionals could do to prevent their own victimization by violent clients. To our knowledge, this is an area without a substantive research foundation. Dr Davies runs practical workshops to assist professionals in avoiding incidents, and we have asked him to convey practical suggestions to the readers of this book. We, like Dr Davies, are aware of the dangers of self-fulfilling prophecies, but are of the opinion that practitioners sometimes give too little thought to their own protection.

13

The Prevention of Assault on Professional Helpers

W. DAVIES
St Andrew's Hospital, Northampton, UK

Professional helpers sometimes work with people who are undergoing considerable traumas; social workers, for example, sometimes have to remove children from their parents, nurses and doctors may have to tell a psychiatric patient that he or she is compulsorily detained, prison staff may have to inform an inmate that he or she has had a parole application turned down; there are numerous examples. Some of these situations are ones which would make many people feel aggressive, and some people habitually show their aggression physically — by throwing objects, destroying property or hitting people.

It is this kind of aggression that those who work in the helping professions therefore need to learn to cope with, both for personal safety and for that of other people. The aim of this chapter is to look at what lessons should be assimilated in order to achieve that ability to cope: lessons in examining our attitudes to clients; in taking precautions, specifically those concerning the design of offices and making home visits; in talking to aggressive people; and in highlighting any learning points which result from incidents of violence in 'helping' organizations.

This chapter considers these points in order. The material stems partly from well-established research findings and partly from the violence-prevention seminars in which the author is involved. These seminars have now been operational for about five years and are attended by nurses, social workers, probation officers and others in the helping professions.

UNDERLYING DYSFUNCTIONAL ATTITUDES AND ASSUMPTIONS

Attitudes and assumptions can be found among professionals which, while they cannot be described as either right or wrong, may be counterproductive to the matter in hand. Attitudes and assumptions may underpin the behaviour shown

Clinical Approaches to Violence. Edited by K. Howells and C. R. Hollin
© 1989 John Wiley & Sons.

to clients. Below are just a few attitudes which seem to be implied by some of the statements made by those attending violence-prevention seminars:

(1) *'They must not be allowed to get away with anything. If you give them an inch they take a yard.'* This is an unfortunate attitude, because it may produce a somewhat antagonistic and confrontational response to clients. Equally, it is a very difficult attitude to change. Most people who exhibit this attitude are able to cite many examples of where its accuracy has been borne out. It may be a form of self-fulfilling prophecy: the helper betrays a confrontational attitude; the client responds in a confrontational way; the helper then feels justified that his or her confrontational attitude was correct.

(2) *'I must not show that I am afraid.'* Certainly, most helpers generally aim not to appear afraid of their clients. However, there are times when the client behaves so aggressively that most helpers would feel intimidated, and the question arises as to what to do in this situation. Attempts to cover up fear may be given away by 'non-verbal leakage', (e.g. Argyle, 1988; Ekman and Friesen, 1969; Haggard and Isaacs, 1966).

Sometimes, of course, the 'leaked' emotion is not correctly interpreted by the client; for example, helpers may attempt to cover their fear by standing very still, by putting their hands in their pockets, etc. This results in a stance which is much more motionless than is normally seen, and therefore creats an unusual impression. Clients may interpret this in various ways; it may be seen as an aggressive or hostile stance — quite the opposite from what in fact is going on in the helper's mind. One way around this is to make a straightforward statement such as 'I wish you wouldn't do that, it really worries me'. This may have the effect of disrupting the intimidatory game that is being played. The New York Police Department, in their hostage-negotiation seminars, have the concept of 'the theatre of terror', whereby the actor (in this case the client) will pursue whatever action he or she is doing until the required response is obtained from the audience (in this case the helper). Therefore if the helper does not give the required response — fear — the client will increase the behaviour until that response is obtained. The helper can therefore benefit by giving a straightforward expression of fear ('I wish you wouldn't do that, it really worries me') early in the sequence to stop the behaviour escalating.

(3) *'I must be calm and relaxed at all times.'* The problem with this, in behavioural terms, is that it is not an achievable goal. Helpers occasionally come across situations in which it is highly unlikely that they are going to maintain a calm and relaxed state of mind. What they can aim for is control of actions and, to some extent, thoughts. Therefore a more reasonable aim might be something along the lines of : 'No matter how agitated I feel, I am going to keep thinking and decide what is best to do'. Research in the British health services (e.g. Drinkwater, 1982) and in the English Prison Department (Davies, 1982; Davies and Burgess,

1988) shows that experienced personnel are much less likely to be assaulted than inexperienced personnel, even while doing the same kinds of tasks. Why this is so is not clear; it may be that, with experience, most individuals learn strategies that they subsequently apply to difficult situations. However, one might also speculate that there are certain second-order factors which come into operation; we would suggest that two of these are that experienced people realize that there is no definitive way of handling a particular situation, whereas inexperienced personnel will frequently think, during a heated interchange, 'I wish I knew the right way of handling this'. Experienced people, therefore, are aware that, no matter how agitated they feel, they are best advised to keep thinking, identify the possible options they have and decide for themselves which to choose.

(4) '*I personally must be able to deal with everyone; I must never pass a client over to a colleague, even if that colleague might be able to deal with the client more effectively.*' It is sometimes difficult to acccept that a client simply does not like us and cannot work with us. We may know this in theory but find it hard to accept in practice. Inevitably, we get on better with some clients than others. There is a distinction to be made here between the client who is always difficult (no matter who they are seeing) and the client who simply does not get on with one personally. All helpers often have to accept their fair share of the very difficult clients, those who are difficult with everyone. On the other hand, there are certain individuals who will perform better with a colleague than with us, even though we persevere and attempt to work through the difficulties we have in the helping relationship. In that small number of cases, where it is felt that we are not helping the client, steps should be taken to transfer that client to a colleague. This is more easily said than done; from personal experience it is apparent that one can have mixed feelings about colleagues succeeding where we have failed!

The question arises as to what to do about attitudes and assumptions. Above, we have described four possibly counterproductive attitudes, and there are, of course, many more. The simplest course of action is to be aware of the attitudes we hold and to examine whether it is a constructive or counterproductive view. To change a particular attitude, it could be argued that a behavioural approach might be the most effective; in other words, every time a situation arose where it was felt that fear should not be shown an attempt would be made to change behaviour directly, so that a helper could say 'I really wish you wouldn't do that, it's worrying me very much'. The problem, fortunately, is that such frightening or worrying situations arise only relatively infrequently, so there is little chance to practise changing our attitudes and behaviours. This implies that the most promising approach may be to rehearse cognitively such situations and their management (Meichenbaum, 1985). Curiously, this seems to be something which many people in the helping professions are reluctant to do; some will even specifically say something along the lines of 'I really don't like thinking about things like that'. We would argue that while one does not want to lose sight of the fact that the principal task of those in the helping professions is to help others (and this is the direction that most of our thoughts will take), it is important that consideration be given to rehearsing what would be done in a range of difficult and threatening situations. Although the specific situations which are rehearsed are unlikely to occur exactly as imagined, the more that are rehearsed, the more likely it is that adequate preparations will have been made. Those preparations may include both overall guidelines and general principles for personal behaviour.

The final point is therefore that helpers should be aware of their attitudes and assumptions, should aim to rehearse a range of potential situations, should know how to behave in them and, more importantly, aim to keep thinking (even though not feeling calm!) in whatever situation presents itself.

PRECAUTIONS FOR OFFICES OR WARDS OR OTHER CLOSED ENVIRONMENTS

Case examples produced by participants on the violence-prevention seminars suggest that many of them might have been avoided or reduced in severity if certain precautions had been taken. Precautions have the additional advantage that they make the helper feel much more relaxed in a situation, and that he or she is working in a relatively safe environment. It is therefore worth examining some of the straightforward and basic measures that can be taken to achieve these kinds of benefits.

It is worth getting together with colleagues, to work out contingency plans for a range of eventualities. This is probably the most cost-effective yet sophisticated precaution that can be taken. It is a relatively complicated measure because of the complexity of the decisions that will need to be resolved. In most work situations there is a wide range of eventualities that could occur, all of them possible crises. The range of contingency plans may therefore also be substantial. Moreover, it may be very difficult for a group of helpers, even working in the same environment, to agree on what the plans should be. Yet more difficult is the process whereby all concerned are kept up to date on the procedures and plans; new staff arrive, old staff leave in a constant changeover of personnel. It is important to ensure that all concerned know what should happen in a range of eventualities, and to make sure what should happen is what does.

On wards, in residential homes and similar settings, the two or more shifts should be approximately matched for experience of staff. Frequently in institutions there is a marked contrast between the abilities of two shifts. Although it is pleasing to imagine that all professionals are equally competent, most people are prepared to admit that this is not so. This informal recognition should be taken into formal account by those responsible for planning the shifts. He or she should make sure that each shift has a certain minimum number of persons who are experienced, 'ward-wise' and have sufficient competence to lead their way through most eventualities.

While it is certainly important to have matched or balanced shifts, it is equally so to have *effective communications or 'handovers' between the shifts*. One hears the explanation, following an incident, that 'I didn't realize' or 'No one had told me that . . .'. The exact mechanism for establishing good communication between shifts will vary from place to place; sometimes it is based on verbal means, sometimes on written handover books, sometimes on both. The overall point remains that staff must be able to judge what is important information to convey and have an efficient and available means of achieving that objective.

Related to the communication between shifts, but an important area in its own right, is the notion of *consistency of approach from staff*. Especially in a ward setting, patients respond to staff being relatively consistent in the rules that they enforce and the approach that they adopt. Equally, a degree of flexibility is desirable. One of the important concepts held by most people is the notion of 'fairness' (Ellis, 1970), and most individuals will react against a system which they perceive as not being fair and equitable. Therefore helpers should aim to ask of patients only what they are able to achieve, remembering that different patients are capable of varying amounts of effort and contribution. The idea of producing a system and ward atmosphere which incorporates both consistency and flexibility is naturally a sophisticated, difficult and demanding objective for which to strive. However, the two concepts are not mutually contradictory, and such a state of affairs can be achieved.

MORE GENERAL PRECAUTIONS

There are certain precautions which are relevant, wherever one works. These depend neither on efficient ward design nor on liaising with colleagues; they are more concerned with one's personal style and personal skill in the work setting.

The first of these is the ability to manage one's time efficiently. The workings of the circadian rhythm means that most people operate better at certain times of day than at others. Curiously, although we may be aware of this, relatively few of us actually take heed of it in planning our working day. One way in which it can be acted upon is by trying to co-ordinate our most efficient times with the most difficult tasks that we face. Therefore, if a difficult client is to be seen, then that person might best be managed at one of the times during which we are at our peak. The same point holds for important meetings or other events, although this is not always possible; only certain tasks are within our control as far as their timings are concerned.

A further element in efficient control of time is simply in not being unduly rushed in dealing with each client. This means having the ability and the will to organize a timetable so that each client is allocated sufficient time and is therefore able to perceive that they are dealt with in a satisfactory and appropriate way.

An occasional cause of friction is when a client is about to talk about what is exceptionally important to him or her just at the time when the helper knows that the interview has to be terminated for another appointment. A way in which some professionals get around this is to state the time constraints at the beginning of the interview. They might therefore say 'We have a maximum of half an hour to talk; maybe we will get finished well before that but either way we have to finish in half an hour'. This usually saves the awkward situation of trying to bring an interview to a close when the real heart of the interchange is just becoming apparent.

Equally, many clients dislike intensely the idea of having to wait for substantial periods of time to see their helper. Sometimes this is difficult to avoid; the situation may make it impossible to see every client immediately. Other times, waiting is caused simply by the fact that the professional in question does not give sufficient importance to punctuality. There is less excuse for this latter state of affairs — punctuality should be given sufficient priority. However, what is to be done when waiting is inevitable? The first rule is to be honest about the situation. If it is known that the client is going to have to wait for three quarters of an hour, it is futile to say 'You may have to wait 10 minutes or so'. The client is certain to notice the discrepancy between 10 minutes and three quarters of an hour! Sometimes a client will work out his or her own salvation and say, sometimes rather aggressively 'I'll come back later, then'.

There is a great disparity between the ways in which different offices set out their waiting areas. Although many professionals recognize that the waiting area indicates how much importance is attached to clients, sometimes these areas are far from adequate. Equally, there exist some excellent examples of what can be done, with coffee and refreshments provided, the availability of amusements and games to while away the time, etc.

Another 'personal skill' is in giving some thought to one's clothing. The first element to be considered is its practicality. If you wish to run away as quickly as possible, will you be hampered by your clothes? Tight skirts and high-heeled shoes are probably not the best apparel in which to make a quick exit. Other aspects of practicality involve ties for men and long hair and earrings for women. Men are sometimes strangled, successfully or not, with their ties; women have long hair pulled and, worse, earrings through pierced ears can be pulled. All these can be distressing and dangerous events for the victim.

One important area outside the direct work setting concerns safety in one's own home. It may be inadvisable for those in the helping professions to let their clients know where they live. It is simple enough not to divulge one's address directly, and, for the same reason, many in the helping professions have an ex-directory telephone number. This prevents publication of one's address in the telephone book. In one instance, for example, a psychologist was held hostage in her own home and cut repeatedly and seriously with a knife. In another, threats were made against the children of a professional helper. Such incidents can be particularly difficult to cope with, sometimes even more so than threats at the workplace.

It is important also to be aware of possibly the most important second-order precaution, remembering that professional helpers should show 'care' and 'respect' for clients. In considering and taking the necessary and straightforward practical measures to avoid putting ourselves at excessive risk it can be the case that clients are regarded with undue suspicion. Fortunately, violent incidents are still very rare (e.g. Brown *et al.*, 1986; Hough and Mayhew, 1985) and preventative measures should be seen in the context of the caring, respect and concern that the great majority of those in the helping professions have for their clients. To maintain this aspect of professional behaviour may well be one of the most effective and pervasive precautions of all.

OFFICE DESIGN

The overall aim in office design should be to make the atmosphere as non-oppressive and conducive to relaxation as possible. At the same time, there should be an absence of heavy ornaments, (or any other objects) which could be used as weapons or missiles by an aggressive person. Similarly, items of sentimental value such as photographs of loved ones, expensive ornaments, etc, are risky to have about because of the personal effect on one if they were destroyed. The helper might turn from victim to aggressor at the sight of treasured objects being destroyed by an aggressive client. In addition to these general guidelines there are some rather more specific areas to address: for example, the chairs of the helper and the client should be roughly equidistant from the door. This would enable the helper to leave the office, if necessary, without being blocked by the client, but it will also enable the *client* to terminate the interview. Perhaps surpisingly, there are many instances where aggressive clients realize that they are becoming out of control, and will voluntarily take themselves out of the situation. The layout of the furniture of an office has been shown to be important in numerous instances, and one needs to be able to direct the client to the chair intented for him or her. Curiously, comments abound, such as 'I got all the furniture planned out right but he came in and sat in the wrong chair'. A simple phrase such as 'Come in and sit yourself down', indicating the approrpiate chair, should result in the client sitting where intended.

When interviewing, some prefer not to be separated from their client by a desk. For those who prefer the absence of a desk, two chairs can be seated to one side of it, and this gives the helper the option of coming round on the same side and talking in an informal setting. Equally, it gives the helper the option of a more formal situation for those who like to be interviewed in that way. However, studies have shown that it is preferable not to have one's own chair and that of the client directly opposite each other; to have them at an angle is seen as more co-operative and less competitive (Argyle, 1988; Cook, 1970; Mehrabian 1972). A possible layout for a small office is shown in Figure 13.1.

The door is also a feature of interest. Ideally, it should have strengthened glass or unbreakable plastic panels to enable colleagues to check easily on one's safety if they hear a commotion coming from one's office. These panels

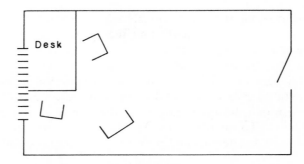

Figure 13.1 A layout for a small office

let someone 'casually' walk past the office and see what is going on; the person doing the reconnaissance does not have to pluck up sufficient courage to actually enter and speak; a straightforward visual inspection can be made instead. The door should not have a lock which can be operated from the inside without the key. There are a number of cases where the latch has been dropped and locked by the client, preventing the helper's colleagues coming to the rescue. Similarly, even if one has a conventional key-operated lock, the benefit can be nullified by leaving the key in it; all the client has to do is to lock the door and leave the key in, again preventing anyone operating the lock from the other side. Once the door is locked in this way it is 'traditional' for the client to barricade the door at leisure and thereby imprison the helper as a hostage. The best option is an outward-opening door, as this is unlikely to be barricaded from within. The normal objections to this (e.g. a client may fling the door open, hitting someone walking in the corridor) can be overcome by very straightforward friction hinges. Many institutions now have such office doors.

All these office design features are important. However, any of them can be undermined if there has been no discussion with colleagues of what should be done in a range of difficult situations. A real-life incident illustrates this.

A probation officer saw a client whom she knew might be aggressive, and therefore left the door slightly ajar so that her colleagues could hear any trouble that ensued. As anticipated, the client became very heated, whereupon after a few minutes a colleague walked along the corridor and poked his head in, saying 'I'll shut the door, we can hear everything that is going on in here'. The colleague shut the door and, with the others in the building, went to lunch. The client then went to the door and dropped the latch and locked it solid. This enabled him to hold the probation officer prisoner for a little over two hours; clearly, a very worrying and disturbing experience for the officer concerned. This is one example of many incidents which could have been prevented with a certain amount of planning and slightly different office design.

HOME VISITS

Home visits, along with the running of residential establishments, are among occasions when a professional helper is more at risk (Brown *et al.*, 1986). Given that this is the case, there are various questions that should be asked before undertaking them. The first of these is, naturally, whether the visit is really necessary; would it be possible to replace the home visit with an office interview? If this is the case, and it can be carried out without losing a significant amount of impact in terms of therapeutic value, then this should be done.

Frequently, the first visit to a person's home is an important one. On the negative side one does not know what one is going into; one may not know the client, and one certainly does not have first-hand knowledge of the domestic situation. In those respects this is a risky undertaking, calling for a certain amount of caution. On the other hand, many clients recognize the necessity and appropriateness of at least one home visit, and are not unduly perturbed about this. It is a relatively formal undertaking and one which many client appear to accept.

However, there is a need to consider visits subsequent to the first, or when a professional helper is regularly visiting an individual's home. There are some helpers who tend to lose sight of the fact that what they are visiting is more than a house, it is a home. This is an easy oversight for someone who is making routine 'home visits', and who can easily lapse into seeing the whole procedure as a matter of course. From the client's position there is rather a different perception; a stranger is entering his or her home — something which may not be at all welcome. The end result is the need to check thoroughly that one gets on well enough with the client to visit his or her home on a regular basis.

Other questions which might be asked are, first, whether the client being visited is generally a non-violent person, judged from his or her previous history. Moreover, is there a particular reason that the client may be violent *today*, because of some unusual circumstance — possibly the news that the helper is taking to him or her? Another, more general, question is whether the helper simply *feels* safe visiting this particular client. Sometimes we will admit things to ourselves at a 'feeling level' which we would not admit more openly; possibly aspects relating to how well we get on with the individual client concerned, etc. If one does not feel safe visiting a client at home, we would suggest that this has implications for future actions.

There are other precautions for home visits. The most simple is to let colleagues know one's movements. This is a very straightforward precaution, yet it is relatively rarely taken. The next most sophisticated measure is to arrange a checking system with colleagues if there is concern about a home visit. An example would be to say that a telephone call will confirm by a set time that all has gone well. Sometimes the practicalities of this intrude; many home visits are, for example, made at the end of the day, and by the time the visit is over most of the staff will have left the office. Such considerations can usually be overcome; many people are perfectly happy to be telephoned at home if asked, and, given that such a system is mutually supportive, it can be an easy and rewarding arrangement to make.

Many (social workers especially) now take colleagues with them when they make a visit they view as particularly risky. Obviously, to take a colleague *every* time you visit is an unwarranted extravagance. Equally, however, never to take a colleague with you — even when you feel especially nervous about a visit — is an unnecessary risk. Surprisingly, there appears to be a wide range of individual variations in preparedness to request a colleague to accompany oneself on a visit. Some individuals seem perfectly ready and willing strongly to request a colleague to accompany them; others equally vociferously maintain that 'It is part of the job to visit on your own'. It is only when one gets representatives of both groups from the same employer in the same room that the ridiculousness of the situation becomes apparent!

Being ready to re-assess the objectives of a visit is also important. Normally, in making a home visit there is a particular aim in mind — important news to give, a particular assessment to make, etc. Occasionally, on arriving at the home one finds that the situation is not as anticipated: perhaps the wife or husband who is normally there is not present, or a person who is usually on his own has a friend with him. The appropriate action here is to re-assess one's aims in the light of the changed setting. Is what was planned still appropriate or would it be too risky? Are there other goals that could be achieved in this new situation — possibly more useful than the original ones?

The final element here is that of routinely noting the exits from a client's house; some of these may not be exits that would be used in conventional circumstances but could be in an emergency. Noting these should be a matter of routine. As always, the aim is not to enter a person's house with a 'siege mentality' but to take ordinary sensible precautions such as calmly making a mental note of the exits.

In summary, there is no doubt that home visits are an important and essential component of the work of many in the helping professions. However, it does not follow that those concerned should put themselves at unnecessary or avoidable risk by making home visits that are not really needed, or by failing to ask some straightforward basic questions, or by omitting to take the simplest of precautions.

CALMING AN AGITATED PERSON—THE SCRIPT

Nearly all the above concerns what can be done in advance of seeing an aggressive and agitated person. This section discusses what can be said to such an individual in order to calm him or her and prevent assault. It therefore deals with verbal behaviour — or the 'script' — and the non-verbal components will be covered in the next section.

Assault sometimes takes place without any warning. More usually, however, there is a build-up of aggression during a conversation. For example, an agitated person may come into our office or start talking to us on a ward, and the task is to calm that agitation and resolve the matter without either being assaulted oneself or leaving the client in a state where he or she is liable to attack another.

Whereas many helpers when confronted with an aggressive and agitated individual will immediately attempt to resolve the problem causing the agitation, in reality this should be the second stage of the 'calming' process. The first step should be simply to diminish the individual's anger. The reason for this is that when individuals are highly over-aroused they are not in the best frame of mind for tackling the complexities of dealing with the task at hand.

The first objective, therefore, is to calm the client's anger by displaying empathy, paraphrasing the content of what is said and reflecting the client's feelings. This stage, during which the anger is calmed, may be quite a short-lived one, perhaps lasting only a few seconds; alternatively, it may last considerably longer, perhaps several minutes. In any case, one needs to be sensitive to whether the client is still in this initial stage of 'needing the anger calmed' or whether he or she is now ready to move on to the problem-solving phase.

The problem-solving stage does, of course, assume that the client is agitated about a specific problem. Very often this is a correct assumption. At this stage one attempts to clarify exactly what the problem is, to generate possible solutions to it and subsequently to evaluate these with the client. This may be a long procedure and a rather more complicated affair than it appears at first. However, this is the task at hand, and there are certainly times when an objective description and analysis of the problem is perfectly possible.

The third stage is to act along the lines of whatever was decided during problem-solving. It is worth being clear what action is required from whom; it is possible to feel such a sense of relief once the client has calmed down and left that the motivation to act disappears. The problem here is, naturally, that the same difficulty may recur.

Within the three-stage process just described there are certain other elements which are worth discussion. Frequently, it may be appropriate to 'depersonalize' the issue in question. If, for example, one's behaviour is governed by departmental rules, make sure the client realizes that, and does not believe that one is simply asserting a whim. A probation officer has given a particularly good example of where depersonalizing the issue would have been appropriate.

A client came into his office asking for money for the bus to get home. The probation officer believed that the money was not to be used for transport but rather for buying a drink, and so said something along the lines of: 'Well, I don't think you are going to spend this money on the bus fare, I think you are going to spend it on drink. For that reason I am not going to give you the money, you have enough problems with drinking already.' In reality, the probation officer was governed by certain rules which specified when he was allowed to give money to clients, and therefore he might well have said something like: 'The situation we are in is that there are rules and regulations which govern when probation officers can hand out money. This means that I am not allowed to give you any money in this case. We are going to have to sort out your problems in some other way.' The latter response would have been one which depersonalized the issue, and indeed corresponded with the true facts of the situation. It would not have resulted in the aggression and violence which occurred as a result of the first response. (This is not to say that confronting a client with what is believed to be the case is never appropriate; rather, that depersonalizing the issue is frequently an effective strategy and, when it corresponds with the facts of the matter, should be given very serious consideration indeed.)

Additional to the notion of depersonalizing the issue is the strategy of personalizing oneself. The principal occasion when this is appropriate is when meeting a client for the first time, or if receiving abuse or aggression simply because of one's role (nurse, social worker, probation officer, policeman, etc.). A social worker recounted that on some housing estates it would be no use seeking help from neighbours because very often 'they would be delighted to hear that the social worker is in trouble'. This may be true in some areas, but there is a great difference between being delighted that 'the social worker' is in trouble and being delighted that John or Sue is in trouble and is about to be assaulted. The effect of this applies not only to neighbours but frequently also to the would-be assailant. If he or she is intent on giving abuse simply because of one's role, then the strategy is to turn oneself from a 'role' into a real person. To do this one needs, preferably, to give one's name and certainly some personal details which stand some chance of bringing one to life: for example, 'I know exactly what you mean because my father had a drink problem too — most Saturdays he would come home to pick an argument with my mother and end up smashing up the place'. The appropriate examples will, of course, vary from person to person, and one situation to another; the important ingredients are that it is true and sincere and fits the situation. Such a strategy has been reported particularly with potential rape victims by Wyre (1986).

The final strategy worth mentioning here is simply to ask the client for the required behaviour. A social worker on a home visit once described a situation in which a father was fighting with his 15-year-old son because he said he was not going to school. The result was that the two men were grappling on the floor and hitting each other with considerable force. The female social worker said that there was nothing she could do, by which she meant she was not physically strong enough to separate them. One strategy she could have used would have been to say repeatedly and authoritatively 'Stop hitting him'. Frequently this is far more effective than one anticipates, especially if said loudly, repeatedly and authoritatively. The reason that such a simple technique is sometimes not tried is the anticipated loss of face if one is not obeyed; what do you do if you tell someone to 'stop hitting him' and he does not? The answer is simple; you simply repeat it until finally you succeed.

Nurses sometimes report that it pays to lose your temper with patients when they are about to hit you. What is usually meant by this is that an utterance such as 'Take your bloody hands off me', said in an appropriately forceful way, results in the required behaviour, i.e. the patient letting go. The effective components of such an utterance are being explicit about what is required and being authoritative in the way it is asked for. This then leads to the observation that many nurses report equal success with a statement such as 'Let go of me' or 'Take your hands off me', said loudly and authoritatively but not necessarily aggressively.

To conclude this section, there are a number of verbal strategies which can be used in a situation where there is a threatening, agitated or aggressive person. Some of these strategies are very straightforward, others are relatively complex. While it is certain that 'the script' is very important, the non-verbal behaviour associated with it is also crucial.

NON-VERBAL BEHAVIOUR

Just as the script is important when managing an agitated person so is the way in which the script is delivered. There are several aspects which bear separate examination and they will be considered in turn.

One of the most commonly cited 'rules' for dealing with aggressive situations is that 'You must always remain calm'. As with so many of the 'always' rules, this is not entirely true. Whereas it is frequently the case that calmness is entirely beneficial to a situation, incidents are described where the very calmness of the potential victim has finally forced the aggressor from agitation into violence. Mood-matching is an important concept here. In conversation one normally matches the other person's non-verbal mood (Argyle, 1983). In talking to someone who is happy, one matches the happy atmosphere; conversing with someone who is depressed, one speaks in a subdued tone. However, when speaking to aggressive people, mood matching is often forgotten. The reason for this is that one would not wish to match aggression with aggression, as this may be the recipe for escalation and a physical confrontation. However, what one can match is the level of arousal; therefore one would match the client's aggression with concern, involvement or interest. The overall impression this conveys is that the seriousness of the situation is appreciated, what the person says is being taken seriously and action is being taken to calm the situation. If one can maintain an arousal level slightly less than the aggressor's, but still 'within the same band', then it is possible simultaneously to model becoming progressively calmer.

In saying that it is sometimes right to remain calm and sometimes right to match the aggressor's level of arousal with one's own arousal (portrayed as concern, involvement or interest) the question arises as to when to be calm and when to be concerned. There are no established general rules for this, although individual reports suggest that one may be generally best advised to be calm when oneself is under threat, but very willing to express concern and involvement when intervening on behalf of someone else. However, even this generalization is contradicted by 'the theatre of terror' mentioned earlier. Perhaps the best summary of the calm versus concerned dilemma is to say that it must be a matter of individual judgement in the particular situation. Obviously, this is no definitive guideline, and it is probably the case that there

Figure 13.2 Angles of standing. (a) Confrontational ($\Rightarrow$ = direction of gaze) (b) attempting to ease away from confrontation

cannot be one, but it is an appropriate step away from the idea that 'you must always remain calm'.

Research on body-buffer zones (Kinzel, 1970; McGurk *et al.*, 1981) suggests that habitually violent people exhibit wider zones than average. The implication of this is that it is probably best to keep slightly further away from those you know are habitually violent than you might otherwise. Similarly, eye contact can be aversive in potentially aggressive situations. In such interchanges this is readily interpreted as hostility (Mehrabian, 1972) and generates psychological arousal (Kleinke, 1986).

The difficulty arises when the potential aggressor fixes one with steady, staring eye contact, and the natural response is to return the stare. It is certainly the case that some people are, even in these heated circumstances, able to gaze at the would-be aggressor with unambiguous docility, obviously not responding to the potential aggression from the client. Others, however, respond with a matching stare which could be interpreted as hostility and so aggravate the situation. The aim should be to return to a normal pattern of eye contact in which gaze is held for perhaps a couple of seconds and then broken, and then held again, and so on. Some people find this easier to do than others, and some can even adopt the strategy of taking notes, which gives a legitimate excuse for making and breaking eye contact. Obviously, however, there are situations where suddenly to start taking notes would be ludicrous.

The other obvious non-verbal signal of aggression that potentially violent people emit is that they will stand directly facing the potential victim, 'toe to toe', 'eyeball to eyeball' or 'head to head' (Figure 13.2(a)). One might aim to transform this 'head-on' stance into a conventionally 'male-friendly' one in which two friends stand at approximately a right angle (Mehrabian, 1972). If the potential aggressor simply re-asserts a front-to-front stance then nothing has been gained. If this happens then ease just slightly away from the head-on position, as in Figure 13.2(b). If one simultaneously places one's weight on one leg while raising one hand to the chin, thereby breaking up bodily symmetry, the position has moved a long way from the face-to-face confrontation of a second or two before. Curiously, this is a surprisingly powerful signal that aggression is not appropriate and the author can report from personal experience that one even feels safer, having eased away from the front-to-front position; this also has a very rapid and marked effect on most would-be aggressors.

In line with the idea of moving away from the front-to-front position when standing it has already been pointed out that this should also be achieved in

Figure 13.3 Positions of chairs. (a) Non-confrontational; (b) possibly confrontational

the placing of office chairs. Should an aggressive discussion develop, it is better to have the chairs positioned at something like 45° to each other rather than in the head-on position (Figure 13.3) (Mehrabian, 1972).

AFTER A VIOLENT INCIDENT

No matter how well prepared we are and how well we carry out precautions and implement strategies, there will be times when violent incidents occur. The nature of the work of those in the helping professions means that it is inevitable that these happen from time to time. This is not to say that these events should be seen entirely in a negative light; although, certainly from the point of view of the victim, there is little immediate benefit to be drawn from such an incident. However, in the long term both from the point of view of the organization and of the individual, there are lessons to be learned. An incident should be seen as an opportunity to strengthen an organization's existing guidelines for such events and to provide learning points not only for the victim but also for other colleagues. The aftermath of an incident can be viewed from three perspectives; those of the victim, a friend or colleague of the victim and the victim's manager. This omits consideration of the aggressor, but we would suggest that this is appropriate in this context.

As a victim, one should endeavour not to become 'helpless'. On many occasions one hears victims say something along the lines of: 'Wouldn't you have thought that Jim would have spoken to me about this?' or 'Wouldn't you have thought that Jim would have had more sense than to keep talking to me about that incident?' Unfortunately, neither Jim nor any other of our colleagues is able to read our mind; it is up to us as a victim to say how we would like others to respond. If we want Jim to talk to us about the incident we should say so. If we would prefer him to forget it, or at least not to talk to us about it, equally we can say that. What we should not do, however, is simply to sit back and hope that other people will respond as we would wish them to; certainly this will happen sometimes, but it is equally likely not to happen.

As the victim, you will probably be well advised to get back to work as quickly as possible, possibly taking no time off at all. The intention of this is to minimize the 'incubation of fear' following a traumatic incident (Eysenck, 1968, 1976). It is quite possible that you will criticize yourself for what happened during the incident. Perhaps you will believe you could have handled it better. Many of us, given the benefit of hindsight, can say how we might have handled situations better; which is not to say that we are in any way at fault. On the other hand, you may be able to see clear learning points for yourself as a result of the incident. If so, this is entirely good; obviously it is much to your benefit if you can identify actions you would take or those you would avoid if a similar situation arises again. To register and act on these learning points is entirely appropriate, to dwell on a fact that you 'made mistakes' is much more negative. Another common phenomenon is that others will blame you for the incident, or imply that it was in some way your fault. There is little one can do to protect oneself from the hurt of this, except to recognize that it is common.

While some may imply that you were at fault, it is a manager's job to assess what happened during the incident. Your task as a victim is not to be offended by this, in that you have to recognize that it is simply part of his or her duty, nothing personal to you. Your manager cannot be prejudiced to the extent that he or she assumes that you acted entirely appropriately or that the aggressor was completely to blame. At the same time, we always hope that managers will investigate such incidents tactfully and in as supportive a manner as possible. It is, however, fair to say that getting the balance right is a difficult task, and you can make this easier simply by registering that a manager's investigation is a necessary evil.

As a friend or colleague of the victim, your initial task is to provide straightforward unconditional reassurance and sympathy. A little later your friends may need time to talk about the incident if they want to; at the same time you should be sensitive enough to judge whether they would really prefer not to talk about it. It can be hurtful to you as a friend if you find that your colleagues do not wish to talk to you — even more so if you find that they would prefer to talk to someone they know less well.

As well as immediately reassuring your colleague you may well wish to travel home with him or her and possibly even to reassure your colleague's spouse. Frequently the spouse can be very anxious about what has happened to their partner or about their partner returning to work. If you colleague lives alone it may be appropriate to contact relatives or neighbours so that they can act accordingly.

In the medium term you should aim to keep in touch with your friend or colleague, and make it clear that you are prepared to talk about the incident, even some time after it has happened. There is, of course, a balance here between inappropriately encouraging your colleague to dwell on past events and being appropriately sympathetic and willing to listen. One of the points that your friend may wish to discuss is the possibility of prosecuting the aggressor. This is highly sensitive, and you would be well advised to be careful about imposing your views here. Perhaps the best approach to adopt is that of the 'sounding board', where you simply give your colleague time and space to work out his or her own opinions.

In the long term you may be able to help your colleague to assimilate any learning points that should have been raised by the incident. This is perhaps the most sensitive task, and one which you may wish to avoid. However, if, some time after the incident, you judge that it would be possible to guide your friend to any appropriate improvements in professional manner then this is something that you would be right to consider.

As the victim's manager you have a very difficult balance to make. You are attempting to balance the necessary administrative tasks of completing all the organization's documentation and establishing a proper account of what happened, while at the same time being understanding and supportive to the victim. You may need to ensure that the aggressor is no longer a danger, either on your own premises or elsewhere. It may be appropriate to inform the police about the incident that has just happened with a view to prosecuting the aggressor. Certainly you will need to ensure that the victim has a colleague or friend who is able to give support in the immediate future and perhaps take him or her home. You will have to consider re-allocating the victim's workload elsewhere, although not without consulting the victim and taking full account of what he or she wishes. In any event, you will need to consider the relationship between the aggressor and the victim if they anticipate working with each other in the future. You must work out and disseminate any learning points for the organization and deal with any anxiety that might have resulted from the incident. Many victims ignore quite serious occurrences, with very little long-term effect, but others may need professional counselling. One task that you have to do is to monitor the victim's reaction and decide whether such support would be appropriate. Overall, the manager has a difficult balancing act to achieve; it is not surprising that few of the victims the author has interviewed speak well of their managers' reactions!

SUMMARY

This chapter considered a range of areas which are relevant to avoiding and coping with violence which may be directed towards professional helpers. We have discussed attitudes and assumptions which may not only be assumed to underly much of our behaviour but also be conveyed to our clients; precautions which, if assiduously followed, would prevent many incidents happening or, at least, escalating to serious dimensions; and finally the verbal and non-verbal techniques we can use to communicate with and calm an agitated, aggressive and potentially violent client. Notwithstanding such preventative and coping techniques, incidents will nevertheless happen, and the final concern must be with what can be done to lessen their impact and to learn constructive lessons to prevent future assault.

References

Argyle, M. (1983). *The Psychology of Interpersonal Behaviour*, Harmondsworth: Penguin.
Argyle, M. (1988). *Bodily Communication*, 2nd edition, London: Methuen.
Brown, R., Bute, S., and Ford, P. (1986). *Social Workers at Risk*, Basingstoke: Macmillan.
Cook, M. (1970). Experiments on orientation and proxemics. *Human Relations*, **23**, 61–76.

Davies, W. (1982). Violence in prisons. In M.P. Feldman (ed.), *Developments in the Study of Criminal Behaviour*, Volume 2 *Violence*, Chichester: Wiley.

Davies, W., and Burgess, P.W. (1988). Prison officers' experience as a predictor of risk of attack: an analysis within the British prison system. *Medicine, Science and the Law*, **28**, 135–8.

Drinkwater, J. (1982). Violence in psychiatric hospitals. In M.P. Feldman (ed.), *Developments in the Study of Criminal Behaviour*, Volume 2, *Violence*, Chichester: Wiley.

Ekman, P., and Friesen, W.V. (1969). Non-verbal leakage and clues to deception. *Psychiatry*, **32**, 88–106.

Ellis, A. (1970). *The Essence of Rational Psychotherapy: A Comprehensive Approach to Treatment*, New York: Institute for Rational Living.

Eysenck, H.J. (1968). A theory of the incubation of anxiety/fear responses. *Behaviour Research and Therapy*, **6**, 309–21.

Eysenck, H.J. (1976). The learning theory model of neurosis: a new approach. *Behaviour Research and Therapy*, **14**, 251–67.

Haggard, E.A. and Isaacs, F.S. (1966). Micromomentary facial expressions as indicators of ego mechanisms in psychotherapy. In La. Gottschalk and A.A. Auerbach (eds). *Methods of Research in Psychotherapy*, New York: Appleton-Century-Crofts.

Hough, M., and Mayhew, P. (1985). *Taking Account of Crime: Key Findings from the Second British Crime Survey*, London: HMSO.

Kinzel, A.F. (1970). Body-buffer zones in violent prisoners. *American Journal of Psychiatry*, **127**, 59–64.

Kleinke, C.L. (1986). Gaze and eye-contact: a research review. *Psychological Bulletin*, **100**, 78–100.

McGurk, B.J., Davies, J.D., and Graham, J. (1981). Assaultive behaviour, personality and personal space. *Aggressive Behaviour*, **7**, 317–24.

Mehrabian, A. (1972). *Non-verbal Communication*, Chicago and New York: Aldine-Atherton.

Meichenbaum, D. (1985). *Stress Innoculation Training*, New York: Pergamon Press.

Wyre, R. (1986). *Women, Men and Rape*, Oxford: Perry Publications.

The Future of Clinical Approaches to Violence: Grounds for Optimism?

Kevin Howells
and
Clive Hollin

We conclude this volume, having read through the preceding chapters, in a spirit of cautious optimism about the existing and potential contribution of applied psychology to understanding and changing violence.

Systematic, clinically oriented assessment, intervention and research into violence have a relatively short history, and yet the knowledge-base available to the practitioner is not inconsiderable. Many professionals are called upon to deal with violence in their everyday work, including nurses, doctors, police officers, social workers, probation officers, psychologists and judges. It is our impression that many go about this task while acutely aware of their difficulties (and often ignorance) in conceptualizing, assessing and modifying this form of behaviour. In our experience, others, understandably, 'make do', adopting makeshift, outmoded or empirically unfounded theories and measures, in the absence of anything better. We would argue (we hope, without grandiosity) that clinical psychological science has much to offer to those looking for a systematic and broadly coherent theoretical and empirical base for their practical work.

Although there are many theoretical differences between the various chapters of this book we are struck by the continuity of particular themes, in spite of the different populations and settings studied. The spirit of cautious optimism seems also to have caught hold of many of our contributors!

In conclusion, throughout the book we discern the implicit conclusion that a 'good start' (but no more) has been made in understanding problems of violence and implementing effective interventions. The need now is for large-scale moral and financial support on the part of government and other institutions for work in this area. Only when such support is forthcoming will the full potential of clinical methods be known.

Clinical Approaches to Violence. Edited by K. Howells and C. R. Hollin
© 1989 John Wiley & Sons.

Author Index

Note: Page numbers in *italic type* indicate where a reference is printed in full

Subject Index